Chronicles of the
Tudor Kings

Chronicles of the
Tudor Kings

General Editor
David Loades

This edition published in 2002 by
Greenwich Editions
10 Blenheim Court
London N7 9NY

A member of the Chrysalis Group plc

ISBN 0-86288-435-7

Printed and bound in Spain

*Half title   The main entrance to Hampton Court,
bearing the arms of Henry VIII. Thomas Wolsey began
building the palace in 1515, but later presented it to
Henry to soothe their strained relationship.*

*Title   A seventeenth century painting of Henry VII's
magnificent Gothic palace at Richmond.*

Project Editor: Terence Monaighan
Designer: Nicholas Maddren

Editorial:
Mark Bryant
Tessa Clark
Tony Hall
Susan Keeling

Production: Georgina McNamara

Picture Research: Jan Croot

Maps: Jeff Edwards

Created and Produced by Phoebe Phillips Editions

Contributors to illustrated spreads:
Christopher Coleman   *Lecturer in History, University College, London*
Dr Anthony Goodman   *Reader in History, University of Edinburgh*
Ralph A. Griffths   *Professor of Medieval History, University College of Swansea*
Dr Charles S. Knighton   *Formerly of Magdalene College, Cambridge*
Dr David Marcombe   *Director, Centre for Local History, University of Nottingham*
Dr Diarmaid MacCulloch   *Leverhulme Research Fellow, Bristol*
Dr Andrew Pettegree   *Lecturer in Modern History, University of St Andrew's*
Dr Glyn Redworth   *Research Fellow, Christ Church, Oxford*
Professor R. L. Storey   *Professor of Medieval History, University of Nottingham*
Dr John A.F. Thomson   *Reader of Medieval History, University of Glasgow*

ACKNOWLEDGMENTS

Our grateful thanks to the many museums, libraries and individuals, including those listed below, who provided us with illustrations.

(b. = bottom; t = top; tl = top left; tr = top right; r = right; l = left)

Biblioteca Universalis, Bologna; 75
Bodleian Library, Oxford; 61, 123b
Bridgeman Art Library; 28, 37t, 47t, 67tr, 74b, 74b, 74t, 75t, 77br, 95/5, 109, 113t, 11?b, 131t, 135t, 138, 163t, 170b, 193tr, 226/7, 235br, 238, 239t, 239b
British Library; 6
British Museum; 233b
British Tourist Authority; 91, 177bl, 177br
Buloz, Paris; 231
Photographie Bulloz; 52t, 66br, 139t
Courtesy of His Grace the Lord Archbishop of Canterbury and the Church Commissioners; 171t
ET Archive; 31t, 39, 125b, 130b, 199tl
Mary Evans Picture Library; 24l
Fitzwilliam Museum Library; 24l
John Freeman; 88, 121, 225
Fitzwilliam Museum, Cambridge; 2/3, 127t
Giraudon, Paris; 119t, 139b

Michael Holford; 34b, 35t, 93t, 94b, 150b, 151, 156, 191b
Robert Harding; 41
Hulton Deutsch Picture Company; 29b, 33t, 51t, 55t, 77t, 115, 135b, 171b, 201b, 211t
Jarrolds Ltd; 185b
Magdalene College, Cambridge; 117b
Mansell Collection; 75b, 134b, 223
Mary Evans 163, 233t
Mary Rose Trust; 116br, 117t
Masters and Fellows of Magdalene College, Oxford 77bl
Colin Molyneux; 22/3, 63
National Portrait Gallery; 123tr, 147t, 173, 187, 197tr, 199tr, 206, 243t
National Trust; 194b
by Kind Permission of HM The Queen; 141b, 175t
Private Collection; 79
Royal Armouries; 110
Royal College of Arms; 111b
Royal Library, Windsor; 183tr
Society of Antiquaries; 211b
Victoria & Albert Museum; 70br, 106tr, 107, 127bl, 127br
Weidenfeld & Nicholson; 33b, 35b, 45b, 71t, 94t, 111t, 143bl, 146/7b, 177bl, 195t, 201t, 209t, 214, 219, 229r, 235tr

Contents

Introduction

The period covered by the reigns of the three Tudor kings, from 1485 to 1553, was one of the most dramatic and formative in English history. When Edward IV died in 1483 a period of stability came to an end. Both his sons were minors, and he had left verbal instructions contradicting his written will, so that the Regency had been claimed both by his widow, Elizabeth, and his brother, Richard of Gloucester, who were also personal enemies. In the summer of 1483 Richard secured not merely the Regency, but the Crown itself as Richard III. His nephews disappeared and the Yorkist party became irreconcilably divided. It was that situation which had turned the last remote Lancastrian hope, Henry of Richmond, into a serious contender for the throne. Henry's victory at Bosworth in August 1485 was decisive because Richard III died in the battle, leaving no natural heir. It was decisive also because Henry VII began immediately to build upon his Yorkist support; he married Edward IV's daughter Elizabeth, and represented himself as the reconciler of strife. Consequently, although he was troubled by Yorkist pretenders for over ten years, none of them commanded major support.

Henry ruled well. Although never a charismatic figure, he provided what England needed at that time, a restoration of confidence. He discouraged faction, had no overweening favourites, and steadily rebuilt the reputation of royal justice. Although the disruption of the two years prior to his reign had been brief, it had been acute, and Richard's reputation for lawless violence, although not entirely justified, had been damaging. The first Tudor was conspicuously successful in two directions. He gained the recognition and respect of his royal neighbours; first Spain, then France, then Scotland, and finally the Holy Roman Empire. With three of these, Spain, Scotland and the Empire, he secured martrimonial alliances, and the twenty four years of his reign saw no major foreign war. Secondly he rebuilt the foundations of the royal authority, using, as it were, the same bricks as his predecessors, but in a different order. In place of the major noble affinities upon which Edward IV had largely relied for provincial government – Warwick, Hastings, Richard of Gloucester – Henry used wherever possible men of knightly or gentle status, working in groups under a royal commission. He did not invent these commissions, but he made much greater use of them. He did not stop employing noblemen, but he used them less and gave them much more restricted powers. It was not a revolution, but a change of emphasis with major significance for the future. He was also able to maintain a good relationship with the papacy. He did not die rich. In spite of all efforts, and at considerable cost to his popularity, he could not raise his revenues by a great deal. By refraining from war he ended solvent, and gave few hostages to a parliament which seldom met in the second half of the reign. But his ministers can have had few illusions about the adequacy of the system to support a more pretentious style of government. In this, as in other respects, Henry VII survived. In spite of discontent, there was no noble rebellion, and his surviving son succeeded him unchallenged. The Crown in 1509 was vastly stronger than it had been in 1485, but it was no nearer to being absolute.

The reign of Henry VIII was substantially longer than that of his father – 38 years as against 24 – and saw much more momentous changes. The first great difference was that the second Tudor was able to start where the first had left off. By embarking almost immediately upon a foreign war the new king created financial problems for himself, but he solved, perhaps unintentionally, the problem of his relationship with his nobles. War offered them congenial employment and attractive rewards.

By displaying all the chivalric virtues Henry also inspired their enthusiastic personal loyalty. He shared a culture which they all understood, in spite of his enthusiasm for unfamiliar Italian learning. Consequently his first great minister, Thomas Wolsey, was able to develop Henry VII's system of local and regional government without provoking major aristocratic resistance. The nobility became increasingly dependent upon office under the Crown, and upon the king's court, to maintain their wealth and political influence. Charles Brandon, duke of Suffolk, a court peer without noble ancestry, died rich, powerful and respected. Edward Stafford, duke of Buckingham, a man who considered his ancestry to be better than the king's, and who disdained routine employment, died on the block and his dukedom disappeared. By the end of his reign, Henry had largely emancipated himself from the remnants of the feudal contract, both in theory and in practice. He had also emancipated himself from the Canon Law. The story of how that came about features largely in the chronicles and correspondance of the period. Very few of his subjects appreciated the full significance of his actions at the time, or took the theoretical claims of the Royal Supremacy seriously, but the king himself was in deadly earnest. By 1540 he had redesigned the law of God to suit himself, and established the principle that it was subjected to the same legislative processes as the common law of England. This made him, in one sense, the most absolute monarch in Christendom, because however great the practical control which the kings of France or Spain might exercise over the church within their dominions, they nevertheless recognized limits which the king of England had transcended. At the same time, in mobilizing the political consent necessary to support such a significant development, Henry placed himself under a different kind of constraint, which in the long run was to transform the constitutional history of the country. From being his accomplices, even his servants, the Lords and Commons assembled in parliament rapidly became his partners – and partners they were to remain, in spite of the fraternal strife of the seventeenth century.

The only way in which Henry could have avoided this outcome would have been to emancipate himself from the necessity for extraordinary revenue, which parliament had the long established right to grant. He could have done that, as his father had done, by refraining from war; but in the sixteenth century such a solution could only have been fragile and temporary, even if the king had not been of a warlike disposition. The alternative was to find a major increase in the ordinary revenues of the Crown. The Royal Supremacy itself created such an opportunity, and by two statutes in 1536 and 1540, all religious houses were dissolved, and their property annexed to the Crown. The capital value of the land thus acquired was in excess of a £1,000,000, at a time when the ordinary annual revenue was about £150,000. Efficiently managed, these vast estates could have added to that figure by about 75 percent. However, the costs of war rapidly used up these resources, and by 1547 the bulk of this great new capital endowment had been dispersed by sale. Henry's debts were reduced, but his chance of financial independence disappeared, and with it any chance of shaking off his new political partners. The dissolution of the monasteries did not, therefore, directly augment the king's authority, but it did so indirectly by creating a vested interest in the ecclesiastical settlement. Those noblemen and gentlemen who had invested good money in church land had no desire to see their title called in question, a fact which Mary I was later to learn to her cost.

The kingdom which Henry bequeathed to his infant son was under considerable economic and social stress, but united as never before in its allegiance to the Tudor dynasty. There was no trace of a challenge to Edward VI, but a steadily growing rural population was placing increasing pressure upon the resources of cultivable land; and a steadily developing urban protestantism threatened the conservative church order of Henry's later years. The second problem was the first to surface, because the coup by which the duke of Somerset gained control of the government also brought the protestants to power. A new church order was legislated, and the conservatives became the opposition, a force which turned from discontent to rebellion in the South Western revolt of 1549. The rebellion was suppressed, but bitter divisions remained. The social crisis was both more widespread and more explosive. Somerset believed in the royal duty of stewardship, and in the king's responsibility to protect the poor against the rich. Unfortunately he had no clear idea how to achieve this, a poor record on his own estates, and an abrasive personality. As a result he succeeded in giving the aggrieved commons who were protesting against the shortage of tenements, and the exploitation of the situation by the gentry, the impression that he sympathized with their position, and was willing to allow them to take the law into their own hands. Nothing could have been further from the truth. However, when widespread disorders broke out in 1548 and 1549 his mind was on the Scottish war and his resources over-committed, so that he moved slowly and with apparent hesitation against the rebels, this confirming the impression. It was the energy of local gentry, defending their own interests, which put down most of the risings, while the major revolts in Devon and Norfolk were suppressed by Lord Russell and the earl of Warwick. Somerset emerged from the crisis without credit, and with his political position crumbling away. In October 1549, after a confrontation which dangerously involved the young king himself, the Protector was arrested and deprived of his office. A fierce factional struggle then ensued between the religious conservatives, who wished to use Somerset's fall to reverse his protestant policies, and the reformers, led by the earl of Warwick, who were mainly concerned to establish themselves in power. Warwick won, and soon after caused himself to be created duke of Northumberland. For the last three years of his reign, Edward's government was controlled by a faction and was characterized by further and more radical religious reform, by a tough and authoritarian stance against civil unrest, and by a precipitate withdrawal from all expensive overseas commitments. It was an unpopular government, with very little support in the country, but it was validated by the king himself who, although a minor, was still deemed to be capable of giving or withholding his confidence. Northumberland's personal ascendency over him was considerable, but it is significant of the prestige of the monarchy that, even in the circumstances of 1552 and 1553, no one challenged the legitimacy of the duke's position as long as Edward lived. Although the last Tudor king was a pathetic figure as he struggled against his last illness, the imposing mantle which his father and grandfather had woven protected him to the end; and protected the rest of their achievements as well.

The Chroniclers

There is a considerable difference between the writer of history and the chronicler of events. A chronicler was not expected to be impartial, or to refrain from comment, but his main task was to record and not to interpret. The renaissance saw a revival of true historical writing in the works of Francesco Guicciardini, Niccolo Machiavelli, and later Johann Sleidan; but this revival affected England very little before the reformation. Of the named writers included in this collection, only Polydore Vergil could be described as an historian in the true sense. A native of Urbino, Vergil came to England in 1502, when he was about thirty, as a papal tax-collector. Through connections with other Italians in England he obtained the favour of King Henry VII. It was the king who invited him to write a history of England, but the first version of his Anglica Historia covering the years down to 1509, was not published until 1534. Towards the end of his

Right   A family tree of the kings of England from Edward III to Henry VII. Henry is the large portrait near the bottom of the page; Richard III is directly above him.

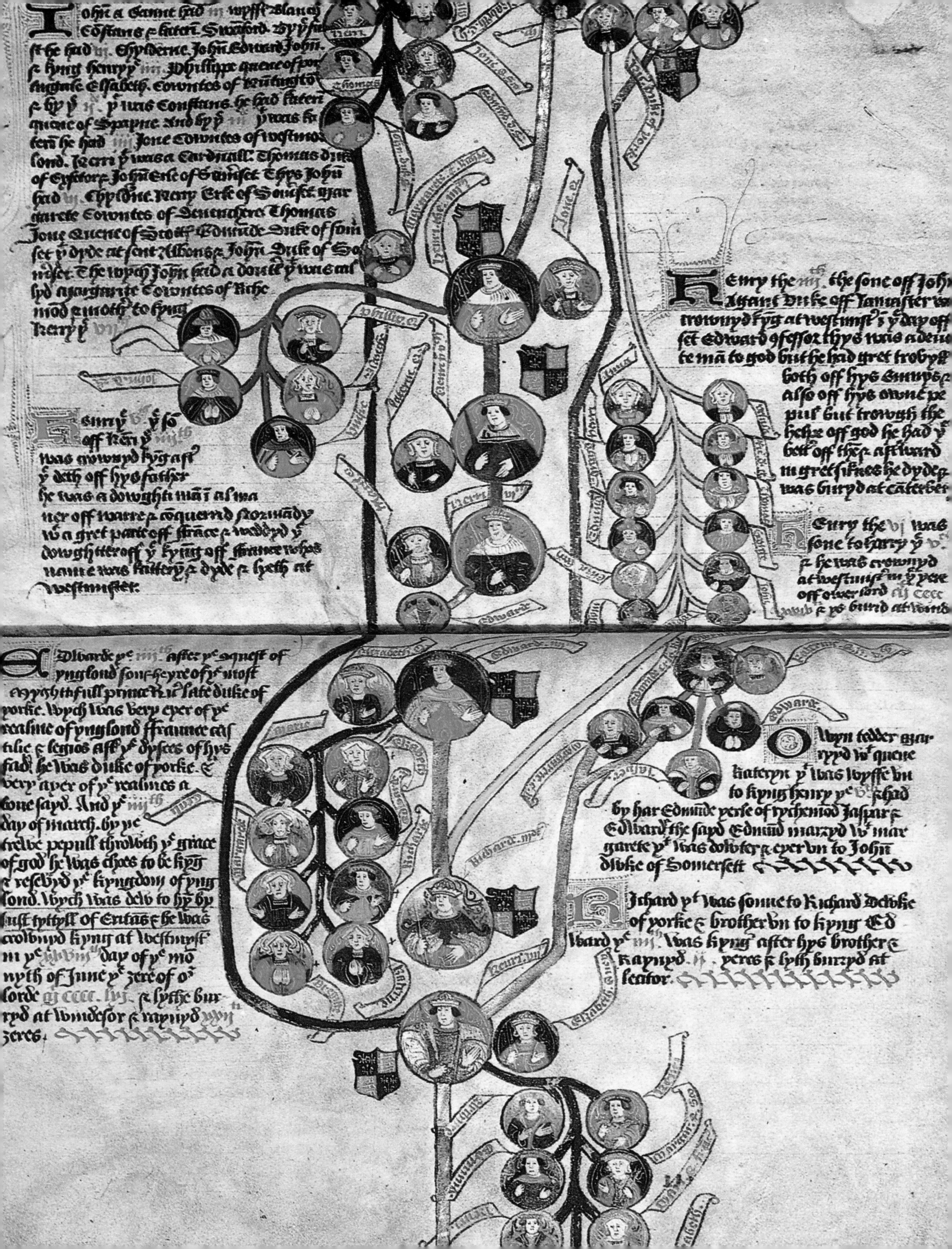

I ohn a Gaunt had in wyffe Blanch
Costans & kateri. & off ye fyr
st he had iij chyldern John Edward John
& kyng henry iiij. whilippe quene of por
tugale. & Elsabeth. cowntes of huntyngto
& by ye ij p̄ was Constans he had kateri
quene of Spayne. and by ye iij p̄ was ka
teri he had iiij Jone cowntes of westmo
lond. Iohn y was cardinall. Thomas duke
of Exforce. Iohn erle of Somset. Thys John
had iij chyldern. Iohn erke of Somset. mar
garete cowntes of Rychemond. Thomas
Ione Quene of Scottes. Edmude duke of som
set ye dyde at seint Albons. John Duke of So
nset. The wych John had a dowter y was al
so ys margarete cowntes of Riche
mond a moth to kyng
henry ye vij

H enry ye v yso
off kateri who
was crownyd kyng aft
ye deth off hys father
he was a dowghti man i al man
ner off warre & coquered stordnady
to a gret parte off fraunce & weddyd ye
dowghter off ye kyng off fraunce whos
name was kateri & dyde & lyeth at
westmynster.

H enry the iiij the sone off John
a Gaunt duke off lancaster was
crownyd kyng at westmynster ye day off
seint edward confessor thys was a deuou
te man to god but he had gret troble
bothe off hys surgye
also off hys owne pe
pull but trowgh ye
helpe off god he had ye
better off them. aftward
in gret sikenes he dyde &
was buryd at caterber

H enry the vj was
sone to henry ye v
& he was crownyd
at westmynst in ye yere
off owre lord M cccc
xxxb & ys buryd at wind

E lwarde ye iiij after ye conquest of
ynglond sonne & eyre of ys most
worshypfull prynce Rychard late duke of
yorke. whych was very eyer of ye
realme of ynglond & france & ca
stile & legion aff ye dysces of hys
fad. he was duke of yorke. &
very ayer of ye realme & a
fore sayd. And ye iiij
day of march. by ye
trelue pepull throwgh ye grace
of god he was chose to be kyng
& resceyd ye kyngdom of yng
lond. whych was deb to hy by
just tytyll of entayl & he was
crobnyd kyng at westmynst
in ye xxviij day of ye mo
nyth of June ye zere of o
lorde M cccc lxj & lyffe bur
yd at Wyndesor & rapnyd xxij
zeres.

Edward

Upon fedder mar
ryed ye quene
kateryn y was wyffe vn
to kyng henry ye v &had
by har Edmude perse of rychemod Jaspar
Edward the sayd Edmud marryd wt mar
garete y was dowter & eyer vn to John
duke of Somersett &

R ichard y was sonne to Richard duke
of yorke & brother vn to kyng Ed
ward ye iiij was kyng after hys brother &
rapnyd ij yeres & lyth buryd at
lestor.

life he extended his history of 1538, and that edition was published in Basle in 1555. Vergil wrote in latin for an international scholarly readership. He was a sharp and sceptical interpreter, who used his sources with great care, and was highly critical of the mythological view of British history which was popular in the England of his time. He liked England, stayed for over forty years, and was a great admirer of both Henry VII and Henry VIII. Cardinal Wolsey, however, he found unpalatable and he became increasingly distressed as the English church began to move in the direction of protestant reform. All these attitudes are reflected in his writing.

John Foxe was also an historian, in spite of his strong apologetic purpose. He was as thorough as Vergil in his use of original sources, if not quite as critical. To Foxe, as to his near contemporary John Bale, human history charted the struggle between Christ and Anti-christ — between the true and false churches. In this cosmic process the history of England played a crucial role, because it was through King John, John Wycliffe and Henry VIII that God had chosen, in different generations, to strike important blows against Anti-christ. He believed that England had a special place in the affection of the Almighty — a view which continued to be influential down to the early years of the twentieth century.

Edward Hall had a great sense of historical drama. He was unashamedly a Tudor propagandist, for whom the oversimplified moral struggles of English history, and particularly of the fifteenth century, had been designed to culminate in the triumphs of Henry VII and Henry VIII. His great advantage as a commentator upon the events of his own day is that he was an active participant, far closer to the centre of politics than was Vergil. Educated at Eton and King's College, Cambridge, he trained as a lawyer at Gray's Inn, became Common Sergeant and Under Sheriff of the city of London, and sat in several of Henry VIII's parliaments. His express purpose in writing was "to enhance lady Fame, and to suppress that deadly beast oblivion", which was more in keeping with the traditions of the Celtic "praise singer" than of the humanist scholar. Nevertheless his work is vivid, and full of detailed observation and incident not otherwise recorded.

Richard Grafton was a printer by trade, and was Hall's publisher and literary executor. His two main works, *An Abridgement of the Chronicles* and *A Chronicle at Large* were published in 1563 and 1568, and were largely derivative, depending mostly upon Hall and Vergil. After their publication he became embroiled in a furious dispute with John Stow, a professional rival, who accused him of every kind of carelessness and malpractice. The charges were not entirely justified, and Grafton makes a useful alternative to Hall because he was less obviously a publicist.

The other chronicles in the book, some anonymous, belong more obviously to the older tradition of local narrative. This is particularly true of the *Chronicles of London and Calais*, with their domestic preoccupations and lists of office holders. Nevertheless each has some contribution to make to our insight, even if it is only to reveal how limited could be the horizons of men who were so close to the centre of events. The chronicle written by the herald Charles Wriothesley is also narrow in its focus, but because Wriothesley was strongly sympathetic to religious reform, he gives us a heightened awareness of those abuses which the Tudors were able to exploit to mobilize support for a religious policy which otherwise commanded little sympathy in its early days. The diaries are very similar, with their day by day progression and inevitable personal angle. The one kept by King Edward VI has all the marks of an academic exercise produced for his tutors, and is much less interesting than the reader might expect. It seldom tells us anything which is not known from other sources, and its lack of spontaneity has often been commented upon, but there are occasional touches which reveal the boy behind the pen, and royal diaries in any form are extremely rare before the nineteenth century. Henry Machyn, the London undertaker, was almost at the opposite end of the social scale, and the notable fact about him is that he was sufficiently literate to keep a diary at all. He was a diligent but disorganized observer, with a strong professional preoccupation and marked conservative sympathies in religion. So he recorded a lot of funeral pageantry, and commented favourably upon the traditional ceremonies of the church.

The remainder of the chronicles included in the book falls broadly into two categories; apologetic or propagandist writings which were intended to be generally read, and correspondance which was intended only for the recipient. In the first category, most obviously, come *The pretended divorce* ..., a late but strongly polemical attack upon Henry VIII; William Patten's laudatory account of Somerset's expedition into Scotland in 1547; and the anonymous *Discourse of the Common Weal*. Less obviously, George Cavendish's *Life and Death of Cardinal Wolsey* should be placed in the same class. Cavendish's work was not published in the sixteenth century, but circulated in manuscript and was probably intended for the printer, if the subject had not failed to find a market. The Bodley manuscript on the Field of Cloth of Gold is harder to place, because neither its author nor its provenance can be identified with certainty. It does not seem to have been intended for publication, and may have been simply a memorandum for private use. Private correspondence is very varied and most of the authors are known, which helps to give the letters their significance. This is most obviously the case with the despatches of Eustace Chapuys and Daniel Barbaro. Chapuys was in the thick of the political action from his arrival in England as Charles V's ambassador in 1529 until his final retirement in 1545. He was an experienced and very shrewd diplomat, but he was totally committed, both by the nature of his position and by personal conviction, to the cause of Catherine of Aragon and her daughter Mary. He frequently overstepped the bounds of diplomatic propriety − even as those were understood at that time − and became actively involved with English opponents of Henry's policies. His opinions were therefore highly partisan, and also designed to tell his master what Chapuys thought he wanted to hear. Consequently his comments upon the fall of Anne Boleyn are particularly informative. Barbaro was in a very different position. As a professional Venetian diplomat he was largely detached from the issues of English politics, but he was extremely well informed, because that was his business. The tradition of the narration which every Venetian ambassador wrote before handing over his mission had been designed to ensure that every representative of the Republic made himself thoroughly familiar with the country in which he was resident, and understood enough of its history, laws, and methods of government to give informed judgements upon events when these were called for. Barbaro's despatch is therefore a very different document from Chapuys's, but no less interesting. The anonymous Italian narration from about 1500 is similar, but being written for a private correspondent rather than as an official report, it has more personal touches, and is often cited as a shrewdly informed opinion of the English and their mores at that time.

A few other individual chronicles have been included, such as an extract from the *Acts of the Privy Council*, which will hopefully give you a feel for the history of the period at first hand, and where the writer's purpose and credentials can be established, the understanding of each individual piece can be enhanced.

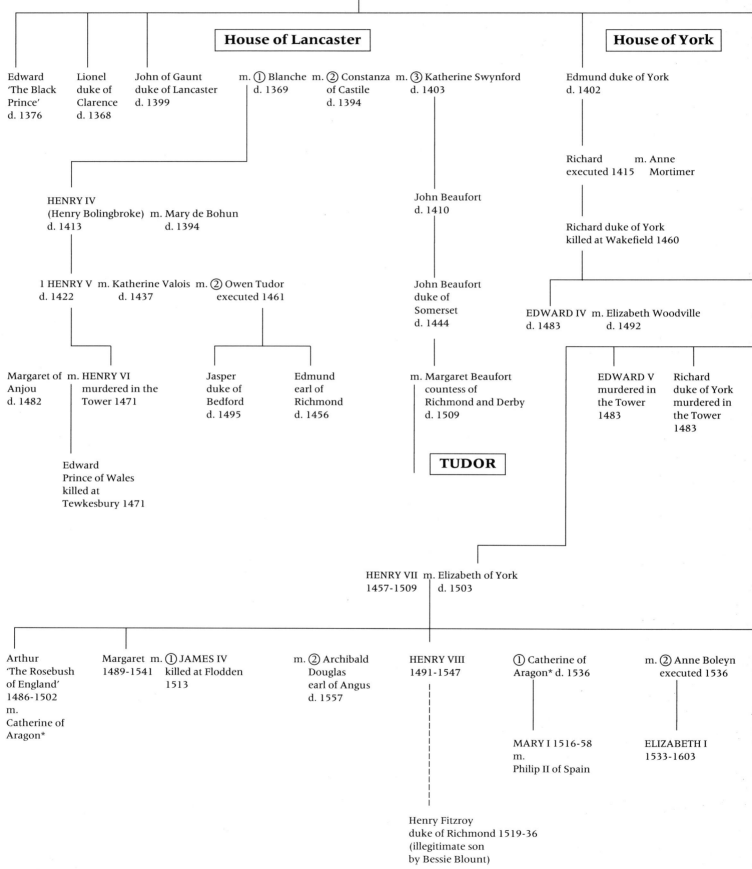

PLANTAGENET

EDWARD III m. Philippa of Hainault
d. 1377   d. 1369

House of Lancaster   **House of York**

Edward 'The Black Prince' d. 1376

Lionel duke of Clarence d. 1368

John of Gaunt duke of Lancaster d. 1399   m. ① Blanche d. 1369   m. ② Constanza of Castile d. 1394   m. ③ Katherine Swynford d. 1403

Edmund duke of York d. 1402

Richard executed 1415   m. Anne Mortimer

HENRY IV (Henry Bolingbroke) m. Mary de Bohun
d. 1413   d. 1394

John Beaufort d. 1410

Richard duke of York killed at Wakefield 1460

1 HENRY V m. Katherine Valois m. ② Owen Tudor
d. 1422   d. 1437   executed 1461

John Beaufort duke of Somerset d. 1444

EDWARD IV m. Elizabeth Woodville
d. 1483   d. 1492

Margaret of Anjou d. 1482   m. HENRY VI murdered in the Tower 1471

Jasper duke of Bedford d. 1495

Edmund earl of Richmond d. 1456

m. Margaret Beaufort countess of Richmond and Derby d. 1509

EDWARD V murdered in the Tower 1483

Richard duke of York murdered in the Tower 1483

Edward Prince of Wales killed at Tewkesbury 1471

TUDOR

HENRY VII m. Elizabeth of York
1457-1509   d. 1503

Arthur 'The Rosebush of England' 1486-1502 m. Catherine of Aragon*

Margaret 1489-1541   m. ① JAMES IV killed at Flodden 1513

m. ② Archibald Douglas earl of Angus d. 1557

HENRY VIII 1491-1547

① Catherine of Aragon* d. 1536

m. ② Anne Boleyn executed 1536

MARY I 1516-58 m. Philip II of Spain

ELIZABETH I 1533-1603

Henry Fitzroy duke of Richmond 1519-36 (illegitimate son by Bessie Blount)

The Tudor Succession

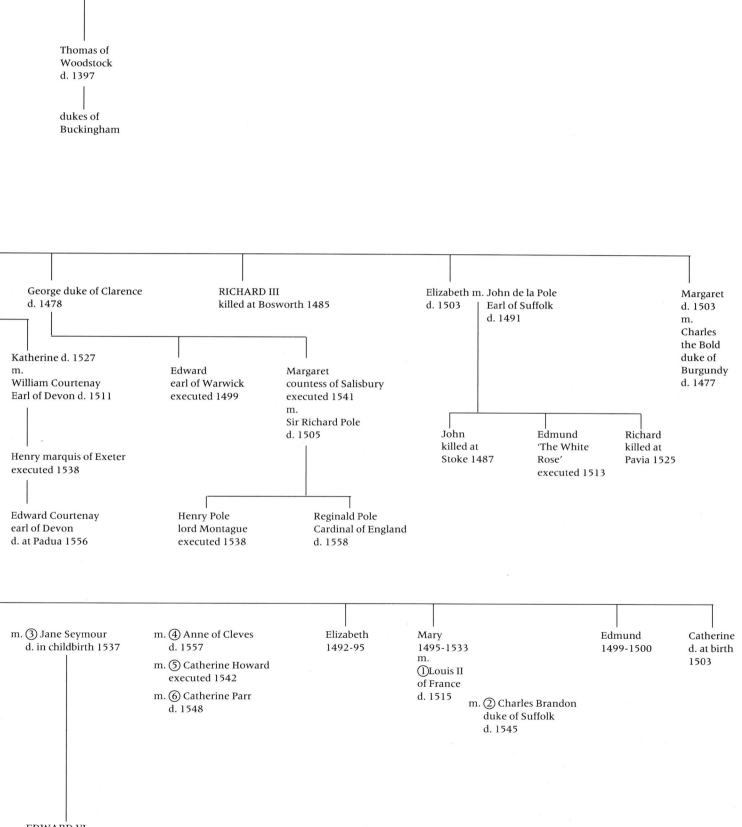

Thomas of
Woodstock
d. 1397

dukes of
Buckingham

George duke of Clarence
d. 1478

RICHARD III
killed at Bosworth 1485

Elizabeth m. John de la Pole
d. 1503   Earl of Suffolk
            d. 1491

Margaret
d. 1503
m.
Charles
the Bold
duke of
Burgundy
d. 1477

Katherine d. 1527
m.
William Courtenay
Earl of Devon d. 1511

Edward
earl of Warwick
executed 1499

Margaret
countess of Salisbury
executed 1541
m.
Sir Richard Pole
d. 1505

John
killed at
Stoke 1487

Edmund
'The White
Rose'
executed 1513

Richard
killed at
Pavia 1525

Henry marquis of Exeter
executed 1538

Edward Courtenay
earl of Devon
d. at Padua 1556

Henry Pole
lord Montague
executed 1538

Reginald Pole
Cardinal of England
d. 1558

m. ③ Jane Seymour
d. in childbirth 1537

m. ④ Anne of Cleves
d. 1557

m. ⑤ Catherine Howard
executed 1542

m. ⑥ Catherine Parr
d. 1548

Elizabeth
1492-95

Mary
1495-1533
m.
①Louis II
of France
d. 1515

      m. ② Charles Brandon
        duke of Suffolk
        d. 1545

Edmund
1499-1500

Catherine
d. at birth
1503

EDWARD VI
1537-53

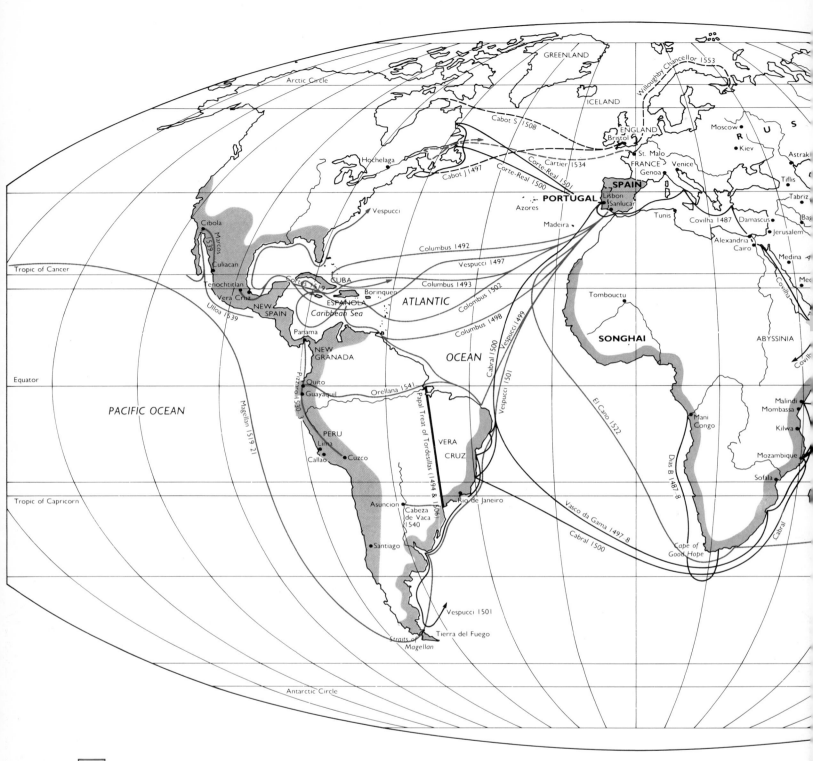

PACIFIC OCEAN

GREENLAND

ICELAND

Arctic Circle

ENGLAND
Bristol

Moscow
Kiev

R U S

Astrak

St. Malo
FRANCE
Venice
Genoa

Tiflis
Tabriz

SPAIN

PORTUGAL
Lisbon
Sanlucar

Azores

Madeira

Covilha 1487
Damascus
Jerusalem

Alexandria
Cairo

Medina

Tunis

Willoughby Chancellor 1553

Cabot S 1508

Cartier 1534

Corte-Real 1501

Cabot J 1497

Corte-Real 1500

Hochelaga

Vespucci

Tropic of Cancer

Cibola
Marcos 1539
Culiacan

Tenochtitlan
Vera Cruz

Ulloa 1539

NEW
SPAIN

Cortes 1519

CUBA

ESPAÑOLA
Caribbean Sea

Borinquen

ATLANTIC

Columbus 1492

Vespucci 1497

Columbus 1493

Columbus 1502

Columbus 1498

OCEAN

Panama

NEW
GRANADA

Cabral 1500

Vespucci 1499

Vespucci 1501

Tombouctu

SONGHAI

ABYSSINIA

Covilha

Equator

Pizarro 1530-3
Quito
Guayaquil

Orellana 1541

Papal Treaty of Tordesillas (1494 & 1506)

VERA
CRUZ

El Cano 1522

Malindi
Mombassa

PERU
Lima
Callao
Cuzco

Magellan 1519-21

Mani
Congo

Kilwa

Mozambique

Dias B 1487-8

Sofala

Tropic of Capricorn

Asuncion
Cabeza
de Vaca
1540

Rio de Janeiro

Vasco da Gama 1497-8

Cabral 1500

Cape of
Good Hope

Cabral

Santiago

Vespucci 1501

Straits of
Magellan

Tierra del Fuego

Antarctic Circle

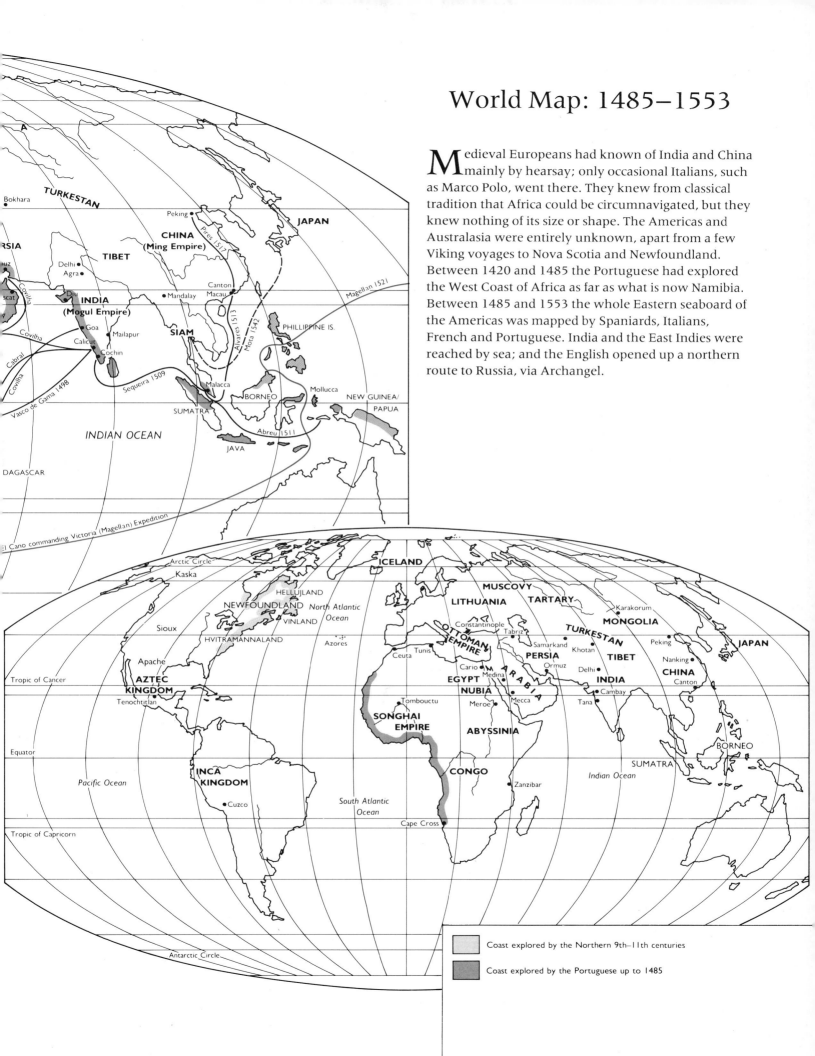

World Map: 1485–1553

Medieval Europeans had known of India and China mainly by hearsay; only occasional Italians, such as Marco Polo, went there. They knew from classical tradition that Africa could be circumnavigated, but they knew nothing of its size or shape. The Americas and Australasia were entirely unknown, apart from a few Viking voyages to Nova Scotia and Newfoundland. Between 1420 and 1485 the Portuguese had explored the West Coast of Africa as far as what is now Namibia. Between 1485 and 1553 the whole Eastern seaboard of the Americas was mapped by Spaniards, Italians, French and Portuguese. India and the East Indies were reached by sea; and the English opened up a northern route to Russia, via Archangel.

Coast explored by the Northern 9th–11th centuries

Coast explored by the Portuguese up to 1485

Part I

Henry VII
1485-1509

The first Tudor king came to the throne because of the mistakes and deficiencies of other men rather than because of any compelling qualities in himself. The deaths of the deposed king Henry VI and his son Prince Edward after the battle of Tewkesbury left the Lancastrian line with no other male representative. The premature death of Edward IV in 1483, leaving his sons as minors, and irreconcilable conflict between his widow, Elizabeth, and his brother, Richard, divided the house of York against itself. It was Richard's usurpation which turned the exiled earl of Richmond into a plausible claimant of the throne. Even then he might not have succeeded if it had not suited Charles VIII of France to embarrass the English by supporting his bid. Henry was not by nature a parsimonious man, but he had known poverty, and was aware of the security which wealth could provide. He was not by nature suspicious, and it was said of him that he could hardly be persuaded to think badly of anyone who had once gained his confidence, but he knew the value of information and established one of the best intelligence services in Europe. Both his sons were highly educated in the most up-to-date manner, and he was strongly influenced by his pious and powerful mother, who briefly outlived him.
(Opposite: Henry VII)

1485

Henry landed near Milford Haven on Sunday, 7 August 1485, and marched up the coast through Cardigan and Llanbadarn to Machynlleth. There, on 12 August he was joined by Rhys ap Thomas, the only powerful man in Wales to declare for him openly. From Machynlleth he proceeded via Shrewsbury and Stafford, confronting Richard III and his army at Bosworth Field on 22 August. Thanks largely to the intervention of the Stanleys on his side in the course of the battle, and the non-participation of Henry Percy, 4th Earl of Northumberland, he was victorious Edward Hall picks up the story after Henry's entry to London.

Henry was conveyed with great pomp to Westminster, and there on 30 October was with all the customary ceremonies anointed and crowned king, by the assent of all the commons and the nobility, and was named King Henry VII of that name. This was in the year 1485, Frederick III then being Emperor of Germany, Maximilian I his son then being newly elected King of the Romans, Charles VIII reigning over the French nation, and James III ruling the realm of Scotland.

King Henry obtained and enjoyed the kingdom as a thing elected and provided by God, and encompassed and achieved by his special favour and gracious aspect. For men commonly report that 797 years ago it was revealed by a heavenly voice to Cadwallader, last King of the Britons, that his stock and progeny should reign and have dominion in this land again. Most men were convinced that by this heavenly voice Henry VII was provided and ordained long ago to enjoy and obtain this kingdom, which King Henry VI also claimed.

Wherefore Henry VII was by right and just title of inheritance, and by divine providence, thus crowned and proclaimed king. First of all, following the ancient example of the Athenians to pardon and put out of mind all crimes and offences perpetrated or committed against him or his laws previously, he called his high court of parliament at Westminster on 7 November to establish all things concerned with the preservation and maintenance of his royal person. In parliament he caused it to be proclaimed that all men were pardoned, acquitted and clearly discharged of all offences, sentences of death and executions, and should be restored to their lands and goods if they would submit themselves to his clemency and take an oath truly to serve and obey him as their sovereign lord. And any who would be obstinate and refuse to return to his cause should be accepted and taken as a public enemy to him and his country. Because of this proclamation a great number who came out of various sanctuaries and places of privilege obtained mercy, clearly forgetting the diversity of factions and the taking of sides. After this he began to remember his special friends and partisans, some of whom he advanced to honour and dignity and some he enriched with possessions and goods, every man according to his deserts and merits.

Firstly his uncle Jasper Tudor, earl of Pembroke, he created duke of Bedford, Thomas Lord Stanley he promoted to be earl of Derby, and Lord Chandée of Brittany his special friend he made earl of Bath. Sir Giles Daubeney was made Lord Daubeney, Sir Robert Willoughby was made Lord Brooke, all in their order barons and peers of the realm. And Edward Stafford, eldest son of Henry late duke of Buckingham, he restored to his name, dignity and possessions which King Richard had confiscated.

Besides this the following notable Act was assented to and concluded in this parliament:

"To the pleasure of almighty God, the wealth prosperity and security of this realm of England, and to the singular comfort of all the King's subjects of that realm, to avoid all ambiguities and questions: be it ordained, established and enacted by this present parliament, that the inheritance of the crown of

Henry's Lancastrian roots

Henry Tudor became king in 1485 as heir to the house of Lancaster, which had seized the throne in 1399 when Richard II was deposed by his kinsman, Henry Bolinbroke, son of John of Gaunt, duke of Lancaster. The Lancastrian dynasty had achieved stability under Bolinbroke (as Henry IV, 1399–1413), and a great military reputation under Henry V (1413–22), and survived the minority and incapacity of Henry VI for a generation (1422–61). The failure of Henry V and his brothers to produce heirs, however, brought their relatives, the Beauforts, descended from John of Gaunt and his mistress Catherine Swynford, to the steps of the throne before the birth of Henry VI's son Edward of Lancaster, in 1453. When John Beaufort, 1st duke of Somerset died in 1444, his daughter Margaret Beaufort, born only the year before, became the family's senior representative.

By 1455, Margaret had married Edmund Tudor, 1st earl of Richmond. He had no royal English blood in his veins, but some French: his father Owen ap Maredudd ap Tudur, a squire from North Wales, had married Catherine of Valois, Henry V's widow. Edmund,

Above   Lady Margaret Beaufort.

Left   The King's Title, an act passed by parliament in 1485 declaring Henry and his heirs to the throne.

Overleaf   Pembroke Castle, the birthplace of Henry VII. Henry's uncle, Jasper Tudor, fled from here to safety with him in 1461.

together with his younger brother Jasper, 1st earl of Pembroke, had been welcomed to court by his half-brother, Henry VI. The marriage of Margaret and Edmund underpinned the Lancastrian dynasty and strengthened the Beaufort's position.

The Wars of the Roses began in 1455, and in 1461 Henry VI was deposed by Edward, son of Richard duke of York. Lancastrian hopes, however, still resided in Henry, who fled to the north, and in his only son, Edward of Lancaster who was taken to France by his strong-willed mother, Margaret of Anjou, to continue the struggle. In 1471 Margaret was defeated at the battle of Tewksbury by the Yorkist king, Edward IV, and

Edward was slain. With the murder immediately afterwards of Henry VI, the main line of the house of Lancaster came to an end.

To be restored, the dynasty needed to champion a junior sprig of the Lancastrian tree. One such was Henry, son of Margaret Beaufort and Edmund Tudor. Born at Pembroke castle in January 1453, three years before his father's death, he had been in Yorkist custody since 1461. His claim, however, with its Beaufort stain of illegitimacy, was not strong, and there were other contenders should Edward IV and his Yorkist line fall or fail. After Tewkesbury, therefore Henry and his uncle Jasper sought refuge in Brittany, where they lived for twelve years in obscurity, with few prospects.

England and also of France, with all the pre-eminence and royal dignity appertaining to the same, and all other territories belonging to the king beyond the sea, with any appurtenances appertaining to them, shall rest, remain and abide in the most royal person of our sovereign lord King Henry VII, and in the lawful heirs of his body, perpetually, with the grace of God, and in no others."

Besides this Act all attainders of the king, enacted by King Edward and King Richard, were annihilated and the record of them adjudged to be defaced and put out of memory, and all persons affected by them were restored to their goods, lands and possessions. And in conclusion, several of the Acts made in the time of King Edward and King Richard were annulled and revoked, and others more expedient for the good of the commonwealth were substituted and agreed. When everything necessary had been ordered discreetly and the parliament dissolved for the time being, the king thought it not necessary to leave in oblivion his friends and hostages overseas, thus with all diligent speed he redeemed Thomas Grey, Marquis of Dorset and Sir John Bourchier whom he had left as pledges in Paris for money borrowed there. He also sent into Flanders for John Morton, bishop of Ely.

Having done this, he established in his house a grave council of wise and politic men by whose judgement, order and determination the people might be governed according to justice and equity, and so that all matters might be finished and ended there without the great trouble and expense of a long debate. To hear and decide these matters justly and speedily, he swore into his council several noble and discreet persons, who were highly esteemed and renowned for their policy, wit and particular gravity.

Henry had committed himself to marry Elizabeth at Christmas 1483, as a part of his attempt to recruit the support of former Yorkists, alienated from Richard III.

Although by this choice of wise and grave councillors all things seemed to be brought to a good and perfect conclusion, yet the harp still needed tuning to set all things in harmony. This tuning was the marriage concluded between the king and Elizabeth, daughter to King Edward. Like a good prince true to his oath and promise, he did solemnize and consummate this soon after on 18 January. Because of this marriage peace was thought to descend out of heaven upon England, since the lines of Lancaster and York, both noble families equal in riches, fame and honour, were now tied and connected together, of whose two bodies one heir might succeed who, after their time, should peaceably rule and enjoy the whole monarchy and realm of England.

After this, although apparently all things seemed to be in good order and set for stability, King Henry, wise and expert from past troubles and mischiefs, remembered that it was wisdom to fear and provide for the crafty wiles and lurking traps of his secret enemies. He remembered that all men who have been much embroiled and exercised in planting division and sowing dissension cannot lightly leave their pestiferous appetite and seditious occupation. So for the safeguard of his own body he constituted and ordained a certain number of good archers and other persons who were hardy, strong and agile to attend daily upon his person, whom he named Yeomen of his Guard.

Men thought he learned this precedent from the French king when he was in France, for men do not remember any King of England before who used such a daily guard of soldiers.

To avoid and eschew all possible dangers and unlooked for perils, campaigns of war are of little avail unless there is security and a steadfast support at home, both for safety and security and for the good government of those left behind. The king therefore summoned again his great court of parliament in order to elect the most prudent and authoritative persons of every county, city, port and borough, especially those counsellors and companions who had helped him through dangers, calamities, miseries and tumultuous concerns to triumph and glorious victory. The minds and thoughts of those people he well knew to be fixed and set for the politic rule and prudent government of the public wealth of his realm and dominion. Not forgetting but having fresh in his memory that for that reason principally he was so sorely desired and instantly called by the English nation, his native countrymen. He esteemed it a chief and principal part of his duty to see his realm adorned and decorated with good and profitable laws and statutes, and to flourish in virtuous acts and good civil manners, which should cause all men to hope that everything would continually improve, from evil to good, from good to better, and from better to the best. This sure foundation King Henry laid at the beginning of his reign.

Welsh roots of a dynasty

Henry Tudor's Welsh ancestors – the family of his grandfather, Owen Tudor – had no royal Welsh blood, but had risen to prominence in the 13th century in North Wales by serving the Welsh princes.

Although they survived Edward I's conquest of the region in 1284 by abandoning their loyalties and siding with the English, they supported the rebel cause during Owen Glyndwr's rebellion of 1400–10, and consequently forfeited their wealth and position in North Wales. Young Owen ap Maredudd Tudur, called Owen Tudor by the English, fled and eventually entered the service of Henry V and his French queen Catherine of Valois. After the king's death he married the widowed queen in secrecy. Two sons, Edmund, 1st earl of Richmond, and Jasper, 1st earl of Pembroke, supported their half-brother, Henry VI and the Lancastrian cause, becoming his representatives in Wales in the 1450s, on the eve of the Wars of the Roses.

In this context they attracted attention and admiration in Wales, especially from poets. Distinguished Welshmen who, like them, were also English nobles – others included the Mortimers and Herberts – became a focus for ancient prophecies of fame and achievement, even if the prophesied achievement was against the English to whom they owed so much. Edmund, Jasper, and later, Edmund's only son Henry, fitted into this mould of "the Son of Prophesy" (Mab Darogan), and in the decade and half before the battle of Bosworth, Jasper and his nephew, forced into exile by the Yorkist king, Edward IV, attracted such sentiment.

Below   Henry VII Tower; Pembroke Castle.

The Plumptons were a Yorkshire family; Thomas Betanson was a priest in Sir Robert Plumpton's service. In the following letter he is reporting the events of Henry's first parliament, which met on 7 November 1485. The Act of Resumption was a intended to be a sign of the king's intention to be a good manager of his resources. Betanson here conveys the impression which Henry was trying to create, both of good husbandry and of strong rule.

Sir, if it please your mastership, I wrote a letter to you before Christmas about such news as I had, but I was deceived for I thought you had had it two days ago; and so you shall have another letter with it. Sir, if it please you, this is the news that I know. The king has resumed into his hands by parliament all manner of patents, gifts and offices which he gave from 2 August to the 3 January, and there are many of his household pleased about this. Also he has resumed into his hands all gifts, patents and offices given from the 33rd year of King Henry VI, by King Edward IV, or by King Edward V his son, or by King Richard III. Also it is enacted in parliament that all manner of hunting in parks, chases and forests belonging to the King is a felony. Also, Sir, the King proposes to travel northwards immediately after the parliament, and it is said he intends to act quickly there against such as have offended against him. Sir, I know of no other tidings as yet. Sir, I beseech you, recommend me to both my good ladies, and I send them a paper of the rosary of Our Lady of Coleyn, and I have registered your name with both my ladies names as the paper says, and you are coupled as brother and sisters. Also, Sir, these lords and gentlemen who were attainted receive no mercy it is said. No more, but I beseech your mastership to be a good master to my father and I shall be your beadsman by the grace of God, who evermore keep you in great joy and felicity. From London, the day after St Valentine's day. Also, Sir, the King will travel with a great company; with 1,000 men in armour, it is said, and with more than five or six score lords and knights. Also the duke of Bedford goes into Wales to see that country. Also it is enacted that all sorts of prophecies be made a felony. Sir, of other tidings I know none as yet, of that you may be certain.
Your servant and beadsman, Sir Thomas Betanson.

1486

A realm which had recently changed hands by battle was inevitably unsettled, and Henry consequently carried out an extended tour, a royal progress, to meet his

Exile and return

In 1485 Henry Tudor was a stranger to England. Born in Pembroke in 1453, in custody in South Wales after 1461, and then from 1471 in exile in Brittany, he may have spent only a few weeks in England – in 1470 and early the following year at his mother's home near London – in the 24 years before Bosworth. His most formative years were years of exile. Duke Francis II of Brittany kept him in castles in southern Brittany, his freedom of movement depending on Breton relations with England and the French king. Breton politics, noble intrigues and diplomatic manoeuvres in a French environment nurtured Henry to manhood.

In 1483 Richard III's usurpation of the English throne changed that: Richard alienated many in England and turned some to rebellion, and when Henry, duke of Buckingham's revolt failed in the autumn of 1483, one alternative to Richard as king was removed. Henry Tudor's mother, Margaret Beaufort, die-hard

Lancastrians and even disgruntled Yorkists now looked to him as the most plausible alternative to King Richard. Henry fled to the French court in 1484 when Richard tried to force Brittany to hand him over. There he was given men, ships and money for his enterprise.

He landed in South Wales, where he and his uncle were regarded as famous Welshmen forced into exile by an unpopular English monarchy, and Henry himself as a Welsh leader who would restore national self-respect. His was not a universal appeal either in England or in Wales and many were cautious or outright hostile as he marched through Wales. He won the battle of Bosworth in August 1485, ''by courtesy of Charles VIII of France'', with support from Scots recruited in France, and Welsh squires from parts of south-west, north-east and the marchland of Wales.

Right   Henry was exposed early to the splendour of the European renaissance. He brought the Merode cup to England from Burgundy.

Below   The bleak Brittany landscape where Henry VII spent his formative years.

people, and suppressing any attempt to raise a Yorkist claimant against him before his power was established. Richard Grafton continues the narrative after Henry's coronation.

When the king had settled all things in London, and had set and appointed all his affairs in good and certain order, as he himself thought, he thought it best to make a progress into the other parts of his realm so that he might weed and root out and purge the minds of men tainted and defiled with the contagious smoke of dissension and privy factions, especially in the county of York, which were secret favourers and comforters of his opponents, and not without cause. For King Richard III loved and regarded the northern men more than any other subjects within his whole realm, a thing not unknown to King Henry. Therefore he attempted all the more to keep them in due obedience and faithful deference because he knew they had for a long time given their hearts and minds to his adversaries.

Therefore in the springtime he took a journey towards York, and because Easter was approaching he turned towards the city of Lincoln where he stayed during that feast. Whilst he was there he was informed for certain that Lord Francis Lovell and Humphrey Stafford had left their sanctuary at Colchester, but where they had gone to no man could as yet tell. Because of that the king took little notice of the tale but continued on his journey to York.

As soon as he had been received there and was settled it was rumoured and openly told to the king himself that Francis, Lord Lovell was nearby with a strong and mighty force, and would speedily invade the city. He was also told that Humphrey Stafford and his brother Thomas were in Worcestershire and had there raised a great band of country people and had cast lots as to which men should assault the gates, which scale the walls of the city of Worcester, and who should guard the roads for the safe passage of helpers and sympathizers. When he first heard this the king judged it to be vain and uncertain and thus was but little moved, but after he was assured by credible letters sent from his friends that all was true which rumour said, he was afflicted with no little fear. And surely not without cause, for he wisely considered that he had neither a competent army ready prepared, nor armour nor weapons for those who were present. Also he was now in such a doubtful place, where he could not conveniently

The Bosworth campaign

On 7 August 1485 a small fleet from France entered Milford Haven in Pembrokeshire. Aboard were Henry Tudor, 2nd earl of Richmond and some 2,000 men, most of them French mercenaries. Others were English exiles who had joined Henry in Brittany. Among these fugitives were former courtiers of the first Yorkist king, Edward IV. Their knowledge of England and experience in its government enabled Henry to plan his campaign to win the crown, organize the

Below right   The battle of Bosworth field marked the beginning of Henry VII's reign. After Henry's march from Wales battle and kingdom was decided beside the River Tweed.

Below   Richard III, slain at Bosworth.

delivery of propaganda in his cause and contact potential supporters.

Unopposed, the invaders hastened northwards along Cardigan Bay to Aberystwyth, where they turned east to Welshpool. Here the Welsh grandee, Rhys ap Thomas brought substantial reinforcements. Sir Gilbert Talbot added 500 more at Newport, the first of Henry's recruits in England.

King Richard had been expecting the invasion since June, when he made Nottingham his base. On 15 August he learned that Henry had reached Shrewsbury and was heading towards him. He marched west, confident, perhaps, that his larger army would overwhelm the invaders. Had he been more popular it would have been larger still; many gentry had ignored his call to arms.

Early on 22 August, Richard drew up his forces on Ambien Hill, in the Leicestershire parish of Market

Bosworth. His vanguard under John Howard, 1st duke of Norfolk, moved down but failed to overcome the hardened contingent led by John de Vere, 13th earl of Oxford. Seeing their deadlock, Richard led a separate charge, aiming to end the battle by killing the Tudor pretender. At this point, Sir William Stanley decided to leave the sideline and lead 3,000 Cheshire men to rescue Henry. Richard was surrounded and killed, fighting to the last. His unengaged rearguard departed for its native north, its leader, Henry Percy, 4th earl of Northumberland was taken prisoner, as was the dead Norfolk's son Thomas Howard, earl of Surrey; the estimated 1,000 dead in Richard's army included many of his immediate subordinates.

Richard's body was sent for public display and an ignominious burial in Leicester. Henry Tudor in the meantime was proclaimed King Henry VII.

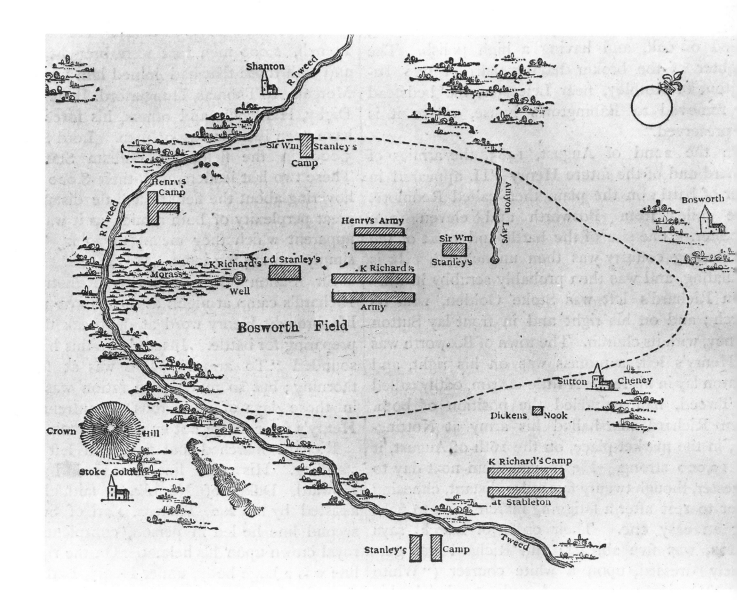

gather an army together, since he was in a city where the memory of his mortal enemy King Richard III was still fresh and lively and not at all forgotten by his friends. Because the matter required diligent speed, least the power of his adversaries might be daily increased and multiplied through a long delay, he commanded the duke of Bedford with 3,000 men, not strongly armed (for their breast plates were mostly made of tanned leather), to undertake a great enterprise. They were to encounter and set upon them with all haste and diligence, and he explained to him what he himself intended to do. After this the king gathered together an army in every place where he might retain them. The duke, setting forward like an eager and fierce captain, came near to the tents and camps of his enemies where he consulted and discussed with certain captains and wise soldiers of his company by what way he might draw and allure them towards peace, without battle or bloodshed. After he had deliberated and taken advice it was decreed that the heralds should proclaim openly that all who would cast down their weapons and armour, and as faithful subjects submit themselves to their natural sovereign lord, should have grace and pardon.

This proclamation was most profitable for Lord Lovell, either for some fear or lack of confidence that he had in his supporters and troops, or being afraid on his own behalf, fled secretly in the night from his company and left them without a leader, as sheep without a shepherd. When his army heard of his departure they put off their armour and came directly to the duke, every man humbly submitting himself and desiring pardon for his offences, wholly trusting on the king's mercy and goodness towards them. So by this politic wisdom and action of the good duke this great rage and fierce company of sturdy and valiant traitors, which had been prepared against the king and were likely to have caused the slaughter of many men, were pacified and repressed and brought into good conformity and obedient subjection. And Lord Lovell, captain and leader of this tumult and rebellion, fearful more of peril and danger than renown or fame in chivalry, did not wait for the doubtful luck of battle but fled posthaste into Lancashire, and there for a while loitered and lurked with Sir Thomas Broughton, who carried great sway in those parts and was of great authority. Humphrey Stafford, hearing what had befallen Lord Lovell, was in great grief and agony, and for fear he also fled and

The king and his council

Henry VII was a novice in government when he rode south from Bosworth in 1485. Most kings of England had served some sort of apprenticeship in its mysteries, or at least been able to observe them as they grew up. By contrast, Henry had no serious prospect of the English throne until two years before he ascended it; he had spent his adult life in exile, and even as a youth may never have set foot outside Wales into England.

A king learning kingship must have a reservoir of experience and good advice in those around him. The institution of a royal council was well-developed by 1485, and it was natural for Henry VII to form his own council. The king could look to a number of able men who had shared his years abroad or who had been involved in the unsuccessful attempt of Henry Stafford, 2nd duke of Buckingham, to overthrow Richard III in 1483. Some, particularly Sir Reginald Bray, Giles Daubeny, Sir Thomas Lovell and Sir Richard Guildford remained with him as his most trusted advisors and men of business.

The most prominent was John Morton, a gifted episcopal politician who had masterminded Henry's emergence as a serious contender for the throne and who was rewarded for his achievement with the archbishopric of Canterbury in 1486 and the lord chancellorship of England in 1487. Morton was present at nearly all recorded meetings of the king's council until his death in 1500.

The new king was also willing to use men who had been at the centre of the Yorkist government, but who were prepared to recognize the new political realities. The most surprising of these to emerge as a royal servant was Thomas Howard, only son of the first duke of Norfolk. Both he and his father had fought against Henry at Bosworth, where the duke had been killed. From 1489 Howard ruled the North in the name of Arthur, prince of Wales, and found high favour with the king, which as a result led Henry to appoint him lord treasurer in 1501.

Of more than two hundred men who were styled royal councillors during Henry's reign, about seventy had the right to claim that proud title at any one time: a mix of noblemen, gentry, lawyers and clerics. Councillors were employed on a variety of business and in a variety of groupings, and recorded meetings of the council show average attendances of about two dozen. Their role was varied. They gathered in the king's presence in the Star Chamber, so named because there were stars on the ceiling, to dispatch legal cases brought by aggrieved individuals, attending to poor men's legal

Above   The Court of Common Pleas allowed ordinary men and women to receive an informal legal service without having to pay large fees.

suits in sessions known as "requests", and taking care of general business.

To establish a system of justice and strong government the king set up two separate tribunals through parliamentary statutes in 1487 and 1495. Both required a small number of leading officials and members of the council to take part. The 1487 tribunal met in the same Star Chamber as the council that dealt with judicial business. This tribunal, however, was establishing the rule of law against rioters or powerful figures who sought to corrupt legal proceedings. The second, in 1495, was intended to specialize in offences of perjury. Neither seem to have been very active, even under Henry, and disappeared after his death.

Henry showed little interest in using parliament as a partner in his rule and the seven which met during his reign did their duty in voting through taxation without apparent fuss or any great change from previous régimes. Instead Henry found more benefit in summoning another traditional institution which faded from sight under later monarchs: the Great Council. In contrast to parliament, with the Great Council he was far freer to select whomsoever he wanted to attend, be it great nobleman and councillor, or on occasion a representative of the chartered corporations of towns and cities.

The five Great Councils which Henry summoned were made partners in vital decisions of policy such as levying taxation, going forward to war, and even confirming his decisions in the course of military campaigns.

took sanctuary in a village called Culham, two miles from Abingdon. But because the sanctuary was not a sufficient legal defence (as it was later proved before the justice of the King's Bench) he was forcibly taken from that place and brought to the Tower of London, and from there conveyed to Tyburn and executed. But his younger brother Thomas who was with him was thought not to have acted of his own will maliciously, but through the evil counsel and mischievous persuasion of his elder brother.

This case created a precedent for not allowing sanctuary, or retreat into the protection of the legal immunity enjoyed by the church, in cases of treason.

After the king had, through his council, appeased and repressed this tumultuous sedition which greatly vexed and disturbed his spirits, and had reduced to reason and conformity the rude and babbling people of the north, especially the inhabitants of the county of York, he returned to London and shortly after that to Winchester where in September Queen Elizabeth his wife was delivered of a fair prince, named Arthur at his baptism. Englishmen no more rejoiced over that name than other nations and foreign princes trembled and quaked, so much was the name terrible and fearful to all nations. And from Winchester he returned to London.

1486

Henry VII was a king, who, from the beginning of his reign, maintained close relations with the City of London, and encouraged the enterprise of its merchants, then entering upon a new phase of expansion. The Great Chronicle looks at him from the City's point of view.

King Henry, upon the day after Hugh Bryse had in London taken his charge as mayor before the Barons of the Exchequer on 30 October, was solemnly crowned at Westminster. And after that solemnization within the monastery was furnished a royal and excellent feast in Westminster Hall.

And this same year the king sent my lord treasurer with master Bray and other honourable personages to the mayor, requiring of him and his citizens a loan of 6,000 marks. The mayor therefore assembled his brethren and the common council on the Tuesday following, and by their authority a loan of £2,000 was granted to the king. It was levied shortly after, and was assessed by the fellowships and not by the wards, for the greater ease of the poor people. Of that loan the fellowships of grocers and drapers lent

£937 6s. The loan was repaid to the grocers and the drapers in the following year.

In mayor Bryse's time there was great altercation among the merchant adventurers trading with Flanders about choosing the master of the fellowship called Adventurers. The reason for this was that all the fellowships of the city were discontented that the master of that company was usually taken from the Mercers, and so all the other adventurers thought that the mercers were in many ways favoured more than other merchants of other trades were. To appease this argument the mayor called before him to his house the wardens of all the companies and fellowships of the city which were trading with Flanders and heard all the arguments of the mercers and likewise from the others. From this he received more labour than thanks, for they departed from him unreconciled, so much so that at the next market the companies of sundry trades held so fast to their opinion that the master who was a mercer was discharged and, to be impartial, Robert Rydon, a man learned in the civil law, was admitted. But after a short while he was again discharged and then a draper named Robert Drayton occupied the office for a time, and some others, to the restfulness of the said adventurers. In this mayor's time wheat was 3s. a bushel, and bay sea salt 2s.8d. a bushel.

1487

Lovell's failure appeared to demonstrate that only a prince of the House of York could be sufficiently popular to challenge the new king. Unfortunately no genuine prince was available as Hall explains...

In the meantime, from a small matter altogether false and invented, an open path and apparent highway was made for greater inconvenience to ensue. The subtle juggling and crafty connivance of this matter, no less deceitful than the legerdemain of a juggler, was thought by all wise men at first too bold and overpresumptuous an act to be attempted. But considering the times it was not so monstrous as to be worthy of great wonder and admiration, since many persons then either borne in the womb of continual dissension or nourished with the milk of civil sedition could not well live at rest nor forbear their usual custom of causing strife and daily debate. They sometimes sat at home planning and imagining hurt and damage towards those who in their hearts they disdained, and sometimes remembered that by the liberty and privilege of war all is fish that comes to

Henry's marriage to Elizabeth

The marriage of Henry Tudor and Elizabeth of York was first planned by their mothers, Lady Margaret Beaufort and Elizabeth Woodville, widow of King Edward IV. This was in the summer of 1483, after Richard III's seizure of the throne when Elizabeth believed that her sons Edward V and Richard, duke of York, the "princes in the Tower", had been done to death. John Morton, bishop of Ely, with other former councillors of Edward IV, took part in this matchmaking.

The object of the conspiracy was to choose an acceptable figurehead for rebellion against Richard III. As the Wars of the Roses had made clear, governments could be changed only by the deposition and coronation of kings; political opposition had to be headed by a claimant with a good royal pedigree.

Henry Tudor was the great, great grandson of John of Gaunt, father of the first Lancastrian king, Henry IV (1399–1413), but his claim to royalty was unimpressive and he had not been seen as a threat by the Yorkist Edward IV, whose parliaments had endorsed the doctrine that the Lancastrians were not legitimate kings.

Nonetheless, Henry was the residuary male legatee of the Lancastrian interest, and still a bachelor at the age of 26. Nine years his junior, Elizabeth was also single. As the eldest child of Edward IV, and her brothers dead, she naturally attracted loyalty from her father's retainers who were outraged by Richard's usurpation. The plan in 1483 was that these courtiers should raise a revolt, and that Henry should return from Brittany and marry Elizabeth. But the risings were uncoordinated and were crushed piecemeal. Survivors fled to Brittany. At Christmas, in Rennes cathedral, Henry promised to marry Elizabeth once he gained the crown, and his assembled supporters swore homage to him as King of England.

He was crowned on 30 October 1485, two months after his victory at Bosworth Field, but his marriage was delayed. Elizabeth was, through her Beaufort grandmother, a descendant of John of Gaunt like Henry, and related to the king according to ecclesiastical law. A papal dispensation was therefore essential for the marriage to be lawful. This was granted on 16 January 1486, on the grounds that the couple were marrying to end the conflict between the houses of Lancaster and York. Tudor historical propaganda claimed that their ambition was realized and England was indeed rescued from the horrors of further civil upheaval.

Top Signatures of Henry VII and Queen Elizabeth his wife.

Above A medallion struck to commemorate the marriage of Henry VII and Elizabeth of York in January 1486, which unified the houses of York and Lancaster.

the net, ever delighting in spoiling, robbing and revenge, vehemently thirsting for the destruction and loss of those they wished to be revenged of, willing to live without law in times of peace and war, and wishing the world never to be at peace. As persons only dedicated and given to mischief and wicked inventions, either for hatred, evil will and malice towards those they favoured not, or for some gain, profit and advantage of those they thought to set up and advance, they were by fraudulent, secret and crafty collusion ready and prepared every day to disquiet the king and his whole realm, thinking that heaven had too much peace and quiet, and hell too little trouble and vexation.

And there was no lack of supporters and encouragers, so that twenty persons would rather prick them forward with a sharp spur than one pull them back with a dull bridle. Among these monsters and limbs of the devil was one Richard Symonds, a priest, a man of low and obscure family who from his birth delighted in fraud and crafty behaviour, and yet he was well-learned, but not so well-learned as wily, nor so wily as ungracious.

This Sir Richard Symonds had chosen a scholar called Lambert Simnel, one of a gentle nature and promising wit, to be the organ and means by which he would implement his false feigned enterprise and attempt. The devil, chief master of mischief, put it into the wicked mind and venomous brain of this most perniciously disloyal and traitorous person to commence to contrive and devise how he might make this child and scholar Lambert into the true inheritor of the crown of England and so make him king, and promote himself to the chief archbishopric or some other high position within the realm.

The chief foundation of his undertaking (which made him the more bold) was the rumour which many men believed that the children of King Edward IV were not dead but had escaped secretly to some remote place and were living there. These rumours, although they were frivolous and vain, and without any likelihood of truth, animated and encouraged this priest much, so that he thought the time had come for this Lambert to take upon himself the person and name of one of King Edward IV's children and to claim a title to the realm and the kingdom, being certain that he would lack neither friends nor aid, since cankered hatred rooted and founded upon most wicked factions and seditious

The development of commerce

Henry VII's attitude to overseas trade, like that of his predecessors, was ambivalent. Although he recognized the potential contribution English merchants could make to his revenues, his overriding aim was to scotch plots against his rule hatched by Yorkists abroad; an aim that sometimes entailed sacrificing commercial interests. Overseas trade was concentrated on the Low Countries, but from 1493 to 1496 when their rulers supported the Yorkist impostors Perkin Warbeck and Lambert Simnel, Henry embargoed direct trade.

His long-term objective, however, was to secure his subjects' right to trade widely at fixed traditional customs rates, and he waged a long diplomatic battle to induce the rulers of the Netherlands to implement the Magnus Intercursus made on these terms in 1496. He used alliances, with Spain in 1489 and Denmark in 1490–1, to secure privileges for English merchants, and the first peace treaties for over a century with France, in 1492, and Scotland, in 1502, to stimulate trade with those countries. Henry's attempts to gain reciprocal privileges from the Hanseatic League for English merchants engaged in Scandinavian, North German and Baltic trade failed, however, and the Venetians jealously guarded their trade monopoly between England and the Eastern Mediterranean.

Henry's reasons for supporting English enterprise abroad were political as well as financial. The fleets that opposed invasions and transported armies to France were composed mainly of hired merchant ships and impressed seamen. The Navigation Acts of 1485 and 1489, were intended to concentrate the carrying trade in English hands by forbidding certain imports in foreign ships. During emergencies the financial and military aid given by England's leading towns was crucial to dynastic security, and kings were judged on how firmly they upheld urban privileges and guarded and fostered overseas trade.

Above all, the Crown needed London's support. Its population of about 60,000 and its wealth, far outstripped those of its rivals – Norwich, one of the

Far left   Two signet rings with tradesmen's marks.

Above   A wool merchant's house in Lavenham, Suffolk, a prospering wool town in the fifteenth century.

Right   A chart of the new standard weights and measures, showing the regulation tables for market supervisors.

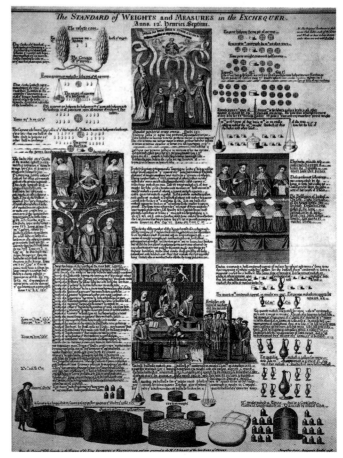

largest, had a population of just over 10,000 – while London merchants dominated the export trade in cloth, which rose by 61 per cent during Henry's reign. The cloth-making industry itself was concentrated in older urban centres such as York, Norwich, Bristol and Salisbury, as well as in some fast-growing rural ones such as Castle Combe in Wiltshire. Lavenham in Suffolk, which by the 1520s had a population of less than 1,000, a typical size for an English country town, was the thirteenth richest town in England. Its eminence rested upon the conversion of English wool into cloth by an industry which had grown phenomenally since the later 14th century.

Henry's awareness of the importance of this industry led him to invest in the import of alum, used in dyeing, and his concern for the harmonious functioning of the Company of Merchant Adventurers, who dominated cloth exports to the Low Countries.

divisions are so enduring and by nature everlasting that they can never be clearly extirpated or dug out of their rotten hearts, but they will if they can further their intended enterprise by hand and foot, tooth and nail.

This poor priest, brought into this fool's paradise by his own fantastical imagination, informed and taught the child diligently at Oxford where he went to school, instructing him in princely behaviour, civil manners and fruitful literature, telling him of what high parentage and from what noble progeny he was lineally descended, thus persuading and teaching him learnedly and craftily for his own purpose so that people hearing the child reciting his pedigree so wisely might give more credit to his deceitful pretense and false-coloured invention.

Richard, duke of York, had resided in Ireland as King's Lieutenant from July 1449 to September 1450, and had created a lasting loyalty to his family among the Irish peerage.

Soon afterwards the rumour was blown abroad that Edward Plantagenet, the young earl of Warwick had broken out of prison. When Symonds heard of this he resolved to bring his intentions to a conclusion; he changed the child's baptismal name and called him Edward like the young earl of Warwick, who was the same age and stature and then sailed with his pupil to Ireland. There he told his plans and business to certain of the Irish nobility whom he knew by true fame and report to bear little favour towards King Henry and his supporters. When they had sworn oaths to him and given promises of aid he showed them how he had saved and preserved the duke of Clarence's son from death and had out of goodwill brought him to that country and region where he knew King Edward IV and all his family were favoured and loved above any other. The nobility believed this straight away and showed forth and published this feigned fable and imagined juggling amongst themselves until at last it was believed to be the gospel truth without any argument, ambiguity or question. So much so that Lord Thomas Fitzgerald, chancellor of Ireland, defrauded by his illusion to believe it the plain truth, received him into his castle and treated him with honour and reverence as one descended from the blood royal and began to aid and help him greatly. Firstly calling all his friends and supporters and others who were bound to him, he told them of the coming of this

child and affirmed that the crown and sceptre of the realm rightly belonged to this young prince as sole male heir of the line of Richard III, duke of York. He exhorted and desired them for the sake of the child who was true heir to the crown and of himself, to help and assist him to obtain the garland and possession of that crown lineally descended to him from his grandfather.

Simnel was crowned in Dublin as King Edward VI on 24 May 1487

When these doings were confirmed to King Henry by messengers sent to England it was no wonder that he was sorely vexed and angered, that by the deceit and fraud of such a dunghill knave and vile born villain such great sedition should be excited and stirred up against him.

Nevertheless, his first reaction was to try the peaceful tactic which had worked so well against Lovell in the previous year.

As a circumspect, ingenious and prudent prince, carefully considering and looking to the future, he realized that if this enterprise was undertaken the final end would be the bloody dart of mortal war, and if they should join and fight in open battle many innocent men on both sides would perish and come undeservedly and without any offence to ruin and confusion. Therefore before all else he determined to see if he could without any battle or blow struck (the end of which is ever ambiguous and doubtful) pacify and reduce the rebels to rule, reason and due subjection, before this evil, newly-planted weed should stray and wander over all the good plants of the realm.

Therefore he called his whole council together at the Charterhouse near his royal manor of Richmond, and there consulted how to pacify this sudden violence secretly begun without any more disturbance or open trouble. It was decided that before anything else was attempted a general pardon should be published to all offenders who were prepared to receive it if afterwards they were true, loving and obedient to the king their sovereign lord, according to their bounden duty and allegiance. It was thought that if the pardon were put off any longer, in the meanwhile (as the proverb says delay attracts and risks peril) Sir Thomas Broughton, who had hidden and kept Lord Lovell from the king for a

Regional and local administration

Local government was chiefly carried out by members of the resident élites in shire, city and borough. In the shires, the Crown controlled the appointment of all officials, except for coroners. The principal official, the sheriff, was responsible for the execution of writs, the standard instrument of royal command, including those ordering the election for parliament of two knights of the shire and two members each from cities and parliamentary boroughs.

Crime was dealt with at regular sessions held by justices of the peace, whose main responsibility was to keep public order. They were, however, increasingly burdened with upholding economic and social regulations that were intended to enforce a just and hierarchically determined behaviour, such as the statutory ban on the lower orders playing tennis or gambling, except at holiday time. Local gentlemen were responsible for the collection of parliamentary taxes, except for customs dues, organizing county militias and, to a large extent, securing for the Crown its lucrative feudal rights. Professional justices of the King's Bench regularly visited shires to deal with serious crimes, and were appointed on commissions to enquire into and settle specific problems.

For the most part, the jurisdiction of shire officials did not intrude into cities and boroughs privileged by royal charter, whose gates, walls and ditches proclaimed their semi-autonomy. Within urban bounds, government and justice were exercised in councils and courts by the mayor and aldermen who were elected annually, mainly from and by the élite of the rich burgesses — to whose ranks prospering commoners might hope to aspire. Burgeoning civic bureaucracies were in control. Leading cities had the right to appoint their own sheriffs and justices of the peace.

For the labourers and craftsmen who made up the bulk of the English population, authority was represented most fully by their lord's manor court, in which the richest and most respected of them had important roles as jurors and court officials, as well as by the village constableship, an office held by the same sort of men.

Royal authority and local order were threatened by magnates and gentry who used their territorial power and positions in shire administrations to further their own interests, and those of the networks of patronage and alliance which they commonly formed. Henry VII's response was to trust certain magnates and their private councils to supervise regional government: Thomas Stanley, 1st earl of Derby, in Lancashire and Cheshire,

Above   A mid-fifteenth century London alderman dressed in the robes of a lord mayor.

and John de Vere, earl of Oxford, in East Anglia. He used offices in, and revenues from Crown lands to retain gentry directly in his service and exact from them loyal and responsible conduct. Statutes and proclamations in 1485, 1487 and 1504, severely restricted the magnates' right to retain and give ''liveries'', uniforms and badges, which might intimidate judicial opponents and sway jurors. Measures like these demonstrated Henry's concern to provide generally for the effective and impartial administration of justice, and to impose a more exacting standard of obedience among the aristocracy.

great while and was at hand with several of his friends, might, in despair and without hope of any grace, suddenly move a new insurrection against the king and cause trouble in some place where he could least resist. For although they were thought to have been confederates and sworn members of this new conspiracy, yet because there was no certain proof or obvious evidence of it, it was thought to be most profitable for the time being to extend no extremity or cruelty to them in any way. But if they were to draw back and be negligent in fulfilling their duty and allegiance, then they should be punished as they deserved according to the common saying: "such bread as they bake, such must they eat".

The king therefore gave a general pardon throughout all England (with no exception for any offence), even to those who had committed high treason against his majesty and royal person. Furthermore after long consultation and mature deliberation it was thought by the whole senate then present most necessary and fitting, to avoid the erroneous rumour rumbling and being proclaimed abroad, that it should be proved that the son of the duke of Clarence was in England, and that he should in person be shown abroad in the city and other public places, so that the opinion falsely affirming that he was in Ireland might be, among the people, put down and counted as an invention and a vain, imagined fable.

In this solemn council many things concerning the realm were debated and decided. Amongst others it was determined that Elizabeth, the wife of King Edward IV, should lose and forfeit all her lands and possessions because she had voluntarily submitted herself and her daughters wholly into the hands of King Richard III against her promise to the lords and nobles of this realm. They, at her desire and request, left all that they had in England and fled to King Henry in Brittany, who was to marry her eldest daughter.

Through her double dealings it was likely to have followed that the marriage could not take place, nor might the noblemen who at her request took King Henry's part return without danger to their lives.

When everything in this council was concluded and agreed according to the king's intent, he returned to the City of London, commanding that the Sunday following, Edward, the young earl of Warwick, be brought from the Tower of London

Managing the economy

The health of England's economy began to improve after 1470. The clearest yardstick for this is provided by totals of woollen cloths exported: under 30,000 in the 1460s, double that number in the 1480s, and treble after 1500. This was the country's principal export, and the customs duties were the largest single source of royal revenue. Because of the demand for wool, and the growth – after a long decline – of the national population, incomes from the land also began to rise. The Yorkist kings had profited from these conditions by improving their methods of estate management and appointing receivers who accounted directly to the king's Chamber Treasury.

Initially Henry VII allowed these new practices to lapse. Revenue from crown lands returned to the Exchequer, where ancient routines did not allow for maximizing profits. A second Act in 1487 for the resumption of royal estates granted mainly to the aristocracy, caused the king to resume the appointment of receivers and auditors for his lands.

The Yorkist structure was renewed under the control of the Chamber, a branch of the king's domestic establishment, where he personally supervised its operations. Henry's legendary application to this work is attested by his daily signatures in the Chamber's account books.

Eventually the bulk of the royal revenues was paid straight into the Chamber, instead of the Exchequer, allowing the king to use them without delay; a vital asset in times of crisis. The Chamber handled £17,000 in 1488, but from 1502 to 1505 its average annual receipts were £105,000. By then, £40,000 came from crown lands, which had been swollen by the estates of attainted rebels, deaths in the royal family, and resumptions. Through the network of receivers, closely directed by the king and his financial experts, potential resources were exploited, rents were raised, and full payments enforced. More were discovered as a result of enquiries to detect possible concealments of revenues due to the king.

It is a myth that Henry amassed a great treasure, but he enjoyed solvency. The splendour of his court which impressed both subjects and foreign visitors is evidence of that.

Right   The Court of Chancery dealing with various writs and subpenas. Two judges preside over the proceedings of the lawyers who are dressed in their party-coloured gowns.

through the most public and frequented streets of London to St Paul's cathedral. The young gentleman showed himself openly to everybody during the procession and stayed for high mass, speaking openly with many noblemen, especially with those who were suspected and thought to have taken part in the action against the king.

However this medicine was no use or profit to evil disposed persons or brainless men. For the earl of Lincoln, John de la Pole and Elizabeth, sister of King Edward IV, did not neglect so open an opportunity for new trouble and mischief and the opportunity to strengthen and bolster the enterprise of the Irishmen. And doubtless the man, being of great wit and intelligence and of no small judgement but half infected with the venomous scab of the late civil war, could not with a quiet mind allow King Henry, the head of the opposing faction, to reign in quiet, but consulting with Sir Thomas Broughton and other trusty friends proposed to sail to Flanders to his aunt, Lady Margaret, duchess of Burgundy, trusting with her help to get a powerful army of men and to join with the supporters of the newly raised rebellion.

Therefore after the king had dissolved the parliament which was then held he fled secretly to Flanders to Lady Margaret where Francis, Lord Lovell had landed a few days before. Being there all together every man according to his own opinion reasoned, argued and debated what it was best to do. After a long discussion they came to a final agreement that the earl of Lincoln and Lovell should go to Ireland and there attend upon her pretended nephew and honour him as king, and with the help of the Irish forces bring him to England and sending for all their supporters should without delay give battle to King Henry. If all their doings prospered and were successful then Lambert should by the consent of the council be deposed and Edward, the true earl of Warwick, be freed from prison, and afterwards by the authority and help of his friends amongst the nobility be proclaimed king.

This sudden move abruptly disabused the king of any illusions about the success following a peaceful policy.

But King Henry, thinking his nobles to be well appeased by the sight of Edward the true son of the duke of Clarence and not thinking any man could be so foolish as to invent, feign or counterfeit anything more about him was only concerned to suppress the

The great noble households

At the end of the 15th century it was generally accepted that a large part of a noble's income should be spent on maintaining a household similar to that of the king, but scaled down according to rank.

The number of a noble's attendants and the lavishness of his or her standard of living were the most public indices of status and wealth. Moreover, a well-ordered household demonstrated a noble's personal ability to govern and his employees usefulness in government. Besides providing the daily spiritual, physical and recreational needs of all its inhabitants, a lord's household was a means for him to gain power in the realm, particularly in the regions where his estates were concentrated.

Its organization was traditional and stereotyped. Interlocking "below stairs" departments were responsible for catering and housekeeping, outdoor sports and transport as well as for the noble's personal attendants, wards and choristers he and his lady were having educated, and for the needs of all other household servants, down to the kitchen grooms who turned the great spits or cleaned out the stables, kennels or mews. Nobles and their companions lived largely apart from the domestic hurly-burly, enjoying a communal sort of privacy in luxurious suites of apartments furnished with ostentatious status symbols such as elaborate beds, tapestried wall-hangings and sets of tableware.

Nobles usually had town houses in or near London and in county towns near their principal estates. They travelled with a skeleton "riding" household to visit these inns or their hunting-lodges, or when attending court, staying with friends or going on pilgrimage. Their great households were also often on the road, and their convoys of carts were a familiar sight as they moved between castles.

The extended noble households were mainly in the country: the public and private governing roles of their lords, in which the households played a pivotal role, were concerned above all with rural affairs. The principal household officers and the noble's attendant knights and esquires were often members of his council, concerned with ordering his propertied affairs. In his presence chamber the lord received petitions from neighbours and tenants and arbitrated with his councillors' advice in their disputes.

In many regions, especially in the North, where Henry VII had few hereditary ties, noble households were important adjuncts of royal government. When a northerner joined one of Henry's regional magnates to revel and dance with the king, or bath and sleep alongside him, a bond of familiarity might be created that would ultimately benefit the king's service and the tranquility of the realm. However, if a noble considered that loyalty to the Crown was in conflict with the honour and profit of his family, the household might become a root of rebellion and regional disorder.

On five occasions between 1461 and 1485, the English throne changed hands because a king was deposed or died. What made these upheavals possible was the ability of a divided nobility to raise armies. Patronage, called "good lordship", was sought by gentry living in the neighbourhood of a noble's estates. Through his favour they could hope to further their own and their children's careers. As respect for the crown and for the law declined, it seemed highly desirable to enjoy the protection of a potent champion. For their part, lords ambitious for regional dominance needed a close relationship with knights and squires whose domestic servants and tenants could supplement their own for a show of force. The size of these retinues wearing a lord's livery signalled his "worship". Some

Below   Penshurst Place in Kent, built and lived in by Edward Stafford, duke of Buckingham.

Below right   A castle built less as a fortress and more of a monument.

retainers were paid fees, but in many cases their lord's promise to uphold their interests was sufficient.

The greatest magnates in many parts of England and Wales naturally had the largest retinues. A few in collusion could concentrate overwhelming might and threaten the stability of the kingdom. When Henry VII came to the throne, however, there were few survivors of the families whose leaders had dominated political life in the mid-15th century. Lands of the duchy of York and earldom of Warwick had become crown property, and Edward Stafford, 3rd duke of Buckingham, was a boy in the king's wardship. By an act of attainder in his first parliament, Henry confiscated lands of John Howard, 1st duke of Norfolk, who had died at Bosworth, together with the lands of Richard III's other supporters in the battle. On the other hand, he restored John de Vere, 13th earl of Oxford and other lords previously attainted for their hostility to the Yorkist kings. His reign therefore began with 50 families whose heads were lords, in that they were personally summoned to parliaments.

Overleaf   Compton Wynyates, Warwickshire, a magnificent manor house built by the Compton family during the reigns of Henry VII and Henry VIII. Henry VIII was a frequent visitor to the home of his friend Sir William Compton.

infamous Irishmen and studied how to subdue and repress their bold enterprise and seditious conspiracy. And hearing suddenly that the earl of Lincoln with others had fled and gone to his adversaries he was much moved and determined with a strong hand and martial power to overcome his enemies and ill-wishers whose malice he could not shun or avoid by counsel or policy. Being so determined he commanded some of his captains to prepare an army of men from every part of his realm, and to bring and lead them to one assigned place, so that when his adversaries should come forward he might with his populous multitude and great power suddenly set upon them and so overcome and vanquish them altogether. And fearing that others would follow the earl of Lincoln to Flanders he caused the eastern part of the country and all the borders thereabouts to be carefully kept so that no others might escape or give them aid. He came to the town of St Edmundsbury and was informed that Lord Thomas, marquis of Dorset, was coming to excuse and purge himself before the king for certain things he was suspected of having done thoughtlessly when he was in France. The king sent John de Vere, earl of Oxford to intercept him while he was still on his journey and convey him to the Tower of London to try his truth and test his patience. For if he were his friend, as he was indeed, he would not be discontent to suffer so little a reproach and rebuke for his prince's pleasure, and if he were not his friend there to remain in safety that he might do him no damage or hurt.

From there the king went to Norwich, and spending Christmas day there left afterwards for Walsingham, and coming there to the church of Our Lady he prayed devoutly and made supplication to almighty God that by his divine power and through the intercession of Our Lady he might avoid the snares and secret workings of his enemies and preserve himself and his country from the imminent danger and reduce again the straying sheep who were amiss to their own fold and true shepherd. His prayers finished he returned from there via Cambridge to London.

In the meantime the earl of Lincoln and Lord Lovell had got with the help of Lady Margaret about 2,000 Germans with Martin Swart, a nobleman in Germany as their leader, and had sailed to Ireland. And so from there with a great multitude of beggarly Irishmen, almost totally naked and unarmed except for skins and cloaks, of whom Lord Thomas Fitz-gerald was captain and leader, they sailed to England with this new-found king and landed deliberately at the tower of Foulney near Lancaster, trusting there to be helped with money by Sir Thomas Broughton one of the chief members of this unhappy conspiracy.

The king, not allowing the matter to rest but mistrusting and smelling the storm which followed, before his enemies arrived sent certain horsemen throughout all the western parts of his realm, chiefly to await the coming and arrival of his enemies, secondly to wait for such spies as came out of Ireland and to apprehend them and compel them to show and declare the secrets of their enemies. When he had gathered all his army together, over which the duke of Bedford and the earl of Oxford were the chief captains, he went to Coventry and there his light horsemen, fulfilling their duty, returned and informed him that the earl of Lincoln had landed at Lancaster with his new king. When the king understood that this was so he consulted with his nobles and counsellors as to whether it was best to confront them out of hand or let them continue for a while, for this matter required both advice and speed. After they had put their heads together and debated the matter well it was decided that they should set upon them without any further delay, lest their power might be increased and greatly multiplied. And so after taking such advice the king removed to Nottingham and pitched his camp there by a little wood called Bowers. Shortly afterwards there came to him George Talbot, earl of Shrewsbury, Lord Strange and Sir John Cheney, all valiant captains, with many other noble and expert men of war. For the king had commanded that all people in the adjoining counties who were able and of strength to carry arms should be ready at an hour's warning in case they were needed. Therefore picked men and hardy persons and such like were chosen in great haste, and a great army was drafted and gathered together.

The battle of East Stoke was to be the last engagement of the Wars of the Roses, and was hard fought, largely because of the presence of the German mercenaries.

During this time the earl of Lincoln, having gone into Yorkshire, passed softly on his journey without spoiling or hurting any man, expecting this to cause men to resort to him, but after he perceived that few or none followed him, and that it was to more purpose to turn back since his enemies were all ready to

Collecting taxes

Historically, the exchequer validated the receipt and issue of royal revenues and operated separately from the royal court. Sheriffs and other royal officials were accounted to the Exchequer of Receipt for their liabilities; royal debtors and defaulters were summoned before the Barons of the Exchequer in the Exchequer of Pleas. Much of the king's revenue was paid at source to a variety of annuitants to whom annual sums had been granted and to creditors and, as a result, the Exchequer received less cash than it accounted for and was often short of funds to pay the royal household's running costs, a major cost.

When he first ascended the throne, Henry VII, inexperienced in government, preferred to trust in Exchequer control of his revenue. However, he soon came to recognize the advantages of chamber finance. By the end of his reign the treasurer of the Chamber was receiver-general of all Crown Lands and most other revenues. Henry himself audited his accounts, initialling the pages of the account books.

However, Henry was poor compared to his Spanish and French counterparts, who had vast taxable resources at their disposal. He died leaving debts, not an accumulated treasure in coin.

Like his Yorkist predecessors, he needed to maintain a suitably luxurious household, retain knights and esquires and fund garrisons on the French borders, and in the Anglo-Scottish Marches. An alternative and potentially more lucrative policy would have been to increase taxation, a step to take with care in the aftermath of civil wars which still occasionally smouldered. To a considerable extent, the public regarded taxation as justifiable only in an emergency, to pay the costs of waging a war or suppressing a rebellion: taxes levied without parliamentary grant might easily raise hackles, and even grants made by the parliament were not guaranteed a good response. The main forms of extra-parliamentary taxation were loans and benevolences or non-returnable gifts, and Henry sent commissioners around England to raise loans in 1486 and 1489.

Below   Henry's tax collectors eagerly counting the day's take.

set upon him, he firmly determined to risk the outcome of battle, remembering that the luck of Mars always stands upon six or seven, and that King Henry not two years before with a small force of men vanquished King Richard III and all his mighty army.

And so putting his confidence in his company he made his way from York to Newark upon Trent where he pitched his camp and lodged there for the night. The earl of Lincoln, informed of his coming, was not afraid but continued on his journey and at a little village called Stoke planted his camp near to the king and his army. The following day the king divided his troops into three battalions and in good array approached near to the town of Stoke where there was a level and flat place for both sides to contest the battle.

On 16 June when the place was appointed and ordained to try the end by battle the earl set forth his army and, giving a token to his company, set upon his adversaries with a manly courage, desiring his soldiers to remember that day his honour and their own lives. And so both the armies joined battle and fought earnestly and sharply, in so much that the Germans being tried and expert in war were in strength and in policy equal and equivalent to the Englishmen, but as for Martin Swart their chief captain and leader, not many Englishmen could be compared or likened to his manhood both for valiant courage and a stout stomach and strength and agility of body. Of the other side the Irishmen, although they fought hard and stuck to it valiantly because after the manner of their country they were almost naked, without harness or armour, were struck down and slain like dull brute beasts, whose deaths and destruction was a great discouragement and abashment to the rest of the company. Thus they fought for a while so hard and so eagerly on both sides that no man could well judge to whom the victory was likely to fall. But at length the king's vanguard, being so full of people and well fortified by wings which both began and continued the fight, set upon their adversaries with such force and violence that first they overcame and killed one by one those captains who resisted their might and power, and afterwards put all the rest to fearful flight. They were either apprehended as captives and prisoners in their flight whilst running away or else slain.

When this battle was finished and fought out to the end, then it clearly appeared what high prowess, what manly stomachs, what courageous hearts and what valiant courage the king's adversaries had. For their chief captains were all slain and found dead. However some say that Lord Lovell took horse and would have fled over the Trent, but he was not able to reach the far side because of the height of the bank and so was drowned in the river.

There were killed at the battle 4,000. Of the king's side there were not half of those who fought in the vanguard and gave the onslaught killed or hurt.

Then Lambert, the youngster falsely reported to be the Duke of Clarence's son, and his master Richard Symonds the priest were both taken, but neither of them were put to death since Lambert was but a poor innocent soul, a mere child and not of such an age as to undertake such an enterprise of his own device, and the other was a priest. But so that he might remember that a stone often falls on the head of him who throws it into the air and that many a man makes a rod for his own back when he intends it for another, this priest was for penance committed to perpetual prison and miserable captivity.

Finally Lambert was made the king's falconer, after he had been a turn-spit and performed other such lowly offices in the king's kitchen and scullery for a while. When Lady Margaret was informed and notified of the outcome in Flanders she was heartily sorry and much lamented and deplored that her imagined purpose had come to such an unfortunate end. Therefore she was incontinently devising, practicing and imagining some great and even more difficult enterprise by which she might vex and perturb once again the King of England and the whole region, as shall be shown plainly later.

1488

Like any king coming to the throne in similar circumstances, Henry was short of money. This was not due so much to a lack of resources, rather a cash flow problem. The Great Chronicle again notices the effect on London.

At the beginning of William Horn's time as mayor of London Queen Elizabeth was crowned at Westminster on St Katherine's Day. 25 November.

In July following another loan was made to the king by the city of £4,000, which was also assessed by the crafts or fellowships, whereof the mercers, grocers and drapers lent £1,615, and the goldsmiths, fishmongers and tailors lent £946 13s. 4d.

Brittany and France

Henry VII followed established practice by entitling himself king of England and France. Although Calais and the Channel Islands were his only French possessions, English pride would have been outraged had its king renounced the title which had been vindicated, it was believed, by the distant victories in the Hundred Years War (1337–1453).

During this war, dukes of Brittany had occasionally asserted their independence of France by allying themselves with England. In 1471, Jasper Tudor had intended to bring his nephew Henry to France, but winds forced them to Brittany. Duke Francis II welcomed them, appreciating Henry's value as a diplomatic pawn. He had English military support against France in 1472, but refused Edward IV's requests to return the Tudors to England, even when Henry's mother Margaret Beaufort added her pleas to that of the king's. Henry did not believe that Edward intended to set him up as an English noble with an Yorkist bride. His gratitude to the duke increased when Francis provided Breton ships and troops for his ill-fated first attempt against Richard III in 1483, and thereafter more shelter for himself and his growing court of exiles.

Henry fled from Brittany in September 1484, when he learnt that the duke's treasurer was about to betray him to Richard III. His last year of exile was thus spent as a guest of the young French king, Charles VIII, who supplied him with the means to invade England in 1485. Soon after his accession, a truce with France was proclaimed. Although it lasted to the end of 1488, in July of that year, a company of English volunteers was sent to aid the Bretons. Henry also entered negotiations with Maximilian I of the Holy Roman Empire and Ferdinand II and Isabella of Spain, to enlist them as champions of Breton independence.

More urgent and direct measures were needed after the death of Duke Francis on 9 September 1488. Breton nobles formed a regency for his daughter Anne, in response to the French king's claim for custody of the duchy. By the Treaty of Redon, 14 February 1489, Henry undertook to provide the young duchess with 6,000 troops, at her expense. They were sent, but only for the agreed six months. Breton resistance collapsed in 1491, and Anne married the French king.

The Breton ports commanding the western approaches were now in French hands. Henry appreciated their strategic importance and parliament granted him taxation to make war with France. His original plan, early in 1492, was to take Brest with the help of anti-French Bretons. However, the plot was detected and Henry's army of baronial retainers

Above   French soldiers defending their territory against the English early in Henry's reign. Mercenaries from countries not involved directly in the war fought with regular soldiers.

remained in England awaiting a move against France. In October of that year, the English forces crossed to Calais and besieged Boulogne. Within nine days, the French offered terms and a treaty was sealed at Etaples on 3 November.

Charles VIII, who was planning to press his hereditary claim to the crown of Naples, had no wish for a war with England, and Henry may well have relied on this. His brief foray into France relieved the frustrations of his own soldiers, but as a war it was a bluff.

The truce endured for the rest of Henry's reign. although he later entered anti-French alliances, he was never an active partner. The southern shores of the Channel were in the French king's control, and sea-faring Bretons were his subjects; conscious of the limitations of his own resources, however, Henry made peace with France the corner-stone of his foreign policy. It was a decision that made a notable contribution to English prosperity by opening French markets and reviving the wine trade with Gascony.

The rest of this £4,000, which was £1,438 6s. 8d. was lent by all the other crafts of the city. Then, a third loan was made to the king of £2,000, which was levied in the same way as the other. They were all repaid in the following year.

Those sums of money, with many more which his grace borrowed from his lords and other honourable men of this land, were to aid the archduke of Burgundy against the duke of Brittany, as will appear more clearly later.

At the end of this mayor's year John Ashley, the son of Sir John Ashley, with two others was drawn from Westminster to Tower Hill and there beheaded.

1489

Henry had spent a significant part of his exile in Brittany. Partly for that reason, and partly in order to frustrate the ambitions of the king of France, he maintained a special relationship with Duke Francis. Charles VIII, on the other hand, sought to annex the Duchy. Charles defeated the Bretons at the battle of St Aubin du Cormiel on 28 July 1488. Duke Francis acknowledged himself to be Charles's vassal, and died three months later. Henry had reluctantly pledged himself to protect Breton independence, and to this end sought the financial aid of Parliament. Edward Hall traces the consequences.

Charles, the French King, having the upper hand of the Bretons and seeing that Maximilian, King of the Romans, was working towards a marriage with Anne, sole heir of Francis, duke of Brittany which would not be to his profit or advantage, concluded a peace with the Bretons. By this treaty he had the lady delivered into his keeping and then he repudiated his marriage to Lady Margaret, daughter of the King of the Romans and married Lady Anne, Duchess of Brittany, by which means the duchy of Brittany was annexed to the crown of France.

The expenses of war were met by parliament, but the northern regions had been accustomed to escape such levies, because they had to meet the cost of their own defence against the Scots. Henry did not adhere to that custom.

Now as to the money laid out because of the costliness of this battle: it was decreed by the three estates in England before any soldiers were sent to Brittany that for the expenses of the war every man should be taxed and assessed on the total of his wealth and should pay the tenth penny of his goods for the support of the war in Brittany. This money most of those living in the bishopric of Durham and in Yorkshire refused to pay, either thinking themselves overcharged and thus grieved with it, or incited and encouraged by the evil advice and seditious persuasion of certain persons who secretly conspired against the king to put him to new trouble and labour.

When the collectors and gatherers of the tax could not get the money according to the commission delivered to them they complained privately to the earl of Northumberland, the chief ruler of the north parts. He immediately informed the king by letters that the people greatly grudged and murmured, saying openly that they had been recently charged with innumerable inconveniences and oppressions without deserving them, and that now there was a huge sum required of them which they were not able to satisfy, nor would they consent to pay one penny of the sum required. The king commanded the earl by any means, by seizure of goods or otherwise according to his discretion, to enforce payment on those who whined most at it, lest it should appear that the decrees, acts and statutes made and confirmed by him and his high court of parliament could be infringed, despised and slighted by his rude and boorish people.

The rude, rash and inadvised people hearing the king's answer by and by violently set upon the earl with the encouragement of a simple fellow called John Chamber. The earl entreated them with fair words to see reason but they charged him with being the chief author and principal cause of this tax and furiously and shamefully murdered and killed him and several of his household servants. Many affirm that the northern men bore a continuing grudge against this earl since the death of King Richard III whom they loved and highly favoured.

Although this offence was great and heinous, there followed after an even greater mischief and inconvenience. For immediately the northern men, to hide the homicide and manslaughter, put on armour and assembled in flocks and chose themselves a captain called Sir John Egremont, a person no less seditious than factious and desirous of trouble. They ordered themselves like warriors, and passing through the countryside they announced and declared that they would challenge the king to battle for the protection and defence of their common liberty and freedom which he wished to pluck and by his extreme power take from them.

But when their cause was to be decided by blows and hand-to-hand fighting their fury was assuaged and cooled, their hearts were in their heels and their stomachs as cold as any stone, and everyone wished that this unrest was removed or quenched, which unrest was now not smouldering but in flames. In conclusion every man ran away, some this way and some that and as men panicking without advice scattered and dispersed in various places.

When every man had returned they thought the matter was ended, but while they diligently sought to save their lives by flight they sought their own destruction. For most of them were punished by death or imprisonment for that offence. The king, hearing of this unrest, sent Thomas Howard, earl of Surrey who he had recently released out of the Tower of London (of which he was well worthy for his wit and fidelity), with a competent crew of men into the north parts; they skirmished with some of the company and took alive John Chamber, the beginner of this rebellion. The king himself rode after the earl into Yorkshire and the slaves and sturdy rebels were so afraid and abashed at his coming that they fled, and were afterwards apprehended and grievously punished according to their deserts.

The king, of his magnificence, pardoned the innocent country people and plagued and executed the instigators and furtherers of the mischief. John Chamber was hanged at York upon a gibbet set upon a square pair of gallows like an arch traitor, and his accomplices and ignorant followers were hanged on the lower gallows round about their master as a terrible example to all others. But Sir John Egremont, whom these seditious persons chose to be their captain, fled to Flanders to Lady Margaret who always envied the prosperity of King Henry.

1490

Maximilian had made his separate peace with France in July 1489, leaving Henry to sustain the Breton campaign alone; but the war was not pursued, and the pope was anxious to free Charles from his commitment. Envoys were exchanged in February 1490, and again in June, but without result. The pope who sent this legate was actually Innocent VIII, as Alexander VI was not elected until 1492. Grafton notes the abortive negotiation.

In the meantime Alexander, bishop of Rome, who succeeded after Innocent, a man full of diligence and of pregnant wit, sent Lionel, bishop of Concord, legate, to the French king about certain matters, and among other things gave him the task of concluding a peace and unity between King Charles and King Henry. When he had declared his message to the French king fully, and had easily obtained all things which he required, then he began to move to the French king and his nobles, and with a long and prolix exhortation, to make and conclude a perpetual peace between him and the king of England. And when he saw that the Frenchmen made no great denial of his request he determined to attempt to move King Henry to consent and agree to the same desire and petition, and took his journey towards England; and at Calais he met the ambassadors both of England and France, who received him into the town of Calais with many ceremonies and great reverence. Where, after they had discussed the matter for a while, as concerning their affairs and business, they departed towards the French King, and the bishop was transported to England.

The king honourably and gently entertained legate Lionel, and gave good ear to his pleasant and eloquent speech, in which he persuaded him with many flattering and soothing words to enter into league and amity with King Charles of France and the French nation. To which request the king answered that he would be glad and joyous if it could be managed and brought about, after long trouble and pernicious dissent, to live in peace and mutual amity with all Christian men. Bishop Lionel, understanding the king's mind and intent, went back again to France with all speed and diligence. He determined to extirpate and drive out of the king's memory all old reckonings and injuries done to him before, and to plant, if possible, in his heart and mind the very good and gracious seed of concord and unity.

1491

In spite of Anglo-Imperial victory at Dixmunde in June 1489, Maximilian, the king of the Romans, son of the Emperor Frederick III, was persuaded to give up his betrothal, and Charles VIII married Duchess Anne of Brittany by proxy early in 1491. The union of France and Brittany greatly enhanced the sea power of the former, and threatened English interests in the channel.

At this very time King Charles of France received Lady Anne as his ward into his hands, and with great solemnity married her, having for her dowry the whole county of Brittany. And so by this means the Bretons became subject to King Charles.

Maximilian being informed of this, fell into a great rage and agony, for Charles had not only forsaken and refused his daughter Lady Margaret but also had taken and ravished away from him his promised wife Lady Anne, duchess of Brittany. Calling upon God for vengeance and punishment for such a heinous and execrable act, cried out and railed against him, wishing him a thousand deaths.

But after he was calmer and came to himself again and had gathered his wits together, he thought it most expedient to revenge his honour and dignity, so manifestly wounded, by the sword. And being of this mind he sent ambassadors to King Henry with his letters, desiring him with all diligence to prepare an army, as he would himself, to invade the King Charles' realm with fire, sword and blood.

King Henry, hearing of this and putting no mistrust in the promise of Maximillian whom he knew to have a deadly hatred and long-held grudge against Charles, caused a muster to be made in all the parts of his realm and put his men of war in readiness with armour and weapons according to their deeds. Besides this he rigged, manned and victualled his navy ready to set forward at any hour, and sent couriers into every county to hurry the soldiers to the coast.

After the message arrived there came without any delay a huge army of men, both the low sort and commoners and noblemen harnessed and armed for battle, glad both to help their prince and do him service and to grapple with the French with whom the Englishmen always desire most willingly to engage and fight in open battle. And immediately, as the order was given, every man repaired to London with his band of soldiers.

After all the army was gathered and ready to set forward, its leaders and chiefs being Jasper, duke of Bedford and John, earl of Oxford and others, the king sent Christopher Urswick, his almoner, and Sir John Risely to Maximilian to assure him that the king was prepared and would shortly arrive on the continent as soon as he knew that Maximilian and his men were ready and prepared to join with him. The ambassadors sailed to Flanders and having delivered their message sent two letters in haste to King

Henry which not only disquieted and vexed him but caused him to take more thought, care and study about him than he had before. For they declared that no prince could be more unprovided or destitute of men and armour, nor more lacking in all things necessary for war than Maximilian was, and that he lay lurking in a corner, sick of dysentery of the purse, so that he had neither men, horses, munitions, armour nor money. His mind and will was good if his power and ability had corresponded to it, but there was no trust to be put in his help or strength.

Their letters dismayed and sorrowed Henry who, like a prudent prince, considered that it was both dangerous and costly to risk so great a war alone. On the other hand if he should desist and leave his intended purpose men might call him a cowardly and craven prince. Besides this he thought that his own nation would not take his waiting at home in good or favourable part, considering that since they had given so much money for the preparation of everything necessary and convenient, they might conceive in their heads and imagine that he had exacted from them notable sums of money under the colour and pretense of a feigned war, and that now the treasure was paid then the war was over, and his coffers well enriched and the commons impoverished.

So at this time he worried and considered perils on every side, and also was not a little sorry that Maximilian, the author of this war, absented himself and deprived him of his company and assistance. And while he studied and mused what counsel he should best take in such a doubtful situation, like a grave prince, remembering the saying of the wise man: "work by counsel and you will not repent", assembled together all his lords and others of his privy council, by whom it was concluded and determined that he should manfully and courageously persevere and proceed in this enterprise he had begun. Plainly, the more difficult and harder chivalry and martial prowess is to attain, the more renowned is the glory and the more immortal the fame of the vanquisher who obtains it.

Therefore by this advice of his friends and senate he proclaimed that every man should set forth to France, and yet without telling how, Judas-like, Maximilian had deceived him, lest knowing all the facts they should not be so courageous to go towards that battle.

The White Rose challenge

The majority of Henry VII's influential subjects and councillors after 1485 could be described as Yorkists, in that they had previously accepted and served Edward IV as their lawful king. Nevertheless, these subjects and councillors had a vested interest in Henry's survival, for recent events had shown that the security of the new regime could not be taken for granted. In response, the king and his advisors had to be tirelessly vigilant, gathering intelligence about potential dangers, and crushing them promptly and decisively as an example to other malcontents.

The first extensive conspiracy centred on Lambert Simnel, an Oxford boy of unknown origin, whose Plantagenet looks prompted a chaplain to groom him as a prince and take him to Ireland in 1487. The real earl, a prisoner in the Tower of London, meanwhile was publicly exhibited to discredit the imposture.

John de la Pole, earl of Lincoln, a genuine Yorkist prince – his mother being Edward IV's sister – suddenly fled from Henry's court to Flanders and Margaret of York, the widowed duchess of Burgundy. She provided 2,000 German mercenaries, who accompanied Lincoln and Lovell to Dublin where Simnel was crowned "Edward" on 24 May 1487. A fortnight later, his troops landed on the southern tip of Cumbria.

The English nobility rallied to the king. He had made Kenilworth castle his headquarters, and as the invaders came south he moved to meet them, his army growing all the time. It greatly outnumbered Simnel's forces and in the battle of East Stoke on 16 June, only the king's vanguard was committed to fight. By midday, his victory was complete. Simnel was a prisoner; Lincoln and the rebellion's other leaders were among the 4,000 slain. The last battle of the Wars of the Roses had proved that England accepted the Tudor monarchy.

Ireland, however, remained outside the king's control until 1494. In the meantime Irish encouragement launched Perkin Warbeck on his career of imposture. He was first noticed at Cork in 1491 where he claimed to be Richard, the younger of the "princes in the Tower", allegedly murdered by Richard III. He was received at royal courts hostile to the English king: Charles VIII of France was his host until he made peace with Henry in 1492, after which Margaret of Burgundy welcomed him as a nephew. Henry's spies learned that Warbeck was a native of Tournai.

After his unsuccessful invasion, the pretender went to Scotland where James IV gave him Lady Catherine Gordon in marriage, and as his ally, invaded England. Failing to enlist any English support for this, Warbeck returned to Ireland where he was rebuffed. In

Top   Perkin Warbeck, the son of a boatman in Flanders, who claimed to be Richard, duke of York.

Above   The Red Gutter at East Stoke, the scene of the massacre of the Yorkist forces on 16 June 1487. The red claylands of Nottinghamshire stained by the blood of 4,000 men.

September 1497 a few thousand Cornishmen came out for him but were easily defeated by Henry's superior forces. Warbeck surrendered. As a foreign adventurer, he could not be put on trial for treason. However he was hanged on 29 November 1499, after trial for a plot to escape from the Tower of London.

1492

When he had thus gathered and assembled his army he sailed to Calais on 6 October and there encamped, waiting there a while to see his men armoured and appareled, so that no weapon or engine necessary for his journey should be neglected. At that place all the army learned from the ambassadors newly returned from Flanders (for they did not know of it before) that Maximilian could make no preparations for lack of money and therefore there was no help to be looked for from him. At which news the Englishmen were not abashed or dismayed, trusting in the strength of their own company.

In the meantime, although Charles was as well supplied with courage as furnished with men fit to fight a battle, he pretended that he desired nothing more than peace, knowing that to obtain peace was of no small value or price. He was afraid that whilst he was diligently resisting the English invasion the Bretons, most of whom bore the yoke of his subjection contrary to their hearts and minds, would suddenly rebel and set themselves free and pluck their heads out of his collar and set up another duke and governor.

At the very same time he was invited by Louis Sforza, duke of Milan, to fight against Ferdinand, King of Naples. He was eager and willing, thinking a chance was sent to him from God for which he had long thirsted and sore wished because he pretended the kingdom of Naples was due to him by succession and had long intended to acquire and conquer it by force of arms as his right and inheritance. Because of this he more busily procured and worked for the amity, favour and friendship of the neighbours round about him, so that when all was appeased and set in good condition at home he might better employ his whole force and strength on his war in Italy.

Therefore being most desirous to have all things pacified and set in perfect concord and security he sent Philip Crevecouer, Lord Cordes, his chief counsellor and diligent officer to entreat and persuade Henry to be reconciled and made as a new friend to the French king.

Not forgetting his message he sent letters to king Henry before he crossed the sea and arrived on dry land, notifying him that because of the bounden duty and observance which he owed to his master the king and to the profit of his realm he would take pains to find some means by which King Henry and King Charles his master, being separated in friendship and made extreme enemies only because of Maximilian the newly elected King of the Romans, should be reduced and brought again to their original state and accustomed familiarity. He doubted not that he would bring his ship to the desired port, if it might please him to send some of his councillors to the edge and border of the English Pale adjoining France, there to hear what reasonable offers should be made and proffered. Which conditions of peace would be so reasonable and so ample that he doubted not that he might with great honour break up his camp and retire with his army to his own territory and dominion.

The Treaty of Etaples was signed 3 November 1492.

Margaret of Burgundy decided to take advantage of his preoccupation in France to raise up a new pretender to the Yorkist claim. This time her choice was a young Fleming who bore a striking physical resemblance to Edward IV, and claimed to be Richard, duke of York. Edward Hall displays his bias unashamedly in explaining what happened.

When this diabolical duchess, had framed her cloth ready for the market and imagined that all things were ready and prepared for the confusion of King Henry, she was suddenly informed that the King of England had prepared a powerful army against Charles, the French king. Then she considered the opportunity offered by the times, as one who saw a wished-for time and a desired day to achieve and bring to pass her old, malicious and cankered inventions, for she always cared nothing for peace and tranquility and desired nothing more than dissension, civil war and the destruction of Henry.

Therefore she sent Perkin Warbeck, her newly found puppet, first into Portugal and thus craftily into the realm of Ireland so that he, being both clever and wily, might move, inveigle and provoke the rude and rustic Irish nation (being by nature more inclined to rebellion than to reasonable order) to a new conflict and seditious commotion.

This worshipful Perkin arriving in Ireland, either by his crafty wit or by the malicious and beastly encouragement of the savage Irish governors, very shortly entered so far into their favours and so seriously persuaded and allured them to his purpose that the greatest lords and princes of that country attached such faith and credit to his words, as if it had been the truth which he untruly and with false proofs set forth and divulged. And they honoured and applauded him with all reverence and due honour, promising to aid, comfort and assist him in all ways necessary for making war.

Meanwhile this news was related to Charles, then in disagreement with King Henry, who without delay sent into Ireland for Perkin, intending to send him against the King of England who was invading France (as you have already heard). Perkin, was not a little joyful at this message, thinking by this one request he had been exalted to heaven when he was called to familiarity and acquaintance with kings and princes. He with all diligence sailed to France, with a very small navy, very meanly furnished. Coming into King Charles' presence he was royally accepted and entertained in a princely fashion. And there came to him at Paris Sir George Neville, a bastard, Sir John Taylor, Roland Robinson and a hundred English rebels. But after the peace already mentioned was appointed and concluded between him and the King of England Charles dismissed the young man and would no longer keep him. Some men who were attending on him there say that, fearing Charles would deliver him to the King of England, he fled from Paris by night. But whether he left with the French King's consent or dissent, deceived in his expectations and despairing he returned to Lady Margaret, his first foolish foundation.

The duchess, thinking every hour from his departure a whole year until she heard from him, and greatly desiring to know which way lady fortune turned her wheel, hearing him to be repudiated and ejected from the French court, was in great agony, much amazed and more appalled. At his coming into her presence she received him with such gladness and with such rejoicing and comfort as if she had never seen or known him before, or as if he were newly crept from his mother's lap. What with her wish to prefer him to the pre-eminence she imagined for him and the hope that she had of destroying King Henry, she fell into such an immeasurable joy that she had almost lost her wits and senses. So that her gladness might be notified and made apparent to all men, she first rejoiced at her nephew's

health and welfare, and secondly much insisted and sorely wished, not once but many times in open audience, to hear him declare and tell by what means he was preserved from death and destruction, and in which countries he had wandered and sought friendship, and finally by what chance of fortune he came to her court and presence. She intended that by the open declaration of these feigned fantasies people might be persuaded to give credit and belief to the claim that he was the truly begotten son of her brother King Edward IV. And after this she assigned him a guard of thirty men dressed in mulberry and blue, the colours of House of York, and highly honoured him as one of great estate, and called him the White Rose, Prince of England.

Because of this the nobility of Flanders treated him assiduously with due reverence and did everything to please him which lay in their power or office. And to be brief, the more that this poetical and feigned invention was shadowed with the pretense of sincere truth, the more faith and undoubting credit was given to it. So much so that many thought him to have been preserved by the will and power of almighty God. The fame and rumour of this conjured miracle was almost in one moment blown over all the country of Flanders and the territories around. But in England it was proclaimed sooner than anyone could think or plan. In that country more than in other places it was received as an infallible truth, not only by the common people but also by various noble and worshipful men of no small estimation, who swore and affirmed it to be true, and not a rumour or fantastically imagined fable.

After it was divulged that Richard, son of King Edward IV, was still living, and held in great honour amongst the Flemings, sedition began to spring up on every side, as in the pleasant season of spring trees are wont to bud and blossom. For not only those who were in sanctuaries for great and heinous offences which they had committed, but many others who had fallen into debt and feared to be brought to captivity and bondage assembled together in a company and crossed over the sea to Flanders, to their counterfeit Richard son of King Edward IV, otherwise named Perkin Warbeck. After this many of the noblemen conspired together, some induced by rashness and temerity, some so earnestly persuaded of their own conceit as if they knew perfectly that this Perkin was undoubtedly the son of

King Edward IV, and they solicited, stirred and attracted to their opinion all who were friends and favourers of the House of York. Others joined them through indignation, envy and greed, ever grudging and thinking they were not suitably rewarded for their pains taken on the king's behalf in his quarrels. Others who it grieved and vexed to see the world stand still in security and all men living in peace and tranquility, desirous of some change, ran headlong into that fury, madness and sedition.

This rumour and vain fable of this twice-born duke Richard divided all England and drew the realm into divisions and several factions, so the minds of all men were vexed either with hope of gain and preferment or with fear of loss and confusion. For no man was quiet in his own mind, but his brains and senses daily laboured and beat about this great and weighty matter, every man according to his intelligence pondering and weighing in equal balance the incommodity and danger that might ensue and the gain and commodity which might be got, and his council and other faithful friends marvelled not a little that anyone being in his right mind could find it in his heart falsely to think and fraudulently to imagine such a pernicious fable and fiction, it being not only strange and marvellous but also prodigious and unnatural to pretend that a dead man had been revived and newly born again.

Henry saw, as far as the lynx with his bright eye, that this new invented rumour and poetical painted fable would cause some trouble and discord in his realm, unless it were clearly published and openly declared to be a feigned fable, a seditious fraud and a crafty imagined mischief. Other persons to whom war, sedition and strife were as pleasant as delicate food and Epicurean living, greatly enjoyed this news, and believed no fraud nor deceit was hidden or cloaked under this golden tale.

Because the matter was weighty and required great aid and assistance they determined to send messengers to Lady Margaret, to know when Richard, duke of York might conveniently come to England, so that being informed of it they might be ready to help and succour him on his arrival.

So by the common consent and agreement of the sworn confederates Sir Robert Clifford and William Barley were sent to Flanders where they explained to the duchess all the secret intentions and private counsels of the friends and favourers of the new-found duke. The duchess gladly accepted and lovingly embraced this message and was made not a little joyful by their tidings, and by her persuasion easily convinced them that all things spoken of duke Richard were true and unfeigned. Afterwards she let them see Perkin who counterfeited the countenance, manner and fashion of Richard, duke of York and she praised the virtues and qualities with which he was endowed above the moon.

Sir Robert Clifford, when he had seen and considered the young man, surely believed that he came of the royal blood and was the real son of King Edward IV, and he wrote letters of credit and confidence in him to his companions and fellows of his conspiracy in England, and to remove all doubt from them he affirmed that he knew him to be King Edward's son by his face and other features of his body.

When these letters came to England the leaders of the business, intending to stir the people to some new commotion and tumult and to set forth some likely seeming matter, caused it openly to be divulged and published that what was spoken and said abroad was true and not feigned, but it was done with such secret craftiness that no one could tell who was the author and founder of that rumour.

When the king perceived that this vain fable was not vanished out of the mad brains of the common people he thought it expedient both for his own safeguard and that of his country, to provide some remedy, not a little suspecting that some conspiracy had been concluded and agreed since Sir Robert Clifford had lately fled secretly to Flanders.

He sent certain knights, chosen and picked warriors, with a band of soldiers into every part to keep the shores and the sea coasts safe, so that no man might pass into any foreign land overseas nor return to this realm without search, or passport, or safe conduct given by the king. All roads, passages and byways were guarded and searched so that no-one could pass to the coast unapprehended, nor hold any meeting or assembly without being espied and taken.

And so that many men, both English and otherwise, inflamed and hardened for very malice by this new invention should run no further in their frenetic madness, he secretly sent wise spies to all the cities of the Low Countries to search and find out what

A woman's life

The Church had always recognized the spiritual equality of male and female, and a religious vocation was accepted as a valid alternative to motherhood – indeed chastity in some respects enjoyed a superior status – but for Englishwomen after the Reformation such an option scarcely existed. A woman's main purpose in life was to bear children, and her principal occupation was to be a wife and mother.

Most marriages were arranged in the interests of a woman's male relatives and the higher her social status, the more likely that was to be the case. The wife of a man of property, whether an aristocrat or a merchant, might be called upon to bear considerable responsibility: to run his estates or his business while he was away, and the domestic side of his household when he was at home. Yet she had no control over her own property and no separate legal identity. She had much more freedom as a widow, provided that she was past the childbearing age and under no immediate pressure to remarry. A lady or gentlewoman in such circumstances could expect to enjoy her own lands and manage her own affairs. The widow of a merchant or artisan might continue to run his business in her own name, and would be accepted into the appropriate guild or fraternity.

Marriage was an honourable estate, but also a hazardous one. The average duration of a first marriage was no more than five years, not because of divorce, which was virtually unknown, but because of death; generally that of the wife in childbirth. Infant mortality was high, even among the aristocracy, and contraceptive techniques primitive and ineffectual; most married women could expect annual pregnancies until their own or their husbands' fertility came to an end.

A girl's education was principally designed to prepare her for this fate, in whatever station of life she was raised. An aristocratic lady might be trained in humanist letters – the daughters of Thomas More are examples – and the daughter of a gentleman or merchant might be taught to read and write. All were instructed in the fundamentals of the Christian faith. All however, were equally taught that their moral and intellectual capacity was less than that of a man. A woman of strong personality might dominate her husband, but, if she was intelligent, would conceal the fact from the outside world. The cultural stereotypings of female behaviour were inhibiting and frustrating, but, as in any age, the enterprising found ways to get around them.

Above and below   In ordinary households the woman was responsible for maintaining a basic level of subsistence for the family. Life expectation was grim.

parentage this misnamed Richard was descended and propagated, promising highly to reward and thank such persons who would make clear and open the secret doubts and devices of the business. Besides this he wrote to his trusted friends to do the same.

They, sailing to France, divided and separated themselves, every man to a certain area and province. And when some of them went to the town of Tournai they were assured by the testimony of many honest persons that this pretended duke came of a low stock and a base parentage and was there called Peter Warbeck. And so shortly after the king's investigators returned to England and reported to the king what they had learned and heard, of which thing the king was also more plainly assured by his trusty and faithful friends, both by letters and trusty messengers.

1493

In the summer of 1493 Henry sent an embassy to the Low Countries to protest against the reception given to Perkin Warbeck, but the Archduke Philip's council replied that it was not responsible for Margaret's actions in her own lands. Henry's own subjects were hurt by his angry response, and vented their anger upon the Hanseatic League, whose merchants were mere bystanders.

King Henry of England was partly grieved with the King of the Romans for breaking his promise when he should have associated with him in his move against the French King, and partly displeased with the Flemings, but principally with Lady Margaret, for keeping and promoting Perkin Warbeck. He not only banished all Flemish wares and merchandise from his realm and dominions, but also restrained all English merchants from their travel to and trade with any of the lands and territories of the King of the Romans, or the archduke his son, causing the market for merchandise and commodities from this realm to be kept at his town of Calais. Because of this the said king and his son banished from their lands and seignories all English cloth, yarn, tin, lead and other commodities, upon great forfeits and penalties. The restraint made by the king sorely grieved and hindered the merchants who were venturers. For as a result of this command they had no occupation to bear their costs and support their continuing credit. And yet one thing sorely nipped their hearts; that the Hanseatic merchants who were free to do so brought into the realm such goods as they were used and accustomed to do, and so served their customers throughout the whole realm. By reason of this the masters, being destitute of sales and trade, neither retained so many covenanted servants and apprentices as before they were accustomed to do, especially mercers, haberdashers and clothworkers, nor gave their servants such great stipends and salaries as they used to before the restraint. Because of this the said servants, intending to vent their malice on the Hanseatic merchants, on the Tuesday before St Edward's day came to the Steelyard in London and began to raid and spoil such chambers and warehouses as they could get into, so that the Hanseatic merchants had a great to do to withstand them and repulse them from their gates. And when their gates were shut and made fast the multitude rushed and beat at the gates with clubs and leavers to enter, but the merchants, with the help of the carpenters and smiths who came to their aid by water from the Borough of Southwark, had so strongly shored up and fortified themselves that they could not prevail. The Mayor of London, hearing of this riot, assembled the magistrates and officers of the City, and being furnished both with men and weapons set forwards towards the Steelyard. As soon as the coming of the Mayor was declared to and known by the riotous persons, they fled away like a flock of sheep.

However he apprehended several of the malefactors and committed them to several prisons. And upon the enquiry before the King's Commissioners there were found guilty above 80 servants and apprentices (and not one householder) who had conspired together to make this attempt and sworn in no way to make known or reveal the same. Some of them, who were the leaders and beginners of this mischievous riot were sent to the Tower of London, and stayed there for a long time.

But in conclusion, because none of their masters were found guilty of this naughty act the king, of his goodness, pardoned their offence, and restored them to their liberty.

1494

Not all the king's time and energy was spent on the serious business of politics. Like any renaissance prince, Henry VII was concerned to project his power and dignity through the magnificence of his court; and one of the recognized features of a magnificent court was jousting. Although Henry VII did not joust himself he was a great

Court entertainment

One of the important functions of the court was to entertain the king, his kinfolk and habitual companions, as well as the guests who swelled the numbers when a foreign prince or embassy was received. It was also to provide diversion for the peers who attended great councils or parliaments, or when celebrations were held for a great Christian feast or a chapter of the Order of the Garter at Windsor castle.

Religious ceremonies were the responsibility of the Chapel Royal, whose clerks and choristers, under its dean, maintained a superlative tradition of polyphony, organ-playing and original composition. Times of feast and celebration were also marked by banquets in the royal apartments and by entertainments, some of which were held in public and even out of doors, visible to the people.

Music, dance, recitation and drama were provided partly by professional minstrels and the companies of mummers – dumb show entertainers – who traditionally sought entry to the court at times of rejoicing. However, courtiers were also expected to entertain; a variety of semi-professional skills were necessary for holders of many chamber offices. The esquires of the King's Body were not only skilled in the profession of arms; they were accomplished in dancing, singing, playing musical instruments and play-acting. Young valets of the King's Chamber and choristers of the Chapel Royal assisted in performances which took place in intervals between courses at banquets. Lords and ladies were often principal players, wearing masks and exotic attire.

Henry VII also enjoyed simple entertainments such as performances by a man who ate fire coals and by a Spanish tightrope walker who displayed "delicious points of tumbling and dancing". He delighted in melody, enjoyed gambling at cards, and provided generously for his courtiers' outdoor recreation. The new palace at Richmond had bowling alleys, butts for archery and tennis courts. He showed no personal enthusiasm for demanding physical activities such as jousting and hunting, but preferred a quieter outdoor life. In his last years he often stayed at his country house at Hanworth in Middlesex. There the song of caged birds and the surrounding gardens, strawberry beds and orchards were a welcome distraction for the careworn king, bereft by the untimely death of Prince Arthur and of his beloved queen, Elizabeth of York, and cynically suspicious of many of the leading men in his realm.

Above   Jousting for a lady's honour. Henry was an enthusiastic spectator, but never a competitor, at tournaments.

Although Henry was careful with money he was not miserly and recognized the importance of spending money freely to keep a royal image. Ambassadors from foreign countries who called were treated to hunting, jousting and lavish outdoor musical entertainments, even though Henry himself preferred more scholarly pursuits such as reading and writing.

promoter of tournaments, understanding the import-ance of martial displays for his own image. His son, the duke of York, later Henry VIII, was thoroughly trained in such exercises from an early age, and later in his life it was to provide an important part of courtly life.

At about three in the afternoon the duke of York, called Lord Henry, the king's second son, came through the city. A child of about four years of age, he sat on a courser and rode to Westminster to the king with a goodly company

Also on 9 November, a Sunday, a solemn joust was held in the Palace of Westminster. There were four challengers, namely Lord Edmund de la Pole, earl of Suffolk, Henry Bourchier, earl of Essex, Sir Robert Curzon and John Peache, then an esquire, who all answered that they would come. On the first day the four challengers had the best of it by the help of John Peache who that day broke four spears. On the second day they ran certain courses and turned afterwards to swords, where the challengers also had the better of it by the help of my Lord Edmund.

It is to be noted that on those two days the chal-lengers came to the palace, on the Sunday, all four were in the king's livery of green and white, both their armour and other apparel, with four badges of the queen's livery of blue and mulberry on their hel-mets. And on Tuesday they all came in the king's mother's livery of blue and white, both armour and other apparel.

On the third day these four challengers became defenders. On that day they were brought into the palace with four fair ladies who laced their bridles with silken laces of white and blue. The ladies rode upon four white palfreys in long-sleeved gowns of white satin with crimson satin in their hair, which was a goodly sight to see. The four challengers were in battle armour with great feathers on their heads. Their horses were armed and caparisoned, the covering was of black velvet embroidered two parts with gold and two parts plain. The crests on the horses' necks were inlaid with a goldsmith's work of black velvet and gold, richly and well-made. With them came in two other persons in blue and white. Of these six persons, the earls of Suffolk and Essex each ran a course against two of the opponents who were the challengers that day. Those two challengers were Sir Edward de Burgh and Sir Edward Darell. After their course Sir Robert Curzon and John

Peache ran again against William de Ryvers, a Bre-ton, and Matthew Baker. And then the other two who came with the lords ran against the other two who came with the challengers, who were but lowly persons. In these six courses only two spears were broken; Sir Edward de Burgh broke one and John Peache the other. After this the earls of Suffolk and Essex fought with Sir Edward de Burgh and Sir Edward Darell to the number of 18 strokes, and then they departed. Then Sir Robert Curzon and John Peache fought together against William de Ryvers and Matthew Baker to the number of 18 strokes. And when they had departed the other four persons ran together and fought, and when this was over all the six challengers ran with their swords against the six defenders and all fought each other, but that con-tinued for only a few strokes.

As well as this there were other jousts and tour-neys on the same two days, but not equal to these, for these were honourable persons and seemly to look at, and many noble gentlemen brought them in, well-horsed and richly appareled, which was honourable and comfortable to the king and queen and many other great people there to watch, and a great pleasure to the common people.

Robert Clifford had gone to the court of Margaret of Bur-gundy in June 1493, after communicating with Sir Wil-liam Stanley, the kings chamberlain. He may have been a royal agent from the start, or have turned "Kings evi-dence" in 1495. Edward Hall describes the consequences of his testimony.

Shortly afterwards Sir Robert Clifford, partly trust-ing the king's promise, and partly mistrusting it, because he knew that several who were accused of taking part in that faction and conspiracy had been executed and thus perceiving that there could not be a more pernicious and desperately begun thing than that devilish enterprise, returned suddenly to England. The king, being forewarned of his coming, went straight to the Tower of London on the day af-ter Epiphany, and there waited until Sir Robert Clif-ford was presented to him in person. If Sir Robert Clifford accused any of the nobility of taking part in this ungracious fraternity and diabolical plot, then all such persons could be summoned there without them suspecting any evil, and there be immediately arrested and kept in prison.

But before I go any further I will explain the opinion which many men then held of this knight's going to Flanders. Some believed that King Henry

The treason of Sir William Stanley

The execution of Sir William Stanley of Holt, on 16 February 1495, is the most notorious and least explicable mystery of Henry VII's reign. His crucial role at Bosworth must have earned him the king's gratitude and ensured his future. He was the younger brother of Thomas Stanley 1st earl of Derby, Henry's stepfather; it is hardly credible that he could have expected any gain from a treasonable conspiracy with Perkin Warbeck. He was convicted on a charge of plotting the king's death on the grounds, apparently, that he had said that he would not fight against Warbeck if the pretender was truly a son of Edward IV. This reported statement could be attributed to excessive caution, but it is as likely that it came from an unappreciated sense of humour.

Stanley's record for changing sides may have been held against him. The Lancastrian parliament of 1459 considered him a supporter of Richard, 3rd duke of York. He subsequently prospered under Edward IV, but in 1483 accepted Richard III as king and strengthened his own hold on the government of North Wales. After Stanley's betrayal of Richard, Henry VII confirmed his possession of grants from the Yorkist kings. Moreover, he appointed him chamberlain of the royal household, a court office with great potential for its holder's enrichment. Stanley became by reputation the richest commoner in England.

He was arrested after the return from Margaret of Burgundy's court of Sir Robert Clifford, in January 1495. Clifford had gone there in 1493, allegedly at Stanley's instigation, in order to make contact with Warbeck. It is possible, however, that Clifford was in the king's service all the time and the source of other reports on Warbeck's English contacts. Henry was said to have been shocked, but reluctantly convinced, by Clifford's denunciation of Stanley. The informer was pardoned and rewarded. Stanley was beheaded as a public example of the king's resolution to show no favour in his treatment of traitors.

Above Margaret, duchess of Burgundy and sister of Edward IV, at prayer. She actively encouraged the Lambert Simnel and Perkin Warbeck rebellion against Henry VII. It was Stanley's misfortune to be closely connected with her court and a former Yorkist.

had deliberately sent him as a spy to Flanders, or else he would not have so soon received him into his grace and favour again. However this was not likely to be true for various reasons and obvious arguments: firstly after the attempt begun by Sir Robert he was in no small danger himself, and his reputation was blemished, and also his friends were suspected and regarded jealously; secondly he was not afterwards held in such great favour or so esteemed by the king as he had been times past, because he was blotted and marked with that crime and offence. And so, favouring the House of York, intending in the beginning to cause displeasure to King Henry, he sailed to France to Lady Margaret, there being seduced and brought to believe that Perkin Warbeck was the true son of King Edward.

But to my purpose: when Sir Robert came into the king's presence he humbly knelt and beseeched grace and pardon, which he shortly obtained. And after that, being asked about the manner and order of the plot and what was done in Flanders, he told everything he knew and afterwards disclosed the names of the helpers and favourers, and of the instigators and beginners. Amongst them he accused Sir William Stanley whom the king had made his chief chamberlain and one of his Privy Council. When he said this the king was greatly dismayed and grieved that he should have taken part in this grievous offence, considering that he had the government of his chamber and the charge and control of all who were next to his body, and remembering the many favours he had received at his hands, and especially not forgetting the benefit above all others, that only by his help and succour had he vanquished and overthrown his mortal enemy King Richard.

Therefore at first he could in no way be induced or persuaded to believe that he was a secret conspirator or malicious offender, but when the crime was openly proved and demonstrably confirmed, then the Henry caused him to be held prisoner in his own chamber in the Tower of London. There the king had him examined by his Privy Council. During this examination he denied nothing, but wisely and seriously assented and agreed to all that he was charged with, if he were culpable or blameworthy in any of them.

The story is that this was his offence. When he and this Sir Robert Clifford spoke about Perkin who falsely usurped the name of King Edward's son, Sir William Stanley said and affirmed that he would

Scotland, Ireland and Wales

Hostility was the normal condition of Anglo-Scottish relations for two centuries before Henry VII's accession. The most recent war had ended with the final English capture of Berwick-upon-Tweed in 1482. Scottish ambition to recover the town persisted but the government of James III was racked by faction, and his murder in 1488 left his young heir, James IV, in the hands of a group of nobles. During Henry's championship of Breton independence, one faction of Scots nobles favoured reviving the "aud alliance" with France. The English king consequently courted their rivals, building up a pro-English party which could, at least, weaken Scotland; it was in England's interest that the Scottish nobility should stay divided.

James IV, however, was more ambitious than his feeble father. After the treaty of Etaples in 1492 between Henry and Charles VIII of France, the French king urged James to keep peace with England, while Henry persistently sought improved relations, offering him the hand of his daughter Margaret in 1495. But James chose to accept Perkin Warbeck as king of England, married him to a cousin, Lady Catherine Gordon, and made a treaty of alliance with Berwick as the price for Scottish military aid. A brief raid over the border in September 1496, however, aroused no support or interest in England. It also persuaded a parliament to grant Henry war subsidies in 1497.

The largest army of Henry VII's reign was raised to crush Warbeck's Scottish champion. Instead, it had to be employed to defeat Cornish rebels who marched to Blackheath because they resented paying a tax for the defence of the northern border. Pressed by English and Spanish ambassadors, James shipped Warbeck to Ireland in July 1497, but continued to show belligerence, attacking Norham castle in August 1497, but withdrawing on the approach of Henry's forces. Both kings were now willing to come to terms, and on 30 September, 1497, the treaty of Ayton declared a truce for seven years. Negotiations for a marriage with Margaret were resumed and were concluded, with a full treaty of peace, early in 1502.

Warbeck's failure to enlist followers in Ireland in 1497 was in striking contrast to Dublin's enthusiastic reception of Lambert Simnel ten years earlier. Ireland had not been visited by a true English king since 1399, although all had claimed to be its lord since 1171. Their effective authority had rarely extended beyond the Pale, the English-speaking hinterland of the east coast. Even here, the king's representative had to contend with Anglo-Irish magnates who were also tribal chiefs beyond the Pale.

Edward IV's lieutenants were absentees, their duties entrusted to the head of the Pale's greatest family, the FitzGerald earls of Kildare. Gerald FitzGerald, the 8th earl, appointed deputy-lieutenant in 1479, remained in office until 1492, despite his support for Simnel.

Prince Henry, then aged three, was appointed lieutenant of Ireland in 1484. His deputy was the king's trusted councillor, Sir Edward Poynings. Kildare was arrested and sent to England. A parliament at Drogheda then enacted 49 measures, one of which became notorious as Poynings' Law; this stipulated that no future Irish parliament might be held without the English kings consent. Poynings established sufficient control to repulse Warbeck, and Kildare was allowed to return as deputy. Henry was a realist: it was cheaper to employ a native magnate, and the earl's exile had converted him to loyalty.

Two other outlying regions of the kingdom were entrusted to councils. Following Yorkist precedent, the council of the prince of Wales, based at Ludlow, was charged to administer his estates in the Principality (Gwynedd and western Dyfed) and to ensure that baronial agents in the marcher lordships properly exercised their judicial powers. In 1489, Prince Arthur was appointed warden-general in the north of England. His lieutenant, first Thomas Howard, earl of Surrey, and from 1501, Thomas Savage, archbishop of York, had a council at York which at times investigated breaches of the peace. In both areas, therefore, Henry delegated authority to his own nominees instead of their traditional ruling families.

Top   Chirk Castle in the marches of Wales, built to provide a centre for administration and to deter rebels.

Above   Chepstow Castle, a similar fortress in the southern marches.

never fight nor bear arms against the young man if he knew for certain that he was undoubtedly the son of King Edward IV. This point argues and proves him at that time being moved by melancholy to bear no great good will to King Henry, from which suspicion first grew, and afterwards followed the accusation of Sir Robert Clifford.

1495

Then the king doubted what to do with him, for he feared lest his brother Lord Thomas Stanley, in whom he had found great friendship, should take the matter badly. He considered whether he should pardon the fault, lest his leniency and mercy allow Stanley to offend and trespass more seriously. In the end severity won and mercy was put behind, and so he was arraigned at Westminster and condemned to die, and according to the judgement was brought to Tower Hill on 16 February and there had his head cut off.

What caused the sincere and faithful mind which Sir William Stanley always bore to King Henry to turn into cankered hatred and spite, and why the special favour the king bore him was changed to disdain and displeasure, different men have different explanations. Some say that (what other mutual benefits they received of each other I will now omit and pass over) in the battle in which King Richard was bereft of his life and his kingdom, when King Henry accompanied by a small number of men was surrounded by King Richard's army and his life was in great danger, Sir William came suddenly and fortunately to the aid of King Henry and saved him from destruction and overthrew King Richard. Surely this was a benefit to be remembered above all benefits as King Henry was not only preserved alive but also obtained the crown and kingdom. After he had obtained the kingdom Henry neither forgot nor left unrewarded William Stanley, giving him great gifts and offices and making him his chief chamberlain.

However, although Sir William was in great favour with the king and held in great and high esteem, he remembered more the benefit he had done to the king than the rewards and gifts he received, thinking that the vessel of oil, according to the gospel, would overflow the brim. Some say he desired to be earl of Chester and being denied that began to bear a grudge and to disdain his high friend the king. One thing also encouraged him much, the

riches and treasure of king Richard which he alone possessed at the battle of Bosworth.

When the king perceived that his stomach began to canker and grow rusty he was not a little displeased with him, and so when both their hearts were inflamed with melancholy both lost the fruit of their long-continued friendship and favour. So it often happens that when men do not consider or regard the great benefits shown to them they give back hatred for liberality, and for bread given they give back a scorpion.

At this time the king thought it best to use some sharp punishment and correction for the offences of his subjects, so that the lately begun sedition might the sooner be suppressed. When knowledge of the slanderous and opprobrious words concerning the expected arrival of the feigned Richard, duke of York, came to the king's ears he caused several people to suffer condign punishment for their heinous offences. By this their accomplices, well perceiving that their enterprise had no prosperous success nor took any good effect, of their own inclination pacified themselves and began to turn to their king and natural liege lord.

As always, when there was trouble in England, Ireland was a source of anxiety, and 1494 and 1495 were no exception. Edward Poynings was sent over as deputy, and Henry Deane as chancellor.

After the death of Sir William Stanley, Lord Daubeney, a man of great fidelity and circumspection was elected and made the king's chief chamberlain. When the king had thus prudently weeded out the evil and corrupt hearts of his English subjects and had pacified and brought all his realm to a quiet life, then he perceived it was necessary also to purge and cleanse his realm of Ireland, so that the venomous seed sown and planted two years ago amongst the wild and savage Irish by Perkin Warbeck might be dug out and rooted up.

Therefore he sent Sir Henry Deane, Bishop of Bangor, a man of great wit and diligence, and Sir Edward Poynings, with an army of men to Ireland to search and purge all the towns and places where Perkin was received, relieved or favoured. And if they found any of his affinity or faction he wished that they should be punished with all extremity as a terrible example to all others who might incline to that unfortunate party.

Firstly, after their arrival in Ireland, they called the nobility of that country to a council in the king's name, and being assembled altogether the chancellor with gentle exhortation required them first to persist in due obedience and fidelity towards their king, and to aid his captain Sir Edward Poynings with their might, power and strength against such rebels who through blindness and folly or through desire and appetite to do evil sustained and aided Perkin with armour, men or money.

Every man promised openly to help with all their power and might. But as quickly as they promised, as slowly did they perform it. When they heard that Sir Edward Poynings had come to persecute all favourers and friends of Perkin Warbeck there was no man, even if he were but a little defiled by that seditious infection, who did not flee out of hand to the woods and marshes for their own defence and safeguard. There they consulted together after the manner of their country where they might best lie in wait to hurt and skirmish with the English men, or if necessary to fight with them hand to hand.

In Ireland there are two kinds of men. One is soft, gentle, civil and courteous and to these people many merchants from adjoining countries daily resort. But because the greatest trade is from the English nation the Irishmen follow and counterfeit their civil manners and honest conditions. And because of the common trade and intercourse between them they have learned the English tongue and can speak and understand it. All these people are under the subjection and dominion of the king of England

The other kind are the direct opposite of this, for they are wild, rustic, foolish, fierce, and for their unmannerly behaviour and rude fashions are called wild and savage Irishmen. These men have many governors and several rulers who continually fight and daily war amongst themselves, which makes them more fierce, more bold and hardy than other Irishmen, and they are very desirous of new things and strange sights and wonders, and after robbery, theft and plunder delight in nothing so much as tumultuous sedition and continual strife. And Perkin Warbeck showed himself first to these wild colts, easily persuading them to believe that he was the very same person whom he falsely feigned and counterfeited.

Sir Edward Poynings intended according to his commission, to punish those who had been aiders and advancers of Perkin's foolish enterprise. He marched forward with his whole army against these wild Irishmen, but when he saw that his intentions were not succeeding as he wished, both because the Irish lords did not send him help as they had promised and since his numbers were not sufficient to set on the wild people who were dispersed amongst woods, mountains and marshes, he was forced to retreat.

Fretting and vexed in his stomach, he suspected that Gerald Fitz Maurice FitzGerald, Earl of Kildare, was the cause of his having no aid sent to him and so he caused the earl to be apprehended and brought to England as a prisoner. When he was examined and certain treasonable matters were laid to his charge he avoided them all and clearly (such was his wit and innocence) acquitted himself, and laid the burden on other men's necks. The king dismissed him and sent him back to Ireland.

The king, like a prudent prince, had many great and weighty considerations which restrained him from using any severity or extremity against this earl, against the minds and wills of his malicious adversaries. One reason was the great authority and sway he had amongst the Irish nation; also the condition and estate of the time, when he smelled some sedition to be brewing.

The king, being free of all fear of battle, took a progress to Lancashire on 25 June, there to recreate his spirits and comfort himself with his mother Lady Margaret, who was then at Lathom in that county.

While these things were thus done in England, Perkin Warbeck in Flanders showed great sorrow and care that his crafty connivance was seen and known openly, and that King Henry had afflicted and punished several of his confederates and allies and he thus despaired of all the aid and help which had been promised and appointed to him.

However he was determined not to give up the hope and trust he had conceived in his mad head to obtain the crown and realm of England, and so gathering a great army of valiant captains of all nations, some bankrupts, some false English sanctuary men, some thieves, robbers and vagabonds who leaving their manual labour desired only to live by robbery and plunder and so came to be his servants and soldiers. Being furnished with this rabble of knaves he took such ships as his friends had provided for him and left Flanders, intending to arrive in England wherever the wind brought him. By chance he was driven upon the Kentish coast, where because the sea was calm he cast his anchors and stayed there and sent some of his retinue to the land to signify to all the country that there was no doubt that the victory would fall to him.

The Kentish men hearing that this feigned duke had come, had heard that he was but a painted image. They considered for a while what to do, whether to help him or to resist his power, and at last remembering what evil luck their forefathers had and how small a profit rebels have gained thought it neither expedient nor profitable for them to aid and assist him who came rather to spoil, destroy and waste the country than to conquer it for their wealth and benefit. This they firmly conjectured because he had none but aliens and foreigners with him who would take and count every church, town, chapel, house and every private man as a prey and profit, and not as their native country. Therefore fearing what would follow they determined to remain true to their king.

They determined that while they were assembling themselves, others should lure and call a great number out of the ships and so give them battle. And so using this guile they all promised to follow him and to fight under his banner.

However, their delaying made Perkin suspicious, remembering that a community is not accustomed sagely to consult, but suddenly and rashly to run headlong into rebellion and newly-stirred commotion. Therefore Perkin determined not to set foot out of his ship until he saw all things to be sure, without any danger.

Although he did not intend to land himself he allowed some of his soldiers to land who, being a fair way from their ships, were suddenly trapped and surrounded by the Kentish men, and at one stroke vanquished and driven back to their ships. Of those taken prisoner, four were captains, Mountford, Corbet, Whitebelt and Quintin or Genyn. These rebels were brought by Sir John Peche, sheriff of Kent, to London fastened in ropes like horses drawing a cart. On their arraignment they confessed their offence and were executed, some in London and others in the towns adjoining the sea coast. Perkin, failing in his purpose, fled back to Flanders and stayed there consulting with his friends until he was better

Burgundy and Spain

There had been strong economic links between England and Flanders since the 11th century. Counts of Flanders were retainers of the French crown, but this did not prevent the citizens of Bruges, Ghent and other Flemish towns from relying on the supply of English wool for their great cloth industry. For a century Flanders was the wealthiest province of the Valois dukes of Burgundy. When their line ended with the death of Charles the Bold in 1477, his daughter Mary married Maximilian Habsburg of Austria in order to protect Flanders from French attack. Unfortunately Mary died in 1482, and as regent to their son Philip (the future Philip I of Castile) Maximilian was unpopular with the Flemings. Moreover, after his election as King of the Romans in 1486, he became increasingly concerned with German affairs.

The court of Margaret, Charles the Bold's third wife and dowager duchess of Burgundy, was permanently resident in the Netherlands. Edward IV's sister, her marriage in 1468 had been intended to seal an anti-French alliance. However until her death in 1503, she welcomed real and feigned nephews, and assisted their schemes against Henry Tudor, whom she regarded as a usurper: thus she provided Lambert Simnel with a small German army in 1487. In 1492, Maximilian allied with Henry VII to defend Brittany against the French, but was detained in Flanders by rebellious subjects. In 1493, however, he received Perkin Warbeck as if he were England's king, and with Margaret equipped him to land in Kent. Henry retaliated with an embargo on trade with the Low Countries.

Above   Margaret, duchess of Burgundy.

Left   Ferdinand of Aragon on his arrival in Spain.

Above right   Emperor Maximilian I, who received Perkin Warbeck as though he was already the King of England.

Henry had also sought aid from Spain to preserve Breton independence, this being the purpose of the preliminary treaty of Medina del Campo in 1489, which also accepted the English king's proposal that his son Arthur should marry Catherine, a younger daughter of Ferdinand of Aragon and Isabella of Castile.

Meanwhile French victories in Italy led in 1495 to the formation of the Holy League, comprising the papacy, German empire and Spain. One consequence was the marriage of Maximilian's son Philip to Joanna, Catherine's older sister. The new allies sought to draw England into the anti-French camp, and to this end, Ferdinand prompted Philip to exclude Warbeck from the Low Countries. In return, by the Intercursus Magnus treaty of 1496, Henry renewed the English trade to Flanders. In 1499, the Treaty of London made further arrangements for Catherine's marriage to Arthur.

As a result of these developments, the Spanish ambassador is reported to have told Henry that his rulers would be happier about their daughter's future if no "drop of doubtful royal blood" survived in England. He was possibly referring to Warbeck, then a prisoner, who was hanged soon after the treaty of marriage. Edward, earl of Warwick, a real Yorkist prince who had been kept in the Tower of London since 1485, was executed for alleged complicity with the pretender, while another nephew to the last Yorkist kings, Edmund de la Pole, earl of Suffolk, took fright and fled abroad.

Negotiations for the Spanish marriage, marked by mutual mistrust, eventually reached fruition after 16 years. Catherine arrived in England in October 1501, and on 14 November was married to prince Arthur in St Paul's cathedral. Although the English kings of the 14th and early 15th centuries had all married foreign princesses, the Yorkists and Henry himself had taken English wives, and indication that the pressures of internal politics had damaged the international standing of the monarchy. The marriage of Arthur and Catherine, and its attendant pageantry, gave Henry's subjects added cause to respect their Tudor king: the sovereigns of Spain had demonstrated their confidence in the security of his rule.

prepared for things to come, more prudently than he had done before.

1496

Rebuffed in Ireland, Perkin Warbeck arrived in Scotland in November 1495, and was received by James IV as Duke of York. James first gave him Lady Catherine Gordon, the daughter of the Earl of Huntly, as his wife; and in September 1496 mounted an invasion of England in his support, which demonstrated that Perkin had no credibility in England.

It is worthwhile to remember here a certain kind of silly mercy and foolish compassion by which the said Perkin was so sorely moved that it made him seem to regard nothing more than the convenience of another man. For while the Scottish king vexed and harried the poor inhabitants of the borders of Northumberland, so that nothing was heard but roaring, weeping and lamenting, this new-invented duke having returned to Scotland, who typically did all things with fraud and deceit, seeing that no concourse of Englishmen openly resorted to him to bring him any aid or help, and fearing not a little that box of his crafty dealing and bag of his secret counterfeiting should be disclosed and set in an open glass, by reason of which he would be hated and held in contempt and disdain by the Scottish people, as though he had been provoked by a natural inclination and pity (with the intent of hiding and cloaking his subtle deceit) cried out openly "Oh, my stony and hard-frozen heart, which is not once moved nor yet afflicted by the loss and slaughter of your own natural subjects and vassals." And at that, gloriously sighing, he beseeched the Scottish king that from henceforth he would not afflict and plague his people, nor deform and deface his native realm and country with such terrible fire, flame and havoc; as if, being overcome with the perfect love of his native region, he began now to have compassion and to lament the cruel destruction of the same. The Scottish king, who began to see which way the wind blew answered him "Sir, I think you take much pain, and very much consider how to preserve the realm of another prince which is not yours, but I think you would gladly have it, but my mind tells me that you are as far from obtaining the same as you are near the soil and sight of the country, considering that you call England your land and realm, and its inhabitants your people and subjects, and yet not one man, neither gentleman nor yeoman, will once show him-

self to aid or assist you in the war begun for your cause and in your name within your realm, to which you are both, as you say, the heir and called and desired by your people."

And so the king reproved the lightness of this young foolish foundling, and every day more and more neglected and less believed and gave credit to him, noting well and wisely that neither his words were fitting and consistent with his deeds nor the succeeding facts with his promises.

1497

Warbeck had been well received by James IV of Scotland, but the invasion on his behalf, launched in September 1496, was little more than a gesture. In January 1497 Parliament voted King Henry money to resist this invasion, which provoked a rebellion in distant Cornwall. Edward Hall, as usual, has no sympathy with rebels.

After the Cornishmen left Wells they went to Salisbury and from there to Winchester, and so to Kent where they looked for help, but they were deceived in their expectation. For George Grey, earl of Kent, George Neville, Lord Abergavenny, and a great number of people were not only willing and ready to defend the country from all mischief and destruction, but were also determined on fight and combat with those who would not be obedient to their natural sovereign lord and to his laws and precepts. Also, the Kentish men themselves, partly remembering that other commotions had been to their damage and great hindrance and partly being under the defence of their nobility, would not so much as come near the rebels nor give them countenance nor once speak to any of them, so that the king should see no untruth or treason.

This so appalled and dismayed the hearts and courage of many of the brutish and rural Cornishmen (who seeing themselves deceived and defrauded of their chief hope of succour and fearing the evil luck which might befall them) and to save themselves they fled secretly in the night from their own company and companions. The captains of the rebels, perceiving they could have no aid from the Kentish people and putting their only hope in their power and fortitude (for surely they were men of great strength and of no less force than valiant courage) went to Blackheath four miles from London and there on a plain on top of a hill they ordered their battalions, ready either to fight with the king if he should attack them, or else to assault and attack the city of London. They truly thought that the king was so afraid of their strength that he intended nothing less than to meet with their army. Being inflamed with arrogance and firmly believing that the victory was certain in their hands, they determined to enter the city of London and to assault the Tower of London, wherein the King (as they thought) had secretly enclosed himself.

But King Henry acted directly contrary to their opinion and expectation, for he never intended to give them battle until he had them far from their homes and native region, so that they should be out of reach of all aid or comfort. When they were wearied and tired by their long and tedious journey, and their fury was somewhat assuaged and they fell to repenting their mad commotion and frantic progress, then he would in some place convenient for his purpose surround them to his advantage and their destruction as he did indeed afterwards.

In the meantime there was great fear throughout the city and cries were made: every man to arms, to arms; some ran to the gates, others mounted on the walls so that no part was undefended and the magistrates of the city kept continual watch lest the rebels, being poor and needy, should descend from their camp and invade the city and spoil and rob the riches and goods of the merchants.

The king however, delivered and purged their hearts of this fear, for after he saw that the Cornishmen were all day ready to fight upon the hill he sent John, earl of Oxford, Henry Bourchier, earl of Essex, Edmund de la Pole, earl of Suffolk and Sir Rhys ap Thomas and Sir Humphrey Stanley, all noble warriors, with a great company of archers and horsemen to surround the hill on the right and left so that all byways should be stopped and closed and all hope of flight be taken from them. Encouraged with manly stomach and desire to fight as furnished with a populous army and company of artillery, Henry set forward out of the city and encamped in St George's Field, where he lodged on the Friday night.

On the Saturday morning he sent Lord Daubeney with a great company to set on them early in the morning. They first attacked a bridge at Deptford Strand which was manfully defended by some of the rebel archers whose arrows it is said were a full yard long. While the earls set upon them on every side,

Lord Daubeney came into the field with his company and the Cornishmen were overcome without a long fight, but first they took Lord Daubeney prisoner and then, whether for fear or for hope of favour, they let him go free without any hurt or detriment to him.

More than 2,000 of the rebels who fought and resisted were slain and an infinite number taken prisoner, amongst them the blacksmith and chief captains who shortly after were put to death. Michael Joseph, surnamed the blacksmith, one of the captains of these dunghill and rubbish-sack ruffians was of such stout stomach and high courage that as he was drawn on the hurdle to his death he said (men do report) that for this mischievous and wicked act he would have a perpetual name and a permanent and immortal fame. So you may see desire and the ambitious greed for vain glory and fame inflames and encourages poor and mean persons as well as the hearts of great lords and powerful princes to work and aspire towards the same. Some affirm that the king planned to fight the rebels on Monday, and anticipating the time deliberately set upon them on the Saturday before when they were unprovided and not in battle array, and so by that policy won the field and victory.

Domestic strife did not drive all other thoughts out of the king's mind. A prolonged battle with the Netherlanders over trading privileges resulted in the treaty called the Magnus Intercursus of 1496, but the archduke Philip attempted to withdraw, and it was only in the summer of 1497 that the dispute was finally settled.

While these things were argued and at last concluded within England and Scotland, King Henry had the French king's ambassadors brought to his presence, and he received them benignly; they, as it was said before, were stopped on their journey at Dover until the Cornish insurrection was suppressed and extinguished. And with similar entertainment he embraced at the same time the Lord of Camphire and other ambassadors of Philip, archduke of Austria and duke of Burgundy who came to him to conclude and continue friendly relations, and to have English merchants resort to their country again from which they had been prohibited and forbidden.

This request, being very agreeable to the quietness and tranquillity of his realm, especially at that time, he favourably granted and benignly assented to. And so being confederated and allied by treaty and league with all his neighbours on every side of his realms and regions, he thanked most heartily King Ferdinand, and the queen his wife, for they were the mediators, organs and instruments by which the truce was concluded between him and the Scottish king, and he rewarded Peter the ambassador liberally and bountifully.

So Englishmen resorted again to the archduke's dominions, and were received in Antwerp with a general procession, so glad was the town with their return since by their absence it had been sorely hindered and impoverished.

1498

The Tudors were always concerned to impress the Italians, who were the leaders of fashion and opinion in the Renaissance, and England was subjected to cool and critical scrutiny in return, in this case by the anonymous regent of a minor Italian prince.

They all from time immemorial wear very fine clothes, and are extremely polite in their language which, although like the Flemish it derives from the German, has lost its natural harshness, and is pleasing enough as they pronounce it. In addition to their civil speeches, they have the incredible courtesy of remaining with their heads uncovered, with an admirable grace, whilst they talk to each other. They are gifted with good understandings, and are very quick at everything they apply their minds to. Few however, excepting the clergy, are addicted to the study of letters, and this is the reason why anyone who has any learning, though he be a layman, is called by them a Clerk. And yet they have great advantages for study, there being two general universities in the kingdom, Oxford and Cambridge, in which many colleges are founded for the maintenance of poor scholars. And your magnificence lodged at one named Magdalen, in the University of Oxford, whose founders were prelates, so its scholars are also ecclesiastics.

The common people apply themselves to trade, or to fishing or else they practice navigation; and they are so diligent in mercantile pursuits that they do not fear to lend money for interest.

Although they all attend mass every day, and say many Our Fathers in public, (the women carry long rosaries in their hands, and any who can read take the office of Our Lady with them, and some com-

Patron of ceremony and culture

The practice of courtly magnificence was a matter of policy, demonstrating to the king's subjects and to foreign courts his worthiness as the pinnacle and moving force of society. When Henry VII met Philip I of Castile in 1506 and escorted him to Windsor castle, an English observer noted with the exactness of a modern fashion correspondent the apparel worn by the two parties, and contrasted Henry's purple velvet raiment, a diamond image of St George hung round his neck, and his peacock nobles, with the sad, black apparel of Philip and his entourage. He also described the state apartments at Windsor: ''the King of Castile's chamber . . . is the richestly hanged that ever I saw; seven chambers together hanged with cloth of arras wrought with gold as thick as could be; and as for three beds of estate, no Christian king can show such three''.

In the 15th century the dukes of Burgundy, rulers of much of the Low Countries, were foremost in the cult of court splendour, and their example was copied by other French dynasties and, to some extent by Edward IV of England.

The staging and themes of the six pageants which greeted Catherine of Aragon on her progress through

et petit serviteur qui nomn

Above   Henry VII receiving a treatise on the nobility. Throughout his reign he curbed the power of the nobility through financial constraints and from 1504 they were not allowed to keep retainers other than household servants.

Left   The Burghley nef, a salt cellar and elegant table decoration.

London, when she was officially received there in 1501 on the occasion of her marriage to prince Arthur, had the sophistication of this style. The wedding tournaments held in the couple's honour at Westminster being probably the first fully-fledged Burgundian ones in England, with a "tree of chivalry" on which the contestants' shields were hung together with their entry on pageant cars: Henry Bourchier, 2nd earl of Essex, for example, arrived on one designed as a green mountain, with rocks, trees, plants and marvellous beasts on its slopes, and at its summit, a maiden clad apparently only in her hair.

Such innovative features in pageantry are probably an indication of Henry's personal taste. They certainly reflect his appreciation of the need to project the glory of his dynasty, the reason behind his huge expenditure on luxuries – over £128,000 on jewels between December 1491 and his death in 1509. He also indulged in building works, rebuilding Woodstock palace in Oxfordshire and transforming his Greenwich dwelling from a country house into a major palace. His greatest achievement, at a cost of more than £20,000, was the new palace of Richmond, on the site of the old one at Sheen in Surrey which had burnt down in 1497.

Although the English court's routines and celebrations remained essentially traditional under Henry, he grafted on to it the idioms and styles of Franco-Burgundian court culture, with their secular classical themes and increasingly their Italianate classical motifs. This trend had already been apparent at Edward IV's court, but Henry was an important influence in encouraging trends which were to lead to the flowering of Renaissance culture at the Tudor court in the 16th century.

71

panion recites it in the church verse by verse in a low voice, after the manner of churchmen) they always hear Mass on Sunday in their parish church, and give liberal alms, because they may not offer less than a coin, fourteen of which are equivalent to a golden ducat. Nor do they omit any form incumbent upon good christians: there are however many who have various opinions concerning religion.

They have a very high reputation in arms, and from the great fear the French entertain of them, one must believe it to be justly acquired. But I have it on the best information that when the war is waging most furiously, they will seek for good eating and all their other comforts, without thinking of what harm might befall them.

They have an antipathy to foreigners, and imagine that they only come into their island to make themselves masters of it and to usurp their goods. Nor do they have any sincere and solid friendships amongst themselves, in that they do not trust each other to discuss either public or private affairs together, confidentially as we do in Italy. And although their dispositions are somewhat licentious, I never have noticed anyone, either at court or amongst the lower orders, to be in love. Whence one must necessarily conclude either that the English are the most discreet lovers in the world, or that they are incapable of love. I say this of the men, for I understand it is quite the contrary with the women, who are very violent in their passions. However, the English keep a very jealous guard over their wives, though any thing may be compensated in the end by the power of money.

The want of affection in the English is strongly manifested towards their children, for having kept them at home till they arrive at the age of seven or nine years at the most, they put them out, both males and females, to hard service in the houses of other people, binding them generally for another seven or nine years. And these are called apprentices, and during that time they perform all the most menial offices. And few are born who are exempted from this fate, for every one, however rich he may be, sends away his children into the houses of others, whilst he in return receives those of strangers into his own. And on inquiring the reason for this severity they answered that they did it in order that their children might learn better manners. But I for my part believe that they do it because they like to enjoy all their comforts themselves, and that they are better served by strangers than they would be by their own children.

1499

Perkin Warbeck had made a final attempt to raise support in England by landing in Cornwall in September 1497. He was soon apprehended, but suffered no more than a loose restraint at court, having confessed his imposture. However, in June 1498 he fled, was recaptured and imprisoned. The following year he became involved in an insubstantial plot with his fellow prisoner, the earl of Warwick, for which both were tried and condemned in November 1499. Edward Hall concludes his story.

Now the fatal day of the death of Perkin Warbeck and Edward, earl of Warwick began to approach.

Perkin, either because it grieved him to be confined, or because he was instigated and enticed by some of his old friends to stir more coals and begin some new seditious faction, studied how to escape and fly away, having perfect hope that he would find a way to bring all things well to pass if he could once convey himself out of English hands. And although he knew that he could not do nor imagine anything without the king hearing of it, he was seduced by the hope of evasion and escape which was the chief comfort of his captivity, and he preferred to put everything to the test and hazard, rather than any longer to tolerate and suffer his present calamity and daily misery.

And so deceiving his keepers he took to his heels, by which he brought himself into stricter custody and imprisonment, and wrapped himself in tortures and punishments. For when he came to the sea coast and had gone a little forward on his journey, the rumour of his flight had spread, and every byway and lane was filled with the king's guard.

So, being sore abashed by the clamour of those who searched and made inquiry for him, and being destitute of wit and counsel, he was forced to change from his planned journey and came to the house of Shene Priory, near Richmond in Surrey, and committed himself to the prior of the monastery, asking him for God's sake to beg for his life and pardon from the king's majesty. The prior, who for his virtuous qualities was held in great esteem, was moved by the calamity and unfortunate state of this man, and came to the king and told him about Perkin, whose pardon he humbly craved and freely obtained.

Exploration and overseas voyages

Henry VII's concern to expand overseas commerce, his interest in founding a new British empire after the decay of the old one in Scotland, Ireland and France, and his alert sensitivity to policy trends at continental courts, are reflected in his grant in 1496 to John Cabot, a Genoese settled in Bristol, and to Cabot's sons and other Bristol merchants, of letters patent authorizing them to discover, investigate and annex lands unknown to Christians. In addition, the letters entitled them to rights of feudal land tenure from the Crown and to a trade monopoly – with a third of the profits going to the Crown. This was four years after Christopher Columbus's claim that he had reached the mainland of Asia on his westward voyage, and discovered an alternative to the overland and Mediterranean route to the lucrative Far Eastern spice trade.

Cabot and his Bristol partners convinced Henry that these claims were mistaken, and that northern Atlantic routes known to Bristol seamen since about 1480, as a result of their voyages to the "Isle of Brasil", would bring voyagers to Asia. In 1497 Cabot made landfall either on Nova Scotia or Newfoundland and reconnoitred the Newfoundland cod banks. He failed to return from a second voyage in 1498, but the ventures from Bristol continued, and in 1508 Henry granted territorial and trading privileges to Cabot's son Sebastian, who, in search of the hoped-for north-west passage to Asia discovered Hudson's Bay.

Henry's patronage of exploration reveals an unexpected imaginativeness and readiness to experiment. His son Henry VIII was more hindbound, concerned in the early years of his reign not to offend his Spanish allies who were suspicious of English interlopers in their Atlantic sphere, and dreaming of re-establishing an old-fashioned English empire in France.

Above all, however, the voyages of discovery are a tribute to the wealth, expertise and vision of the Bristol élite, whose city by the 15th century had emerged as the major western port of the British Isles, exporting cloth from a wide hinterland that stretched into the Midlands, importing and re-exporting Mediterranean delicacies, and developing a shipbuilding industry whose boats could tackle the North Atlantic.

Top   Christopher Columbus, whose voyage across the Atlantic discovered America.

Above   Vasco da Gama, the Portuguese explorer who found the sea routes to India in 1498.

73

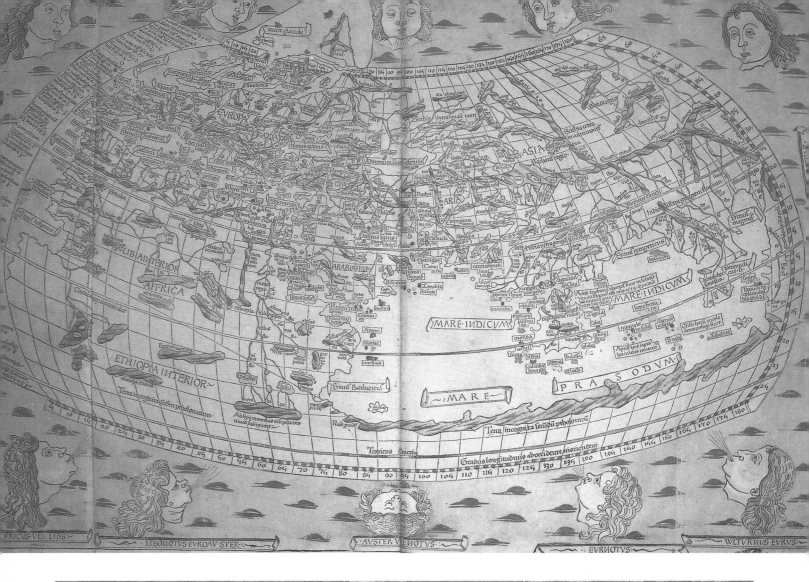

Left   Ptolemy's map, printed in 1482, shows the boundaries of the world ten years before Columbus discovered the New World.

Below left   A map of the world drawn after 1492 with the South Pole at the top.

Above   The Spanish conquistadors first view of South America – a mixture of fact and fantasy.

Below   The caravel, to the left of the galley ship, was a versatile vessel capable of sailing close to the wind and therefore very speedy.

Immediately after this Perkin was brought again to the court at Westminster with many a curse and reproach, and one day he was fettered in a pair of stocks before the door of Westminster Hall, and stood there the whole day with innumerable reproaches, mockings and scornings. The next day he was carried through London and set upon a similar scaffold in Cheapside, with similar bolts and stocks as he occupied the day before, and stood there all day and read openly his own confession written in his own hand, the true copy of which follows:

"First it is to be known that I was born in the town of Tournai in Flanders, and my father's name is John Osbeck, he was controller of that town, and my mother's name is Katherine de Faro. And one of my grandsires upon my father's side was named Dirck Osbeck which died, after whose death my grandmother was married unto Peter Flaue, that was Receiver of the town of Tournai, and Dean of the boatmen who ran upon the river called Leochelde. And my grandfather upon my mother's side was Peter de Faro, who had in his keeping the keys of the gate of St Johns within the town of Tournai. Also I had an uncle called Master John Stalyn, living in the parish of St Pious in the same town who had married my father's sister, whose name was Jan, with whom I lived for a while.

Afterwards I was taken by my mother to Antwerp to learn Flemish in the house of a cousin of mine, an officer of the town, called John Stienbeck, who I was with for half a year. After that I returned to Tournai because of the wars in Flanders. And within a year I was sent with a merchant of Tournai named Barlo, whose master's name was Alexander, to the market of Antwerp where I fell sick for five months. The said Barlo sent me to board in the house of a skinner who lived beside the house of the English nation. And by him I was carried from there to Barow market, and I lodged at the Sign of the Old Man where I stayed for two months. And after this the said Barlo put me to service with a merchant of Middleboroughe to learn the language; his name was John Strewe and I stayed with him from Christmas until Easter and then I went to Portugal in the company of Sir Edward Brampton's wife in a ship called the Queen's ship. When I arrived there I was put in service to a knight who lived in Lisbon called Peter Vacz de Cogn, with whom I stayed a whole year, which same knight had but one eye. And because I desired to see other

Intellectual and educational developments

Romances were the handbooks of courtly values and manners, and for the nobility chivalrous accomplishments were of practical use, as well as a mark of caste and a source of immense pleasure. Most sons of peers were educated in these subjects in the great households, while the sons of gentlefolk used the universities of Oxford and Cambridge and the London inns of court as finishing schools, and as a means to acquire skills useful in administrative careers and the management of their estates.

Young men in noble households also learnt Latin grammar, the foundation skill of learning, as did gentlefolk and commoners in the grammer schools founded by pious benefactors, often with endowed places. The start of an educational revolution was underway, with curricula that included classical Latin and the works of the Roman poets, orators and historians. These areas of teaching were soon well established at Magdalen College Grammar School under masters such as John Ankwykyll, who published a new grammar using the works of Cicero and Horace. When John Colet, dean of St Paul's cathedral, planned his new school in the early 16th century, his emphasis on the study of the late classical Christian poets brought a Christian rather than a pagan influence to humanist education. The foundation statutes of some new university colleges and lectureships specifically provided for the more intense study of Latin grammar: Margaret Beaufort's refoundation in 1506 of the Cambridge college renamed Christ's for example.

Henry VII was the first English king to enjoy the courtly aspects of humanist learning. He appreciated the usefulness of humanists in helping his dynasty to gain international respect, and took care that his sons Arthur and Henry had the best of modern education. Both were given a thorough grounding in Latin classics. The Dutch scholar, Erasmus, was impressed by the future Henry VIII's erudite manner at the age of eight, when he visited the royal nursery at Eltham in Kent, in 1499. His initial scepticism about the authorship of a precocious Latin letter he had received from the boy was soon overcome. In later years Erasmus claimed that Henry's style in his anti-Lutheran writings was similar to his own, because the king had been encouraged to read his works when young.

Although Henry VII was not a great patron of the academic side of humanism, he established classical culture as the English court style in literature, and ensured that his sons were taught the new grounding in arts, which was to be the basis of gentlemanly education for the next four centuries. Subsequent generations would refer to Henry VIII as the first English king with a modern mind. But it is his father who should be regarded as England's first Renaissance ruler.

Above   Children at school, a woodcut printed by Wynkyn de Worde in 1512.

Far left   William Caxton's History of Troy, the first book to be printed in English.

Below left   Henry encouraged scholarship and learning to develop as it had been doing in Europe during the Renaissance.

Below   A page from Leonardo da Vinci's notes written in Florence in 1508.

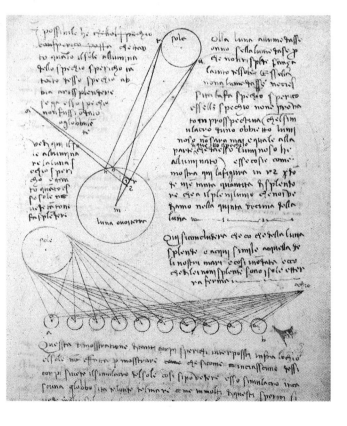

countries. I took licence of him, and then I put myself in service with a Breton called Pregent Meno, who brought me with him to Ireland, and when we were arrived there in the town of Cork, they of the town, because I was arrayed in some clothes of silk belonging to my mistress, came to me and claimed that I must be the duke of Clarence's son who had been previously at Dublin. And when I denied it, the mayor of the town brought me the blessed sacrament and the cross, and there in the presence of the same John Wellen and others I took my oath as the truth was, that I was not the dukes son, nor any of his blood. And after this there came to me an Englishman whose name was Stephen Poytron with another called John Water and said to me and swore great oaths that they knew well that I was King Richard's bastard son. To them I answered with like oaths that I was not. Then they advised me not to be afraid, but to take it upon me boldly, and if I would do so they would aid and assist me with all their power against the King of England, and not only they but they were certain the earls of Desmond and Kildare would do the same. For they did not care which party they took, so long as they might be revenged upon the king of England. And so against my will they made me learn English and taught me what I should do and say. And after this they called me duke of York, second son of King Edward IV, because King Richard's bastard son was in the hands of the King of England. And in this way John Water, Stephen Poytron, John Tyler, Hubert Burgh and many others entered into this false quarrel. Within a short time after the French king sent an ambassador to Ireland, called Loyte Lucas, to admonish me to come to England."

When the night of 15 June had come (partly because the king had pardoned his life and partly so he should no more run away and put the king in doubt of any mishap or misfortune to come) he was committed to the Tower of London, where his wickedness boiling so hot within his cankered stomach would not allow him to escape the punishment and vengeance of God, but shortly afterwards he was most justly and deservedly put to death.

1500

In May 1500, in the midst of a sharp outbreak of plague, Henry crossed to Calais for a meeting with the archduke Philip. This meeting took place an 9 June, and was inconclusive, as Richard Grafton explains.

Soon after, when this plague had abated, the king returned again to England, about the end of June, and soon after there came to him one Gaspar Pous, a Spaniard, very excellent both in learning and good behaviour, sent from Alexander, bishop of Rome, to show Englishmen the right way to heaven. Therefore that year was called the year of Jubilee, which was the year of our lord 1500.

And so that the people from far countries might be eased of their labour and effort in travelling there, the charitable father sent his legates to every country to distribute the heavenly grace, as he called it, to all Christian people who, prevented by war, enemies, infirmity, weakness or the tediousness of the long journey, were not able to make their journey to the holy city of Rome.

But this benevolent liberality was not so frankly and freely given: for the holy bishop Alexander, while helping and looking to the health of men's souls, thought to do something for his own private benefit and singular wealth, and therefore he limited and set a certain price on this grace and pardon. And so that the king should not hinder or stand in the way of his purpose, he offered part of his gain to the king. And so that the people might the sooner diminish their purses and enrich his chests he promised he would at the beginning of the year make war with all haste against the Great Turk.

By this means and policy this Alexander got and heaped up a great sum of money, and yet no battle was begun against the Turk, who in the meantime had taken, conquered and destroyed many regions, cities and towns that had to many centuries belonged to Christian men.

1501

A marriage between Arthur and Catherine, the third daughter of Ferdinand and Isabella of Spain, had first been agreed at the treaty of Medina del Campo in 1489. The marriage had been celebrated by proxy in May 1499. In September 1501 Arthur was fifteen and Catherine seventeen. The preparations for her arrival were meticulous, as the following document, probably drawn up by the lord chamberlain reveals.

Memorandum for the transportation of the Princess Catherine, daughter to the right high and mighty Princes the King and Queen of Spain:

Arthur and Catherine

Henry VII's son and heir Prince Arthur was only eighteen months old when in March 1488 formal negotiations began for his future marriage with an equally tiny princess, Catherine, daughter of Ferdinand II and Isabella of Spain. Henry was seeking a rich prize in the match. The Spanish rulers had united the kingdoms of Castile and Aragon by their marriage, and were about to drive the last remnants of Islamic power out of Spain. By contrast Henry had still to prove his ability to survive. Of course, hindsight was to show that his victory at the battle of Stoke in 1487 had ended the most serious challenge to his rule. He was also anxious to prevent Spain from supporting English rebels. By 1491 when the Treaty of Medina del Campo was signed with Spain, he had achieved his objectives: a definite prospect of the most important foreign royal marriage alliance since Henry V had married the king of France's daughter.

The promised pair, however, were still infants and their union was still subject to pressures of diplomacy. Spanish confidence in Henry was quickly shaken by the English monarch's trials by rebellion throughout the 1490s. The Flemish impostor Perkin Warbeck attempted to pass himself off as a Yorkist claimant to the throne until he was caught and hanged. His execution was soon followed by that of Edward, 2nd earl of Warwick, long imprisoned for being the only surviving son of George, duke of Clarence, and the genuine heir to the house of York.

The Spanish were delighted at this confirmation that the English alliance was a safe option, and the marriage took place by proxy on 20 January 1500 – the first of three proxy ceremonies to take place before the final wedding. This was staged on 14 November 1501, soon after Catherine's arrival in England. The festivities were accompanied by spectacular pageantry – a pioneering venture in the great shows which were to become a feature of the English court during the 16th century. The inspiration for this was the lavish court of the dukes of Burgundy, which set the fashions for all 15th century Europe: clearly Henry was determined in this celebration of his son's match to show that England was no longer on the edge of Europe but had arrived among the continental powers.

Fate mocked the king's theatrical investment, however, when on 2 April 1502 Arthur died at his castle of Ludlow. Catherine's marriage to the prince's younger brother Henry was mooted shortly afterwards, but because of the tangled diplomacy of Henry VII's last years it was postponed until his son was actually on the throne. The papal dispensations which made that

Above   A Flemish tapestry showing the betrothal of Arthur, Prince of Wales, and Catherine of Aragon, which gave Henry a powerful alliance with Spain.

marriage possible would cast a long shadow over the years to come.

Disputes at the time of Arthur's death, and in the momentous struggles around Henry VIII's divorce of Catherine, have obscured our knowledge of that brief marriage. It is difficult to know whether the union was consummated. Henry VII had a strong interest in asserting consummation, in order to secure the remainder of the dowry owed to him by the Spaniards. In the future, Henry VIII was to be equally insistent that it had taken place in order to fulfill the conditions of the Levitical prohibition. Yet Catherine, a lady with an uncomfortably straightforward relish for truth, always insisted that she had remained a virgin, and only hearsay and reports of Arthur's gauche adolescent sexual boasting can oppose her firm insistence.

1. It is agreed that in the month of August or September next the said Princess Catherine, with her company, shall be transported, God willing, to Southampton Water. It is thought good, since the ships which carry her noble person shall not come nearer than three or four miles to the king's port and town of Southampton, that the two barks which the king our sovereign lord caused to be rigged for the last voyage of his army by water to Scotland should be richly appointed, and other barges and great boats to attend upon her company be likewise well arrayed and furnished, to bring her noble grace and her company more easily and safely to the king's town and port aforesaid.

2. It is agreed that in the two barks there should be some noble personages of mine to receive the princess at her ship.

3. There are lords, spiritual and temporal, who have been appointed to attend upon her landing, whose names are written in the roll of the first meeting, and therefore letters must be sent to them for this purpose at a convenient time.

4. Ladies have also been appointed to attend the princess on her landing, whose names are specified in a roll. Therefore it is necessary that the queen's letters be sent in the same way to those ladies with the same intent.

5. That a presentation should be made at the first receiving of the Princess into the hands of my Lord Steward, Lord Willoughby de Broke, by one who my lord shall move the king to do the act. And since upon the landing of the princess it seems fitting that she and her company should enter into the king's charge, he should appoint some officers and others of his noble household to provide for her costs.

6. That the nine following persons should be appointed to attend upon my Lord Steward when he shall call or send for them:

The Lord St John	Sir Robert Poyntes
Sir John Risley	Sir Edward Wingfield
Sir James Tyrrell	Sir William Sandys
Sir Walter Hungerford	Sir Edward Darrell
Sir David Owen	

so that he and they may debate and commune together from time to time about the ordering of the reception of the Princess off the water, for the first meeting on land, for the conveyance, lodging and dislodging of her and her company, and so inform the bishops and earls of the first meeting, to have their advice and agreement about it.

7. These persons, that is my Lord Steward, my Lord St John and so forth, shall see everything duly executed as it shall be agreed between the lords for the first meeting. And they are to remember that servants should not be allowed to ride in front, but there must be a sufficient number of horsemen to ride behind, for the better order and the greater honour. And in the same say for the second and third meetings it is thought good for my Lord Steward and the other nine to inform the lords and to do for those two later meetings what is planned and rehearsed for the first.

8. The following persons are appointed to attend upon my Lord Steward at the first meeting: Richmond, king of arms; Somerset, Herald, Rouge dragon and Bluemantle pursuivants: John of Roydon; Thomas Footman; Lionel Chawford; and John of Leighe.

9. My Lord Steward should have the rolls of the estates and the noblemen appointed for the first, second and third meetings, for himself and for the information of the lords and knights appointed to assist him, the better and more assuredly to conduct everything in due order.

10. It were good, so that he should know the whole ordering of these traditions, that he should have a book thereof, better to direct all that is contained in the same to his charge.

11. Certain officers should be assigned to provide for litters, chairs and palfreys for the princess and her ladies.

12. Boats should be provided to bring the baggage of her and her company from their ships to land, and horses should be obtained for the company to travel by land, and carriages for the baggage.

13. Two litters should be prepared for the princess herself, one to carry her to Croydon, the other, more richly decorated than the first, for her entry into London.

Catherine reached London on 12 November, and was received into the City of London with six magnificent allegorical pageants, over which no pains and expense had been spared. The first was at London Bridge, the second at Grace Church Street, the third at Cornhill, the fourth at Soper Lane, the fifth at the Standard in Cheapside and the sixth at the end of Friday Street.

After these speeches were ended she passed through and so came to Cheapside where against Soper Lanes the fourth pageant was set. It was in the manner of a heaven in which were painted twelve signs, and over them was Arthur, fully armed, in his golden chariot. And in the firmament were three young striplings of twelve or thirteen years, fully armed, who moved always towards Arthur's chariot, but never passed a certain height.

"Welcome! fair lady, fairer than Hesperus,
Welcome, noble princess, unto Britain!
The land of Arthur, your spouse most bounteous,
Whose exact image and figure certain
You may behold all armed, not in vain
With corporal armour only but likewise
With the spiritual armour of justice.

Which armour of Justice, as the prophet says,
Is of every realm the peaceable conservator;
Wherefore as you see this chariot here on high
Stands in his company always firm and sure,
Likewise the realm of your worthy spouse Arthur
Shining in virtue shall stand perpetually
With the compass of his noble progeny.

Wherefore, Madam, greatly rejoice you may,
For whose marriage as a special favour
It has pleased almighty God to purvey
A prince of all princes the very flower,
With whom you shall aspire to great honour;
Go ye forth to the joyful semblance now
Of the marriage between your spouse and you."

After this speech was ended she rode towards St Paul's Cathedral, but when she came to the Standard in Cheapside there was a right costly pageant prepared, like a heaven with seven gold candlesticks, and wax candles burning on them, and a man dressed to represent the father of heaven. He had a speech which follows. (In a house where William Geffrey, haberdasher, lived stood the king, the queen and many great dignitaries of the realm.)

"I am beginning and end, that made each creature
Myself and for myself, but man specially,
Both male and female, made after my own figure;
Whom I joined together in matrimony,
and that in paradise, declaring openly,

That men shall weddings in my church solemnise
Figured and signified by the earthly paradise.

In this my church I am always resident,
As my chief tabernacle and most chosen place,
Among these golden candlesticks, which represent
My catholic church, shining before my face
With light of faith, wisdom, doctrine and grace;
and marvellously also inflamed towards me
With the inextinguishable fire of charity.

Wherefore my wellbeloved daughter Catherine,
Since I have made you in my own semblance
In my church to be married and your noble children
To reign in this land as in their inheritance,
See that you have me in special remembrance;
Love me and my church, your spiritual mother;
For ye despising the one despise the other.

Look that you walk in my precepts and obey them well,
And here I give you the same blessing that I
Gave my wellbeloved children of Israel:
Blessed be the fruit of your belly,
Your substance and fruits I shall increase and multiply,
Your rebellious enemies I shall put in your hand.
Increasing in honour both you and your land."

This done she went on her way, and when she came a little beyond the Cross in Cheapside, at the end of Friday Street, there the mayor, on horseback accompanied by the recorder, advanced a little towards the princess, and the recorder in the name of the mayor, his brethren and the citizens of London welcomed her grace with appropriate words and greeting; this done the mayor and recorder returned to their places. And she rode on past all the aldermen who sat in order on horseback along the street from there to the old Exchange, doing her grace due obeisance.

Arthur's wedding was in many ways the high point of Henry's reign, both diplomatically and dynastically, but he was never safe from the dangers of conspiracy, even after Perkin Warbeck's death, as this dispassionate extract from Polydore Vergil reveals.

When the nobility as a whole were occupied in the games and knightly tournaments of Arthur and Catherine's marriage feast, Edmund de la Pole, earl of Suffolk with his brother Richard, having secretly boarded a ship, fled across to their mother's sister

Margaret in Flanders. The earl was the son of John, duke of Suffolk by King Edward's sister Elizabeth, and was bold, impetuous and readily roused to anger; shortly before this, incited so it was believed by his aunt Margaret, he had secretly fled from the kingdom. But since he was a cunning fellow he was able to produce a thoroughly detailed excuse for his action; and having obtained pardon from King Henry, he immediatelly returned.

However after that he was not well disposed to Henry, and finally, partly because of party feeling and because he was eager for a revolution, partly because he was embarrassed by very heavy debts, he again crossed to the continent without the king's authority, and took with him his brother Richard. When the king learnt of Edmund's flight he was greatly disturbed, regretted that he had spared him on the first occasion and began to fear fresh upheavals.

That these things should befall King Henry came as no surprise to many of his counsellors who, forseeing precisely what would happen, had accordingly warned him to treat Edmund with rigorous severity since he was corrupted by the evil advice of the king's enemies; otherwise the earl would become more overbearing, partly because of the forgiveness of his recent offence, partly because of the favours he was at present enjoying, and would again engineer some most dangerous assault against the state.

But the king, with an even shrewder plan, dealt gently with the earl after his first flight, so that by maintaining this attitude for a period he might at length acquire information concerning some conspiracy, which he considered had been hatched between the earl and several other persons. Wherefore, when immediately after the earl's return to England Sir Robert Curzon, commander of the castle of Hammes, in the Calais Pale, fled to Flanders to all intents and purposes as one of the conspirators, many people suspected that he had not really abandoned his king, but had been sent by the king to spy out at Margaret's court all the plans of the conspirators. And even today many people hold this view. For Robert Curzon was of humble origin and was knighted by the king; so far as was known he had not been in any way offended but betook himself to the rebels enticed only by a foolish hope; and finally, when the plot was laid bare and many of the conspirators punished by death, he returned into the king's favour.

When these things are thought of it may easily be believed that all he did was done on Henry's orders. However this may have been, after the marriage celebrations were over, the king acted with so much application that he learnt who all the conspirators were by name. Accordingly within a few days he ordered the arrest of William Courtenay, son of Edward, earl of Devon to whom had been married King Edward's daughter Catherine; another William, the brother of earl Edmund himself; Sir James Tyrrell, commander of the town of Guisnes, in the Calais Pale, Sir John Wyndham, and many others of the common people. All of these, except William Courtenay and the other William de la Pole since they were less incriminated, he ordered to be punished with death. The two nobles whose lives he had spared he flung into prison there to suffer for a long time for their offences. But see now how God remembers all the crimes we have committed! At length even James Tyrrell came to the scaffold.

He was the same James to whom King Richard deputed the business of arranging the death of the two wretched sons of King Edward; which business he thoroughly performed. On that occasion James could – without danger to his own life – have spared the boys, rescued them from death and carried them to safety; for beyond doubt the entire population would have risen in arms to defend them. But he would not do this in order that he might afterwards try, against all human and divine injunctions, to help earl Edmund, son of Edward's sister; for this at length he paid by his own death the appropriate penalty for his previous crimes.

When duke Edmund heard that his fellow conspirators in England were either executed or imprisoned he began to despair of success and postponed trying his luck until some later occasion. And wandering for long among many German and French peoples he at last put himself at the mercy of archduke Philip. But his brother Richard, in order to get far away from danger, went to Hungary.

1502

The success and dynastic triumph promised by Catherine's marriage to Arthur was short-lived, and the relationship was probably never consumated.

Dynastic marriages and family deaths

The death of Prince Arthur on 2 April 1502 was not allowed to break the Anglo-Spanish alliance. His parents-in-law, Ferdinand II and Isabella of Spain, instructed their ambassador in England to negotiate for their daughter Catherine of Aragon's marriage to Henry VII's younger son, the future Henry VIII. The formal treaty for this was concluded in 1502. A papal dispensation was needed, because Arthur and Catherine's marriage was thought to have been consummated, but because of delays at Rome, the bulls did not arrive until 1505.

In the interval, two more deaths complicated international relations. With the death of the king's wife, Elizabeth of York, he was now able to offer his own hand in the course of diplomacy. When Isabella of Castile died on 26 November 1504, Spanish unity was endangered by Castilians unwilling to accept Ferdinand as their governor, preferring instead Philip of Flanders, husband of the Infanta Joanna. Ferdinand found a new wife, Germaine de Foix, niece of the French king, Louis XII.

Henry's own treaty with Philip, negotiated during his visit to England in 1506, helps to explain why Catherine languished in widowhood, a virtual prisoner

Above   Ode by the Welsh Bard Rhys Nanmor on the death of the young prince written in 1502.

Left   Arthur, Prince of Wales, from the north window in Great Malvern Priory.

of her father-in-law. Philip had no desire to see Catherine's position strengthened while he was trying to press his own wife's claim to Castile. The suggestion that Henry contemplated marrying her himself cannot be substantiated. He entertained the idea of marrying Joanna after Philip died in September 1506, and also negotiated for his daughter Mary to marry Charles, the son of Philip and Joanna – the future Holy Roman Emperor Charles V. The hectic diplomacy of his last years saw Henry VII desperate to secure continental friends.

One achievement of his diplomacy was of long-term importance: on 8 August 1503, James IV of Scotland and Henry's daughter Margaret were married in Holyrood House. The Treaty of Ayton (1502), brought peace but did not endure, and James was killed at Flodden in 1513. The marriage, however, paved the way for the union of the crowns of England and Scotland in 1603.

Richard Grafton describes the misfortunes which followed.

When the king by his high policy had completed his alliance with Spain in this way, there suddenly came a lamentable mischance and loss to the king, queen and all the people. For that noble prince Arthur, the king's first begotten son, after he had been married to the Lady Catherine for five months, departed this transitory life at Ludlow on 2 April 1502.

With great funeral obsequies he was buried in the cathedral church of Worcester. After his death the name of prince belonged to his brother the duke of York, since his brother died without any issue, and so without being thus created he ought to be called, unless some apparent cause was a let or obstacle to it. But the duke, suspecting that his brother's wife was with child, as was thought possible by the expert and wise men of the prince's council, was by a month or more delayed from his title, name and pre-eminence, in which time the truth might easily appear to women.

It is reported that this lady Catherine thought and feared such an unhappy chance might come, for when she had embraced her father and taken leave of her noble and prudent mother, and sailed towards England, she was continually so tossed and tumbled hither and thither with boisterous winds that what with the raging of the water and the contrary winds her ship was prevented many times from approaching the shore and landing.

1503

The following year Queen Elizabeth, lying in the tower of London, was brought to bed on Candlemas day of a fair daughter who was there christened and named Catherine, and on 11 February, the most virtuous princess and gracious queen there died, and was with all funeral pomp carried through the City of London to Westminster, and there buried, whose daughter also lived but a little time after her mother.

The Emperor Maximilian, hearing that Queen Elizabeth had died, sent to England a solemn embassy, of which the chief ambassador was Lord Cazimir, marquis of Brandenberg, his cousin, accompanied by a bishop, an earl, and a great number of well-appareled gentlemen. He was triumphantly received in London and was lodged at Crosby's Place. This embassy was sent for three reasons: one to visit and comfort the king, being sorrowful and sad at the death of so good a queen and wife; the second to renew the old league and friendship; the third, which was not so apparent, was to persuade the king to marry the emperor's daughter, Lady Margaret, dowager duchess of Savoy.

The first two took effect, for the king on Passion Sunday rode to St Paul's Cathedral in great triumph with the marquis riding at his left side. And there the bishop made an excellent and comfortable oration to the king concerning the death of the queen. There also the king openly swore to keep the renewed league and friendship during their two lives. But the third request, whether the hindrance was on the man's part or the woman's side, never came to any effect or conclusion. And so these things done the ambassadors returned sumptuously and honourably rewarded.

All this winter preparation was made for the conveyance of Lady Margaret, betrothed to the king of Scots, into Scotland. And when all things were ready and prepared the king moved on the last day of June from Richmond, in the company of this daughter, and came to Colyweston, where his mother the countess of Richmond then was. And at the end of certain days of recreation the king gave her his blessing with a fatherly exhortation, and committed her conveyance to the king her husband's presence to the earl of Surrey: and Henry Algernon Percy, earl of Northumberland was appointed as Warden of the Marches, to deliver her at the border of both the Marches.

Thus this fair lady was conveyed with a great company of lords, ladies, knights, esquires and gentlemen until she came to Berwick and from there to a village called Lambton Kirk in Scotland where the king with the flower of Scotland was ready to receive her, to whom the earl of Northumberland according to his commission delivered her.

The Scots that day, I assure you, were not behind the English but far above, both in dress and rich jewels and weighty chains. But above all others was the earl of Northumberland, what with the riches of his coat, being goldsmith's work garnished with pearls and stones, and what with the costly dress of his henchmen and the gallant trappings of their horses, besides four hundred tall men, well-horsed and dressed in his colours, he was esteemed by both the English and Scots to be more like a prince than a subject.

Then this lady was taken to the town of Edinburgh, and there the day after King James IV in the presence of all his nobility married the said fair princess, and feasted the English lords, and showed them jousts and other pastimes, very honourably, after the fashion of his rude country. When all things were done and finished according to their commission the earl of Surrey with all the English lords and ladies returned to their country, giving more praise to the manhood than to the good manner and nurture of Scotland.

Henry's main building project hitherto had been his great palace of Richmond. He now set out to build himself a suitable mausoleum, in the most developed gothic style, and imported the Italian renaissance sculptor, Torrigiano, to prepare his funeral monument.

In this year began the new work of the King's chapel at Westminster, which is one of the most excellent pieces of work wrought in stone in Christendom.

In this year the King kept his high court of parliament, in which various acts were concluded which were thought necessary and expedient for the preservation of the public good. Amongst other things it was determined that thieves and murderers duly convicted by the law to die should be burned on the hand and committed to the bishops' custody, as I have before declared. After this money was granted to the king by the whole parliament, and the goods of outlawed men were forfeited and confiscated. There was also called as is usual a congregation of the clergy so that they with their treasure and money might advance the common wealth of the realm.

Hitherto we have showed you rough and sharp battles, pernicious and seditious strife, tumult and the death of many noble and mean persons. Now therefore let us here rehearse the dispute of familiar things, the gnawing at the hearts and the fretting of minds and of vows, promises and requests made of various persons.

1504

The latter part of the king's reign was dominated by his attempts to place his heir beyond challenge, by bequeathing him a secure realm and a full treasury.

King Henry, now growing old, before this time had always been vexed and provoked by the scrupulous stings of sedition and civil commotion, so that he detested and abhorred internal and private war more than death or anything more terrible. Therefore he determined to provide so prudently that all causes of such unquietness and mischief to come should be rooted out and banished. This intention and purpose he doubted not to compass and bring to effect if he reduced and lessened the courage of his subjects and vassals, especially the richest sort, remembering the old proverb that men through abundance of riches grow more insolent and headstrong, and that nothing is more acceptable or desirable to them than the abundance of treasure and plenty of money, for fear of losing which, or hope of gaining worldly riches, they desire either peace or war.

But so that men should not think or report that he, who is their king and instituted by God to revenge all injuries done and committed against them, should oppress and wrongfully plunder and exact money from his subjects, he debated with himself by what honest means he might accomplish it. And thus debating with himself, it came into his head that Englishmen cared little for the observation and keeping of penal laws and statutes made and ordained for the preservation of the common good and wealth. And therefore if inquisition were made about such penal statutes, there would be few noblemen, merchants, farmers, husbandmen, graziers or occupiers not found to be transgressors and violators of those statutes.

After he had taken this advice he sought out the penal laws and put them into execution, and those who were found to be offenders were easily at the beginning fined and scourged. After this he appointed two masters and surveyors of his forfeits, Sir Richard Empson and Edmund Dudley, both learned in the laws of the realm. And these two competed as to which by most profit might most please and satisfy their master's desire and appetite. Therefore in the beginning, armed with a company of accusers (commonly called promoters) who brought them the names of offenders, they valued and regarded so much the gaining of money that they clearly forgot and banished from their memory their present duty, the danger which might follow, and the thanks and goodwill which they might have obtained, although they were warned by various wise persons to keep their hands from such uncharitable doings and cruel extremities, according to the adage that the extremity of justice is extreme injury.

The king, after he had got a large and ample sum of money, had pity on the people who daily cried to God for an end to their pilfering, and of his mercy and gracious goodness thought it best and thus determined that these two extreme officers should be deprived of that office, and the money be wholly restored and delivered again to those from whom it had been unjustly exacted and extorted. He was prevented from this by death, but ordered it by his last will and testament to be duly and truly performed, but in the mean time many men's coffers were emptied.

1505

After the death of Arthur, a fresh treaty in 1503 had agreed that Catherine should marry Henry, Arthur's younger brother, when the necessary dispensation had been obtained. After Elizabeth's death, the king also considered remarrying himself. His first choice was Joan, the recently widowed Queen of Naples, niece of King Ferdinand I, and consequently Catherine's cousin, but the negotiations came to nothing. In order to find out whether Joan might be suitable for him, Henry gave strict instructions for his ambassadors to follow, among them the following:

Instruction given by the king's highness to his trusty and well beloved servants, Francis Marsin, James Braybrooke, and John Stile, showing how they shall order themselves when they come into the presence of the old Queen of Naples and the young queen her daughter.

First, after presentation and delivery of such letters as they shall have with them to be delivered to the said queens from the Lady Catherine, Princess of Wales, making her recommendation and declaration of such charges and words as shall be showed and committed to them by the said princess to be opened and declared on her behalf the said queens, they shall well note and mark the estate which they keep, and how they are accompanied with nobles and ladies.

Response: At our coming to the said queens we knelt down before them and kissed their hands, and delivered my lady princess's letters to the said queens to each of them separately, with the report of the recommendations on behalf of my lady the princess, which the said queens received and took

very thankfully, each of them making answer separately to the said recommendations, and giving their thanks for them with a grave and steadfast countenance. The young queen said little more than to thank the princess her cousin for her good and loving mind to write to her, and asked about the welfare of my lady the princess, whom she said she was glad to hear of, for she had never seen her. The old queen said similar words and many more, which we passed in communication. As we are informed the two queens each have their own separate lodging by themselves, and each has their servants, men, women and slaves, to themselves, although the said queens do keep their estates and households together as one household, and commonly the young queen and the old queen both sleep in one chamber, and they keep a great household of gentlemen, ladies, gentlewomen and slaves, and the old queen keeps a great estate with a great gravity, for she has the king's power to rule all the realm of Valencia, and so she rules and is obeyed in all things, and no manner of person does what is contrary to her commandment. As we can perceive and hear the said queens do keep a noble firm rule and order in their household and servants.

Item, they shall also endeavour to understand whether the young queen speaks any languages other than Spanish and Italian, and whether she can speak any French or Latin.

Response: As to this article, as far as we can understand and know, the said young queen can speak no languages except Spanish and Italian. It is said that she understands both Latin and French, but she speaks none.

Item, specially to mark and note well the age and stature of the said young queen and the features of her body.

Response: As to this article, as to the age of the said young queen, it is 27 years and not much more; and as to the stature of her person we cannot perfectly understand or know, for commonly when we came into her presence her grace was sitting on a cushion, and another twice we saw her on foot going across a chamber which was not wide, where she came in at a door and came to her mother the queen in the same room and sat down by her, and at both times she wore slippers after the manner of the country, in such a way that we could not come to

Money and the nobility

An important aspect of Henry's love of money, and probably his best known characteristic is his use of bonds and recognisances in dealings with his nobility. A bond, or obligation, was a legal document by which someone engaged to observe some condition on penalty of forfeiting an agreed sum of money; a recognisance was a type of bond by which someone recognized or acknowledged a past debt or agreement, often made conditional on future behaviour.

Henry's government used such instruments extensively, with the king taking a close personal interest in their details and exploitation. Their attraction was only partly financial, for more importantly, Henry could regulate their effect with subtle flexibility. Anyone who broke the conditions could face the full penalty specified in the bond, or a smaller fine decided by the king. Recognisances could be used without any control from the law courts with their cumbersome public procedures and their tendency to insist on legal correctness in all details.

At one extreme, both bonds and recognisances were part of everyday administration – agreements with merchants for instance, or routine stages in legal transactions – and in any case a recognisance usually involved some genuine previous debt to the king. However, they were more clearly instruments of power when they concerned criminal or political matters – the release of a prisoner or the pardon of a rebel or dynastic opponent. In this way they enabled the king to curb the nobility's retention of military forces, and the exercise of personal control over what he considered breaches of law and public peace.

Henry's use of recognisances increased after 1500. Many recorded bonds specifically mention that those giving them must keep their allegiance to the king, probably because in the years after the death of Arthur, prince of Wales, and with Prince Henry still only a teenager, Henry VII suffered renewed anxiety as to whether his achievements would be lasting.

During his reign, more than two-thirds of all aristocratic families were forced to enter conditional agreements with the king binding them to loyalty, and, particularly in the last decade from 1499 to 1509, many were bound more than once. The result was a state of nagging anxiety and fear among the English nobility that the king just might exercise his rights and demand the often huge sums involved.

Although Henry rarely demanded payment in full, bonds and recognisances provided a substantial income for the royal coffers. The king's former minister and financial agent, Edmund Dudley, in a remarkable secret

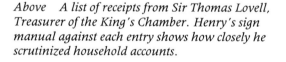

Above   A list of receipts from Sir Thomas Lovell, Treasurer of the King's Chamber. Henry's sign manual against each entry shows how closely he scrutinized household accounts.

confession on the eve of his execution by Henry VIII in 1510, acknowledged that many bonds had unjustly raised sums of money and that his royal master had often been personally involved. Dudley knew there was little to gain from maligning the dead king in his last desperate stage of his life. Nevertheless he explicitly stated that Henry had taken such bonds, "to have many persons in his danger at his pleasure". Sir Richard Empson, another of the king's financial agents was also beheaded in 1510. In both cases, the only explanation for their fates is that they were portrayed as criminally responsible for the wrongs of the past.

In his will Henry specified that a committee be set up to consider any wrongs anyone might have suffered at his hands: a firm indication that he knew all had not been well with the government. Equally telling was that Henry VIII cancelled at least 175 of his father's recognisances over five years, and that 51 of these cancellations recorded that they had been levied unjustly. Henry VII's policy may have been unjust but it succeeded: there were no serious uprisings against the government after 1497.

any perfect knowledge of the height of the said queen.

And as to the features of the body of the said young queen, since at all times that we have seen her grace she always had a great mantle of cloth on her after the manner of that country, in such a way that a man cannot easily see anything except the face, therefore we could not be certain of any features of her body, but as far as we can perceive and judge she is not of high stature but of middle stature in our opinion, because of the height of her slippers of which we have seen an example.

Specially to mark the favour of her visage, whether she be painted or not, and whether it be fat or lean, sharp or round, and whether her countenance be cheerful and amiable, frowning or melancholy, steadfast or light, or blushing in conversation.

Response: As to this article, as far as we can see or tell the queen is not painted, and the favour of her visage is after her stature, of a very good compass, and amiable, and somewhat round and fat, and the countenance cheerful, not frowning, and steadfast, and not light nor presumptuous in speech, but with a demure womanly modest countenance, and of few words as we saw, but we think that she uttered fewer words because the queen her mother was present, who did all the talking, and the young queen sat as demure as a maiden, sometimes talking with the ladies who sat around her with a womanly laughing cheer and face, and with a good dignity, the ladies talking with her always having their faces turned towards her grace with reverence and honour.

Item, to mark whether her neck be long or short, small or great.

Response: As to this article, the neck of the said queen is full and comely, and not misshapen, not very short nor very long, but fitting for the size of her personage, but her neck looks shorter because her breasts are full and somewhat big.

Item, to mark her breasts, whether they be big or small.

Response: As to this article, the said queen's breasts are somewhat large and full, inasmuch as they were trussed somewhat high, in the manner of the country, which caused her grace to seem much plumper and her neck to look shorter.

Item, to mark whether there appears any hair about her lips or not.

Response: As to this article, as far as we can tell and see the said queen has no hair appearing about her lips or mouth, but is very clear skinned.

Item, that they try to speak to the young queen fasting, and that she might talk to them of something at length, and they approach as near to her mouth as they honestly may, so that they may feel the condition of her breath, whether it be sweet or not, and to mark every time they speak with her if they feel any savour of spices, rosewater or musk on her breath or not.

Response: To this article we could never come to speak with the said queen fasting, therefore we could not answer that part of this article, although at other times when we have spoken and had conversation with the said queen we have approached as near to her face as we conveniently might do, and we could feel no savour of any spices and waters, and we truly think the favour of her face and the cleanness of her complexion and of her mouth, that the said queen is likely to be of a sweet savour, and good breath.

Henry's relations with the papacy were consistently good, and a major source of strength to his government from the start of his reign. In consequence he was also much praised by ecclesiastical writers, such as Bernard Andreas.

The pious love for God and devotion to the sacred Church, the love of virtue and zeal for the honour of God shown by our most modest and wise King Henry VII, his piety towards to the poor, his compassion for guests and foreigners, in short, his conscientious fulfilment of all pious works and of God's worship, caused the popes of the Holy Roman Church, Innocent VIII, Alexander VI and finally Julius II, to present this king with the most famous and noble insignia of the Christian faith, namely the cap and sword of our religion for the protection and safeguard of the entire Church militant.

Nor was this without justification; for although our church can boast many other great princes who are truly devoted to God and who, moreover, are conspicuous for the integrity of their lives and the probity of their ways, yet none of them, to our knowledge, has been honoured with gifts. Is there anyone, I ask, who from the very beginnings of his

The search for a new wife

Elizabeth of York died in childbirth in February 1503 and although Henry VII was genuinely grief-stricken his practical turn of mind led him to explore new possibilities: another wife might build up further dynastic capital. The future of the Tudors was still at risk; a number of Plantagenet candidates such as the earl of Suffolk and duke of Buckingham waited in the wings, and Henry, his only surviving son, was still in his early teens. The king's first marriage had established his dynastic position at home, uniting the houses of Lancaster and York, a second might clear up the ever-present danger that any continental power – including his supposed Spanish ally – might support one of the pretenders who threatened his son's title. It was also important that no single kingdom should gain domination, especially in the rivalry between Spain and France, as a balance of power was safer in Europe.

Henry's first enquiries concerned Joan, queen of Naples, niece of Ferdinand II and Isabella of Spain; although Germaine de Foix, niece of Louis XII of France was also a candidate. An alliance with the duchy of Burgundy, long an important trading partner and English ally was potentially more advantageous: Joanna, wife of Philip, duke of Burgundy, was the daughter of Isabella of Castile, and it was she, rather than Isabella's husband Ferdinand, who was heir to Castile. After Isabella's death in 1504, Henry worked hard with Philip and Joanna and concluded a secret treaty at Windsor in 1506, closely followed by agreement on his marriage to the duke's widowed sister, Margaret of Savoy, governor of the Low Countries.

Philip's death within months of the agreement being reached, prompted plans for an even more ambitious marriage – to Joanna herself. However, she was imprisoned on a dubious claim of insanity by Ferdinand who became regent of Castile. Henry genuinely upset and angry at these moves, kept Catherine of Aragon in England, but would not allow her planned marriage to prince Henry to proceed.

He never married again – yet the diplomatic weavings, of which his quest for a remarriage formed a part, left England in its strongest international position for nearly a century.

Above   Henry thought that Margaret of Savoy, the eldest daughter of the Emperor Maximilian I, would be the perfect wife for him. However, Margaret was not very excited at the prospect.

life and throughout the rest of his time has enjoyed such widespread renown, such glory for his virtues, and such success in all his undertakings as this king of ours? Indeed, the histories record that some in past ages received such a distinction just once, and from a single pope; yet a third cap and a threefold sword now decorate our king.

I shall leave aside the famous and wise men who brought these insignia and the most honourable legates; all of these, in my judgement, were surpassed in wealth, ancestry, grace, worthiness, probity and faith by the reverend, the father and lord, Lord Silvester de Liliis, Bishop of Worcester by the will of divine and royal grace. These blessed men were present in Richmond on the holy birthday of the Mother of Christ; words cannot convey the mass of illustrious noblemen and common people gathering round for such an uncommon spectacle, whose like had never before been seen, or the skilful and harmonious song sung by men of the Church and of the army alike, while people hurried from all sides to the sound of the sweetest singing to meet him, just as the Jews hurried to meet our Saviour.

Finally, when this great and glorious throng of nobles had arrived in the royal shrine with melodious voices, our most pious king was seated there upon a golden throne, with the whole band of heroes massed around. The Bishop of Worcester, distinguished by his fine linen of purple and gold, pronounced agreeably and with great eloquence a splendid and well wrought speech to his most magnificent majesty, who shone with gold and gems. After he brought forth the mandates and the distinguished insignia of the bishop of Rome, our most christian king gave devoted thanks in a most humble manner. Then, once melodic and angelic voices had rendered praise and thanks to God, the same bishop performed the holy service with singular humility and pious devotion. After this, a sermon which was no less sacred than eloquent, was delivered to the people concerning the merit and excellence of such insignia and once the solemn rites had been accomplished the king proceeded to the royal banquet, escorted by a huge crowd of prelates and nobles.

I shall not describe the lavish preparations for that most joyful feast in which the ambassadors of the King of Castille, who were amongst this splendid procession, were received with great generosity and

Henry's personal piety

English medieval kingship was a religious office: through the anointment at his coronation, the king received a divine power that was revealed in his ability to cure swelling of the glands by touch and to alleviate muscular problems and epilepsy through sufferers' contact with ''cramp rings'' made from coins offered by the king on Good Friday. The king was obliged to protect the Christian faith and church, and to set an example of piety in his conduct and in the rule of his household.

Henry VII conformed remarkably to this ideal: no breath of scandal touched him or his court. Although he was no scholar of mystical theology, as his uncle Henry VI had been nor an amateur theologian, as Henry VIII was to prove, he was punctilious in discharging religious duties. His young chaplain Thomas Wolsey correctly gauged that the way to win his favour was to display a seemly gravity of speech and behaviour, as well as promptitude and sense in the dispatch of business.

Henry was the first English king for over 70 years to found new religious houses, reflecting French enthusiasm for the Observant Franciscans who strove to follow the teaching of St Francis of Assissi. He endowed a hospital, The Savoy, modelled on one in Florence, and intended a new chapel in Westminster Abbey to be the shrine of a canonised Henry VI; instead it became his own mausoleum, more splendid than that of any previous English king. The chapel's elaborate

heraldic panels, sculptures and glass proclaimed Tudor glory with a new propagandist intensity.

In his will Henry made provisions for masses to be celebrated for his soul on an unusually large scale, and for its executors to act as a court to hear complaints about any wrongs he had done; reflecting the troubled conscience of a king who was perhaps painfully aware that, despite his care to uphold the religious facade of his office, he had committed harsh acts against individual subjects to enforce his often precarious rule.

Above   Henry VII Chapel in Westminster Abbey. A magnificent setting for the tombs of Henry and Elizabeth of York.

Far left   Henry VII's will, in which he left detailed instructions on the erection of a monument to himself and his queen.

91

festivity. Nor shall I recall the indescribable dress and ornaments worn on that day by the most serene Elizabeth, wife of the king, and her royal daughter Mary, nor the splendid costumes of the other illustrious ladies. What more? Such was the greatness and the dignity of that occasion that I hardly think that even the most eloquent of men could describe it in words.

Thus the pope judged that this prince, who was both beloved of and sent by God, should be honoured with divine rewards, for he had long been aware of how his reknown was spreading throughout the world. Indeed, if you compare any previous king who has a reputation for prudence, which is the first source of honesty, to King Henry, you will find that our king far surpasses him in political virtues. To find that another exceeds him in justice and equity is to commit an offence against the dignity of justice itself; so far does Henry excel in his goodness. Henry, by his magnanimity and his strength of mind, would surpass any other king who has been singled out for praise for his fortitude. If, finally, any king thought that he himself took the prize for temperance and modesty, by whatever path he reached the summit of such virtue he would find our king leading the way. Truly, if anyone should wish to observe a living effigy of all the virtues in a clear light and to look inside let him fix his mind's eye upon this man with complete concentration, and he will see a king who is made an object of wonder by the splendour of all his virtues. Thus the leader of Christendom, seeing that this one prince was so gifted, graced, magnificent and virtuous in soul as well as in body, wished to honour the king who was extolled by such great praise with divine rather than human favours. And this will suffice on this matter; for with a single voice the entire world calls him the lover of peace, the protector and defender of all kings, like another Octavius, so that without doubt, he first of all the kings to come in future years, deserves to be crowned with the title of the 'peace-making king'.

1506

Philip of Habsburg, archduke of Austria and duke of Burgundy, was King of Castile, in the right of his wife, Joanna, the eldest daughter of Ferdinand and Isabella, who had died in 1504. In attempting to travel to Spain to claim his crown, he was driven ashore in England by bad weather.

And on the next day, Sunday 1 February, King Henry, being lodged in the Queen's Lodging, went from his chamber to the chapel, having so many noblemen with him that it was a long time before they could all pass. Lord Henry Stafford carried the sword, and on the right hand at the upper end of the choir of the chapel there was arranged a screen of cloth of gold, within which the king sat and heard mass, which was sung by the bishop of Chichester. And after mass King Henry went to visit the King of Castile, who that day heard mass in his closet in his own lodging, and when the King of Castile realized that King Henry was coming to him, he hastily came and met him at the second chamber door, for in the third chamber stood his guard all the time.

At the meeting the King of Castile took off his bonnet and made a low bow and bade King Henry good morning. And the king said that he could not have dined happily that day unless he had seen him and bade him good morning. The King of Castile thanked King Henry for his great courtesy and trouble; and so with various other good words they both proceeded together to the King of Castile's dining room and both stood by the fire together.

After they had spoken together for a while King Philip asked him to stay there still, but he excused himself and said he would convey the King of Castile to his lodging; and so King Henry took him on his left hand and went to the second chamber. And there the king desired King Henry to stay there, but he would not. And from there they went together to the third chamber door, where the king stopped and said that he had given King Henry too much trouble to have gone so far; and there the king had much ado to make King Henry stay, and said that he would rather take him back than that he should go any further. Then the King of Castile answered: "I see right well that I must do as you command, and obey reasonably". And the sword which was borne after mass was not borne within the King of Castile's lodgings. So for that time King Henry left and returned to his chamber for dinner.

After dinner King Henry sent to the King of Castile to find out if it would please him to see the ladies dance for entertainment, since it was a holy day and they might not hunt; and he answered that he would gladly do so. A little before by King Henry's command my Lord Herbert emptied all the king's chamber, except for lords and officers and certain knights

The Church

In the late 15th century, the characteristic monk took deep pleasure in studying devout literature or genteelly mixing in local society. Only the small Carthusian Order had a reputation for austerity and holiness, although the orders of friars were still held in reverence as preachers and confessors.

Anticlericalism existed at all social levels, but on a small scale with little political significance. The remarks admitted to by a humble Lollard in 1489, that "the Pope is an old whore, sitting upon many waters, having a cup of poison in his hand", may have been common sentiments among radical dissidents, but they would have shocked the devout Henry VII. Policy, especially as he was a usurper, and temperament, inclined him to avoid antagonizing the Church: the papacy had sanctioned his crucial dynastic marriage to Elizabeth of York and his rule, and had provided his nominees to bishoprics. The king handled the Church's privileges circumspectly, cautiously curtailing the rights of sanctuary in churches and clerical judicial immunity.

The Crown's complacency towards clerical privileges and shortcomings may have given a boost to Lollardy, the heresy of the late 14th century which survived clandestinely, mainly among pockets of the lesser gentry, merchants and artisans, linked by itinerant preachers and a diverse theology based heavily on communal Bible-study. There was an increase in prosecutions for heresy during the reign – over seventy persons were put on trial, three probably being burnt. Bishops, often heavily involved in service to the Crown, showed more ardour in rooting out heretics than in tackling the perennial problems of raising the moral and educational standards of the rural parish clergy. On the whole the parish clergy probably conscientiously provided the reconciliatory and beneficial magic sought by their quarrelsome and wonder-seeking flocks.

Literate clergymen and laymen may have looked askance on such expedients as using holy water as farmyard medicine; the literate concentrated as they were in towns and manor-houses, shared with monks, friars and secular clergy a widespread devotion which focussed partly on miraculous cults, it must be admitted, but also on developing the individual's sense of relationship with Christ and appreciation of the significance of the Passion. These trends were catered for by the large proportion of early printed books whose subjects were the liturgy, saints' lives, sermons and mystical theology.

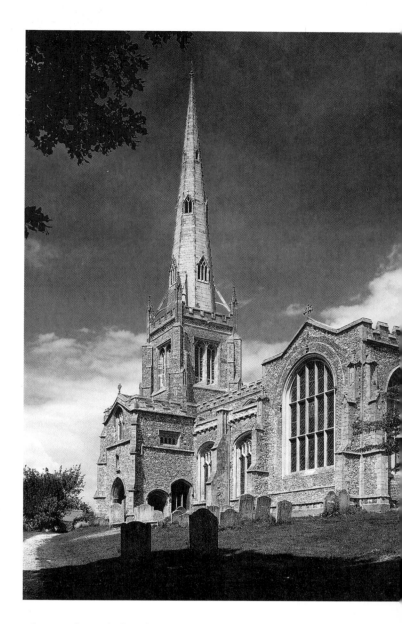

Above   Thaxted Church in Essex built in the Perpendicular style with enormous windows. Often built with the profits from the wool trade, such churches served a very small community.

HENRY VII (1485–1509)

Right   Pilgrims arriving at Canterbury.

Below   A document developed by Henry VII, with the help of the archbishop of Canterbury and bishop of Winchester, that arranges the distribution of alms in Westminster Abbey.

Bottom   A hammerbeam roof in a rural church built in Suffolk during Henry's reign.

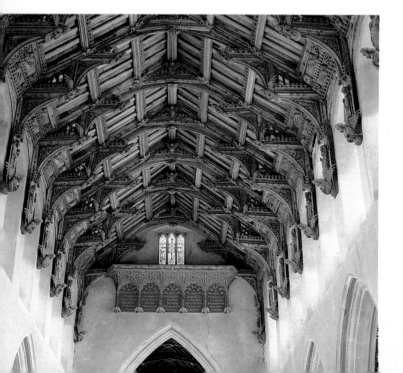

of great good behaviour who still remained there. And when King Henry knew that the King of Castile was coming he went to the door of the great chamber and there received him and desired him to take him by the arm, for the King of Castile would not have taken so much upon himself except by King Henry's desire. And so both together they went through that chamber, the dining chamber, and from there to an inner chamber where was my Lady Catherine, Princess of Wales and my Lady Mary, King Henry's daughter, and various other ladies. And after the King of Castile had kissed them and spoken for a while with King Henry and the ladies, they all came into the dining chamber where my lady princess danced with a Spanish lady in Spanish array.

After she had danced two or three dances she left, and then my Lady Mary danced and an English lady with her. And all the time the lady princess desired the king of Castile to dance, who, after he had excused himself once or twice answered that he was a sailor, "And yet," said he, "you would make me dance!" And so he danced, but talked still with King Henry. And after my Lady Mary had danced two or three dances she went and sat by my lady princess on the end of the carpet which was under the cloth of state and near to where King Henry and the King of Castile stood. And then one of the foreign lords danced with an English lady.

That done my Lady Mary played on the lute and after upon the clavichord. She played very well and all the people there praised her greatly that despite her youth in everything she behaved herself so very well.

1507

Following the death of his queen, Isabella, in 1504, Ferdinand of Spain strengthened his position by securing a treaty with France, and married Louis XII's niece, Germaine de Foix. In 1506, in response to the anxious representations of the French estates, Louis provided for the succession by betrothing his daughter Claude to Francis of Angoulême. As Grafton explains, this had consequences for Henry, and Mary and Charles were betrothed in December 1507.

While these things were happening Louis, the French king, doubting that he would ever have a male child, married his eldest daughter Lady Claude to Francis de Valois, Dauphin of Vienne and Duke of Angouleme; which lady had been promised a little before to Charles, the King of Castile. When King Henry learned of this he thought it best to marry his daughter Lady Mary to this Charles King of Castille, being almost both of one age, and therefore ambassadors were sent to and fro, and at last the marriage was concluded and confirmed by the bishop of Winchester, chief ambassador for the king at Calais; and so the Lady Mary, being aged 10 years, was promised to King Charles. For the conclusion of this marriage various great ambassadors were sent to England from the Emperor Maximilian, who received great rewards and returned.

1508

Even in the last year of his reign, Henry's preoccupations with the security of his dynasty remained unchanged, and his suspicion of the house of York had increased again after Elizabeth's death. Thomas Grey, marquis of Dorset, was her nephew, and later in favour with Henry VIII. The betrothal of his daughter Mary to Charles of Burgundy, Philip's son, who was later to be both King of Spain and Holy Roman Emperor, was Henry's last diplomatic coup. The Calais chroniclers juxtaposition of high policies with natural phenomena was more typical of an earlier generation.

Sir Richard Carew, lieutenant of the castle of Calais, brought out of England by the King's command, lord marquis of Dorset and Lord William of Devonshire, the earl of Devonshire's son and heir, who were both related to the late Queen Elizabeth and of her blood. They had been in the Tower of London for a long time. They were kept prisoners in the castle of Calais as long as King Henry VII lived, and would have been put to death if he had lived longer. They were brought to the castle of Calais on 18 October 1508.

On 27 October there came from England the bishop of Winchester, Lord Privy Seal, the earl of Surrey, Lord Treasurer, and the Lord of St John's, with Doctor Weston, all ambassadors. They landed at Temperlto in Picardy, and on 2 November there came to Calais out of Flanders from the Duke of Burgundy the earl of Fynes, the lord of Barowe, and the president of Flanders, with others of that country, and they were met by Sir Richard Carew, lieutenant of the castle of Calais and Sir John Wilshere, comptroller of Calais and Walter Culpeper, undermarshal of Calais, and all the spears and archers on horseback and many soldiers in armour, for these foreigners feared the Frenchmen. But being brought in safety to Calais, there the lords on both sides agreed the marriage between Charles duke of Burgundy and the Lady Mary, daughter of King Henry VII, and on St Thomas the Apostle's day, 21 December a great triumph was made in Calais.

On 9 July, being Relic Sunday, there was seen at Calais an innumerable swarm of white butterflies coming from the north-east and flying south-eastwards, as thick as snowflakes, so that men shooting in St Peter's Field outside the town of Calais could not see the town at four o'clock in the afternoon, they flew so high and so thick.

1509

Edward Hall concludes the story of the reign in a suitably sympathetic vein.

Now approached the end term of the three years of peace that I spoke of before, at which time King Henry thought his fatal day to be at hand. For his sickness increased daily more and more, so that he could easily see that death was not far from hounding his prey.

Therefore, like a good prince, desiring to show some generosity to his people so that he might be remembered after his death, he granted of his great liberality a general pardon to all men, for all offences done and perpetrated against his laws and statutes. But because murderers and thieves did not only offend against him but against others he excepted them and some others from his pardon.

He also paid the fees of all prisoners in gaols in and about London who were there only for those debts. He also paid the debts of all such persons as lay in the prisons of London or Ludgate for 40s. or less, and some he relieved who were condemned for £10. Because of his goodness and pity shown to his people, who were sore vexed with inquisitors, taxers and informers, general processions were held daily in every city and parish to pray to almighty God to restore his health, with long continuance of the same.

Nevertheless he was consumed by his long illness that nature could no longer sustain his life, and so he departed out of this world on 22 April 1509 at his palace of Richmond. His body was taken with funeral pomp to Westminster and there buried next to the good queen his wife in a sumptuous and solemn chapel, which not long before he had had built. He reigned for twenty-three years and more than seven months, and lived fifty-two years. He had by his queen Elizabeth eight children, four boys and four girls, of whom three remained alive after him: Henry, Prince of Wales who succeeded him as king; Lady Margaret, Queen of Scots, and Lady Mary, promised to Charles, King of Castile.

Henry was a man of lean and spare body, but very strong, somewhat taller than the average sort of men, of a wonderful beauty and fair complexion, of a merry and smiling countenance, especially in conversation, his eyes grey, his teeth single, his hair thin, in all things quick and prompt of wit, of a princely stomach and high courage. In great perils, troublesome affairs and matters of weighty importance he seemed supernatural and in a way divine, for such things as he undertook he did advisedly, and not without great deliberation and consideration, so that amongst all men his wit and prudence might be noted, regarded and spoken of. For he was not ignorant that his acts and doings were especially noted and marked by the eyes of many people, and therefore a prince ought far to excel and surmount all mean persons in wisdom and policy, as he precedes all others in estate and dignity.

Surely this good and modest prince did not devour and consume the substance and riches of his realm, for by his high policy he marvellously enriched his realm and himself, and yet left his subjects in high wealth and prosperity. The proof of this is manifestly apparent in the great abundance of gold and silver yearly brought into this realm, in plate, money and bullion, by merchants passing and returning out of and into this realm with merchandise. To whom he himself of his own goodness lent money largely without any gain or profit, so that trade employed in his realms and dominions.

And so the king, living all his time in the favour of fortune, in high honour, riches and glory, and, for his noble acts and prudent policies, worthy to be registered in the book of fame, gave up his spirit at the last, which is undoubtedly ascended into the celestial mansion where he has the sure fruition of the godhead, and the joy that is prepared for such as shall sit on the right hand of our saviour, for ever world without end.

Part II

Henry VIII
1509-1547

Coming to the throne in 1509 when he was barely eighteen, Henry VIII had never known insecurity. He may well have been protected, and was as innocent of political experience before his accession as his father had been, but there the resemblance began and ended. Over six feet tall and powerfully built, he was physically imposing, handsome and athletic. Intellectually he was less imposing, but his mind was well trained, sharp and inquisitive. He lacked his father's qualities of patience and stamina, both major political assets, particularly in adversity. His early ambition was to be the most magnificent and triumphant prince in Europe. His title to the crown was never challenged, but from about 1520, when it had become clear that his queen, Catherine of Aragon, would bear no more children, his anxiety over the succession became increasingly obsessive.

(Opposite   Henry VIII)

1509

Henry, prince of Wales, the king's only surviving son, was two months short of his eighteenth birthday when his father died. He succeeded without challenge, and without any need for a regency. One of his first actions was to punish his father's chief financial agents, who were used as scapegoats for the most unpopular aspect of the late king's policy, as Edward Hall explains.

After the death of Henry VII, his son, King Henry VIII, began his reign on 22 April in the year of our Lord 1509 when he was 18 years old. Maximilian I was then Holy Roman Emperor, Louis XII reigned in France, Ferdinand was king of Aragon and Castile, and James IV ruled over the Scots.

Henry's accession was proclaimed by the blast of a trumpet in the City of London on 23 April and there was much rejoicing amongst the people.

The same day, he left his manor at Richmond and went to the Tower of London where he remained, alone with his advisors, until the funeral arrangements for his father had been concluded. Also that day, Sir Richard Empson, knight, and Edmund Dudley esquire, close advisors of the late king, were arrested and brought to the Tower, to the great pleasure of many who had suffered under them. Indeed, their arrest was rumoured to have been an act of malice by those who had been made to suffer under their authority in the days of the late king and

Western Europe in 1519

In 1518 it looked as though the cycle of wars which had been triggered off by the French invasion of Italy in 1494 had been brought to an end. However, in that year the Emperor Maximilian I died, and his grandson Charles, already King of Spain and the ruler of the Netherlands, was elected to succeed him. This immediately gave England a new strategic importance With an English alliance, Charles was in a position to attack France from three sides. If England allied with France, the Netherlands became vulnerable. Henry VIII generally favoured the Habsburgs, and fought two unsuccessful wars as Charles' ally, in 1523 and 1544–5.

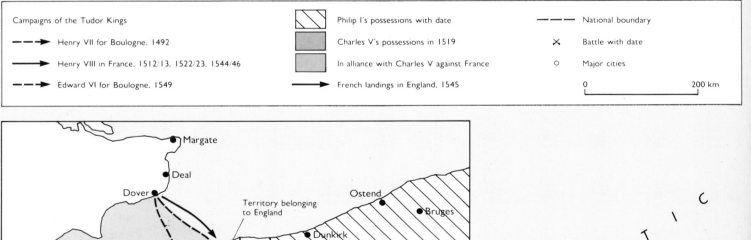

Campaigns of the Tudor Kings		
Henry VII for Boulogne, 1492		Philip I's possessions with date
Henry VIII in France, 1512/13, 1522/23, 1544/46		Charles V's possessions in 1519
Edward VI for Boulogne, 1549		In alliance with Charles V against France

National boundary

× Battle with date

○ Major cities

French landings in England, 1545

0   200 km

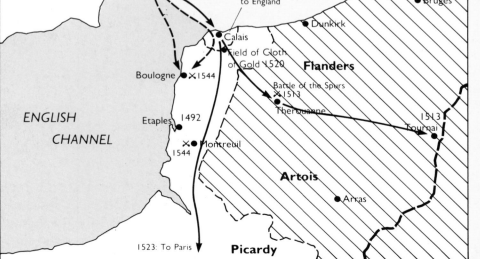

Margate

Deal

Dover

Ostend

Bruges

Dunkirk

Calais

Territory belonging to England

Field of Cloth of Gold 1520

Flanders

Boulogne ×1544

Battle of the Spurs ×1513

Therouanne

1513
Tournai

ENGLISH CHANNEL

Etaples 1492

×● Montreuil
1544

Artois

Arras

1523: To Paris

Picardy

ATLANTIC

PORTUGAL

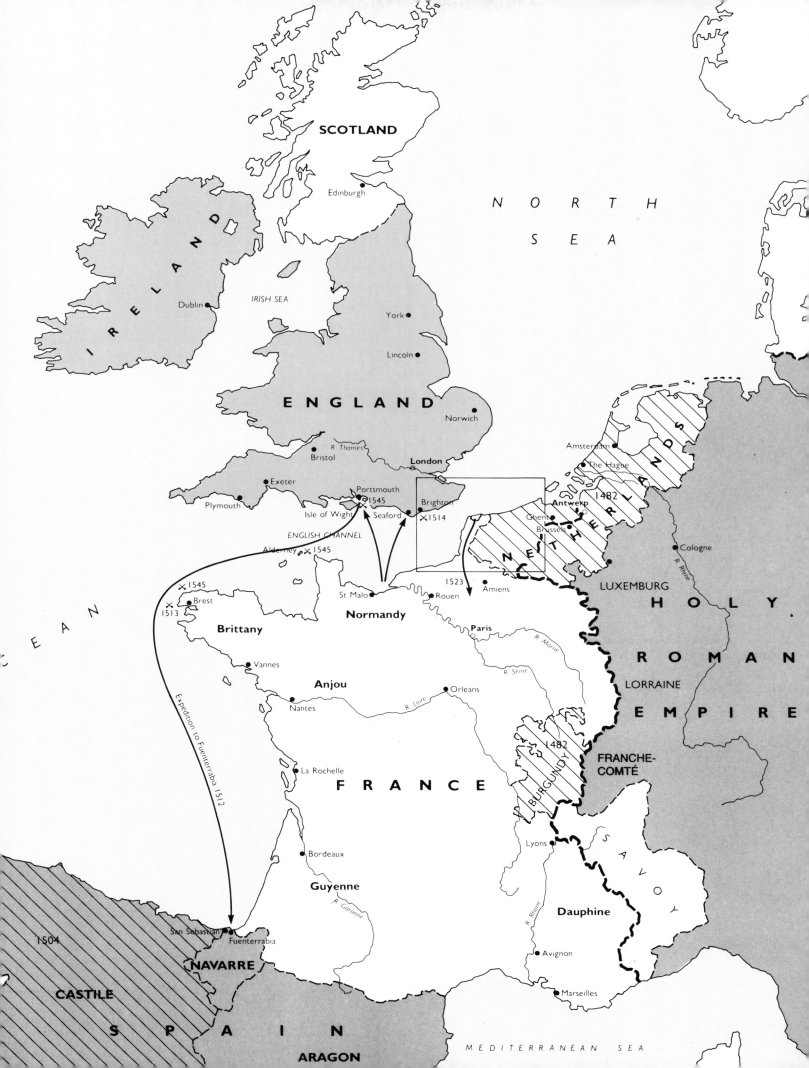

SCOTLAND

Edinburgh

NORTH
SEA

IRELAND

Dublin

IRISH SEA

York

Lincoln

ENGLAND

Norwich

Amsterdam

The Hague

R Thames

Bristol

London

Exeter

Portsmouth
⦿1545

Brighton
✕1514

Antwerp

Ghent
Brussels

1482

Cologne

R. Rhine

Plymouth

Isle of Wight

Seaford

ENGLISH CHANNEL

Alderney ✕1545

St Malo

Rouen

1523

Amiens

LUXEMBURG

HOLY.

Brest

✕1513

✕1545

Normandy

Paris

ROMAN

Brittany

R. Marne

Vannes

Anjou

Orleans

R. Seine

LORRAINE

EMPIRE

Nantes

R. Loire

Expedition to Fuenterrabia 1512

La Rochelle

FRANCE

1482

FRANCHE-
COMTÉ

BURGUNDY

Lyons

SAVOY

Bordeaux

Guyenne

R. Garonne

Dauphine

R. Rhone

San Sebastian

Fuenterrabia

Avignon

1504

NAVARRE

CASTILE

S P A I N

ARAGON

Marseilles

MEDITERRANEAN SEA

ATLANTIC OCEAN

Derry

Armagh

Achonry

I R E L A N D

The Pale
1537

Athlone

1534

Dublin

Kildare

R. Shannon

Limerick

Kilkenny

Waterford

Wexford

Cork

Rebellions against Henry VII, 1485–1509

Rebellions against Henry VIII, 1509–1547

Rebellions against Edward VI, 1547–1553

Main routes taken by rebels during Pilgrimage of Grace
against Henry VIII

Monastery involved in Pilgrimage of Grace

Principality of Wales before 1536

New Welsh counties after 1536

X   Battle with date

o   Major cities

0 ————————— 100 km

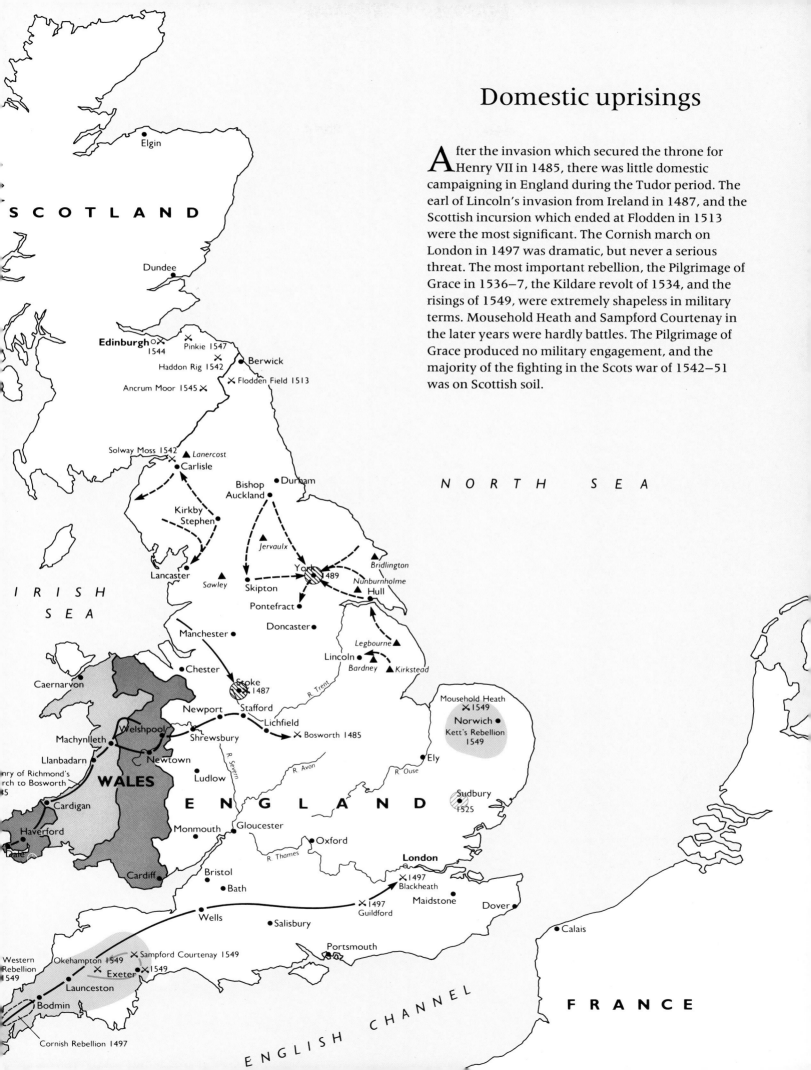

Domestic uprisings

After the invasion which secured the throne for Henry VII in 1485, there was little domestic campaigning in England during the Tudor period. The earl of Lincoln's invasion from Ireland in 1487, and the Scottish incursion which ended at Flodden in 1513 were the most significant. The Cornish march on London in 1497 was dramatic, but never a serious threat. The most important rebellion, the Pilgrimage of Grace in 1536–7, the Kildare revolt of 1534, and the risings of 1549, were extremely shapeless in military terms. Mousehold Heath and Sampford Courtenay in the later years were hardly battles. The Pilgrimage of Grace produced no military engagement, and the majority of the fighting in the Scots war of 1542–51 was on Scottish soil.

SCOTLAND

Elgin

Dundee

Edinburgh 1544
Pinkie 1547
Haddon Rig 1542
Berwick
Ancrum Moor 1545
Flodden Field 1513

NORTH SEA

Solway Moss 1542
Lanercost
Carlisle
Bishop Auckland
Durham
Kirkby Stephen
Jervaulx
Lancaster
Sawley
Skipton
York 1489
Bridlington
Nunburnholme
Hull
Pontefract
Doncaster

IRISH SEA

Manchester
Legbourne
Lincoln
Chester
Stoke 1487
Bardney
Kirkstead
R. Trent
Caernarvon
Newport
Stafford
Mousehold Heath
1549
Welshpool
Lichfield
Norwich
Kett's Rebellion
1549
Machynlleth
Shrewsbury
Bosworth 1485
Llanbadarn
Newtown
R. Severn
Ely
R. Ouse
Henry of Richmond's march to Bosworth 1485
WALES
Ludlow
R. Avon
Sudbury
1525
Cardigan
ENGLAND
Haverford
Monmouth
Gloucester
Dale
Oxford
R. Thames
Cardiff
Bristol
London
Bath
1497
Blackheath
Maidstone
Wells
Salisbury
1497
Guildford
Dover
Portsmouth
Calais

Western Rebellion 1549
Okehampton 1549
Sampford Courtenay 1549
Exeter 1549
Launceston
Bodmin

Cornish Rebellion 1497

ENGLISH CHANNEL

FRANCE

who now wished to punish their oppressors to satisfy public opinion. On the same day too lord Henry Stafford, brother of the duke of Buckingham, was also arrested and sent to the Tower, but the charge was not thought to be serious as he was soon released and later the same year was created earl of Wiltshire. Also on 23 April Doctor Ruthall was named bishop of Durham.

Soon after this a number of agents of Empson and Dudley were arrested and stood in the pillories. However, the craftiest knave of them all, John Baptist Brimald, managed to escape to Westminster Abbey where he took sanctuary.

On 25 April it was proclaimed that all pardons granted by the king's father would be honoured and that all prisoners, except those on trial for treason, murder and felony, would be released.

This done, all the necessary arrangements for the sumptuous interment and funeral of the late king were made with due regard to pomp and decorum. The corpse of the dead monarch was brought out of the privy chamber into the Great Chamber where it rested for three days, on each of which a mitred bishop in full regalia sung dirges and masses over the body. From the great chamber it was brought to the hall where it also lay three days and then to the chapel, again for three days, in each place receiving the same ministrations by the clergy. And in each of these three places there was an ornate hearse, framed with banners, and nine mourners in constant attendance during the service. Black cloth hung everywhere and every day offerings were received. On Wednesday 9 May the corpse was laid in a carriage covered with black cloth-of-gold with gold cushions and drawn by five huge chargers covered in black velvet. Over the body, laid again on gold cushions, was an image of the late king dressed in his robes of state, wearing his crown and holding the ball and sceptre in his hands. The chariot itself was decorated with banners and pennants depicting his titles, dominions and pedigree. When the chariot had been prepared, the members of the king's chapel choir and a large number of bishops led off the procession, praying all the while. Then followed his servants, dressed in black, and the chariot itself. Behind the chariot came nine mourners and on both sides were men carrying long and short funeral candles, six hundred in all. In this manner the procession left Richmond and arrived at St George's

Field where all the priests, clerics and religious men from both the city of London and elsewhere joined the front of the cortege in front of the members of the king's chapel choir.

The following day the body was transported to Westminster, Sir Edward Howard carrying the king's banner on a charger covered in trappings bearing the arms of the late monarch.

In Westminster Abbey there was a curious hearse made of nine poles, all covered with candles which were lit at the approach of the corpse. Six lords removed the body from the carriage and laid it within the hearse, the effigy being placed on a cushion on a large gold pall-cloth.

The hearse had two sets of railings surrounding it. Inside the first sat the official mourners, inside the second stood knights bearing banners depicting the saints, and outside of these stood soldiers. When the mourners were seated, Garter King of Arms declaimed his official cry for the soul of the noble prince King Henry VII, late king of this realm. Then the choir began *Placebo* and sung dirges. These finished, the mourners returned to the palace, where rooms had been kept for them, and rested for the night.

The next day, three masses were solemnly sung by bishops and during the last of these the late king's banner, charger, coat of arms, sword, shield and helmet were presented as offerings. At the end of the mass the mourners also offered rich pall-cloths made of cloth of gold. The body was then lowered into the earth while the choir sang *Libera me* and the lord treasurer lord steward, lord chamberlain, treasurer and comptroller of the king's household all broke their official staves and cast them into the grave. Then garter king of arms cried out in a loud voice: "Vive le Roi Henri le huitième, Roi d'Angleterre et de France, et Sire d'Irlande." After which all the official mourners and all the others that had attended the funeral service went off to the palace where they had a great and sumptous feast.

It is indeed truly remarkable to record the great lamentation amongst the king's household and nobles at this death and the equally great joy expressed by those who had suffered under his iron rule. Yet the promise of the future, which showed itself in the young king, both healed and comforted the heavy hearts of those who had felt the loss of such a wise prince and at the same time cleansed all grudges and rancour from those gladdened by his death, whose joy was further increased by the granting of their pardons.

Within a few days of his accession, Henry VIII announced that he would honour his father's long-standing undertaking that he would marry Catherine of Aragon, his brother Arthur's widow, who had remained in England. The ceremony took place at Greenwich on 11 June and they then shared a joint coronation.

The following day being a Sunday, and also Mid-summer's Day, the noble prince with his queen left the palace for Westminster Abbey at the appointed hour. The barons of the Cinq Ports held canopies over the royal couple who trod on striped cloth of ray, which was immediately cut up by the crowd when they had entered the abbey. Inside, according to sacred tradition and ancient custom, his grace and the queen were anointed and crowned by the arch-bishop of Canterbury in the presence of other pre-lates of the realm and the nobility and a large number of civic dignitaries. The people were asked if they would take this most noble prince as their king and obey him. With great reverence, love and will-ingness they responded with the cry "Yea, Yea".

When the ceremony was finished, the lords spiri-tual and temporal paid homage to the king and, with the queen's permission, returned to Westminster Hall – each one beneath his canopy – where the lord marshall bearing his staff of office ushered all to their seats. Each noble and lord proceeded to his allotted place arranged earlier according seniority. The nine-piece table being set with the king's estate seated on the right and the queen's estate on the left, the first course of the banquet was announced with a fanfare. At the sound the duke of Buckingham entered riding a huge charger covered with richly embroidered trappings, together with the lord steward mounted on a horse decked with cloth of gold. The two of them led in the banquet which was truly sumptous, and as well as a great number of delicacies also included unusual heraldic devices and mottoes.

How can I describe the abundance of fine and del-icate fare prepared for this magnificent and lordly feast, produced both abroad and in the many and various parts of this realm to which God has granted his bounty. Or indeed the exemplary execution of the service of the meal itself, the clean handling and

distribution of the food and the efficient ordering of the courses, such that no person of any estate lacked for anything.

After the second course had been served, a fully armed knight entered the hall riding on a huge horse decorated in tissue-cloth and embroidered with the arms of England and France. The knight himself wore a skirt to his armour made of richly embroid-ered tissue and a great plume of ostrich feathers stood out from his helmet. Preceded by a herald of arms, he presented himself to His Majesty with due ceremony, at which the garter herald of arms cried: "Sir knight, whence come you and what is your busi-ness?' The knight, who was none other than Sir Rob-ert Dimmocke, the king's hereditary champion, replied: "Sir, the place from which I come is of no consequence and the reason I come hither concerns no other place or country than this." At that point he commanded his herald to declare "O yea". He then addressed the garter herald of arms saying, "Now you shall hear the reason for my coming and my business here."

He then commanded his own herald to make the following proclamation: "If there be any person here, of whatever estate or degree, who says or wishes to prove that King Henry VIII is not the right-ful inheritor of the throne of this realm, I, Sir Robert Dimmocke his champion, hereby throw down the gauntlet and offer to fight such a person." This pro-clamation was repeated in various parts of the hall and each time he cast down his gauntlet to prove his earnest. Having made several of these challenges the knight returned to the king's presence and requested something to drink. At the king's com-mand he was given a golden cup filled with wine which he drank and then asked for the cup's cover. This was also delivered to him, which done the knight left the hall, taking the cup and its cover with him.

The explanation of all this is that on the cor-onation of the king, his official champion tra-ditionally goes to the armoury and takes the king's second-best harness, armour-skirts, plumes and other things for decorating his crest or helmet. Then he proceeds to the stable and takes the second-best charger and the second-best armour and then, fitted out with all this equipment, enters the coronation banquet as above described and, having performed his ceremonial duties, is allowed to keep all the trappings, including the gold cup and its cover, for his own use.

After the departure of the aforementioned champion, the garter king of arms, together with all the other heralds and officers of arms, went round the hall with the ceremonial cry of "Largesse".

But to return to the end of this noble feast – when the tables had been cleared the wafers were brought in. At this point, Sir Stephen Jenyns, then lord mayor of London, whom the king had dubbed a knight before he had sat down to dine, arose from his seat to serve the king with hippocras cordial in a gold cup. When the king had drunk from it the cup, with its cover, was presented to Sir Stephen as the customary gift to mayors of the city on the event of a royal coronation. Then, after the a cloth had been laid and the tables had again been cleared, the king and queen washed themselves and departed into their private chambers.

To further enhance the triumphal coronation, jousts and tourneys were organized, to be held in the grounds of the palace of Westminster. For the comfort of the royal spectators a pavilion was constructed covered with tapestries and hung with rich Arras cloth. And nearby there was a curious fountain over which was built a sort of castle with an imperial crown on the top and battlements of roses and gilded pomegranates. A vine with gilded leaves and grapes grew up it and on its walls were painted while and green lozenges, each containing a rose, a pomegranate, a quiver of arrows or the letters H and K – all gilded – and the castle itself was supported by gilded arches and turrets.

The shields of arms of the jousters also appeared on the walls and on certain days, notably the day of the coronation as well as those of the jousts and tourneys, red, white and claret wine ran from the mouths of the castle's gargoyles.

The organizers of these jousts were lord Thomas Howard, heir apparent to the earl of Surrey, admiral Sir Edward Howard, his brother, lord Richard Grey, brother of the marquess of Dorset, Sir Edmund Howard, Sir Thomas Knevet and Charles Brandon esquire.

The trumpets sounded and the fresh young gallants and noblemen took the field and positioned their horses. All the participants were magnificently attired in exquisitely cut and embroidered outfits,

A renaissance king

As the king's younger son, Henry VIII might well have been destined for a clerical career and was perhaps educated accordingly. There is no strong evidence for this, and he seems to have received the same education as his elder brother – a diet of Latin secular authors. His grandmother, Margaret Beaufort, supervised his studies and possibly imported Cambridge scholars such as the poet John Skelton to tutor her grandson. At an early age, Henry was proficient in Latin and French, and developed a passionate interest in performing and composing music.

After his brother's death in 1502, when Henry was 11, the now future king was placed under strict supervision by his father; a Spanish envoy commented that he was brought up more like a girl than a boy. But nothing could impair Henry's physical development. Tall and muscular, with a fine shock of reddish hair, he was said to be far handsomer than his great rival, Francis I of France. He was nimble at tennis yet strong

Below left   Design for a triumphal arch representing the apotheosis of the Renaissance Prince.

Below   Henry VIII's writing desk made from walnut and leather, and bearing the arms of the king and Catherine of Aragon.

enough to wrestle; he could ride a horse to exhaustion and still be prepared to dance the night away.

Most of all, Henry loved to show-off. He would argue theology with theologians, and risk his own life in jousting with the young bloods with whom he packed his court. But whether sparring in his privy apartments or at the tournament, or even with his ministers, the king needed to win the day. When he did so, he could be magnanimous to a fault, but when he lost, he became ruthless.

both for themselves and their mounts – some in gold, some in silver, some in tinselled cloth and a variety of other attractive products of the goldsmith's imagination. Then a number of men brought on another castle-like structure made of cloth of gold. The top of this was covered with roses and pomegranates which hung down on all sides, and inside sat a lady holding a shield made of crystal bearing the name "Pallas". Lord Howard and his companions – each fully armed and with their armour skirts and trappers made of green velvet inlaid with golden roses and pomegranates and fringed with gold damask – formed up behind the castle and followed its progress.

The castle was then brought before the king and the lady Pallas presented her retinue – which also included about a hundred men on foot, all freshly appareled in variously coloured outfits of velvet with matching hose and bonnets. The knights she called her "scholars" and beseeched his majesty to accept them as such, declaring that they wished only to serve him and increase their honour in his eyes. To which the lady added that, if it would please his grace, her scholars would be pleased to take on all comers in his name, the king gave his consent to this.

Next appeared another band of horsemen, three score in number and all dressed in fine cloth of gold, silver and elaborately embroidered costumes, with trappers on their steeds to match. And each man wore a golden helmet on his head from which sprouted a great plume of feathers, some of one colour, some of another. In this manner the band entered the field, accompanied by a large number of drums and fifes, each man conducting his mount with great skill, both to impress the ladies and to earn praise for his horsemanship. Following these came a large crowd of hearty men on foot, dressed in finely cut and embroidered clothes of velvet and silk with matching hose and bonnets.

Next came eight men on horseback, namely sir John Pechy, Sir Edward Nevell, Sir Edward Guildforde, Sir John Carre, Sir William Parre, Sir Giles Capell and Sir Griffith Dun. They too were fully armed and carried shields bearing their heraldic devices. Rich plumes and other such stuff crowned their headgear and their armour-skirts were made of tissue-cloth, cloth-of-gold, silver and velvet.

Leading them in was a gentleman on horseback

dressed in a coat of blue velvet embroidered with gold, his steed being adorned in like manner, and carrying a golden lance at his thigh. This man presented himself to the queen, saying that the knights of his company had learnt that the lady Pallas had presented six of her "scholars" to the king but did not know whether these men had come to learn or to teach feats of arms. He then added that, for their part, his knights had indeed come to perform such feats for the love of the ladies and thus requested her majesty to permit his men to prove themselves against lady Pallas's scholars. Also, if it should so happen that the scholars should , in the view of the judges, and as announced by their heralds, break more lances than his knights then the scholars may take his golden lance as their prize. But if his knights should break more lances than the scholars then they should win the crystal shield. This request being granted, the jousts begun and every man acquitted himself well and valiantly, but who won which prize when the night came on and the jousts ended, I know not.

The following day the aforementioned defending team, lady Pallas's scholars, presented themselves before the king ready for the tourney. All on horseback and armed from head to foot they each had one side of their armour-skirts and horse-trappings made of white velvet embroidered with gold roses and other devices, and the other made of green velvet embroidered with gold pomegranates. On their headpieces each wore a plume of gold damask.

At the same time the other side rode in, the aforementioned eight knights fully armed and dressed, like their mounts, in green satin embroidered with fine golden bramble branches. Following them, blowing horns, came a number of men dressed as foresters or gamekeepers in green cloth, with caps and hose to match, who arranged a set like a park with white and green fencing around it. Inside this paddock were fallow deer and artificial trees, bushes, ferns and so forth. Once set up before the queen the paddock gates were unlocked and the deer ran out into the palace grounds. Greyhounds were then let loose which killed the deer, the bodies of which were then presented to the queen and the assembled ladies by the above-mentioned knights.

Crocheman, who had brought in the golden lance the previous day, then declared that his knights were the servants of the goddess Diana and whilst

Catherine of Aragon

Catherine of Aragon was born in 1485, an *infanta* of the two Spanish kingdoms of Castile and Aragon, which were precariously united by the marriage of her parents, the so-called "Catholic Kings", Ferdinand and Isabella. Her father, the "Fox of Aragon", was determined that his daughters should be diplomatic pawns who would increase his influence by alliances with the major ruling families of Europe. His daughters were therefore to be highly educated for their roles as diligent promoters of their father's interests.

Accordingly, Catherine was tutored to a level that even the daughters of Sir Thomas More would have been hard put to rival. The basis of her education was classical. She studied the Roman poets and orators, and the religious works of Christian Fathers such as Augustine and Jerome. Her command of Latin was such that it was natural for her to write to Henry VII in that language, and it is said that her letters to her first husband Arthur, were worthy of Cicero himself. She was sent to France to learn French, so that she could converse the more easily with her English ladies-in-waiting; although she eventually mastered English, her accent never ceased to betray her Spanish origins. Passionately interested in literature, she sponsored the spread of humanism in the universities of Oxford and Cambridge, and ensured that her daughter, Mary Tudor, had an education that befitted her rank.

Catherine's fate was sealed by the Treaty of Medina del Campo, 27 March 1489. In return for her betrothal to Arthur, Prince of Wales, Spain promised not to assist Yorkist pretenders and also granted important trading concessions. As she was only a few years old, there was time to review the agreement, but in 1496 it was finally agreed that she should arrive in England in 1500, when Arthur would be 14 years old. In fact she came ashore in October 1501, and a month later, on November 14, married the Prince of Wales. The rejoicing lasted well over a week and was designed to show to all other Christian princes that the Tudors were worthy of marriage into one of the oldest royal houses in Europe.

Catherine's marriage was already tainted with tragedy, however. It was rumoured that her father had obliged Henry VII to execute the pretender Perkin Warbeck and Edward, the imprisoned 2nd earl of Warwick, before he would part with his daughter. A far greater tragedy overtook her, when, on 2 April 1502, Arthur died at Ludlow castle, where he was nominally presiding over the government of Wales and the Marches. For the next seven years Catherine remained in England. Despite being betrothed a little over a year after his death to her late husband's brother, she often

Above   Catherine of Aragon, the eligible daughter of mighty Spain, who was genuinely loved by Henry during the early years of their marriage.

felt abandoned and unwanted. One problem was the need for a papal dispensation to marry her former brother-in-law; although Catherine claimed that her first marriage had never been consummated. Another was her father's reluctance to pay the additional dowry of £100,000 the English demanded. Unhappy and depressed, she threw herself into intense religious observance, and convinced herself that it was the will of God that she should marry Henry.

Catherine finally became queen of England on 11 June 1509, in the church of her beloved Franciscans in Greenwich, some six weeks after Henry VIII's accession. The first 15 years of the marriage were surprisingly felicitous. Not only did Catherine make Henry happy, he also often relied on her political advice. When he went with his army to invade France in 1513, it was natural for him to name his popular and pious wife governor of the realm. However, one shadow loomed over the marriage. Catherine bore only one child that survived – Mary – and her numerous miscarriages aged her prematurely and planted in the king's mind a fear that God was taunting him for breaking the Levitical injunction against marrying a brother's wife.

they had been indulging in their pastime of hunting had received news that lady Pallas's knights had come into these parts to perform feats of arms. Thereupon they had left off the chase and come hither to encounter these knights and to fight with them for the love of the ladies.

He added that if lady Pallas's knights vanquished them or forced them to leave the field of battle then they would receive the deer that had been killed and the greyhounds that slew them. But if Diana's knights overpowered their opponents they were to be given the swords of those knights and nothing more.

Hearing this, the queen and her ladies asked the king for his advice on the matter. The king, thinking that perhaps there was some grudge between the two parties and believing that to grant the request might lead to some unpleasantness, decided not to consent to these terms. Instead, to defuse the situation, it was decided that both parties should fight the tourney but that only a limited number of strokes would be permitted.

This was done and the two sides then left the field. The jousts then came to and end and prizes were awarded to each man according to his deserts.

1510

Jousting was more than a pastime for Henry VIII; it was a passion. England had never seen so many, or so splendid, tournaments as followed in rapid succession during the early years of his reign. The king was immensely proud of his own skill, and similar skill was a sure passport to his favour, as the career of Charles Brandon demonstrated.

Then on the opposite side entered Sir Charles Brandon on horseback, wearing a long robe of russet satin like a hermit or monk, with his steed similarly attired. Without any kind of drumroll or accompanying music he petitioned the queen, the gist of which was that if it would please her majesty to permit him to joust in her presence then he would do so gladly. If not, then he would depart in the manner in which he came. After his request had been granted he took off his monk's habit to reveal that he was fully armed and that his armour-skirt and horse-trappings were all finely decorated. He then rode his horse to the end of the tiltyard where various men on foot, also clothed in russet satin, awaited him.

The jouster as statesman

Charles Brandon, 1st duke of Suffolk, sprang to prominence from moderate but respectable gentry origins as the friend and boon companion of the youthful Henry VIII. His prowess in the lists commended him especially to the king's favour: he showed conspicuous valour, but also the common sense to fall off his horse from time to time whilst tilting against his lord and master. His advancement was meteoric, and he was promoted to a knighthood, viscountcy and dukedom within the space of two years. In 1515 he took the incredible risk of marrying the king's sister Mary, the widowed queen of France, without Henry's consent; technically an act of treason which he survived because of his unique place in the king's affections. The links of family and friendship that were thus formed were broken only by the duke's death in 1545.

Suffolk served the king as a soldier, diplomat and administrator. He was active in the French wars of the 1520s; against the Lincolnshire rebels in 1536; and against the Scots and French in the 1540s. He sat on innumerable commissions connected with the legislative changes of the period, and undertook expeditions overseas to convince foreign powers of Henry's good faith or even-handedness. He remained remarkably aloof from faction, and his attitude to religion displayed this same detached pragmatism.

Instinctively rooted, like Henry himself, in the mores of pre-Reformation catholicism, Suffolk displayed a

respectable interest in protestantism without getting carried away by it. He established good working relationships with Cardinal Wolsey and Thomas Cromwell, and in his last years counted both Thomas Howard, 3rd duke of Norfolk and Edward Seymour 1st earl of Hertford among his friends. This was partly because of his personality – affable, tolerant and non-controversial – and partly because his loyalty to the king superceded all factional alignments. With the exception of a brief period of eclipse during Anne Boleyn's ascendancy in the early 1530s, his role as courtier, soldier and factotum was central; although he never dominated affairs, his power was everywhere to be seen.

Because of his origins, Suffolk did not enjoy a great family estate; his landed wealth (and income derived from sources such as wardships) depended largely on the largesse of his royal patron, and the land and prestige that might accrue through marriage. Henry was happy to reward Suffolk, but only in a way which fitted in with the wider scheme of events. For example, before Mary's death in 1533, the emphasis was on building up a power base in East Anglia as a counterweight to the duke of Norfolk and the continued influence of the Yorkist de la Poles. However, with Suffolk's marriage to the Lincolnshire heiress, Lady Catherine Willoughby, and the disturbances of the Lincolnshire Rising in 1536, Henry felt convinced that it would be more useful to move the duke's centre of operations north, so towards the end of his life his main base became Lincolnshire.

Above   Charles Brandon, duke of Suffolk, with his wife, Henry's sister Mary.

Far left   The armour for Henry VIII and his horse, made for Henry at Greenwich by Italian and Flemish craftsmen.

Below   Henry jousting before Catherine of Aragon.

Next came young Henry Guildford esquire, clothed, like his horse, in russet cloth of gold and cloth of silver surmounted by an emblem showing a castle or tower fashioned out of russet florence and picked out in gold and incorporating his motto. All his men were dressed in russet and white satin with hose and bonnets to match. He also requested the queen's favour to enter the joust and, permission granted, took his place at the end of the tiltyard.

Then came the marquess of Dorset and Sir Thomas Bulleyn dressed like two pilgrims in black velvet tabards with pilgrims' hats over their helmets and carrying Jacob's staffs in their hands. Their horses were similarly covered with black-velvet trappings and their tabards, hats and cloaks were decorated with golden scallop shells and strips of black velvet, each strip being itself set with a scallop shell. Their servants were likewise clothed in black satin with golden scallop shells on their breasts.

Soon afterwards appeared lord Henry Stafford, earl of Wiltshire, both himself and his horse dressed in cloth of silver embroidered with his motto and arrows of gold set in a circle formed by the words "La Maison du Refuge", the letters themselves made of crimson damask and embroidered with golden arrows and roses, surmounted by a silver greyhound bearing a gold pomegranate tree, its branches so large that they spread over the whole design. Then came Sir Giles Capell, and Sir Rowland with many other knights, all fully armed and richly dressed.

And so began the jousts, which were won by the king and his companions, His Majesty receiving the prize. The jousts then being completed, each man withdrew from the field and the king was disarmed. Later he and the queen attended evensong and that night a great banquet was held attended by the king and all the ambassadors. After supper, his grace, together with the queen and the lords and ladies, entered the white hall of the palace, which had been decorated with ornamental hangings and in which pews had been constructed and surrounded by railings. There then followed a performance by the choristers of the king's chapel, featuring a number of new songs. When this had finished his majesty summoned a lord from Ireland called O'Donnell to his presence and dubbed him a knight before the assembled ambassadors. After this the minstrels began to play and the lords and ladies started to dance.

The pageants which accompanied tournaments took a number of traditional forms, and the characters were given allegorical names taken from the romances of chivalry. They formed a link between the martial exercises of the joust and the cult of courtly love.

During this time, when most of the company were concentrating on the dancing, the king suddenly disappeared, unnoticed by all except perhaps the queen and one or two others. A little while after his departure there was a fanfare of trumpets at the end of the hall and a wheeled tableau was brought in. Out of this device appeared a gentleman dressed in rich apparel who described a pleasure garden in which there was a golden arbour containing lords and ladies who would like to entertain the queen and her ladies if they would so permit them. The queen answered that she and all those present would very much like to see these people and and their play. Then a great screen that hung over the front of the device was taken away and the tableau moved closer. It was wonderfully made and a pleasure to behold, being both sumptuous and richly fashioned. Every pillar and post was covered with gold and it contained hawthorn trees, eglantine, rose-bushes, vines, pleasant flowers of various colours, gillyflowers and herbs – all made of satin, damask, silk, silver and gold, just like real trees, herbs and flowers.

In this arbour sat six ladies, all dressed in white and green satin embroidered in gold with the letters H and K knitted together with lace of gold damask. All their garments were covered with glittering gilt spangles and on their heads they wore bonnets open on three sides and embroidered with golden damask. The orrellettes were made of rolls, fashioned from glossy crêpe so that the gold showed through the crêpe and the fassis of their heads were all set in the latest fashions. In this garden also sat in the king and five others, all dressed in purple satin clothes marked with the letters H and K. Every hem was bordered with gold and every garment was decorated with mottoes picked out in solid gold lettering and each of the six had his own motto. The first was "Cuer Loyal" (Loyal Heart), the second "Bon Volure" (Good Courage), the third "Bon Espoier" (Good Hope), the fourth "Valiant Desire" the fifth "Bon Foi" (Good Faith) and the sixth "Amour Loyal" (Loyal Love). Their hose, caps and coats were also covered with mottoes and the letters H and K, all in solid gold such that you could hardly see the ground, every space being filled with gold spangles.

Courtly fashion

Costume was an important aspect of courtly magnificence, and the image projected by a king was greatly influenced by what he wore. In the 15th century it was said of Henry VI, who was not interested in such matters, that he always appeared in the same blue gown: "more like a beggar than a prince", and was held in contempt as a result. The Tudors did not make that mistake; Henry VII dressed sombrely, but in rich fabrics; Henry VIII, when he was not engaged in athletic pursuits, glittered like a peacock. Jewels worn by men and women were sewn into embroidered bodices and doublets, made into pendants or rings, and covered gloves and kerchieves. When a king made a ceremonial entry at a major court festivity, he might be accompanied by a team of noblemen identically dressed, whose liveries would have been made in the royal wardrobe.

The English, however, were never trend setters. In the 16th century, the courtiers drawn and painted by Hans Holbein were generally dressed in French fashion, with puffed and slashed doublets over loose-fitting silk shirts, broad padded shoulders and short cloaks. Some wore jackets with longer skirts, and cloaks that resembled sleeveless coats, a style which they had probably picked up in Italy. Most foreign observers agreed that English women were badly dressed, and were immodest in both costume and behaviour. The freedom with which kisses were exchanged as greeting by both sexes was probably responsible for the latter observation, but the reason for the former is not immediately obvious. The ladies of the court were no more *décolleté* than their continental sisters. One reason may be that skirts were worn somewhat shorter in England to allow more freedom of movement: the Spaniards, in particular, were horrified by the sight of any part of a woman's leg.

Colours, flowers and embroidered emblems and designs often had a symbolic or allegorical significance, indicating chastity, availability or political allegiance; accessories were used to send out similar signals. When Princess Mary and her retinue appeared in London in 1553 armed with large black rosary beads, no one would have mistaken the religious significance of the gesture.

Top   Preparing for the court was a time-consuming affair, with help often needed to create exactly the right image.

Above   The fabrics and styles of Tudor fashion were influenced a great deal by the renaissance of mid-fifteenth century Europe.

Later the tableau was moved again and the lords and ladies descended from it, couple by couple, followed by the disguised minstrels in the arbour. Then everyone, minstrels, lords and ladies, began to dance and it was a pleasure to behold.

1511

As a part of his preparations for war against France, in 1511 Henry sent out two small scale military expeditions: one to aid Margaret, regent of the Netherlands, against the duke of Gelders, and the other to assist Ferdinand of Spain against the Moors. When the latter expedition arrived at Cadiz, it discovered that it was no longer needed, and after an outbreak of indiscipline, returned after about two weeks.

Then, when the wind served their purpose, and all the army were aboard their ships, which were victualled and prepared in all ways, the captain and others departed from Plymouth haven on the Monday in the week in which Ascension Day falls with three royal ships, and the wind was so favourable to them that on the 1st of June, the eve of the feast of Pentecost, he arrived at the port of Cadiz in southern Spain. Immediately, on the advice of his council, he sent to the king of Aragon two gentlemen, called John Bartholomew and William Symond, with letters to inform the king and his council of their arrival, and what pains they had taken to come to his country, in fulfilling the king, their master's command. The messengers did so much that they came to the king, beside the city of Seville, where he then was, and told him how the Lord Darcy by the appointment of the king their master, had come there with 1,600 archers, according to the said King of Aragon's request, and waited at Cadiz to know his pleasure. The King of Aragon answered them politely, that the Lord Darcy and all others who had come from his most best beloved son were welcome, and he heartily thanked them for their pains, and asked the messengers to return to their captain and tell him that the king in all haste would send his council to him. And so they departed from the king and reported to the Lord Darcy, who stayed on his ship in great state, and would not land, but only allowed those who were sick or weak and a few others to land.

The Englishmen who did land fell to drinking strong wines and were scarcely in control of themselves; some ran to the brothels, some broke down hedges and spoiled orchards and vineyards and unripe oranges, and did many other outrageous deeds. Therefore the chief governor of the town of Cadiz came to complain to the Lord Darcy in his ship, who sent forth his provost marshal, who scarcely with force could restrain the yeomen archers, they were so hot and wilful, but by orders and policy they were all brought on board their ships.

1512

From the moment of his accession, Henry was looking for an opportunity to renew the war against France. In November 1511 he joined the Holy League, with Spain and the Papacy. The summer campaign of 1512 in Gascony was a complete failure, and towards the end of August the French prepared to counter-attack by sea.

At about this time king Henry had been informed by spies that a large fleet had been prepared by king Louis XII at Brest, a port in Brittany, and would shortly be ready to set sail and begin harrying the sea-lanes. On hearing this, Henry immediately ordered out the fleet he had prepared for just such a purpose, with the intention of sailing along the English coast to deter any attack on England itself or, if a favourable opportunity was offered, to engage the French fleet at sea.

There were two great ships in the English fleet, one the *Sovereign* under the command of Sir Charles Brandon, the other the *Regent* captained by another knight of great courage, Sir Thomas Knyvet. These two were the first to set sail for Brittany, competing in their desire for glory. Brandon, however, made the greater speed and was the first to spy from mid-ocean what looked more like a French castle than a ship the *Cordelière*, lying at anchor off the port of Brest and at a considerable distance from the other ships. He headed for it with all speed.

Seeing the English ships coming at them, the French deployed themselves and when the first vessel came in range they received it with a volley from their bow cannon. Brandon retaliated in like manner and pressed forward, eager to join in the hand-to-hand fighting. However, the mast of his ship had been broken by cannon-fire and he was forced to fall back. When Sir Thomas saw from a distance that Brandon had turned away, he quickly moved in and, accompanied by only one small escort, made a direct and savage attack on the *Cordelière*, revealing more spirit than prudence.

Henry's early government

Henry VIII was barely 18 when he ascended the throne in 1509, and although he was headstrong and wilful in some ways, at first he allowed himself to be ruled by his father's mature councillors.

It soon became apparent, however, that his priorities were different from those of his father. He yearned to be a warlord and to lead his army into battle. Inevitably the chosen enemy was France, and with equal inevitability this also involved war with France's ancient ally, Scotland. Although this was the policy of an ardent and inexperienced king, it could be justified.

For over a generation, the English nobility had been subjected to constant fiscal harrassment, and denied their natural role in fighting, with the rewards and profits which it could be expected to bring. A new war with France was the ideal remedy for their frustration. While William Warham, the Lord Chancellor, and Richard Fox, bishop of Winchester, tried to dissuade Henry from his intention, his younger nobles and courtiers looked forward to their new opportunities.

While the Council put Henry VII's chamber finance on a statutory basis, brought the general surveyors of the Crown lands under the control of the Exchequer, and continued to collect most of the old king's bonds, the new king was winning hearts in a dashing and spectacular manner. Henry found routine business tedious, and writing a painful exercise, but was always eager to show off his numerous accomplishments, whether as jouster, courtier or politician. The executions of Richard Empson and Edmund Dudley, Henry VII's unpopular fiscal agents on trumped-up charges of treason, were meant to capitalize on people's reaction against his father's severity. Special commissions established in July 1509, to hear grievances were part of the same tactic, but were wound up in November.

Above all, Henry courted the admiration of scholars and men of letters who, scenting a lavish patron, showered him with praise which was more desired than deserved.

Three years after his accession, the king was master in his own house. By April 1512 he had declared war on France – but needed ministers of his own choosing to carry out his policies effectively. The first year of the war was a failure, but produced the man Henry needed: Thomas Wolsey, his almoner, whose energy and efficiency in organizing the campaign of 1513 made his fortune. By the end of that year, Wolsey was the political equal of Warham and Fox, and far more in tune with the king. The first phase of Henry's reign had come to an end, and a celebrated partnership in government had begun.

Below   Henry, accompanied by his lords, on the way to parliament in 1512. He found it difficult to keep his mind on parliamentary business, preferring a ceaseless round of merry-making.

Grappling irons having been thrown, a fierce struggle ensued between the two ships, of a character more typical of land warefare as it was possible to cross from one ship to the other. Many of the crew on both sides were either cut down at once or flung into the sea. Meanwhile the little escort vessel sailed around the French ship and holed it in a number of places with cannon fire until it began to leak badly.

In the normal course of events it would now have only been a matter of time before the English gained the upper hand, had it not come about that, in the midst of the fighting – either by an enemy ploy or by pure chance, which might well have been the case – a huge tongue of flame spurted from the French ship in the direction of the English vessel and started a terrible fire. Then the combatants on both sides, surrounded by flames, stopped their fighting and tried to put out the fire.

But as the ships were joined together by grappling irons the flames inevitably triumphed and could not be arrested by any human agency until they had finally and hideously engulfed the two ships and all their men. To avoid the flames many leapt into the sea and some were saved by the arrival of boats manned by their countrymen.

Thus the engagement was a sad one for both sides. Of the English about 600 men, including their commander Sir Thomas, perished, whilst a further 1,000 Frenchmen – the garrison of the huge ship – also died. The action was begun so suddenly and was so quickly terminated by the fire that neither side had time to come to the aid of the doomed men.

While Henry was winning the Battle of the Spurs and capturing Tournai, James IV of Scotland decided to take advantage of his preoccupation. Ignoring papal threats, he crossed the Tweed at the head of a large army in late August.

Meanwhile James, king of Scotland, incited by the bribes and exhortations of King Louis of France, began to muster an army of 60,000 men with the intention of making a sudden attack on the English borders to distract Henry from his campaign in France. However, so that his actions might not appear dishonourable, James first sent a herald to King Henry who was at that time fighting against the French at Tournai. The messenger was to announce that because of past grievances and the English king's current invasion of the territory of his friend

Preparing the navy for war

Although Henry VIII inherited only seven ships from his father, these included two large carracks *Regent* and *Sovereign*. Custom-built warships of over 600 tons burden, they were nearly 20 years old but still among the best in Europe. The king was interested in guns, particularly big guns, as well as ships, and immediately after his accession laid down two more large warships, the *Mary Rose* and the *Peter Pomegranate*. Unlike their predecessors they were designed to mount heavy guns broadside, in addition to the lighter anti-personnel weapons carried in the castles, fore and aft. Heavy guns had been carried before by Portugese carracks in the Far East, but were mounted on the deck in the waist of the ship and therefore had to be severely limited in number, for fear of making the vessel top-heavy. Henry overcame this problem by adapting the French device of a port or loading door, which opened in the side of the ship between the decks. The new warships had several small ports on each side, with guns mounted to fire through them. In this way the centre of gravity was lowered making the ships more stable.

Together with the *Regent* and the *Sovereign* they formed the nucleus of a fleet of 18 vessels which the lord admiral, Sir Edward Howard, was commissioned to command in April 1512. Most of them were raised by the traditional method of requisitioning from the merchant community, and then armed and fitted out at the king's expense. At Blackheath of 16 April, 3,000 men were mustered to serve in the fleet. In addition, transport ships were bought and hired: the main purpose of the fleet being to carry an English expeditionary force to Guienne.

In spite of his interest in the navy, Henry did not regard it as an independent fighting force, let alone a standing service which would be constantly available for policing the seas. These developments were among the results of the wars which were about to begin.

Below left   Objects recovered from the Mary Rose.

Left   Henry enjoyed seeing heavy guns "fired again and again, marking their range, as he is curious about matters of this kind".

Below   The pride of Henry's navy, the Mary Rose, was to overturn in Portsmouth harbour in 1545 because of a freak accident with the lower gun ports.

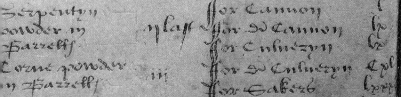

King Louis, James would attack England with his army unless Henry immediately withdrew his forces from France. The herald departed for the continent and diligently executed his king's commands.

Henry's reply, it is said, was that James had no grounds for complaint as he had suffered no wrong-doing at Henry's hands and the war was being waged on behalf of the Church, a very just cause. Thus he couldn't see why James, as a Christian prince, should want to attack him when there were such positive human and divine reasons not to. However, were he to persist in his designs he should know that king Henry would be his enemy for ever and would make sure that at some time or other James would pay the penalty for breaking his trust in this way. With these words Henry sent the herald away.

James, however, was not pacified by this reply and regardless of his alliance with England, both by treaties and by marriage, swiftly crossed the border. In the first attack he stormed Norham Castle on the frontier itself and practically razed it to the ground. He then pushed on for another six miles, laying waste everything with fire and sword as he went, until he came to the hill known as Flodden. Here he made his camp and destroyed the surrounding area.

When Thomas Howard, earl of Surrey, military commander of the northern provinces, heard of this while travelling in Yorkshire he immediately ordered the north-country folk to take up arms. He himself then made for Newcastle with all speed and thence to Alnwick where he had instructed all the local nobles with their armed retinues to meet him. Amongst these were Thomas, lord Dacre, a fine commander and advisor, Henry, lord Clifford, Richard, lord Latimer, Henry, lord Scrope, William, lord Conyers, and Thomas, lord Howard, and a number of other knights and powerful citizens of high birth, each contributing armed men in greater or lesser numbers according to his resources.

The army grew in this way until it amounted to 30,000 men and, having conferred with his generals, the earl instructed the troops to form a column and march against the enemy. About a mile from Alnwick he pitched camp on the near side of the river known locally as the Till. Then, as his men were eager for battle, he decided it would be better to cross the river and get quickly to grips with the enemy. So at dawn on 9 September he formed up his army in full battle order.

Wars with France and Scotland

The quarrel between Louis XII of France and Pope Julius II provided a diplomatic pretext for the war which Henry chose to launch in April 1512.

In May 1511 the French king summoned a schismatic General Council of the Church, and in October that year Henry joined the pope's Holy League against France, assuring himself of a war, and with allies in the Holy Roman Emperor Maximilian I, and Ferdinand II of Spain. In June 1512 an English expeditionary force was sent to Gascony to collaborate with the Spaniards in a campaign against Aquitaine. However, Ferdinand was interested only in taking Navarre, and, when he had done so, withdrew from the campaign. The English commander, Thomas Grey, marquis of Dorset, had no option but to bring his frustrated and mutinous troops home.

In March 1512 Julius stripped Louis XII of his title of Most Christian King and of his kingdom, and bestowed both upon Henry. However, for these grants to be effective, Louis had to be defeated and his kingdom conquered. In 1513 Henry planned a new campaign,

The Battle of

this time with Maximilian, and took an army of 40,000 men to Calais at the end of June. On 16 August the English won the battle of the Spurs and captured the towns of Thérouanne and Tournai. Although this was a long way from the kind of victory they needed, it satisfied Henry's immediate craving for military glory.

On August 11, James IV of Scotland, seizing his opportunity while Henry was in France, declared war on England. The English were expecting such a move, however, and a powerful army under Thomas Howard, earl of Surrey, was ready in the North. On 9 September the two armies met at Flodden, where the Scots were defeated and James killed.

After Julius' death in March 1513, Louis made peace with his successor, Leo X, thus removing Henry's justification for the war with France. More seriously, first Ferdinand and then Maximilian signed truces with the French king in February 1514, leaving Henry to carry on alone. Although he at first seemed fully prepared to do so, pressure from the pope and, probably, Thomas Wolsey, archbishop of York, brought him to the negotiating table in June. In August a peace treaty was signed as a result of which Louis married Henry's younger sister Mary and the English retained possession of Tournai.

Above   The battle of Flodden, 1513, where James IV of Scotland died.

Below   Victory at The Battle of Spurs satisfied Henry's immediate craving for glory.

When James learnt that the English were crossing the river, he assumed that they were hurrying to occupy a small hill which lay between the two armies. So in order to reach it first he had great fires lit to blind the English with smoke and, having broken camp, hastened to the hill in full battle order. He was convinced that the English wouldn't fight and that they just wanted to occupy the hill so that they could set up a well-appointed camp from which they could harry James's lines of communications. And he deemed it a foregone conclusion that if it came to a fight the English would quickly flee. In this belief he was greatly mistaken, as will be shown and as a result he was defeated. To despise your enemy is always dangerous, even for great generals.

Meanwhile the English, who had by now crossed the river, advanced towards Flodden hill and remained close to it, both to avoid the enemy cannon fire and in turn to harass with their own guns the enemy coming down the hill. It was this tactic that led to their final victory.

Both armies then met at the foot of the hill and the battle began. Edmund Howard advanced on the right flank with about 3,000 men who were attacked in the first Scottish charge. Howard pressed on valiantly but his troops panicked and took flight. Seeing this from a distance King James thought the whole army had taken to its heels, as he had earlier anticipated it would. Thus he quickly dismounted, seized a weapon and marched into battle very inadequately armed. He then thrust himself into the front line, followed by the majority of the nobility. But the English were by no means intimidated and put up fierce resistance.

For a time both sides fought hard until the Scottish front line, completely surrounded, had been almost entirely destroyed. The remaining Scottish troops behind the battlefield didn't enter the fray, perhaps by God's will, perhaps because of the fool-hardiness of their king's actions, or perhaps because they didn't dare enter the battle after the death of their monarch (they believed, correctly that he had fallen in the first charge). They thus withdrew into Scotland, taking with them a large number of captured men and cattle.

The fighting had lasted about three hours and of the 15,000 men that fell about 5,000 were English.

In gathering up the spoils of battle James's body was found, wounded in two places and showing great dignity even though the life was gone out of it. This gave the victors great joy as they had not believed earlier that they had indeed defeated the king himself.

This then was the death that James had to suffer in order to atone for his violation of the treaty with England. His body was later carried to the Carthusian monastery at Sheen, seven miles from London, where it lay unburied for some time as, by violating the treaty, James has been excommunicated.

1513

On 25 April 1513 the Holy League was extended to include the Emperor Maximilian, and on 30 June Henry landed at Calais at the head of a large expeditionary force. By the beginning of August he had reached, and besieged, the small town of Tournai. Maximilian, in order to avoid commitment to an expensive campaign, offered to serve under Henry. Such flattery could hardly be refused, and the king accepted.

Knowing that he would have to fight the English king, the French monarch sent the duc de Vandôme, the duc de Longuyle and various other courageous officers of Blangoy. It was then decided that the duc d'Alençon should take 5,000 men and attack the earl of Shrewsbury, or at the very least prevent him or lord Herbert coming to aid Henry's forces.

Meanwhile Vendôme and Longuyle's men would engage the king, thereby covering the entrance of supplies to the besieged town. To carry out this plan the Frenchmen began large-scale manoeuvres on horseback which the English king got wind of, and sent word to Maximilian, who was camped at Ayre, to join Henry in his headquarters for a conference on the situation. Maximilian had not been aware of the French troop movements and replied that he would come the following day.

The king, meanwhile, sent out detachments of light cavalry at regular intervals to scout the surrounding countryside for any sign of the enemy so that they wouldn't be unprepared in the event of a sudden attack.

While all this was going on, Maximilian and his entourage, all in the pay of the king and wearing his colours of a St George's cross with a rose, set off for

A soldier's life

Most men became soldiers because they were conscripted by their landlord or the authorities of the village or town in which they lived. Some volunteered to serve under individual captains who were known to be recruiting, but most were drafted to fill the quota allocated to their particular community. All able-bodied men were supposed to serve in the militia, a home defence force, and provide their own weapons.

A man recruited for an overseas campaign was paid coat and conduct money which enabled him to clothe himself suitably and paid his expenses to the port of embarkation, or to the general muster point. Local contingents were normally mustered in their home areas and travelled together under their officers to reduce the risk of desertion. A deserter was liable to execution under martial law if caught, but many men considered that a lesser risk than actual service.

Once mustered, soldiers were issued with weapons and trained in their use. All other matters including food, clothing and discipline were the responsibility of the military command. Officers were invariably gentlemen, while non-commissioned officers were often veterans who had begun their careers as volunteers and had served in many campaigns. They were significantly better paid than the ordinary soldiers.

Although pay was theoretically regular, at about 6d. a day, it was often far in arrears as a campaign proceeded, and this was the commonest cause of mutiny and disorder.

Disease, malnutrition and exposure, rather than enemy action were the main dangers on campaign: although medical services existed, they were extremely primitive, and as little help as civilian medicine in the face of plague, typhoid or syphilis. Troops were billeted whenever possible, but accommodation was usually inadequate, if it existed at all. Discipline was draconian in theory, but in practice troops often got out of hand: plunder, authorized or not, was the average soldier's only chance of making any profit from his service. The taking of prisoners for ransom was largely confined to officers.

At the end of a campaign survivors were shipped home and demobilized. They were paid their conduct money home at the port of arrival, and any who were sick or disabled might be harried from parish to parish, lest they become a charge on the community. Discharged soldiers were often unwelcome until they had shed all traces of their military service. A soldier's life was not regarded with much respect in Tudor England.

Below   This contemporary woodcut of the siege of Boulogne shows soldiers using firearms to attack the town, while knights in full armour wait to advance.

Henry's camp and arrived on Friday 13 August. Here Maximilian was received with great ceremony and conducted to a tent made from cloth of gold and decorated inside with cloth of gold and blue velvet embroidered in fine gold with the letters H and K. Every service was laid on for his benefit and officers were assigned to wait on him. He remained in Henry's camp until Sunday and then returned to Ayre.

Meanwhile, the king and his advisers had been informed by their spies and from the confessions of some prisoners that the French army stationed at Blangoy intended to try and get supplies through to Thérouanne. Thus, on the night of Friday 13 August, the duke of Buckingham, Edward Stafford, the earl of Essex, Henry Bourchier, lord Burgayne, George Neville, lord Abergavenny, the marquess of Dorset, Thomas Grey, lord Willoughby and various others – together with 6,000 foot soldiers and lord Walon and lord Ligny's cavalry brigades – took up their positions in full battle order at Gyngate to the south of Thérouanne and waited for the French supply-train. However, the English forces were spotted and the French broke off their mission and the duke of Buckingham and his companions returned to camp.

On Monday 6 August an unfortunate incident occurred when, without any apparent cause, violent argument and fighting broke out between the English and German troops under Henry's command, which ensued in considerable loss of life. The Germans suddenly seized hold of the artillery and turned it on the Englishmen who replied by turning their archers and pikemen on the Germans. However, luckily the situation was defused by the officers before things got out of hand, just as Maximilian arrived from Ayre. The emperor praised the skill of the officers and went on to join the king and his generals, where he was informed that they were not certain that the French were intending to relieve the city of Tournai. It was then agreed that the master of ordnance should construct five bridges over the river as quickly as possible, in order that the army could lay seige to the city. The carpenters worked all night at their duty and by daylight the bridges had been built and the light cavalry crossed to spy out the land.

On Tuesday 17 August the king struck camp and crossed the river with all his heavy artillery and transport. At this point Sir John Nevell rode up to him with his light cavalry group and informed him that behind the tower castle at Gyngate there was a large company of horsemen. At about the same time as these tidings were being received, Sir John Peche and a group of lancers had encountered this very force and after a number of skirmishes had beaten the Frenchmen, who had fled. One of the French horseman had been taken hostage and in lieu of ransom informed them that 15,000 French heavy cavalry were en route from Blangoy to relieve Tournai from this side of the river. And to ensure that the armies of the lord steward and the lord chamberlain didn't come to the aid of King Henry, 5,000 of the French horsemen were being directed to the other side of the river.

As this news was being heard a messenger arrived from Sir Rhys (ap Thomas) with the information that a prisoner he had taken that day had confessed that the relief of the city was intended for that very day and that approximately 6,000 enemy horsemen had been spotted heading in their direction. Then the northernmost spies arrived to confirm that they had indeed seen the French army advancing in full battle order, but that they didn't estimate them to number more than 12,000.

The king then drew up his battle lines and positioned his artillery. Some of his advisers beseeched him to take down his tents and retire from the front line but the king replied that he would arrange his battlefield in as royal a manner as possible and command all his sumptuous headquarters to be set up. This having been done he then summoned Lord Darcy and commanded him to look after his treasure and personal effects.

Every man then readied himself for battle and rallied to the standard, the cavalry leading the foot-soldiers by the distance of about a mile. As messengers arrived with the news that the French army was near, the king gave the order to advance under his banner in the name of God and St George. At this point, for some unknown reason, the German troops suddenly moved to the left flank of the king's forces, leaving his front unprotected. As the king thus advanced into battle, the Emperor Maximilian and 30 men-at-arms – all dressed in red crosses – approached him. After some consultation the king then ordered a number of small artillery pieces to be positioned on the top of a long hill to take care of any outriders. This done he continued his advance with

The rise of Wolsey

Thomas Wolsey's emergence to power as Henry VIII's lord chancellor, demonstrates the extent to which the Church provided opportunities for men of talent, and the need of those men to acquire the support of influential patrons. Ability took Wolsey to Oxford at an early age – he was a Bachelor of Arts at the age of 15 – but he was in his late twenties before he won the favour of Elizabeth of York's half-brother, Thomas Grey, marquess of Dorset, in 1500. After Dorset's death in 1501, he became chaplain to Henry Deane, archbishop of Canterbury and keeper of the Great Seal, and to Sir Richard Nanfan, Governor of Calais. These contacts gave Wolsey experience in government. When Nanfan died in 1507, he was appointed a royal chaplain and secretary to Richard Fox, bishop of Winchester, Henry VII's lord privy seal. Henry VII appointed him dean of Lincoln in 1509, and Henry VIII, on his accession that same year, made him almoner, a post that gave him personal access to the young king.

His immense industry made him an ideal royal servant. Henry was inclined to neglect routine matters of administration in favour of his personal pleasure, and Wolsey, willing to deal with all matters of government business, became indispensable. He was the principal organizer of the king's French campaign which culminated in Henry's victory in the Battle of the Spurs in 1513, and played an active role in subsequent peace negotiations. Rewards followed fast: the bishoprics of Tournai (1513) and Lincoln (1514), and finally, also in 1514, the archbishopric of York. In 1515 the pope, Leo

Above   Cardinal Wolsey, Henry's omnipotent lord chancellor.

Below   Illustration from the biography of Wolsey, written by his servant George Cavendish. This scene shows Wolsey travelling to France.

X, prompted by Henry, made him a cardinal. A month later the king appointed him lord chancellor. In 1518 he became papal legate. As the incumbent of high offices in both Church and State, Wolsey became a dominant influence in England for over a decade.

his cavalry and mounted archers but was persuaded by his generals not to be in the front of the battle, so he tarried with the emperor and the foot soldiers at the back of the field.

The French advanced in three ranks, each 36 men deep, and could easily make out the king's foot-soldiers coming towards them with the earl of Essex's cavalry, while Sir John Peche, leading the king's cavalry and 1,100 Burgundians, stood in a valley with raised banner. Lord Walonne, and lord Ligny, with his bastard son Emery then moved their group of 400 Burgundian horseman away from the Englishmen, the 700 remaining riding up to the top of the adjoining hill with their banner where they met up with Sir John Guilforde and 100 mounted longbowmen who had spotted the French troops.

On the top of the hill was a plain of good ground, on the left was a small wood and on the right a fallow field. Lord Walonne and the Burgundians were still apart when the French appeared in full view with their banners and standards.

At this point an English officer called Clarenseux went up to the English general and said: "In God's name attack and the victory will be yours. I am convinced that they won't stand their ground and I will accompany you wearing my coat of arms." So then the archers dismounted and deployed behind a hedge that ran the length of a village called Bomye. The Frenchmen advanced bearing 36 standards and were resisted by the English, the archers cutting down their horses whilst the lancers fought valiantly hand to hand crying: "For God and St George".

Dust flew everywhere and the hue and cry was great when suddenly the French abandoned their standards, threw away their lances, swords and maces, cut the armour off their horses to make them run quicker and rode off at great speed. When the rearmost forces saw the vanguard running they fled too, especially when they saw what else was happening. For as the English cavalry mounted the hill the stradiates were advancing down one side of it in front of the French host which, suddenly seeing the Engish cavalry followed by the footsoldiers coming up as well, thought they were all mounted troops and turned and fled. Indeed the Frenchmen fled at such speed that the stradiates couldn't keep up with them. When it was seen that the French were in full flight the Burgundians took up the chase. It was a complete rout of the French cavalry, who outnumbered the English by ten to one, and made history in being the first time that French troops had been defeated entirely by English horsemen. The French call this battle the Battle of the Spurs, because the cavalry ran away so swiftly, and it took place on 16 August.

Prisoners captured included the duc de Longuyle, brother of the comte du Dunoys who had married the daughter of the marquis de Rutilons, Cleremounde and twenty score other noblemen who were all brought into the king's presence with their standards and banners. The Burgundians, however, kept their prisoners and didn't parade them before Henry, and rumour had it that monsieur de la Palayce had been captured by them and then released.

The English forces pursued the French for three miles from the battlefield until they reached a river in a valley. At this point a Frenchman turned to Sir Giles Capell and said that one day they would return, to which sir Giles retorted in French that he'd heard that old French boast before.

The English forces then returned to the king, who praised them greatly for their valiant actions and on the spot made Sir John Peche a banneret and knighted the badly wounded John Car. After this the king returned to Gyngate where he was told how the Frenchmen has skirmished all day with his troops on the far side of the river. The earl of Shrewsbury, with banner held high, had been hard-pressed against the forces of the duc d'Alençon, the comte de St Polle and the sire de Florenges who as earlier related, had been sent with 5,000 men to defend the town on the side where Shrewsbury's forces were ranged and prevent him from reaching the king. As it turned out, the French didn't descend and do battle but only skirmished with Sir Rhys's troops. However, when the citizens of Tournai saw their saviours approaching they sallied forth proudly and attacked lord Herbert's forces, letting off artillery from every side all the while. Lord Herbert and his men counterattacked with considerable courage and so sorely beset the Frenchmen that they drove them back to the gate of the city and a great many were slain.

That night the king sent for the duc de Longuyle, Cleremounde and various other captured nobles and they dined with him at his table.

Courtly magnificence

The politics of magnificence, or *maiestas*, was designed to dazzle and impress. It was also a royal monopoly which no great nobleman could emulate.

Partly in a race with his great rival Francis I of France, Henry VIII continued his father's policy of spending lavishly on his court, with the aim to attract men of influence to his service, and his alone. However, there were two significant developments. First, and in complete contrast to the undemonstrative Henry VII, the king joined in the pageantry of his court and took part in its numerous sporting events, as well as in the dancing and acting which became a feature of royal domestic life. Unlike his father, in another respect, he was not aloof from court intrigue.

The second major development, the politicization of the members of the Privy Chamber, thrust the king even further into court rivalries. The Privy Chamber was in fact a set of apartments which Henry VII had set up in the 1490s to provide a degree of privacy away from the semi-public rooms of the Chamber. Henry VIII replaced the humble servants with which his father had staffed the Privy Chamber with gentlemen of the highest rank. Far from being a retreat from the affairs of state, his most private apartments became the headquarters. Not even the king's ministers had a right of access to the Privy Chamber, and behind its closed doors its officers soon became political rivals to privy councillors who had been officially appointed to advise the king – they even began to rival the king's chief ministers.

As a result of these changes, the king could be monopolised by personal servants who were themselves politically ambitious. Conflicting advice was not necessarily bad, but that of the "Gentlemen of the Privy Chamber" was often given in ignorance of the state of the treasury or the latest diplomatic dispatches, information which was largely restricted to holders of the great offices of state in the Privy Council. Moreover, the traditional patterns of government were disrupted when, in the scramble for office, the king's attendants became more important than his ministers in the distribution of patronage.

On one occasion, in 1517, when the court had to move away from London because of the plague, Cardinal Wolsey, who had remained in the city, discovered that the Groom of the Stool and his friends were persuading the king to look favourably upon their clients, and that they had contradicted Wolsey's wishes in writing. In 1519 Wolsey felt constrained to act, and with his fellow Councillors persuaded the king to exclude many from the court.

Above   Henry eating dinner in his private apartments, where informal policy discussions often took place.

There was a more sinister side to these factional politics. Edward Stafford, 3rd duke of Buckingham had royal blood in his veins. A Privy Councillor, he was no friend of either Thomas Wolsey, or of the gentlemen of the Privy Chamber. He complained that Henry "would give his fees, offices and rewards, rather to boys than to noblemen", and made a particular enemy of one of the leading gentlemen, Sir William Compton, who with Wolsey brought their joint-enemy to the block in May 1521 on trumped-up charges of treason.

Wolsey never completely solved the problems which the new-style court created for him and when his arch-rival, Anne Boleyn, insinuated her friends and family into the Privy Chamber in 1528, his end was in sight.

Lacteur.

Pres ce la dicte dame prist la
voye plus oultre iusques a sa
porte aux painctres ou y auoit
vng eschauffault richement prepare. Au
hault du quel estoit come au ciel dedans
vne nuee vng dieu le pere tenant en sa

Above A late sixteenth century painting of Nonsuch Palace in Surrey. Continental craftsmen created a palace to rival Francis I's chateau at Chambord. However, this testimony to Renaissance kingship no longer stands today.

Right A Chinese crystal bottle for keeping spices and The Howard Grace Cup made from silver.

Left Mary Tudor, Henry's sister, at the court of Louis XII of France. She married the elderly Louis in 1514. Such relationships with Europeans brought Renaissance culture to England.

1514

In the later years of the 14th century an Oxford theologian named John Wycliffe had criticized many of the sacramental doctrines and ritual practices of the Church. After his death his views obtained wide popular currency. Although persecuted intermittently throughout the 15th century, these Lollards survived as an underground organization. For the most part they were humble people, but their number included a few substantial merchants and craftsmen, particularly in London. One of the characteristics of those who held these beliefs was hostility to the jurisdiction of the clergy. They later became absorbed by the rising protestant movement and later protestants, like John Foxe, looked back to them with partisan sympathy. One such victim was Richard Hun, whose fate at the hands of the bishop of London's officers became a cause célèbre of English anticlericalism.

In the year of our Lord 1514 there dwelt in the city of London a merchant tailor and freeman of the city called Richard Hun. He was greatly esteemed in his lifetime and had a good reputation, being not only a man of fair dealing and good substances but also a good Catholic. This Richard Hun had a child in the care of a nurse in Middlesex, in the parish of St Mary Matsilon, which died. Whereupon, the parson of the said parish, one Thomas Dryfield, sued Richard Hun in the spiritual court for non-payment of a bearing-sheet which he unjustly claimed he should have received from Hun for the burial of his son Stephen who had died at the age of five weeks. Hun's defence was that, being only 5 weeks old, the child had not owned the sheet and thus he would refuse to pay for it and the parson should not receive any money for it. At this point, motivated by greed and loath to relinquish his supposed right to payment, the priest had Hun summoned to appear in the spiritual court to decide the case there.

However, Richard Hun (having suffered at the hands of the spiritual court) took it upon himself to seek legal advice and issued a writ of praemunire, against Thomas Dryfield and his advisers, the results of which are outlined below.

Praemunire alleges that there has been an abuse of ecclesiastical power.

When the priests heard of this, they were so outraged that a layman should take such an action against them – and equally so fearful that if this priest was condemned through Hun's prosecution then the laity might feel free to issue writs against the clergy in any similar cases – that they determined to take all measures to try and trap him within the framework of their own legislation – both in revenge on Hun himself and to put an end to the matter for good.

Thus after much secret and diligent research, not leaving a stone unturned, they at last found a means by which he could be accused of heresy. They put their case to Richard Fitzjames, then bishop of London, who, eager to satisfy his chaplains' desire for revenge, ordered Hun's arrest and incarceration in the Lollards' tower in St Paul's cathedral where none of his friends could visit him.

And so it came about that Richard Hun, having been locked in the Lollards' tower, was shortly thereafter brought before the bishop at his manor in Fulham at the express wish of the bishop's chancellor, a man more disposed to the cruel tyranny of the clergy than to the truth of Christ's gospel. Thus on 2 December in the year already mentioned the bishop examined Hun's case in his chapel, based on the following articles of indictment compiled by the aforementioned chancellor and his accomplices:

1. That he had believed taught, preached, published and obstinately defended the view, against the laws of almighty God, that the paying of tithes [to the church] had never been officially sanctioned except by the greed of the priesthood.

2. That he had declared, taught, preached, published and obstinately defended the view that bishops and priests were like the scribes and pharisees who crucified Christ and condemned him to death.

3. That he had declared, taught, preached, etc. that bishops and priests were just teachers and preachers who neither followed the law of God nor carried out the commandments themselves; all they ever did was take and receive, never giving or ministering to others.

4. When Joan Baker, a London Lollard who had been condemned a few years earlier, was caught and recanted all her heresies, the same Richard Hun declared, published, taught, preached and obstinately insisted that he would defend her and her opinions even if it cost him 500 marks.

5. When the same Joan Baker had recanted and

had been forced to make public penance for her sins, the said Richard Hun declared, published, taught and obstinately protested her innocence, saying: "The bishop of London and his council have done manifest injustice to Joan Baker in punishing her for heresy as her sayings and opinions are all according to the laws of God. Indeed the bishops and his council are more worthy of punishment for heresy than she is."

6. That the said Richard Hun had in his possession various books that were prohibited and banned by law, such as the apocalypse, epistles and gospels in English, Wycliffe's damnable works and other books containing numerous falsities, all of which he had studied and taught from daily for many years.

I could find no specific replies to any of these several indictments in the official record of the trial, just the following words which appeared immediately after them and written in his name, but not in his handwriting:

"Concerning these articles of indictment, I have not said the things I am therein accused of. However, I have somewhat ill-advisedly spoken words of a similar nature, for which I am sorry and for which I beg God's forgiveness and submit myself to the bishop's benevolent correction."

This, it is affirmed, was written in Hun's own hand, but how close to the truth that is I shall let the wisdom of the reader judge in the light of the trial. And if indeed he had written it then why did they murder him so cruelly afterwards? Especially since he had so willingly already confessed his crimes and submitted himself to the mercy and corrective measures of the bishop, following which punishments, even by their own laws, they eventually pardoned cases of even the most severe heresy – unless of course vile murder can be counted amongst the bishop's instruments of "charitable correction".

In addition, it appears that they produced very few reliable witnesses that this was his reply and handwriting. Indeed the records clerk, or whoever he had appointed to enter the details in the register, only certified the entry as being confirmed through hearsay and not from his own personal knowledge, as the words written in the margin of the register next to the reply clearly prove: "Hoc fuit scriptum manu propria Ricardi Hunne, *ut dicitur*". ['This was written in Richard Hun's own hand, *as it is said*'.]

Surely, if he had been able to verify the statement then he would have done so, and instead of writing "ut dicitur" would have entered the names of the assistants who were present at the trial. He had admitted that there were a number of them. This is normal practice, especially in cases of so-called heresy.

But how scrupulous the actions of such good fellows who were able to murder Hun so shamelessly might be when it came to lying about him once dead I can only leave to the impartial judgement of others.

The trial ended, the bishop sent Hun back to the Lollards' tower where the chancellor, ostensibly transferred him from the custody of Charles Joseph the summoning officer of the court into the charge of John Spalding, the bell-ringer – a man through whose simplemindedness and general wickedness the scheming chancellor hoped he could make the intended "accidental death" that much easier. Which is indeed what happened when, within two nights, the cruel deed was done, by agents whom he had suborned – all this having since been plainly proved by diligent research and the final verdict of the coroner of London's inquest, as required by law.

However, once the papists had committed this deed they made every effort to cover up their actions. To this end, the morning following the murder, Spalding, undoubtedly on the advice of his chancellor left for the city and gave the keys of the prison to one of his colleagues with the instruction to pass them on to the summoning officer's boy, who had been used to bringing Hun his food and other requirements. The idea of this was that it was hoped that the boy would find the prisoner hanging dead in his cell and that his narration of the discovery would free the others of any suspicion in the matter.

All this seemed to go according to plan at first. At about ten o'clock on the morning of 4 December the boy, having received the keys, went to the prisoner's cell as he was wont to do, accompanied by two other summoning officers of the bishop's court. Here they found Hun hanged with his face turned to the wall. Astonished at this sight, the summoning officers immediately conveyed the news to the chancellor who was then in the church – no doubt awaiting just such a report. He then gathered up a number of his colleagues and went with them to the person to see for himself what his wicked conscience knew full well he would see. At the time, however, he made a remarkable display of surprise, bruiting it abroad that in desperation Hun had hanged himself.

Be that as it may, the people themselves, knowing well the honesty and godliness of Hun and equally the evil malice of his adversaries the priests, judged that he had in fact been secretly murdered by their will.

1515

Thomas Wolsey commenced his career at court as a chaplain to Henry VII. He became almoner on Henry VIII's accession in 1509 and distinguished himself in managing the logistics of the Tournai campaign of 1513. He became first bishop of Tournai, then of Lincoln, and within a year archibishop of York. In 1515 he became lord chancellor and the most powerful man in the realm after the king. This power, together with his flamboyant style of wielding it, made him many enemies of all ranks. Among them the chronicler Polydore Vergil.

When Wolsey had reached the summit of his power he opened a law shop – and what a Charybdis, what a whirlpool, what an abyss of every kind of plundering it was! For over this new court he appointed as its head Dr John Allen – a creature himself so far removed from the study and love of justice that he had recently been convicted not only of flagrant crimes but of perjury on the testimony of a great many people. And yet this same man became a judge, a guardian of morals, a teacher of old-fashioned and proper virtues!

His first act was to review the administration of justice within the whole city and to examine the conduct of certain individual citizens. If any slight suspicion of misdemeanour fell on any men or women he could harrass them and fine them heavily, whether this was legal or not. For some, however, this practice proved less burdensome, as a single penalty was applied to all cases and those who could afford it were thereby able to redeem themselves in the eyes of the judge and the law and be acquitted of the offence with minimal damage to their reputations – a positive incitement to crime.

Allen's deputies diligently applied, practised and upheld this scheme throughout the country and there was in addition a group of civil servants who toured the villages and sniffed out the dying and the executors of their wills in order to bring the wills rapidly to the new legate's court. For it is the custom in England that heirs and executors of the deceased

Diet of the common people

Bread and cheese was the staple diet of all classes in 16th-century England, their quality varying according to the wealth of the household. "Carter's bread", the cheapest, was a mixture of wheat and rye; "Ravel" or yeoman's bread was made of wholemeal; and "Manchet", the most expensive, of white wheat flour. Beer brewed without hops, and not particularly alcoholic, was consumed in large quantities at all levels of society, although the wealthy also drank imported French wines. Water was often contaminated, and soft drinks unknown.

All except the very poor had small patches of land attached to their houses, gardens and paddocks, whether they lived in towns or villages. Many kept chickens, and often pigs or cows. Animals were regularly slaughtered in November, and the meat salted, smoked or dried for later consumption. Although beef was readily available, bacon was the commonest meat of the poor.

Other sources of meat could be had but at a risk. For though it was permitted to take rabbits and pigeons

Left   Meat was seldom fresh and people lived through the winter months on smoked bacon and salted beef.

Above   For most of the population bread was the staple diet and poor harvests meant starvation. There were no potatoes or rice, or tomatoes, but fruit was in abundance, especially pears, apples and plums.

from the wild, they were more than likely to belong to the lord's warren or dovecote. The safest alternative source of meat for those who lived close to a coast or a river estuary was wild-fowling. It was obligatory for the people, as Catholics, to eat fish on Fridays, generally in the form of salted herring or dried cod – fresh fish did not travel far in the slow transport system of the period.

Apples, cherries and strawberries were eaten in season, but citrus fruits were exotic rarities, available only to the rich. Green vegetables, particularly peas and beans were eaten when available, as were carrots and onions; salad herbs were gathered from the hedgerows rather than cultivated. Potatoes and tomatoes were unknown.

Famine was rare in England, although two runs of bad harvests, in the mid-1550s and the mid-1590s, produced widespread hardship. If the harvest failed there was no flour for bread, no feed for cattle and so no butter or cheese. Under normal circumstances, however, the everyday English diet was varied and reasonably plentiful during summer, but monotonous in winter.

should present a document, showing how the deceased's property will be bequeathed, in front of a bishop or archdeacon, swearing in their presence that they will carry out the deceased wishes as detailed therein. The bishops and archdeacons then take a proportion of the value of the property as tax – and sometimes this can be a substantial amount and considerably affect the heirs' inheritance. For this reason King Henry had previously reduced this tax to a nominal sum and by this deed, as devout and blessed as it was equitable, he truly protected the interests of his subjects. To my knowledge this taxing of wills is not found amongst any other nations.

But to return to the duties of these civil servants, they had also to make a careful note of all vacant estates which the legate would then grant to whomsoever he pleased.

Meanwhile in London, Wolsey, who had decided from the start to make a profit from his work, summoned monks of all orders to his presence. As they flung themselves at his feet, Wolsey assumed a very sanctimonious attitude and reproved them on many counts, saying that they no longer conducted themselves as they should and that instead of busying themselves with the pursuit of literature and virtuous activities they were more concerned with acquiring wealth, which they did with considerable zeal. He thus asserted that he would take it upon himself to correct these abuses, lest their religion should be ruined. And in order to show them that he meant business he immediately went to Westminster abbey and there instigated a thorough inquiry into the conduct of the monks. He carried this out in such a manner that he caused great anxiety amongst them, as it was his intention to do, thereby exhibiting his power and creating fear of him amongst the other monks. The whole performance was deliberately engineered so that the monks who had been called to account for their actions would prefer to pay cash voluntarily for their misdemeanours rather than change their way of life. He was not mistaken in this supposition.

The monks themselves quickly perceived why this physician, who was so unconcerned for his own health, should be so preoccupied with theirs and though they appeased Wolsey with gifts, they all secretly wished that at some point this practice might lead to his undoing. Indeed, so objectionable and excessive was this power of Wolsey's, which

should have been based on regard for his devoutness, charity and good will, that the archbishop of Canterbury, William Warham warned the king about it. As soon as the latter heard of this he replied: "Indeed I know nothing of these matters. Nor should this be surprising, for if anything bad ever happens in a household, the head of the house is usually the last to hear about it. However, I beseech you, holy father, to go to Wolsey and recount all those things to him so that, if there has been some offence committed, he may be given the opportunity of putting the record straight himself."

The archbishop promptly carried out the king's wishes and visited Wolsey, remonstrating with in him in a brotherly manner about his conduct. He recounted the charges individually. First that each day religion and true devotion were being debased by the corrupt use of bribery for the forgiveness of sins, and that any payment received through such practice should in any case be given to the church and not to the individual who instigated the punishment. Also offenders should be punished with penalties suited to their misconduct so that an example will be set for others. And the general wellbeing of society would be improved if those who vehemently demanded penalties for crimes committed were not themselves tainted with even greater misdemeanours themselves – it being intolerable and inequitable that someone not free from sin himself should punish another. Such a travesty of justice offended against all the principles of virtuous living. And finally that the proving of wills of deceased persons was beyond his legatine power – even the pope himself did not exercise this right – and the bestowing of the estates of the gentry which came into the power of the church was not Wolsey's privilege, this ancient right having long since fallen into disuse in England.

Wolsey listened to these criticisms with considerable unease. He gave a short but somewhat ambiguous reply, perhaps because he felt that either way the truth would be open to misinterpretation, but more likely because he sensed that his evil practices had reached the ears of the king himself. However, as a result of his intervention in this matter, Wolsey's hatred for the archbishop of Canterbury grew greater still.

Another factor also contributed to a decline in Wolsey's harsh practices. Such was popular offence

The Imperial connection

In the middle of the fifteenth century the ruling families of Castile and Aragon were branches of the same Trastamara dynasty. Henry III of Castile (1388–1406) and Ferdinand I of Aragon (1412–1416) had been half-brothers. Henry's son, John II (1406–54) married twice, and the Castilian succession became uncertain. John was succeeded by his son through his first marriage, Henry V (1454–74), but Henry had no issue of undoubted legitimacy and by 1465 his heir was John's son through his second marriage, Prince Alfonso. However, Alfonso died in 1468, leaving his sister Isabella as the only survivor of the Castilian branch. This situation, which was confused by the fact that Henry IV had a daughter, Juana, who was generally thought to be illegitimate, was watched keenly by Ferdinand's son, John II of Aragon (1458–79). Immediately after Alfonso's death he despatched a diplomatic mission to Castile to suggest a marriage between Isabella and his own son, Ferdinand. Henry IV, who had accepted Isabella as his heir, agreed, and the marriage took place in 1469. No institutional union of the two kingdoms was provided for, and none took place, but when Henry IV died Ferdinand claimed a share of the Castilian succession as the only surviving male of the Trastamara line. It was then agreed that a form of dual sovereignty should apply in Castile, although when Ferdinand inherited Aragon in 1479, no such arrangement applied to that kingdom, Isabella being merely the queen-consort.

The joint rule of Ferninand II and Isabella, known as the Catholic Kings, had two major achievements. First, the centuries long *reconquista* was brought to an end by the conquest of the last Moorish principality, the Emirate of Granada, in 1491. Second, the foundations of Spain's immense empire in the New World were laid in the same year when the Genoese seaman Christopher Columbus, crossed the Atlantic and claimed his discoveries for his patrons and employers. However, the security of their success came to rest, once again, upon the knife-edge of dynastic chance. Isabella bore Ferdinand three daughters and one son who survived infancy, and their marriage strategy was carefully planned. Isabella, the eldest, married Alfonso of Portugal, strengthening the already close ties which bound the neighbouring kingdoms together. Catherine, the youngest, married Arthur, Prince of Wales, and in spite of Arthur's death the English alliance served Ferdinand well, particularly in the later part of his life. However, the most important bargain was struck with Maximilian of Austria, the Holy Roman Emperor, whose son Philip married their second daughter, Juana,

Above   Ferdinand of Aragon in council from a contemporary illustration made in Barcelona.

and whose daughter Margaret married their son Juan. Had Juan lived and begotten heirs of his own, the fragile unity of the Spanish crowns would have been preserved without great difficulty, but he died in 1497, and the succession immediately became contentious, so taht the death of Queen Isabella in 1504 provoked a crisis. Despite the fact that Ferdinand's own claim to Castile had been partly recognised in 1474, and in spite of all that they had jointly achieved, Isabella unquivocally bequeathed the crown to her eldest surviving child, Juana, ignoring her husband's rights. Ferdinand however, was not easily defeated. In 1505 he married the French princess Germaine de Foix, re-opening the possibility of a male heir and although Juana and her husband Philip were accepted as King and Queen in November of that year, Ferdinand retained control of Naples, and retreated there with his French wife.

at these injustices that John Allen, the head of the legatine court, was publicly accused of perpetrating, criminal acts by an upright and learned London priest called John. However, Allen suffered no more than the shame of public condemnation for his sins and, by the aid of his friends – clandestinely supported by his master Wolsey – he managed to escape any real danger. Nonetheless, by the very fact of these accusations it was sufficiently proven that the crimes with which the archbishop of Canterbury had charged Wolsey were in fact genuine. The king thus reprimanded Wolsey in the most severe language and thereafter he managed to restrain himself somewhat from indulging in such flagrant looting.

1516

After the death of Louis XII the new king of France, Francis I, had renewed the treaty with England in April 1515, but the goodwill did not last long. John Stewart, duke of Albany, cousin of James V of Scotland, returned to the north from France, and Henry's sister Margaret and her second husband the Earl of Angus were compelled to seek refuge in England.

This year the new league between the king and the French king was openly proclaimed through the city of London with a trumpet. This year also Margaret, queen of the Scots, wife of James IV killed at Flodden in the fifth year of the king's reign, and elder sister of the king, after the death of her late husband married Archibald Douglas, earl of Angus, without the consent of the king her brother or the council of Scotland, with which he was not well pleased. But after that there arose such strife between the lords of Scotland that she and her husband came into England like banished persons, and wrote to the king for mercy and comfort. The king, ever inclined to mercy, sent them clothing and vessels and all things necessary, wishing them to stay in Northumberland until they knew further of his wishes. And the queen was there delivered of a fair lady called Margaret, and all the country were commanded by the king to do them pleasure.

This year on 18 February at Greenwich was born a fair princess, and christened with great solemnity and named Mary.

This year the king of Aragon, the queen's father, died; a solemn obsequy was kept for him in the cathedral church of St Paul's.

The pre-reformation church

When Henry VIII came to the throne the Church appeared to be both powerful and stable. In many matters it was virtually independent of Rome. Its leaders were chosen primarily from men who had shown loyal service to the crown and who continued to be amenable to the king's wishes. The Church paid taxes to the crown, and the ecclesiastical courts and state acknowledged each others' jurisdiction. Although clerical privileges such as sanctuary occasionally aroused antagonism, particularly in legal circles, the worst abuses were gradually being restricted.

Relations with Rome were also stable. Litigants appealed to the Curia for redress of alleged failures in England's ecclesiastical courts, and petitioners sought dispensations from the pope on matters ranging from the holding of benefices in plurality to marriages within the prohibited degrees. The news of a papal election would be celebrated in London by a civic procession to St. Paul's to sing a *Te Deum*. Only the small surviving groups of Lollards remained hostile to Rome.

Hardcore anticlericalism had little support. The case of Richard Hun, a London merchant allegedly murdered for challenging ecclesiastical authority, created strong feelings at the time, but was a unique example. Most parishioners acknowledged their obligations to their church, and many also supported it voluntarily. There were numerous parish guilds, and substantial sums of money were devoted to church

Above   Martin Luther, the German reformer,

OPERIBVS CREDITE

building: the parish accounts of Louth in Lincolnshire record funding work on a new spire, and also record a parish celebration when it was complete in 1515.

However, with increasing literacy which extended to the artisan class, more people had access to religious literature, the largest single element in the publications of early English printers. Reading could not be separated from thinking about material, and the church authorities were never able to channel the spiritual enthusiasm and desire for personal religion that the texts aroused into practices which they regarded as safe. At the popular level, Lollard traditions of dissent dating from the early 15th century had never been entirely suppressed, and this is reflected in an increase in the level of persecution between 1500 and 1521.

The influence of Italian humanism began to penetrate the universities. Erasmus, the Dutch humanist and the greatest scholar of his day, taught for a time at Cambridge where bishop John Fisher also helped to found St. John's College. At Oxford, Corpus Christi College, founded by Richard Fox, bishop of Winchester and Cardinal College, founded by Wolsey and now Christ Church, were also intended to serve the new learning. Traditionalist reaction was exemplified by Richard Fitzjames, bishop of London, when he accused the dean of St. Paul's, whose preaching was strongly influenced by the new ideas, of heresy. This intellectual diversity was cause for debate when Lutheran ideas began to spread into England in the 1520s.

Above   Bishop Sherburne asking Henry VIII to confirm a religious charter in 1519.

Below   Richard Hun was imprisoned and later found hanged in his cell, for non-payment of a burial fee for his baby.

Attempts were made to modernize aspects of church life. Although monasticism no longer expressed the most urgent spiritual need as it had done in the early Middle Ages, the most austere orders such as the Carthusians and the Observant Franciscans were still attracting support. Their main problems, however, were financial and administrative, with a shortage of funds often leading to problems of fabric maintenance, problems exacerbated by the demands of royal taxation.

1517

Hostility against the alien merchant communities, and particularly the Flemings, had long been festering in the city of London. Towards the end of April 1517 this latent xenophobia was stirred up by the inflammatory preaching of certain friars, and on 1 May a large-scale riot, known as Evil May Day, resulted. The war with France had ended in 1514, and England was officially at peace with all her neighbours, a circumstance which made this demonstration particularly embarrassing.

This year there were great disturbances in the city of London caused by the apprentices, that is to say, those who serve the merchants for an agreed period to learn the trade. These apprentices had often been resentful of the foreign craftsmen and merchants, usually because they were envious of their skills in buying and selling, though according to Plato and Cicero we should all co-operate to help one another.

However, such sentiments of co-operation have sometimes even been condemned by the very men whose duty it is to teach the people the gospel and the laws of God. They have even preached from the pulpit views full of sedition, bewailing the shortages (especially in London) and saying that foreign merchants come from far and wide to steal the wealth and livelihood of our citizens. As a result, such ignorant fellows ruin the very commercial business which helps to make the products of any country in the world as readily available as if they were home-produced: wine for instance is not made in England yet the English nevertheless enjoy it in great abundance.

From amongst the ranks of these so-called scholars there were two particular monks, one a Dominican, the other the more usual kind. Though well-intentioned, they quickly stirred up the masses with their sermons, arguing that the damage and loss and various other misdemeanours done by the foreigners were no longer tolerable. The apprentices heard their evil counsel readily and soon after, at the instigation of one John Lincoln, they began to conspire together against the foreign workmen and merchants. Their plan was that, early in the morning on May Day, they would go out into the fields in the traditional manner and bring back leafy branches, thereby arousing no suspicions of what was to follow. They would then attack the foreigners and beat them up, killing some and depriving others of their wealth.

However, as they went about the city, murmuring and boasting that they would soon be avenged on the foreigners who had seized their livelihood and wronged them in other ways, their plans were exposed. As a result the foreign merchants sought the aid of the king and asked that he would protect them from injury. The king then summoned the mayor and the entire town council and commanded them to keep the apprentices in order and to take all possible steps to prevent the occurrence of any public disturbance. Consequently the council proclaimed that on the forthcoming May Day no apprentices or servants of any kind should be allowed out of doors before nine o'clock in the morning.

The anticipated civic unrest thus seemed to have been scotched when suddenly, at dawn on the day itself, an enormous band of apprentices and riverboatmen burst into the parish of St Martin's, where many craftsmen worked in cobbler's shops, and pillaged and plundered everything – beating all who resisted. When this was reported the mayor took action and ordered Thomas Howard, admiral of the fleet, to send in a large body of soldiers.

Meanwhile, the noise of the raving mob caused great anxiety among the other foreigners in the city who though barricaded in their houses, felt extremely threatened. However, the arrival of Howard's men soon calmed them as the apprentices, like sheep before a wolf, immediately scattered and hid themselves in fright.

At this point, Thomas, duke of Norfolk, George Talbot, earl of Shrewsbury, Thomas Docwra, a knight of Rhodes and prior of the order of St John, and George Neville, lord Bergavenny, all arrived and, having immediately sealed off all the roads in the area, started to take prisoners.

In the subsequent investigation it was established that John Lincoln has been the instigator of the wicked plot. He was in the country at the time, in order not to seem part of the conspiracy, but was none the less ordered to be arrested and imprisoned. This done and the disturbance quelled, a full judicial inquiry was opened regarding its origins.

As no blood had been shed during the upheaval it was decided that only those who had done the most damage or created the most violence should be punished and the rest should be pardoned. Those who suffered most were the men who had fallen in with the rabble by accident rather than by design and yet shared the same punishments. In consequence, John Lincoln and four of his associates were put to death, their dismembered bodies being hung on each of the city gates, and ten others were executed by hanging elsewhere. However, such was the offence to the citizens at seeing so many gallows erected throughout the city that they were taken down after 15 days. The remaining criminals who had not been condemned to death were made to suffer the indignity of having halters placed around their necks and being led in the greatest shame to Westminster where the king, sitting on his throne of judgement, granted them pardon when they all raised their hands in supplication.

However, the monks who had incited the crowd were spared any serious punishment, no doubt for religious reasons. At first they were imprisoned and later confined in church in order that they might learn prudence in their preaching and, instead of bringing dissension into the city, might learn to be an example to others.

Later on, all the property that had been taken during the upheaval and which had been found in the possession of the apprentices was restored to those who had lost it. Nevertheless, many of the foreigners remained terror-stricken and preferred to return to their own lands voluntarily, fearing that they might once more come up against the apprentices and their clubs, which they carried with them like swords.

1518

By the summer of 1518 the intricacies of Anglo-French diplomacy had again brought the two parties into line, and a new treaty was in prospect. This was partly designed to solve the problem of Tournai – in English hands since 1513 – and partly to form the basis for an ambitious scheme of general peace, which Wolsey and Henry were promoting for their own purposes.

On Monday 27 September the earl of Surrey, high admiral of England, in a coat of rich tissue cut on cloth of silver, on a great courser richly bedecked, and with a great whistle of gold set with stones and pearls hanging on a great and heavy chain like a baldrick, accompanied by 160 gentlemen richly dressed on goodly horses, came to Blackheath and there amiably received the ambassadors of France.

The young gallants of France had coats trimmed with one colour, cut in 10 or 12 parts very elaborately. And so all the Englishmen accompanied the Frenchmen, and lovingly together they rode to London. After the two admirals followed 24 of the French king's guard who accompanied 24 of the king's guard. And after them a great number of archers, to the number of 400 and in this order they passed through the city to the Tailor's Hall; there the chief ambassadors were lodged, and the rest in merchants' houses around. When these lords were in their lodgings, then the French traders opened their wares, and made the Tailor's Hall like a marketplace. Many of the Englishmen objected to this, but to no avail. On the last day of September the French ambassadors took barge and came to Greenwich. The admiral was in a gown of cloth of silver with a raised nap, trimmed with rich sables, and almost all his company were in a new fashion of garment called a chemise, which was in effect a gown, cut in the middle. The gentlemen of France were brought into the king's presence, where the bishop of Paris made a solemn oration. When this was ended and an answer made to it the king richly entertained the the admiral and his company, and so did all the English lords and gentlemen. While the ambassadors were in daily council at Greenwich the other gentlemen danced and passed the time in the queen's chamber with ladies and gentlewomen. After long discussion and much pleading by the French king and his council it was agreed that the city of Tournai should be delivered to the French king, him paying 600,000 crowns for the city and 400,000 crowns for the castle which the king had built, but it was not fully performed; and also he should pay 23,000 pounds Tournais, which sum the citizens of Tournai owed the king of England for their liberties and franchises.

When these conditions were fulfilled it was agreed that the city of Tournai should be delivered to the French king. The Frenchmen, the sooner to achieve their purpose, made a pretence of a marriage to be arranged between the dauphin, son and heir to the French king, and the Lady Mary the king's daughter, which was agreed upon this condition, that if they both consented when of lawful age then it should be firm and stable, and otherwise not for they were both very young. And so all matters were concluded, and the earl of Worcester and the bishop of Ely were appointed to go to France to deliver the city of Tournai and perform the other agreements. And to ensure payment of the sums of money to be paid to the King of England upon the said agreements four gentlemen of the realm of France were left in England as hostages: their names were Monsieur Montmorency, Monsieur Monpesart, Monsieur Moy, Monsieur Morret. Of these four the first two named were of noble blood, but the last two were only of mean houses. And because they were young there were older gentlemen appointed as governors to them.

In 1518 Wolsey brought off the biggest diplomatic coup of his career, a treaty binding over twenty European states, including France and the Empire, to perpetual peace and amity. This Treaty of London was, however, put under great strain in the following year by the election of Charles I of Spain as Holy Roman Emperor. In an effort to preserve his treaty, and his own and his master's prestige, Wolsey set up meetings between Henry and Charles, and then between Henry and Francis I of France, which took place in May and June 1520. The latter was planned and carried out as a great renaissance festival, which became known as the Field of Cloth of Gold. A central feature of the celebrations was the tilting. This letter from the earl of Worcester to Henry VIII, concerns the preparations for the tilt.

May it please your excellent highness to be informed that Marshal Chastillon and I, with variious carpenters of both your majesty's and the king of France's service, have examined the ground for the camp in both length and width. You will recall that this site was chosen by myself and the aforementioned Chastillon and I wrote to you concerning it. You then sent me via Clarenceux a plan for the tilt and, as I mentioned, the site is indeed suitable.

However, we find from the said plan that the tilt is to be 208 feet from the pavilion where the queen and ladies will stand and 88 feet from the pavilion on the far side of the field which faces the queen's pavillion. This the aforementioned Lord Chastillon and myself, together with others here, think is not practicable because the queen and her ladies will not have a good view of those running at the tilt since they will be 208 feet away from where they stand. thus we have decided, if it please your grace, that it would be better to place the tilt right in the middle of the camp.

The place your grace has allocated for fighting on foot is fine where it is and we hope, and so do all

European Diplomacy

Europe had been unstable since 1494, when Charles VIII of France had invaded Italy. After Charles' death in 1498, Louis XII, the Holy Roman Emperor Maximilian I, and the Spanish rulers Ferdinand and Isabella sought to exploit the rivalries of Milan, Florence and Genoa for their own purposes. England, geographically on the edge of Europe, had no direct interest in these struggles; and Henry VII, naturally cautious and concerned to establish his own position, avoided all entanglements which did not affect the security of his throne. However, traditional English distrust for France led him to establish a naval base at Portsmouth in 1496 and, more significantly, to arrange a diplomatic marriage for his son Arthur, Prince of Wales, with Catherine of Aragon, the younger daughter of Ferdinand and Isabella. Catherine's elder sister, Juana, was already married to Maximilian's son, the Archduke Philip, and her son, Charles would eventually succeed both his grandfathers, becoming Charles I of Spain in 1516 and the Emperor Charles V in 1519.

England became more aggressive when Henry VIII succeeded his father in 1509, and a desire for glory superseded caution as the main characteristic of royal policy. Although Henry enjoyed the active support of his military aristocracy, who nurtured nostalgic

fantasies about past triumphs, and fretted to recover their favourite occupation, the men who had served his father initially tried to put a curb on the new king's impetuosity. During the first decade of Henry VIII's reign there was continual tension between the doves and the hawks in the king's council, but it was the signing of the Holy League against France in October 1511 which first persuaded the clerical doves to war on the Pope's behalf. The subsequent campaigns of 1512 and 1513 enjoyed some success, including the capture of Tournai, the battle of the Spurs, and a decisive victory against France's Scottish allies at Flodden. However, in spite of Wolsey's efficient planning, financial difficulties rapidly began to mount, and a peace settlement was reached in 1514, which involved the marriage of Henry's sister Mary to Louis VII.

In 1515 Francis I succeeded Louis as king of France, and Mary returned to England as the bride of the duke of Suffolk. Francis renewed the war in Italy, winning a decisive victory at Marignano in the same year. In 1516 Ferdinand II of Spain died, and his successor Charles was less inclined to continue hostilities. At the same time Pope Leo X, who had succeeded Julius II in 1513, was also more peaceful than his predecessor, and perhaps more concerned with defending Christendom against the threat from Islam. In 1518, after intense diplomatic activity, France, the Empire, the Papacy, Spain, England and over twenty lesser powers signed the Treaty of London, which provided that, if any party to it committed aggression against another, the remainder would assist the victim.

Above   Henry's great rival Francis I of France surrounded by his children and court.

Below left   Francis in his splendour as he liked the world to see him.

Below   The French army was heavily defeated by Charles V the Holy Roman Emperor at Pavia in 1525, and Francis was captured.

your skilled craftsmen, that you and the queen and ladies will be pleased with the finished result and that all the partitions and railings will be satisfactory and that there will be a good view of the sport.

However, the marshal and everyone who has looked at the plan thinks that the little ditch which your grace has indicated to run alongside each of the pavilions will do rather more harm than good, for if it should happen to rain then it will damage the foundations on both sides. Also, in order to make it, it will be a great effort to carry all the earth out of the site, and this will also take a long time. In addition, it will be impossible to take the earth across the field itself as this would make the surface uneven thus making it difficult to gallop and control the horses properly.

As an alternative, it was thought that a railing situated 8 feet from the pavilion to keep the people away would serve just as well, for a ditch 4 feet deep and 8 feet wide is really no deterrent if evil persons were so disposed to any evil deeds, which I trust to God will not be the case.

Also, Marshal Chastillon informed me that he thought the tilt would be on firmer ground if it were set up at the Ardes end of the camp rather than where I had intended it to be, at the Guisnes end. For in the latter place the ground is not good, nor could it be made so by a thousand men if they worked for a month. In this I was in agreement with him and in the end resolved the matter by suggesting that the course should be extended by 50 feet in the direction of Ardes, to be sure that the ground was good and firm, and he was happy with this.

He then suggested that the barrier for the feats of arms performed on foot should also be constructed at the Ardes end, where your grace had planned the tiltyard to be, and that both should be in the same place, the barrier being removed each night and the tiltyard prepared anew each morning.

I replied that I didn't want to move it from its appointed position, and I saw no reason for changing your grace's plans in this regard and that the tiltyard and the barrier area would be fine as they were, especially if, as above mentioned, the tiltyard itself was placed centrally in the middle of the field.

His answer to this was that it would make little difference to your grace where the barrier area was situated as the whole camp was laid out according to

your grace's wishes, and if I would just write to you about this then he would be satisfied.

I told him that I would not write to your grace about this as I already knew your mind on the matter, but concerning the little ditch and moving the tiltyard so that it was equally placed between the two pavilions, as outlined above, I would write to discover what was your pleasure. With this answer he seemed content and thus departed, and if this all accords with the wishes of your grace then it will be carried out accordingly and I am sure the lord Chastillon will be satisfied with it.

Therefore I most humbly beseech your grace to let me know your opinion and pleasure concerning these matters, for until I have your reply I will put nothing in motion. Everything else has been diligently looked into by both parties and all are agreed – the lord Chastillon, myself and the builders – in all things, except on these two issues.

However, I have my reservations that it will be possible to finish all the pavilions by the day appointed; but, that said, I can assure your grace that very effort possible will be made – to the limit of my small power and with the aid of God, to whom I pray to give your most excellent highness a long and victorious life – to carry out your most noble desires.

From your town of Calais the 19th day of May.

1519

Searching for increased privacy in the latter part of his reign, Henry VII had created a new intimate service department called the "Privy Chamber". After Henry's accession he began to appoint his young noble and gentle friends to the Privy Chamber, and to call them after the French fashion "Gentlemen of the Privy Chamber". By 1519 the influence of these minions over the king was beginning to cause alarm among his senior councillors.

In the beginning of this year the king, with all the knights of his order of St George who were in England, rode on double horses, with the squires following the king, from Colbrook to Windsor, in gorgeous apparel, and there he kept with great solemnity the feast of St George and dined in the hall. And the bishop of Winchester, prelate of the order, sat at the end of the table alone. And the king was solemnly served and the cloth spread as at a coronation feast. All things were plentiful for strangers who resorted there. At the Requiem Mass were offered the banner and other hatchments of honour

The Field of Cloth of Gold

Thomas Wolsey, the lord chancellor, was anxious to create a new order in Europe, and in October 1518, after months of careful negotiation, he secured a new Anglo-French relationship and invited the other European powers to join a long-lasting non-aggression treaty. The great majority did so, including Spain and the Holy Roman Empire, but less than a year later the scheme created by this Treaty of London was threatened with total collapse when Charles I of Spain was elected to be Holy Roman Emperor, Charles V.

Wolsey, in an attempt to preserve his achievement and the prestige it conferred on him and his master, arranged two summit meetings: between Henry and the new emperor, and between Henry and Francis I of France. Charles visited England briefly in late May 1520, on his way from Spain to the Netherlands. His meeting with Henry was cordial, but inconclusive, and the two men agreed to meet again in the following year.

Within days of the emperor's departure, Henry was in Calais preparing for his meeting with Francis. Accompanied by his queen, Catherine and more than 5,000 attendants, he was determined to impress, regardless of cost or effort. The meeting-place was near Ardres, within France but on the borders of Calais. On the chosen ground he erected a huge temporary palace of timber and canvas, surrounded by pavilions, galleries and tilting grounds. Hundreds of pounds worth of velvet, satin, cloth of gold and other luxurious fabrics were shipped across for the courtiers' liveries and for furnishings and hangings of all kinds. Not to be outdone, Francis replied with a sumptuous retinue and city of tents. It was a massive display of conspicuous consumption, and caught the imagination of contemporaries and historians alike.

On 5 June there was a stage-managed meeting between two monarchs, but the lavish festivities and sporting competitions which followed gave little opportunity for any real political understanding. Despite much talk of brotherhood, and a number of carefully displayed exhibitions of mutual trust, when the celebrations came to an end on 23 June, it is doubtful whether either the kings or their courtiers were any closer. A Venetian observer declared that Francis and Henry hated each other. It was nevertheless an achievement that two such ancient enemies had met in more or less friendly competition instead of in battle and at the same time Henry had defended his honour as effectively as by a striking victory.

The amity created by the Field of Cloth of Gold lasted about 18 months. Charles V, who cared nothing for Wolsey's priorities, kept up his pressure for an anti-French alliance and eventually succeeded in his objective in November 1521. By the time he returned to England for his second promised visit, in May 1522, he had obtained Henry's full commitment to war. Wolsey had gained no more than a year's delay. In August 1523 another English army landed in France, not to joust this time but to wage battle.

Below   The embarkation of the king and his court at Dover as they prepared to cross to Boulogne in 1520 on the way to the Field of the Cloth of Gold.

Above   Henry and Cardinal Wolsey arriving in procession at the Field of the Cloth of Gold. An eye-witness called the meeting the ''eighth wonder of the world''.

Right and far right   Drawing of tents as they were planned for Henry's encampment and how they finally looked.

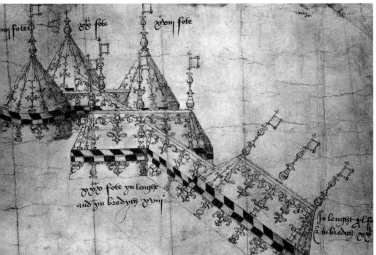

belonging to the late Emperor Maximillian. After this feast ended the king came to Richmond, and so to Greenwich and there stayed all of May.

In that month the king's council secretly discussed together the king's kindness and liberality to all persons; by which they saw that certain young men in his Privy Chamber, regardless of his estate and degree were so familiar and at home with him and played such jokes with him that they forgot themselves. Which things, although the king because of his gentle nature suffered them and neither rebuked nor reproved them, yet the king's council thought it not fit to be allowed for the king's honour; and therefore they all together came to the king, beseeching him to redress all these enormities and this lightness. The king answered them that he had chosen them for his council, both for the maintenance of his honour and defence against all things which might blemish it; therefore if they saw any about him misbehave themselves, he committed it to their reformation. Then the king's council caused the lord chamberlain to call before them [Nicholas] Carew (and another who is still alive and therefore shall not at this time be named) with several others also of the Privy Chamber who had been in the French court, and banished them from the court for various reasons, laying nothing particular to their charge. Those who had offices were commanded to go to them; which dismissal from the court sorely grieved the hearts of these young men who were called the king's minions. Then four grave and elderly knights were put into the King's Privy Chamber, namely Sir Richard Wingfield, Sir Richard Jerningham, Sir Richard Weston and Sir William Kingston; and several officers were changed in all places.

Then Sir John Pechey was made deputy of Calais in place of Sir Richard Wingfield, and Nicholas Carew made captain of Ricebanke, and ordered to go there, which much displeased him. These young minions who were separated from the king had been in France, and so highly praised the French king and his court that in a way they thought little of the king and his court in comparison, they were so much in love with the French court, therefore their fall was little mourned among wise men.

1520

By the end of the previous year Henry and Wolsey were striving to maintain the general peace achieved at the Treaty of London. The new Holy Roman Emperor, Charles V, was trying to break it down, and Wolsey arranged meetings between Henry and the Emperor, and Henry and Francis I, both in 1520. The latter was to be one of the most celebrated competitions of display in the whole century.

On Monday 21 May in the seventh year of the reign of our sovereign lord, Henry VIII, the king left Greenwich for Otford, where he stayed the night. On Tuesday he reached Ledde, then Charing on Wednesday and on Thursday was at Canterbury where His Grace remained all that week and the whole week following until the Emperor landed at Dover on the Saturday.

Accompanying the Emperor was the queen of Aragon and a number of nobles, all of whom were received by the lord cardinal and various other dignitaries at the seafront and conducted to Dover Castle at ten o'clock at night by torchlight, where they rested the night. Once at the castle, Sir Edward Ponynge, then lord warden of the cinq ports, presented the keys of the castle to the emperor, who in turn, like a true prince, said he would not accept them as he knew well that he was in no danger and was as safe there as he would be in his own kingdom. That same night, about two o'clock in the morning, King Henry arrived in Dover by torchlight and as soon as the emperor heard of his coming he got out of bed and greeted the king at the top of the staircase where each embraced the other warmly. It was a sight most pleasing to see these two princes talking so familiarly and at such length, the king always with the emperor at his right hand.

On the following day, which was Whitsunday, the king and the emperor, together with all their retinue, rode to Canterbury, Thomas Stanley, earl of Derby, riding between the two princes brandishing a sword as the king had commanded. In this manner they arrived at Canterbury and proceeded to Christchurch Cathedral where they were met by the archbishop of Canterbury. They then joined a procession and both the king and the emperor went under a canopy into St Thomas's shrine where they said their prayers and made their offerings to the blessed saint.

This done, the king and the emperor departed for the bishop's palace where the queen of England met the emperor at the door. After this, the king and the emperor rested themselves and then went to high mass where first the emperor then the king made his offerings and then each returned to his separate box-pew. When this had been completed they went in to dinner which was served to a fanfare of the emperor's trumpets rather than the king's.

On the following Monday at nine o'clock in the evening there was a great banquet which continued until three o'clock the next morning. At this banquet the king, queen and emperor all washed together, Edward Stafford, the duke of Buckingham providing the water and Charles Brandon, the duke of Suffolk holding the towel. The next to wash were the lord cardinal, the French queen Mary and the queen of Aragon.

At the table itself everything was in proper order: the king sat on the emperor's left hand, next to him was the French queen and on the other side of the her was the lord cardinal and the queen of Aragon. The food was served by the emperor's own carvers, stewards and cupbearers and the noble company passed the night in great merriment and pleasure.

On Tuesday their highnesses left Canterbury and the emperor accompanied the Queen on horseback to Dover. He then continued on with the king till they reached the Downs where they parted company, the emperor proceeding to Sandwich where a great number of ships from his fleet were moored. The king meanwhile returned to Dover where he remained that night and all day Wednesday, sailing to Calais on Thursday, where he stayed for a further six days.

Thursday 8 June being Corpus Christi day, Henry and the French king Francis I, met in a valley called the Golden Dale which lay midway between Guisnes and Arde where the French king had been staying. In this valley Henry pitched his marquee made of cloth of gold near where a banquet had been prepared. His Grace was accompanied by 500 horsemen and 3,000 foot-soldiers, and the French king had a similar number of each.

When the two great princes met, proclamations were made by the heralds and officers-of-arms of both parties, to the effect that everyone should stand absolutely still – the king of England and his company or one side of the valley and the king of France with his retinue on the other. They were commanded to stand thus, completely still, on pain of death whilst the two kings rode down the valley. At the bottom of the valley they embraced each other in great friendship and then, dismounting, embraced each other again, taking off their hats. Henry's sword was held, unsheathed, by the marquess of Dorset whilst the duc de Bourbon bore the French king's sword similarly all the while.

After this had continued for a little time, twenty of the noblest men of both kingdoms came to wait on their highnesses in the marquee. The meeting of both these parties was itself a very honourable affair: on Henry's side there were the duke of Buckingham, Charles Brandon, the duke of Suffolk, Henry Algernon Percy, earl of Northumberland, Henry Courtenay, earl of Devonshire and six others from the noblest families in England. And on the French side there were the king of Navarre, the duc D'Alencon, the duc de Vendôme, the duc de Lorraine, the comte de St Pole, monsieur de Guys, grand senechal de Normandie and admiral de la Tremoulle amongst others. Each party saluted the other with perfect decorum. When their Royal Highnesses had both eaten and drunk their fill they departed, the French king to Arde and King Henry to Guisnes.

On Friday 9 June the two kings met at the camp where a tiltyard had been set up with a pretty green tree with damask leaves nearby. On Saturday two shields bearing the arms of the two kings were hung upon this tree and a proclamation made to the effect that anyone who intended to attend the royal jousts and compete in feats of arms – such as running at the tilt, fighting tourneys on horseback and fighting on foot at the barriers with swords should bring their shields of arms and have their names entered into the records kept by Clarencieux and Lancaster, officers-at-arms. Challengers at these royal jousts were the king of England, the king of France, the duke of Suffolk, the marquess of Dorset, sir William Kingeston, sir Richard Jermingham and Nicholas Carew and Anthony Knevett with their aides. Also present were monsieur de Vendôme and various other French nobles.

On Sunday 11 June the French king came to Guisnes to dine with the queen of England and was graciously received by the lord cardinal, the duke of Buckingham, the duke of Suffolk, the earl of Northumberland and various other noblemen, together with a large number of ladies and gentlemen all richly dressed in cloth of gold, velvet and silks. That day too the French king was himself magnificently dressed in tissue-cloth set with precious stones and pearls.

When dinner was over, some time was spent dancing in the banqueting hall. Before he started to dance the French king went from one end of the room to the other, carrying his hat in his hand and kissing all the ladies on both sides – except for four or five who were too old and ugly. He then returned to the queen and spoke with her for a while before spending the rest of the day dancing.

At the same moment King Henry was dining with the French queen at Arde where he spent the time in a similar manner until seven o'clock in the evening when he returned to Guisnes and the French king likewise returned to Arde.

On Monday 12 June both kings and their men-at-arms met at the aforementioned camp. Also present were the queen of England and the queen of France, wife of Francis I with her ladies-in-waiting – all riding in litters and sedan chairs covered in sumptuous embroidery. Some other ladies also arrived mounted on richly decorated palfreys.

Then the two kings with their teams of challenges and their sides entered the field, every one fully armed and magnificently dressed. The French king started the jousts and did extremely well, even though the first lance was broken by King Henry, who managed to break one on each charge. The French king broke a good number of lances but not as many as Henry. The defenders on this day were a fine company drawn from the followers of Monsieur duc de Vendôme and the lord admiral of France. Well armed and handsomely dressed in cloth of gold decorated with a plume motif they acquitted themselves well on the field and then departed.

On Tuesday 13 June the kings and their companions again entered the field where they met a number of other noble challengers. And on this day, in the presence of both monarchs, there was a contest between an Englishman and a Breton, in which the Frenchman had suffered a terrible blow and the Englishman emerged unscathed.

Thursday 20 June saw Henry in the field again, fully armoured and challenging all comers. Opponents that day included two French noblemen with their men-at-arms, all well-mounted and finely dressed, who acquitted themselves well. On Friday 16 June there was no contest at the camp because of a tremendous gale. On Saturday both kings entered the field and king Henry's armour-skirt and horse-trapper were decorated with 2,000 ounces of gold and 1,100 huge pearls, the price of which was incalculable, the earl of Devonshire also appeared that

The end of the Tudor line?

England had no law of succession. With no heir, the inheritance of the Crown was uncertain, and during the Wars of the Roses the throne had passed to the strongest who could make a plausible claim – namely Edward IV, Richard III and Henry VII.

Tudor historians saw the wars as God's judgement for the deposition of a consecrated king, Richard II, and regarded the new Tudor dynasty as an instrument for reconciling feuds and restoring order. Their views provided justification for the Tudors' presence and their autocratic rule, but left a legacy of fear that troubles would recur if the succession was insecure. By the 1520s, this insecurity was apparent.

Henry VIII was the only survivor of his father's three sons, and although his wife, Catherine of Aragon had numerous pregnancies, most ended in miscarriages, stillbirths or death on delivery. Only Mary, born in 1516, survived beyond infancy, and after 1518 Catherine did not become pregnant again.

England had never had a female ruler, and fear of the possible consequences made Henry suspicious of any family of royal blood. Edmund de la Pole, earl of

Suffolk, the son of Edward IV's sister, Elizabeth, was first exiled, then imprisoned, and finally executed in 1513. Edward Stafford, 3rd duke of Buckingham, a descendant of Edward III's youngest son, Thomas of Woodstock, and the most powerful magnate in England, was sent to the scaffold in 1521 on a dubious charge of treason.

There was no prospect of a male heir as long as Catherine remained queen. If Mary succeeded to the throne, effective power would be in the hands of her husband. To choose her partner from the English nobility would give rise to intolerable factional jealousy. To select a foreign bridegroom of the appropriate rank such as Francis, dauphin of France, James V of Scotland, or the Holy Roman Emperor Charles V, would run the risk of subjecting English interests to those of another power.

An alternative scheme was for Henry to legitimize his bastard son by his early mistress Elizabeth Blount; the boy, Henry Fitzroy, was created 1st duke of Richmond in 1525. The title was significant: Henry VII had been the second earl of that creation before his victory at Bosworth. The plan, however, was impractical. If the throne was to pass to an heir of the king's line, he would have to be from a lawful marriage. The only possibility for Henry was to replace Catherine.

Above   Princess Mary.

Below   ''The Succession of Henry VIII'', painted in Elizabeth's reign show Mary and Philip followed by Mars, the god of war, and Elizabeth followed by Flora holding the fruits of prosperity. Edward VI kneels beside his father.

day wearing cloth of gold, tissue-cloth and cloth of silver, all elaborately embroidered, with his retinue wearing the same uniform.

When the French king and the earl of Devonshire charged at each other, so fierce was their encounter that both their lances broke. In all they ran off eight times, during which the French king broke three lances while the earl broke two lances and the French king's nose. The rest of his men completed their jousts and then lord Edmund Howard and his men appeared in suitable finery to finish the contest.

On Sunday 18 June the French king and some of his men suddenly entered the castle at Guisnes where they met King Henry in the middle of the great courtyard. This was all a ceremony betokening mutual trust and when both had warmly embraced, with their hats off, the French king declared: "I have come into your castle stronghold to yield myself up to you as your prisoner, should you so wish it." The king of England's reply was to place the French king on his right hand and lead him to the new banqueting hall where they passed the rest of the day. That evening the French king again dined with the English queen and Henry, wearing a mask, rode over to Arde to dine with the French queen, returning later still wearing the mask.

On the 19th June the two kings appeared at the camp as they had done on previous days. Every contestant from both parties, challengers and defenders, performed to the best of his ability, but the general opinion was that the duke of Suffolk had been the best that day, as he had been on many previous occasions and would have certainly continued to do so had his hand not been injured in an accident.

On Wednesday 21 June the earl of Devonshire and lord Howard appeared with their entourages and fought well, both defenders and challengers being highly praised. And on Friday the 23 all the noble parties above mentioned came into the camp to see the fighting at the barriers in which both Englishmen and Frenchmen gave good account of themselves.

On Saturday 23 June a large and well-appointed chapel was set up in the grounds, decorated with ornate hangings and filled with statues of saints and holy relics. Later the lord cardinal said mass in the chapel – which has been built and fitted out entirely at king Henry's expense. During the service the chaplains of both kings took it in turns to sing the refrains, which was heavenly to listen to. The mass completed, the kings and queens, together with their noble retinues, proceeded to the gallery beside the chapel to dine in great style.

Dinner over, the two kings and their companions, challengers as well as defenders, returned once more to the camp to officially close the contest.

On this Sunday the French king dined with the queen of England at Guisnes in the company of 28 lords and even more ladies and ladies-in-waiting – all with face-masks covering up their features. Likewise King Henry dined with the queen of France at Arde with 40 lords, ladies and ladies-in-waiting, notably his own sister Mary, the queen dowager of France, whom the duc de Bourbon desired and who could be seen filling her goblet with great grace and politeness. And equally everyone was dressed in masking clothes made of tissue-cloth, cloth of gold and cloth of silver.

At about 5 o'clock in the afternoon, Henry had left the queen of France and was riding towards Guisnes in his masking gear when just outside Guisnes itself he came across the French king, also in a mask, and neither recognized the other. However, the French king did nonetheless remove his hat until he had passed all the masked company of Englishmen, whereupon both kings turned their horses around and talked for a while.

In spite of the apparent amity of these meetings and celebrations, they achieved nothing for the stability of Anglo-French relations. As soon as he had parted from Francis, Henry returned to Calais, and then proceeded to Gravelines for another meeting with the Emperor. It was agreed that Charles would visit England again in the following year.

1521

Edward Stafford, duke of Buckingham, was a remote kinsman of the king by descent from Thomas of Woodstock, the youngest son of Edward III, and was related by marriage to the Percys, the Poles and the Howards. He was a powerful nobleman of the old school, with great estates and many retainers. By the end of 1520 Henry had become deeply suspicious of him, having discovered via Wolsey that the duke had made a number of rash statements about his proximity to the throne. This was a subject about which Henry had become acutely sensitive because of his lack of a legitimate son.

At about this time investigations were being carried

out in the various shires concerning the activities of Edward, duke of Buckingham who had been imprisoned in the Tower of London. He had been incarcerated there after being indicted for high treason following public statements he had made in Bletchingly to Lord Abergavenny. Lord Abergavenny had himself also been arrested for conspiracy along with the king's cousin, Lord Montague. Both had been sent to the Tower of London and Sir Edward Nevell had been banned from court.

The duke of Norfolk was to hear the appeals of peers of the realm, judge their claims, etc. And so, shortly after the incarceration a platform was erected in the great hall of Westminster for the peers of the realm and a place set apart and railed off for the adjudicator to sit in. The chief justice was the duke of Norfolk and many other peers sat as judges on the duke of Buckingham.

When the lords had taken their places, Sir Thomas Lovell and Sir Richard Chomley brought the accused duke to the bar of the court. Here, with the executioner's axe from the tower in front of him, he removed his hat and humbly made due reverence to the duke of Norfolk and then to all the assembled lords and the king's learned council. Then the clerk of the council said: "Sir Edward, duke of Buckingham, hold up thy hand. Thou art indicted for high treason, having traitorously conspired and plotted to shorten the life of our sovereign lord, the king. How will you be tried for this treason?" The duke answered: "By my fellow peers."

When the indictment had been read to the court the duke said: "It is false and untrue, and has been deliberately forged to bring about my death. And this I will prove." He then proceeded to give many arguments to show the falsity of the indictment. However, against his arguments the king's attorney produced the sworn testimony and confessions of a number of witnesses.

The duke of Norfolk asked for the witnesses to be brought forward, which was duly done. His first accuser was his own chancellor, Sir Gilbert Perke, a priest, and the duke's personal confessor, John Delacourt even produced a testimonial in his own handwriting condemning the duke. Charles Knevett esquire, the duke's cousin, and a monk – the prior of the Charterhouse near Bath – also accused him hypocritically, having themselves incited the duke to treason, and on a number of occasions had said that

he should be king of England. But the duke denied that he had ever entertained the idea. The depositions were read out and, that done, the witnesses were led away to be imprisoned in the Tower.

Then the duke of Norfolk spoke: "My lord, the king our sovereign lord has commanded that his laws should be administered with the utmost righteousness with regard to your case. Thus if there is anything further you would like to say in your defence then you may say it. As nothing further was said, he then ordered the prisoner to be taken away and he was accordingly led off to a house named Paradise.

The assembled lords then went off to discuss the matter for a considerable time and later returned to their places. Then the duke of Norfolk said to the duke of Suffolk: "What is your verdict on the duke of Buckingham and the indictment for high treason?" The duke of Suffolk answered: "He is guilty," and so said the marquess and all the other earls and lords. And thus the duke of Buckingham was found guilty of high treason by a duke, a marquess, seven earls and twelve barons.

The duke was then brought back to the bar of the court, sweating profusely and considerably agitated. After he had made due obeisance, he calmed for a while. The duke of Norfolk in his role of presiding officer said: "Sir Edward, you have heard how you have been indicted for high treason. You pleaded not guilty to this charge, asking to be judged by your fellow peers of the realm, who have found you guilty." Then the duke of Norfolk wept and said: "You shall be led from this place to the king's prison and then taken to the place of execution. There you will be hanged, cut down while still alive, your limbs amputated and cast into the flames, your bowels burnt before you, your head smitten off and your body quartered and divided, by the king's will. May God have mercy on your soul. Amen."

The duke of Buckingham then said: "You have spoken to me as you would to a traitor, yet I never was one. But, my lords, I do not blame you for what you have done to me; and may eternal God forgive you for my death, as I do. I shall not plead with the king to spare my life, though he is surely a gracious prince and more grace comes from him than I could possibly desire. I beg you, my lords and all my friends, to pray for me."

Then the edge of the axe was turned towards him

and he was led off to a barge on the river outside. Sir Thomas Lovell asked him to sit on the cushions and carpet provided but he said; "No, for when I went to Westminster I was duke of Buckingham, but now I am just plain Edward Bowhen, the most despicable villain in the world."

And in this manner they arrived at the Temple, where he was received by Sir Nicholas Vawse and Sir William Sandes, bannerets, who led him through the city. And as they went they asked the people to pray for him, and many wept and lamented, saying: "This is the end of an evil life. God forgive him, for he was a proud prince. It is a pity that he behaved in such a manner against his king and liège lord, whom God preserve." In this way he was brought to the Tower, a broken man, at about four o'clock.

On Friday 17 May at about eleven o'clock, the duke was delivered up to John Kyeme and John Ske-vyngton, sheriffs, who led him to the scaffold on Tower Hill. Here he declared that he had offended the king's majesty through negligence and lack of grace and urged all noblemen to take his example as a warning. And he asked all to pray for him and said that he believed he went to his death as the king's devoted subject. In this manner he meekly received the axe, and on his soul may Jesus have mercy.

Then the Augustine friars took his body and head and buried them. Alas that truth should have have deserted such a noble man, that he should not have been in allegiance to his king as was his duty. Such is the end of ambition, of false prophecies, of evil life and of evil advice.

1522

A new Anglo-Imperial treaty was signed, binding England to war with France in the summer of 1522. Wolsey then attempted to use this Treaty of Bruges to extract concessions from the French, and the Emperor began to fear that England would renege on its obligations. In March he sent an embassy to England to find out what was happening, and was reassured.

On the night of Shrove Tuesday, the king's cardinal and the visiting ambassadors had supper, and after supper they entered a great chamber hung with Arras cloth. At the lower end of this chamber was a castle which had a main tower housing a burning cresset and two minor towers, both battlemented. On each tower flew a banner: one of three broken hearts; one showing a lady's hand holding man's

The nobles

The wealthiest and most powerful subjects held their Crown lands by military tenure, and considered their relationship with the king to be one of unwritten contract. Only the monarch could create or promote a peer. However, although the judicial process of attainder was required to unmake a noble, the law offered little protection to anyone who incurred the king's wrath.

When Henry destroyed Edward Stafford, 3rd duke of Buckingham, in 1521, without provoking armed resistance, or even adverse political reaction from Stafford's fellow peers, the king's ascendancy was sufficiently demonstrated. Henry was of a naturally suspicious turn of mind, but the circumstances which might arouse his suspicions were unpredictable. The duke of Buckingham was certainly guilty of extreme clumsiness when he pressed his claim to the hereditary Constableship of England, against Henry's express wish, and drew attention to his royal lineage at a time when the succession was in serious doubt.

Edmund de la Pole, earl of Suffolk, had also died, in 1513, because of his proximity to the throne, but others of Yorkist blood had survived unscathed, and were even in favour in court, until the king was reminded of the threat they could still represent. Henry Courtenay,

promoted marquess of Exeter in 1525, and Henry Pole, Lord Montague, drew attention to themselves by their opposition to the king's marriage to Anne Boleyn, though it was their Plantagenet connections rather than any acts of treason which brought them to the block in 1538. The same was true of Margaret Pole, daughter of George, duke of Clarence, Edward IV's brother. She was restored in blood in 1514, and became countess of Salisbury in her own right. But she sympathized strongly with Catherine of Aragon. Imprisoned in 1538, she was executed in 1541.

At the same time, Henry was more generous than his father in granting peerage titles, and with the rewards of land and office. The spate of creations that promoted the warriors of the 1513 French war included two dukes; Thomas Howard, earl of Surrey, recovered the family title of Norfolk as 2nd duke, and Charles Brandon became 1st duke of Suffolk. In 1525 more creations accompanied the elevation of the king's illegitimate son, Henry FitzRoy to the dukedom of Richmond. Thomas Manners, Lord Ros, became earl of Rutland; Henry, Lord Clifford, became earl of Cumberland; Robert Radcliffe became Viscount FitzWalter; and Sir Thomas Boleyn, Viscount Rochford. The brothers of two of Henry's later queens were also made nobles. Jane Seymour's brother Edward became earl of Hertford in 1537, and William Parr, the brother of Catherine, was created earl of Essex in 1543. Although by 1547 over half the contemporary peerages were of Henry's own creation, this was achieved without any particular hostility between new and old peers. The overall size of the group remained the same, at about 50 families, and in fact its average wealth increased.

The semi-independence of the old-style magnates disappeared. The Howards remained dominant in Norfolk until the attainder of the 3rd duke in 1546, but Henry moved the duke of Suffolk from place to place in accordance with his whim and convenience. He was given estates in the marches of Wales when the king wished to increase his influence there, and was compelled to surrender lands in East Anglia and accept others in Lincolnshire. The most autonomous of all the old noble families was that of Percy, headed by the earl of Northumberland, but the king achieved such a personal ascendancy over him that when the 6th earl died he made the Crown his heir.

Henry used his peers in high office – Norfolk was lord treasurer for many years – and compelled them to look to office and the court to maintain their positions; great fortunes were made, or secured, only in close proximity to the king. The fierce competition for monastic land in the 1540s reinforced this truth: no nobleman was too proud to enter, along with gentlemen and others, the competitive petitioning which redistributed about 20

Above   Caister Castle in Norfolk, built by Sir John Falstoff, was one of the first brick-built castles.

Left   The windows and parapets of Marney Tower in Essex have renaissance style terracotta decoration.

per cent of the country's landed wealth between 1540 and 1553. The king also used his peers in war, and many of them owed their elevation to their traditional expertise. Henry's appetite for chivalric romances and feats of arms helped to reconcile many nobles to his radical policies.

Both Henry's great ministers, Thomas Wolsey and Thomas Cromwell, strove to increase the king's direct influence in the provinces, and this was inevitably achieved at the expense of the informal networks traditionally operated by the nobility. ''We will not be bound of a necessity to be served with lords'', Henry declared after the Pilgrimage of Grace in 1537, ''but we will be served with such men of what degree soever as we shall appoint to the same''. He reorganized his council, strengthened the position of office holders, and excluded most of those magnates who had been accustomed to attend on a casual basis. However, because many office holders were noblemen, the changes were not seen to be anti-aristocratic.

heart; and the third depicting a lady's hand turning a man's heart. This castle was occupied by ladies with strange names: Beauty, Honour, Perseverance, Kindness, Constancy, Bounty, Mercy and Pity. All eight ladies wore Milan-point lace gowns made of white satin and each had her name embroidered in gold on her headgear and Milan bonnets of gold encrusted with jewels. Underneath the fortress of the castle were more ladies whose names were: Danger, Disdain, Jealousy, Unkindness, Scorn, Sharp Tongue and Strangeness. These ladies were dressed like Indian women.

Then eight lords entered wearing cloth-of-gold hats and great cloaks made of blue satin. They were named: Love, Nobleness, Youth, Devotion, Loyalty, Pleasure, Gentleness and Liberty. This group, one member of which was the king himself, was led in by one man dressed all in crimson satin with [a motif of] burning flames of gold. His name was Ardent Desire and the ladies were so moved by his appearance that they might have given up the castle, but Scorn and Disdain said that they would hold the fort.

Then Desire said that the ladies must be won over, and encouraged the knights to attack. The lords then ran to the castle, at which point there was a great sound of gunfire, and the ladies defended it with rose-water and comfits. The lords replied with dates, oranges and other pleasurable fruits and eventually the castle was taken. However, Lady Scorn and her companions kept up a stubborn defence with bows and balls, till they were driven out again and fled. Then the lords took the ladies by the hands and led them out as prisoners, bringing them down to the floor-level and dancing with them, which pleased the foreign guests immensely.

When they had danced their fill, everyone then unmasked themselves and revealed who they really were. After this there was an extravagant banquet and when all was over the visitors took their leave of the king and the cardinal and departed for Flanders, praising the king greatly.

1523

Anne Boleyn, daughter of Sir Thomas Boleyn, returned to England from the French court towards the end of 1521. At that time her father was negotiating a marriage for her with James Butler, heir to the earldom of Ormond. Her romance with Henry Percy probably took place in the spring of 1523, and the king had nothing to do with Wolsey's decision to break it up. By the summer of 1523 that negotiation had been abandoned, possibly as a result of Anne's behaviour. Some years later George Cavendish, Wolsey's gentleman usher, recounted events as he had seen them.

I will tell you as best I can how the king's love came about and what followed thereafter. When this lady, Mistress Anne Boleyn, was very young she was sent to France to be a lady-in-waiting to the French queen. When the queen died she was sent back to her father who arranged for her to become a lady-in-waiting to queen Catherine, wife of Henry. Such was her success in this post, shown both by her exemplary behaviour and excellent deportment that she quickly outshone all the others. To such an extent, in fact, that the flames of desire began to burn secretly in the king's breast, unknown to all, least of all to Anne herself.

At this time Lord Percy, the son and heir of the earl of Northumberland, was aide and secretary to Wolsey, the lord cardinal, and whenever the lord cardinal happened to be at court Lord Percy would pass the time in the queen's quarters where he would dally with the ladies-in-waiting. Of these, he was most familiar with mistress Anne Boleyn, to such an extent that a secret love grew up between them and they pledged that, in time, they intended to wed. When knowledge of this reached the king's ears he was greatly distraught. Realizing that he could no longer hide his secret love, he revealed all to the lord cardinal and discussed with him ways of sundering the couple's engagement to each other.

When the lord cardinal had left the court and returned to Westminster, he remembered Henry's request and summoned Lord Percy to his presence, saying in front of us, his servants: "I am amazed at your foolishness in getting entangled, even engaged, to this silly girl at court – I mean Anne Boleyn. Have you not considered your position? After the death of your noble father you stand to inherit one of the greatest earldoms in the country. It would thus have been more proper if you had sought the consent of your father in this affair and to have made his highness the king privy to it, requesting his royal blessing. Had you done so, he would not only have welcomed your request but would, I can assure you, have promoted you to a position more suited to your noble estate. And thence you might have gained the king's favour by your conduct and wise council and thus risen further still in his estimation.

But now look what you have done by your thoughtlessness. You have not only offended your own father but also your sovereign and pledged yourself to someone whom neither would agree to be suitable. And do not doubt that I shall send for your father and when he comes he will break off this engagement or disinherit you forever. The king himself will make a complaint to your father and demand no less an action than I have suggested. Indeed, I happen to know that the king has already promised this lady to someone else and that though she is not yet aware of it, the arrangements are already far advanced. The king however, being a man of great prudence and diplomacy, is confident that, once she is aware of the situation, she will agree to the union gladly."

"Sir," said Lord Percy, weeping, "I knew nothing of the king's involvement in all this, and I am sorry to have incurred his displeasure. I considered myself to be of sufficient age and in a good enough situation to be able to take a wife of my own choosing and never doubted that my father would have accepted my decision. And though she is just a simple maid and her father is only a knight, yet she is of very noble descent. On her mother's side she has Norfolk blood and on her father's side she is a direct descendant of the earl of Ormond. Why then, sir, should I query the suitability of the match when her pedigree is of equal worth to mine? Thus I humbly beg your favour in this matter and ask you to beg the king to be benevolent concerning this issue of my engagement, which I cannot deny, still less break off."

"See, gentlemen," said the lord cardinal to us, "what nonsense there is in this wilful boy's head! I thought that when you heard me explain the king's involvement in this business you would have relented in your suit and have submitted yourself to the king's will, allowing his highness to decide on the matter as he thinks fit."

"Sir, and so I would," said Lord Percy, "but in this matter I have gone so far that I am no longer able to renounce my commitment in full conscience."

"What?" said the cardinal, "Do you think, that the king and I do not know what to do in such a serious matter as this? One thing's for sure, I can see no point in your making any further pleas in this case."

"Very well," said Lord Percy, "if it please you, I will submit myself completely to the king's will in this matter and will release my conscience from the heavy burden of the engagement." "So be it, then," said the cardinal. "I will send for your father in the north and he, the king and I will take whatever measures for the annulment of this hasty folly the king thinks necessary. And in the meantime, I order you – and in the king's name command you – not to see her again if you intend to avoid the full wrath of his majesty". Having said this, he got up and went off to his study.

Then the earl of Northumberland was sent for, who, learning of the request being at the king's command, made great speed to court. His first port of call after leaving the north was to the lord cardinal, by whom he was briefed about the cause of his hasty summons and with whom he spent a considerable time in secret discussions. After their long talk, the cardinal ordered some wine and after they had drunk together the meeting broke up and the earl left.

As he was leaving, he sat down on a bench that the servants used and called his son Lord Percy to him, saying, in our presence: "Son, you have always been a proud, presumptuous, headstrong wastrel. And you have so proved yourself once more. What possible joy, comfort, pleasure or solace could I ever receive from you who have so misconducted yourself without discretion and in such secrecy. With no regard for your own father, nor for your sovereign to whom all honest and loyal subjects give faithful and humble obedience, nor even for your own noble estate, you have ill-advisedly become engaged to this girl and thereby incurred the king's displeasure – an action intolerable in any of his subjects!

If it wasn't for the wisdom of the king and his benevolence towards your empty-headedness and wilful stupidity, his wrath would have been sufficient to cast me and all my family for generations to come into abject poverty and desolation. But by the supreme goodness of his grace and the worthy lord cardinal, I have been excused your transgression – they have decided to pity your stupidity rather than blame it – and have presented me with a command concerning you and your future conduct.

I pray to God that this may serve as sufficient warning to you to conduct yourself with more care hereafter, for I can assure you that, if you do not amend your ways, you will be the last earl of the house of Northumberland if I have anything to do with it. You do nothing but waste and consume everything that all your ancestors have built up and cherished with great honour. But in the name of the good and gracious king, I intend – God willing – so to arrange my succession that you will benefit from it but little. For I have no intention, I can assure you, of making you my heir. I have, after all, praise be to God, a wide choice of sons who will, I am sure, prove themselves worthier than you and abler to conduct themselves as true nobles should. And from these I will choose the best as my successor."

"Now gentlemen," he said to us servants, "it may so happen that when I am dead you will see these things that I have spoken of to my son prove to be the case. Yet in the meantime, I would be grateful if you could be his friends and tell him when he strays from the path or is at fault." And with that he took his leave of us and said to his son: "Go on your way and serve the lord cardinal, your master, and make sure you carry out your duty." And thus he departed and went down through the hall and out to his barge.

After much debate and consultation about lord Percy's case it was finally decided that his engagement to Anne Boleyn should be dissolved and that he should instead marry one of the earl of Shrewsbury's daughters Mary Talbot, which he later did.

1524

By now Henry was coming to the end of his jousting career. He had suffered a number of falls, but this accident, and the fact that he still had no son and heir, probably caused him to heed the advice of his council and retire from such a strenuous pastime.

On 10 March the king, having a new armour made to his own design and fashion, such as no armourer before that time had seen, thought to test the same at the tilt, and ordered a joust for the purpose. The lord marquis of Dorset and the earl of Surrey were appointed to be on foot: the king came to one end of the tilt and the duke of Suffolk to the other. Then a gentleman said to the duke: "Sir the king is come to the end of the tilt." "I see him not," said the duke, "by my faith, for my headpiece blocks my sight." With these words, God knows by what chance, the king had his spear delivered to him by the lord Marquis, the visor of his headpiece being up and not down or fastened, so that his face was quite naked. Then the gentleman said to the duke: "Sir the king is coming."

Then the duke set forward and charged with his spear, and the king likewise inadvisedly set off towards the duke. The people, seeing the king's face bare, cried hold, hold; the duke neither saw nor heard, and whether the king remembered his visor was up or not few could tell. Alas, what sorrow was it to the people when they saw the splinters of the duke's spear strike the king's headpiece. For most certainly the duke struck the king on the brow right under the guard of the headpiece on the very skull cap or basinet piece to which the barbette is hinged for strength and safety, which skull cap or basinet no armourer takes heed of, for it is always covered by the visor, barbette and volant piece, and thus that piece is so protected that it takes no weight. But when the spear landed on that place there was great danger of death since the face was bare, for the duke's spear broke into splinters and pushed the king's visor or barbette so far back with the counter blow that all the King's head piece was full of splinters. The armourers were much blamed for this, and so was the lord marquis for delivering the spear blow when his face was open, but the king said that no one was to blame but himself, for he intended to have saved himself and his sight.

The duke immediately disarmed and came to the king, showing him the closeness of his sight, and he swore that he would never run against the king again. But if the king had been even a little hurt, his servants would have put the duke in jeopardy. Then the king called his armourers and put all his pieces of armour together and then took a spear and ran 6 courses very well, by which all men could see that he had taken no hurt, which was a great joy and comfort to all his subjects present.

1525

Two years earlier Wolsey had made an unsuccessful attempt to extract from parliament enough money to pay for the French war to which he was committed. He then compounded his mistake by endeavouring to anticipate the subsidy which was granted. By January 1525 the war chest was empty, and in March and April Wolsey sent out commissioners to demand a non-parliamentary tax, which they optimistically called an "amicable grant".

In the same season through all the realm this demand was utterly denied so that the commissioners could achieve nothing, and yet they tried both by fair means and foul. Some spoke fair and flattered,

The Boleyns and their Enemies

Anne Boleyn, Henry VIII's second and most controversial wife, was the daughter of a courtier and a lady of considerable lineage. Her paternal grandmother, Margaret, was a daughter and co-heir of Thomas Butler, 7th earl of Ormonde, who died in 1515. Anne's mother Elizabeth, was the daughter of Thomas Howard, 2nd duke of Norfolk, and sister of the 3rd duke. Her father, Sir Thomas Boleyn, was not originally in possession of a great estate. His connections enabled him to enter Henry VIII's service in 1501, and by 1509 he had been appointed Esquire of the Body. A man of charm with many skills, particularly in languages, he undertook his first diplomatic mission, to Margaret of Austria Regent of the Netherlands, in 1512, which enabled him to place his eldest daughter Anne, then aged about 12, in Margaret's service in 1513.

Thomas's career in the king's service continued to develop. In 1519 he was ambassador at the court of France, and in 1520 he was a leading figure at the Field of Cloth of Gold, soon afterwards being engaged in negotiations with the Holy Roman Emperor, Charles V. He also became a member of the king's council. He introduced his young son George to the court in 1514, and secured for him the position of page in the royal Chamber. His younger daughter, Mary, accompanied the king's sister Mary to France when she married the French king, Louis XII in 1514. Shortly afterwards, Anne transferred her service from Margaret of Austria to Claude, the wife of Francis I of France, who succeeded Louis in 1515, in response to Henry VIII's shifting diplomatic priorities, and remained in France, acquiring a first class courtly education, until the breakdown of relations with England led to her recall in 1521.

Meanwhile, Sir Thomas had been trying to secure his rights in the earldom of Ormonde, which were blocked

Above   Anne Boleyn, whose beauty and vivacity are not particularly apparent in this contemporary portrait.

Below left   Hever Castle, home of the Boleyn family.

by the Irish claimant, Piers Butler. It was suggested that Anne should marry James, Piers' son, to end the dispute. Although she did not do so, this was not on account of the king's interest. In 1522 Henry was more interested in her younger sister, Mary, who became his mistress. Sir Thomas' complaisance, and even connivance in this, as well as his general record of good service, led to his creation as Viscount Rochford in 1525.

Henry's relationship with Anne started in 1527, when he had already decided that his marriage offended the law of God. Captivated by her wit and charm, he always intended to make her his wife. The consequences for her family were dramatic. The Boleyns became the enemies, first of Cardinal Wolsey, who wanted the king to re-marry in France, and then of Catherine of Aragon's supporters, notably the Poles and the Courtenays, who tried to dissuade the king from his intention.

others spoke cruelly and threatened, and yet they could not achieve their purpose. In Kent Lord Cobham was commissioner and he handled men roughly, and because one John Skudder answered him clownishly he sent him to the Tower of London. As a result of which the people muttered and grumbled against Lord Cobham, and expressly said that they would pay no money.

In Essex the people would not assemble before the commissioners in any houses, but only in open places; and in Huntingdonshire several resisted the commissioners' sitting, and they were apprehended and sent to prison at the Fleet.

The duke of Suffolk sat in Suffolk at this time on a similar commission, and by gentle handling he persuaded the rich clothiers to assent and grant to give a sixth, and when they returned home to their houses they called their spinners, carders, fullers, weavers and other craftsmen, who were used to be set to work and earn their livings by making cloth, and said: "Sirs, we are not able to set you to work, our goods are taken from us, therefore look to yourselves and not to us, for it cannot be otherwise." Then women began to weep and young folk to cry, and men who had no work to rage and assemble themselves in companies. The duke of Suffolk, hearing of this, ordered the constables that every man's armour should be taken from him; but when that was known then rumours grew greater and the people railed openly against the duke of Suffolk and Sir Robert Drury, and threatened them with death, and Cardinal Wolsey also, and so 4,000 men of Lavenham, Sudbury, Hadleigh and other towns around rebelled and put themselves in armour, and rang the alarm bells and began to gather more men.

Then the duke of Suffolk realizing this, began to raise men, but he could get only a small number, and they who came to him said that they would defend him from all perils if he did not hurt their neighbours, but they would not fight against their neighbours. But the gentlemen who were with the duke did so much that all the bridges were broken, so their assembly was somewhat hindered.

The duke of Norfolk, high treasurer and admiral of England, hearing of this, gathered a great force in Norfolk and came towards those commoners, and of his nobility he sent to them to find out their intentions. They answered that they would live and die in the king's causes and be obedient to the king. When the duke knew that he came to them, and then they all spoke at once, so that he knew not what they meant. Then he asked who was their captain and ordered him to speak. Then a well-aged man of over fifty years asked leave of the duke to speak, which was granted with goodwill. "My lord," said this man, whose name was John Green, "since you ask who is our captain, truly his name is poverty, for he and his cousin necessity have brought us to this, for all these persons and many more, who I wish were not here, live not of ourselves, but we all live by the substantial occupiers of this county, and yet they give us such little wages for our work that we are scarcely able to live, and thus we pass our time in penury with our wives and children. And if they by whom we live are brought to the situation where they of their little cannot help us to earn our living, then we must perish and die miserably. I tell you my lord, that the clothmakers have put all these people and a far greater number out of work, the husbandmen have put away their servants and given up their households, they say that the king asks so much that they are not able to do as they have done in the past, and so of necessity we must die wretchedly. Therefore my lord now, according to your wisdom, consider our need."

The duke was sorry to hear their complaint, and he knew well that it was true. Then he said: "Neighbours, separate yourselves, let every man depart to his home, and chose four who will answer for the rest, and on my honour I will send to the king and make humble intercession for your pardon, which I trust to obtain if you will depart." Then they all answered that they would, and so they went home.

At the request of the two dukes, commissioners of great authority were sent to them; then the duke of Norfolk and the duke of Suffolk came to Bury, and there came many people of the country in their shirts with halters around their necks meekly desiring pardon for their offences. Then the demand for money ceased in all the realm, for it was clearly seen that the commons would pay none.

After this the two dukes came to London, and brought with them the chief captains of the rebellion who were put in prison in the Fleet, and then the king came to Westminster, to Hampton Court palace, home of Cardinal Wolsey. There he assem-

Financial reform

Tudor England's finances suffered from medieval England's achievement in creating relatively sophisticated financial institutions long before other European monarchies. As a result a 12th century Exchequer and a 14th century tax system needed drastic overhaul. The Yorkist kings had tackled the conservative bureaucracy of the Exchequer by sidestepping it. Land revenues were collected by local officers, chiefly surveyors who personally accounted in cash to central officers under the close control of the landowner. In the king's case, they dealt with his private apartments or Chamber. After initial hesitation, Henry VII followed Yorkist precedent, and the Chamber became the centre for collecting parliamentary subsidies, customs revenues and other kinds of royal revenue; not just those from land. Although not a sophisticated system, it was easy to work and suited Henry's urge to keep close eye on his money.

As Chancellor under Henry VIII, Cardinal Wolsey did little to modify Chamber finance until 1522 when, with the introduction of informal methods of revenue collection, such as "loans", a lot of money began to come under the control of the king's gentlemen favourites in his innermost apartments, the Privy Chamber. Calling for financial caution, Wolsey swiftly introduced a ceiling of £10,000 on Privy Chamber revenue holdings. He sponsored more genuine reform when he established a new national tax, the subsidy; assessed on individuals, and more flexible than the two-centuries-old community tax, known as Fifteenths and Tenths, alongside which it ranked. However, Henry's ·massive expenditure on war with France and his love of lavish building and court display, meant that ever more money was needed. Wolsey's efforts to provide funds for the king became increasingly desperate. In 1525 the taxpayers of southern England, goaded beyond endurance by his demand for a Amicable Grant, simply refused to pay.

After Wolsey's fall in 1529, the new minister Thomas Cromwell turned his attention to succeeding where the earlier régimes had failed, namely in providing secure and regular income. Part of his strategy was to continue adapting parliamentary taxation. In 1534, he asked for taxes on a new principle: that the king's maintenance of peace deserved a gift from his grateful subjects.

Parliamentary taxes were thus justified in peacetime as well as when the country was at war. However, the cornerstone of Cromwell's revenue strategy was an assault on the Church's wealth. The confiscation of Wolsey's spreading estates was followed by royal appropriation of clerical taxes, chiefly the First Fruits and Tenths, paid originally to the Pope. Most spectacular of all was the dissolution of all England's monasteries, nunneries and friaries, and the confiscation of their lands. Cromwell created a new set of ministries to deal with the assets that poured in alongside funds from older revenue agencies. The king was able to watch money stream into coffers scattered around London, some placed close to his private apartments.

By the time Henry died in 1547, the dissolution policy had raised £1.3 million, but most of this came not from the rents of settled estates, but from the sale of monastic lands to his subjects. Sales started even before Cromwell's fall, and during the hideously expensive French campaigns of 1544–5, they mushroomed. By the end of James I's reign, practically everything had been disposed of. Cromwell's revolution in Tudor government finance was short-lived, and it was the next generation of royal ministers under Mary and Elizabeth I who gathered his scattered revenue departments into a relatively unified structure, once more under the control of the ancient Exchequer although it incorporated lessons learnt from the Chamber phase of land management.

Below   Building accounts for the extension and embellishment of Hampton Court, 1538.

157

bled a great council about this matter, and he openly said that he never intended to ask anything of his commons which might lead to his dishonour or to the breach of his laws; therefore he wished to know from those it concerned why the commissioners were so strict as to demand the sixth part of every man's substance. Cardinal Wolsey excused himself and said that when it was raised in council, how to make the king rich, the king's council, and especially the judges, said he might lawfully demand any sum by commission, and that it was done by the assent of the whole council, and he called God to witness that he had never maligned nor desired the harm of the commons, but like a true councillor planned to enrich the king.

And the spiritual men say that it accords with God's law, for Joseph caused the king of Egypt to take the fifth part of every man's goods. But Wolsey said since every man refuses the burden I am content to take it upon me, and to endure the fame and evil report of the people for my good will towards the king and the comfort of you, my lords, and the king's other councillors, but God eternal knows all. "Well," said the king, "some have told me that my realm was never so rich, and that trouble should never have risen from that demand, and that men would pay at the first request, but now I find to the contrary." Then every man held his peace.

The king was greatly moved that his subjects were thus troubled, and also he was informed of the denial which the spiritual men had made, and of their sayings, therefore he thought it touched his honour that his council should attempt such a doubtful matter in his name, and that it should be refused both by the spirituality and temporality, for although some agreed to it in fear before the commissioners, when they had departed they denied it again. Then the king said: "I will have no more of this trouble. Let letters be sent to all shires that this matter may no more be spoken of; I will pardon all those who have denied the demand, openly or secretly. Then all the lords knelt down and heartily thanked the king. Then letters were sent to all the commissioners to cease, with instructions how to declare the king's pardon.

This declaration showed that Cardinal Wolsey never assented to the first demand, and the instructions included the information that the lords and the judges and others of the king's council devised the demand and that Wolsey followed the decision of the whole council; these two points contradicted each other, which was well marked. And further, the instructions were that by the humble petition and supplication of cardinal Wolsey the great sums which were demanded by the king's royal authority were clearly pardoned and remitted, therefore the commissioners wished the people to pray for the cardinal. But the people took all this for a joke and said: "God Save the King," for commoners would hear no praise spoken of Wolsey, they hated him so much.

1526

After his defeat at Pavia, and subsequent imprisonment, Francis I signed the treaty of Madrid with the Emperor Charles V, making numerous political concessions, and surrendering his two sons as hostages. In spite of this, as soon as he was released, he began to seek pretexts to repudiate the treaty, as Edward Hall explains.

Because all summer the king took pleasure in hunting, nothing happened worthy to be written about. So, I wil tell you about the French king, now returned to his realm'

When he was in Paris, he wrote to the Emperor that he would observe and keep his promises on every point, but what he really thought I will not judge, for shortly after he published a book going against the agreement made between the Emperor and him at Madrid, alleging that he was forced to make the ageement, or else it would never have happened. He alleged further that his lawyers had clearly determined all promises and covenants made by any person that harmed themselves should not be effective. He also said the governors of the law, determined that no other promise should take effect if it puts a man in jeopardy of his life, might be imprisoned or put under bondage, especially when it is done with a threat.

Moreover he said that he might give away nothing in connection with his Crown without the assent of his peers and the estates of his realm, to which he was sworn at the time of his coronation.

1527

By this time Henry had decided that the only remedy for his lack of a son was to annul his marriage to Catherine

Henry's divorce

In England, the crisis caused by Henry's wish to divorce Catherine was complicated by his choice of Anne Boleyn as her successor, because Anne's family ties had major political implications. Her father, Sir Thomas Boleyn, was a councillor and a diplomat, and her uncle Thomas Howard, 3rd duke of Norfolk, was lord treasurer. Both men disliked Wolsey, as did Anne, and her access to the king was a valuable weapon in their hands and in the hands of the cardinal's other enemies.

Anne attracted Henry's attention in the mid-1520s. The problems of the succession were then becoming apparent, and awareness of the situation may have prompted her for several years to pursue a path of virtue in response to the king's infatuation, rather than follow the example of her sister Mary and become his mistress. Her apparent inaccessibility seems to have fuelled rather than dampened Henry's desire.

By 1529 Wolsey's political power was crumbling. When the continental powers resolved their differences at the Peace of Cambrai, without reference to England, he could no longer maintain his old prestige. His failure to procure the annulment of Henry's marriage to Catherine showed that his influence at Rome was negligible. Henry made him a scapegoat, and his dimissal in September from all his offices except the archbishopric of York made him the first political casualty of the English Reformation crisis.

Wolsey's successor as lord chancellor, Sir Thomas More, accepted the office only on condition that the divorce would be handled only by those honestly supporting it, and clerical opposition was even more seirous than that. Catherine's strongest and most articulate supporter was John Fisher, bishop of Rochester, who stood firmly at her side from 1527 until his death on the scaffold in 1535. William Peto, provincial of the Grey Friars compared Henry to Ahab, with the implication that Anne was like Jezebel. William Warham, archbishop of Canterbury was also hostile, and it was his death in 1532 that gave Henry the opportunity to appoint the reformer Thomas Cranmer as his successor, in 1533. Cranmer declared the marriage with Catherine null and void, empowered to do so without regard to Rome by the Act in Restraint of Appeals, passed by a parliament which probably had few strong feelings on the marriage issue, but which did wish the security of a peaceful succession.

Anne's acceptance by the English people was to be hindered by Catherine's continuing popularity, however. On the eve of the queen's appearance before Cardinals Campeggio and Wolsey, in 1529, she was

Above   John Fisher, bishop of Rochester, Catherine's most courageous and out-spoken English champion.

loudly applauded by the crowd and throughout the succeeding years she and her daughter retained widespread affection. They were greeted with enthusiasm when they appeared in public, even after Anne's coronation in 1535; it was about this time in fact that a Suffolk woman described the new queen a ''goggle-eyed whore''. At court, too Catherine had continued support from a number of influential families; even men who had been happy to use Anne as a weapon against Wolsey had little affection for the king's second wife.

and take a second wife. This he determined to do on the grounds that his first marriage had been contrary to the law of God, in that it had broken the rule, apparently laid down in the Book of Leviticus, that a man should not marry his brother's widow. Convinced of the veracity of his interpretation, he sought an annulment from Pope Clement VII. Clement was unsympathetic to his interpretation of Leviticus, and in any case helpless to oblige him because of the power of Catherine's nephew, the Emperor Charles V. Both sides, however, continued to go through the judicial motions.

Cardinal Campeggio came to England in September 1528, and after he had rested and reposed himself for a while he spoke with the king at Bridewell, where his secretary made an eloquent oration in latin, setting forth and exaggerating the great spoil recently made at Rome, and the ransacking of the city by the Imperials, and putting forward the king's particular favour and benefits shown to the pope, the cardinals and the whole city. Nothing was said openly at this time of the king's great matter. But much and various talk and rumour went abroad after this legate's arrival; men did not hesitate to say freely and frankly that the king, to serve his own appetite and pleasure more than for any just impediment in his marriage, had caused the legate to be sent for so that he might be divorced from the queen, who was almost universally unpopular, especially among the common people.

To repress this talk the king assembled at his palace of Bridewell in November, his nobility, judges and counsellors, with various other persons, to whom he declared the great worthiness of his wife, both for her nobility and virtue and all princely qualities, to be such that if he were to marry again he would marry her of all women, if the marriage were found to be good and lawful. But, despite her worthiness and the fact that he had a fair daughter by her, he said that he was wonderfully tormented in his conscience, for he understood from many great clerks whom he had consulted, that he had lived all this time in detestable and abominable adultery. Therefore to settle his conscience, and the sure and firm succession of the realm, he advocated this legate as a man most impartial, and said that if by the law of God she should be judged to be his lawful wife, nothing would be more pleasant and acceptable to him in his whole life. He added that when his ambassador was last in France, and mention was made about his daughter's marriage with the earl of Orleans, one of the French king's most notable counsellors had said it was expedient first to know whether she was the king's lawful daughter or not. This was in effect the king's oration. Our chronicles record that the same doubt was cast in the council of Spain also, after the emperor had agreed with our king to marry his daughter.

Not long after this both the legates went to the queen, and told her they were appointed by the pope as judges to hear and determine the controversy which had arisen over her marriage with the king, and to give a final judgement as to whether it was consonant with the law of God or not. The queen, hearing this, was abashed and astonished and pausing a while, at length spoke thus: "Alas, my lords," she said, "that now after almost twenty years such a question should be raised, and that men should now try to dissolve and undo this marriage as wicked and detestable" – imputing the origin of all her trouble to Cardinal Wolsey and his deadly feud against the emperor, whom he most resented and hated of all the princes in Europe, because he would not serve and satisfy his immoderate ambition in his wish to be made pope. The cardinal, on the other side, denied all blame and said the thing was much against his will; he said he was assigned by the pope to be a judge in this case, and swore by his faith that he would, in hearing it, administer justice and right impartially.

1528

Henry was pathologically nervous of infection, and every so often fled into a secure retreat until the threat abated. During such periods the business of state was virtually in abeyance. Edward Hall refers briefly to once such episode.

In the very end of May there began in the City of London a sickness called the sweating sickness, which went all round the realm almost, of which many people died within five or six hours. By reason of that sickness the term of parliament was adjourned and the judges' circuit also. The king was sorely troubled with this plague, for many died in care. One of these was Sir Francis Poynes, who was ambassador to Spain. The king moved away almost every day to Tattenhanger, a place of the bishop of St Alban's, where he was prepared to bide the time that God would allow him.

On 28 May the legates sat solemnly at Blackfriars, where the king appeared with his two proctors, the queen in person with four bishops and other counsellors, refusing to stand for the legates' judgement as incompetent judges, and appealing from them to Rome. The legates proceeded notwithstanding, and cited the king and queen to appear again on 18 June, when both of them appeared in person. At that time the king openly declared the great disquiet, vexation and trouble with which he was grievously encumbered over his marriage, so that he could scarcely attend to anything concerning the necessary business of the realm; therefore he desired the matter might be most quickly and speedily determined, according to justice and right. He commended also at that time the queen's womanhood, wisdom, nobility and gentleness. When the king had ended the queen made her protestation, and put in her plea of objection, and renewed her provocation, alleging the case to be advocated by his holiness the pope, desiring it to be admitted to proof, and to have a term competent for this. Whereupon a day was set by the legates for 21 June for the declaration of their opinions and intentions. On that day both the king and queen appeared in person; and although the legates declared their sincere intention to proceed directly and justly without favour, fear, affection or partiality, and that no objection, appeal or term could or might be admitted by them, the queen nevertheless persisting in her former opinion submitted her appeal, which the legates refused. Since they intended to proceed further with the case the queen would remain no longer to hear what they would further decide, even though the king also asked and commanded her to stay, about which she seemed afterwards to suffer some remorse, as for some disobedience towards her husband. And she reported afterwards to some who were then her counsellors (from whom I heard of it) that she had never before in her life in anything in the world disobeyed the king, her husband, and she would not have done so now, but the necessary defence of her cause forced her to. Her proctor, notwithstanding, answered for her and said she would stick to her appeal. But the legates caused her to be three times summoned by name and called forthwith to return and appear. When she refused to do this she was denounced as contumacious by the legates, and a citation decreed for her appearance the following Friday to answer such objections as should be made against her.

Upon this the king wrote on 23 June to his ambassadors then resident at the court of Rome about the matters already mentioned, willing them to have special care and regard that nothing should pass or be granted by the pope's holiness which might give either delay or disappointment to the direct and speedy process to be used in his case.

Now, the said appeal notwithstanding, the judges proceeded and still went forward in hearing and examining the matter. Hot and fervent reasoning was there at Rome, to further the said divorce. The summer drew quickly on, and the king importunately called for speed and full sentence in the matter. But the legates made no great haste, and Campeggio brought forward a reason why they could not proceed until October following. The king hearing of this, complained to the dukes of Norfolk and Suffolk and other nobles of his council, noblemen were sitting with the legates on 30 July and expected that day or the next to give a final judgement in the matter. Campeggio swore on his honour and the faith he bore to the church of Rome that the practice of the courts there is to suspend all matters at the end of July until 4 October, and that all judgements given in between were void; therefore he asked the king to bear with him until that date (before which they could no longer sit), trusting that then they would make a conclusion which would content the king.

This answer greatly offended the noblemen and the duke of Suffolk, giving a great clap on the table with his hand, swore that there was never a cardinal who did good in England, and forthwith departed in great anger.

1530

Wolsey's failure to secure the success of the Legatine court cost him the king's favour. In the autumn of 1529 he was deprived of the lord chancellorship, and indicted of praemunire, the offence of exercising ecclesiastical jurisdiction without the king's consent. Ridiculous as the charge was, Wolsey surrendered to it, and recovered enough favour to be allowed to retire to his archdiocese. The following account of his subsequent fate is heavily coloured by the chronicler Hall's hostility.

You have heard under the last year how the cardinal of York was attainted in praemunire, and despite that the king had given him the bishoprics of York and Winchester, with great possessions, and had licensed him to live in his diocese of York. Being thus in his diocese, grudging his fall and not remembering the kindness the King showed to him, he wrote to the court of Rome and to several other princes letters reproachign the king, and as much as he was able stirred them to revenge his case against the King and his realm; so much so that various opprobrious words about the king were spoken to Dr Edward Kern, the king's orator at Rome, and it was said to him that for the cardinal's sake the king's matrimonial suit would have the worse speed. The cardinal would also speak fair to the people to win their hearts, and always declared that he was unjustly and untruly commanded, which fair speaking made many men believe that he spoke the truth. And to be held in higher repute by the people he determined to be installed or enthroned at York with all possible pomp, and caused a throne to be erected in the Cathedral Church of such a height and design as was never seen before; and he sent to all the lords, abbots, priors, knights, esquires and gentlemen of his diocese to be at his manor of Cawood on 6 November, and so to bring him to York with all pomp and solemnity.

The King, who knew of his doings and secret communications, all this year pretended to ignore them to see what he would eventually do, until he saw his proud heart so highly exalted that he intended to be so triumphantly installed without informing the king, even as if in disdain of the king. Then the king thought it was not fitting or convenient to let him any longer continue in his malicious and proud purposes and attempts. Therefore he sent letters to Henry, the sixth earl of Northumberland, willing him with all diligence to arrest the cardinal, and to deliver him to the earl of Shrewsbury, great steward of the king's household. When the earl had seen the letter, with a suitable number of men he came to the manor of Cawood on 4 November, and when he was brought to the cardinal in his chamber he said to him: "My Lord, I pray you have patience, for here I arrest you." "Arrest me," said the cardinal; "Yes," said the earl, "I have orders to do so." "You have no such power," said the cardinal, "for I am both a cardinal and a peer of the College of Rome, and ought not to be arrested by any temporal power, for I am not subject to that power, therefore if you arrest me I will withstand it." "Well," said the Earl, "here is the king's commission, and

A new Church head

There were profound and far-reaching consequences for the country when Henry made himself supreme head of the Church of England. For Henry personally, it enabled him to rid himself of Catherine of Aragon in spite of the pope's opposition; to marry Anne Boleyn, and to ensure that any children born from this marriage would be legitimate and therefore entitled to take their proper place in the line of succession to the throne. It also increased his authority and prestige, turning him into the magnificent and awe-inspiring figure represented in the portraits of the 1530s. Rather less happily, it drew him ever deeper into the religious turmoil of the day, and ensured that he was constantly subjected to pressure from conflicting factions in court.

The Act of Supremacy greatly increased the power of the Crown. It enabled Henry and his successors to take possession of much of the wealth of the clergy – by appropriating to themselves, and significantly extending, taxes formerly paid to the papacy; by dissolving the monasteries and chantries; and by compelling the high clergy to make exchanges of their lands which were markedly advantageous to the Crown. It also greatly expanded the Crown's powers of patronage since the monarch was able to appoint men of his choice to the most important and desirable posts in the Church. After the dissolution of the monasteries, the Crown had a huge quantity of land which could be exploited for purposes of patronage.

For the Church, the Act of Supremacy did much more than subject the English clergy and their wealth, lands and courts to royal rather than papal authority. In effect it created the Church of England as a separate national church. The sees of York and Canterbury were unified, enabling the king to provide them with the same doctrine, to enforce it, and keep control of the various clerical factions.

Before the Reformation the king was significantly less than sole master of his own house. In spiritual matters he was subject to the canon law of the universal Catholic Church, whose ruler was the pope, and his authority over his subjects was limited, since the clergy owed allegiance to Rome. Parliament could not legislate freely upon all matters. As a result, when Henry wished to have his marriage to Catherine of Aragon annulled, he had no choice but to refer to Clement VII.

The pope's obstinate refusal to settle his "Great Matter" for him left Henry with two stark alternatives: either give up his efforts to secure an annulment, and therefore his hopes of marrying Anne Boleyn, or to challenge the whole basis of papal authority in England. Henry chose the latter course, adopting the legal

argument that within his own realm he was the superior of the pope. He allowed himself to be convinced by dutiful scholars, who combed the archives of Europe for favourable precedents, that the pope's jurisdiction was false, and forced upon him, and that he himself was already, by God's will, the head of the Church of England.

Claiming the Supremacy was one thing: enforcing it was another. Henry was therefore obliged to turn to parliament to pass Acts which would confirm the clergy's subjection to the royal will, and sever existing ties with Rome. Parliament's extensive and prolonged co-operation was necessary to develop the legislation.

Above   Thomas Cromwell, Henry's leading minister thoughout the 1530's and chief planner of the English Reformation.

Below   A medal depicting Henry as Supreme Head of the Church.

therefore I charge you to obey." The Cardinal somewhat remembered himself, and said, "Well, my lord, I am content to obey, but although by negligence I fell under punishment of the praemunire and lost by law all my lands and goods, yet my person was in the king's protection and I was pardoned that offence. Therefore I wonder why I now should be arrested, especially considering that I am a member of the apostolic See, on whom no temporal man should lay violent hands. Well, I see the King lacks good counsel." "Well," said the earl, "when I was sworn warden of the marches you yourself told me that I might with my staff arrest all men under the degree of king, and now I am stronger for I have a commission for what I do as you have seen." The cardinal at length obeyed, and was kept in his private chamber, and his goods seized and his officers discharged, and his physician, Dr Augustine, was also arrested, and brought to the Tower by Sir Walter Welshe, one of the king's chamber. On 6 November the cardinal was conveyed from Cawood to Sheffield Castle, and there delivered into the keeping of the earl of Shrewsbury until the king's pleasure was known. About this arrest there was much talk among the common people, and many were glad, for surely he was not in favour with the commons.

When the cardinal was thus arrested the king sent Sir William Kingston Knight, captain of the guard and constable of the Tower of London with some of the yeomen of the guard to Sheffield, to fetch the cardinal to the Tower. When the cardinal saw the captain of the guard he was much astonished and shortly became ill, for he foresaw some great trouble, and for that reason men said he willingly took so much strong purgative that his constitution could not bear it. But Sir William Kingston comforted him, and by easy journeys he brought him to the Abbey of Leicester on 27 November, where through weakness caused by purgatives and vomiting he died the second night following, and is buried in the same Abbey.

1531

While the issue over his marriage remained unresolved, the King canvassed theological opinion, particularly in the universities, in support of his case. His opponents were not impressed, and controversy raged. Meanwhile Henry separated from Catherine for the first time.

At this time there were many preachings in the realm, one contradicting the other, about the king's marriage, and especially one Thomas Able, clerk, both preached and wrote a book that the marriage was lawful, which caused many simple men to believe his opinion. This Able was the queen's chaplain, and wrote this book to please her. Therefore the king ordered a disputation in the universities, and all the judgements of great clerks to be compiled into a book and printed, which book satisfied the minds of all impartial and discerning persons, but some men were partial, so that neither learning nor reason could satisfy their willful minds.

This year the king kept his Christmas at Greenwich with great solemnity, but all men said that there was no mirth in that Christmas because the queen and the ladies were absent.

1532

As the obstacle to the fulfillment of his wishes was ecclesiastical jurisdiction, the King began to encourage his lay subjects to complain on that score. Some needed little encouragement, and the House of Commons produced a list of grievances, which were then passed to the Convocation for their comments. Not seeing the danger signals and the problems that they were going to face in the near future, the clergy dismissed the complaints as trivial and unjustified. Meanwhile, controversy over the king's marriage continued.

On the last day of April, while parliament was sitting, the king sent for Thomas Audley, Speaker of the House of Commons, and certain others, and declared to them how they had exhibited last year a book of their grievances against the spirituality which, at their request he had delivered to his spiritual subjects, for them to answer, but he had had no answer until three days ago, which answer he delivered to the Speaker, saying: "We think their answer will please you little, for it seems to us very slender. You being wise men I doubt not but that you will look circumspectly at this matter, and we will be impartial between you." And truly their answer was very sophistical, and did nothing about the grievances of the lay people. And further the king said, that he wondered not a little why someone in Parliament spoke openly about the absence of the queen from him, which matter was not to be determined there; for, he said, it touched his soul, and he wished the marriage had been valid, for then he would never have been troubled in his conscience; but the doctors of the univerities, said he, have determined the marriage to be void, and detestable before God, which conscientious doubt caused me to abstain from her company, and not foolish or wanton appetite. "For I am," said he, "41 years old, at which age man's lust is not so quick as in lusty youth. And except in Spain and Portugal it has never been seen that one man married two sisters, having carnally known one of them before; but for the brother to marry the brother's wife was so abhorred amongst all nations that I have never heard that any christian man did it except myself. Therefore you see my conscience troubled, and so I pray you report it." So the Speaker departed, and told the Commons of the king's words, both about the clergy's answer and about the king's marriage; and the slight answer displeased the Commons.

1533

Having persevered until 1531 in his hopeless quest for an annulment, and having by 1527 chosen Anne Boleyn as his second wife, Henry then decided to take the matter into his own hands. Convinced that he was entitled by divine law to exercise ecclesiastical authority in England, he forced the clergy to accept him as Supreme Head of the Church, and to submit the legislation of convocation to his approval. In 1533, having appointed Thomas Cranmer to the archbishopric of Canterbury, he announced his divorce and married Anne Boleyn.

The king at the beginning of this year kept St George's day at his manor of Greenwich with great solemnity, and the court was greatly replenished with lords, knights, ladies and gentlewomen to a great number, with all enjoyment and pleasure. The previous year parliament had enacted that no person should, after a particular day, appeal to Rome for any cause whatsoever as laid down in the Act in Restraint of Appeals, and that the queen, now called the princess dowager, had appealed to the court of Rome before the act was passed, so it was doubted whether the appeal was good or not. This question was well handled in parliament, and much better in the Convocation house, but in both houses it was alleged and shown by books, that in the Councils of Chalcedon, Africa, Toledo and various other famous councils in the primitive church, and in the time of St Augustine, it was affirmed, declared and determined that a case arising in one province should be determined there, and that the patriarch of Constantinople should not meddle in cases moved in the jurisdiction of the patriarch of Antioch, and no bishop should meddle within another's province or country. These things were so cleverly opened, so cunningly set forth for attention, that every man who had wisdom and was determined to follow the truth, and was not partial or wilfully wedded to his own opinion, might plainly see that all appeals made to Rome were clearly void and of no effect. These doctrines and councils were shown to the Lady Catherine, princess dowager, but she (since women love to lose no dignity) still continued in her old song, trusting more to the pope's partiality than to the determination of Christ's truth. Whereupon the archbishop of Canterbury, accompanied by the bishops of London, Winchester, Bath, Lincoln and several other great clerics rode in a great number to Dunstable, which is six miles from Ampthill where the princess dowager was, and there by a doctor called Dr Lee she was cited to appear before the said archbishop in a matrimonial cause, in the town of Dunstable, and at the day appointed she would not appear but made default, and so she was called peremptorily every day for 15 days, and at last for failing to appear and for contumacy, by the assent of all the learned men there present, she was divorced from the king, and their marriage declared to be void and of no effect. After the sentence was given the archbishop and all the others returned wherever they pleased.

After he had sued for this divorce many wise men said that the king was not well advised to marry Anne Boleyn before the divorce was pronounced, for by marrying before the first marriage was dissolved they said the second marriage might be called into question, and they said truly, for so it was in May, three years later, as you will hear after when I come to that time. Of this divorce, everyone spoke according to his discretion and wisdom; for wise men said it was Godly and honourably done for the discharge of the king's conscience, and profitable for the safety of the realm, and that God loved the marriage since the new queen was so soon with child. Others said that the bishop of Rome would curse all Englishmen, and that he and the Emperor Charles V would invade the realm and destroy the people, and the Spaniards especially boasted much, but, thanks be to God, their deeds were much less than their words. But after every man had talked enough there was no more discussion of the matter, but all was at peace.

Anne Boleyn was not popular, and the king's decision to annul his first marriage was poorly received. Conse-

quently Henry made a great effort to ensure that Anne's coronation was lavishly celebrated, and put heavy pressure upon both his courtiers and the City of London to put on a suitable show.

On Thursday 29 May, Lady Anne, marquess of Pembroke, was received as queen of England by all the lords of England. And the mayor and aldermen, with all the guilds of the City of London, went to Greenwich in their barges after the best fashion, with also a barge of bachelors of the mayor's guild richly hung with cloth of gold with a great number to wait on her. And so all the lords with the mayor and all the guilds of London brought her by water from Greenwich to the Tower of London, and there the king's grace received her as she landed, and then over a thousand guns were fired at the Tower, and others were fired at Limehouse, and on other ships lying in the Thames.

And on Saturday, the last day of May, she rode from the Tower of London through the City with a goodly company of lords, knights and gentlemen, with all the peers of the realm, richly apparelled. She herself rode in a rich chariot covered with cloth of silver, and a rich canopy of cloth of silver borne over her head by the four Lords of the Ports, in gowns of scarlet, followed by four richly hung chariots of ladies; and also several other ladies and gentlewomen riding on horseback, all in gowns made of crimson velvet. And there were various pageants made on scaffolds in the city; and all the guilds were standing in their liveries, every one in order, the mayor and aldermen standing in Cheapside. And when she came before them the Recorder of London made a goodly presentation to her, and then the mayor gave her a purse of cloth of gold with a thousand marks of angel nobles in it, as a present from the whole of the city; and so the lords brought her to the palace at Westminster, and left her there that night.

On 1 June Queen Anne was brought from Westminster Hall to St Peter's Abbey in procession, with all the monks of Westminster going in rich copes of gold, with thirteen mitred abbots; and after them all the king's chapel in rich copes with four bishops and two mitred archbishops, and all the lords going in their parliament robes, and the crown borne before her by the duke of Suffolk, and her two sceptres by two earls, and she herself going under a rich canopy of cloth of gold, dressed in a kirtle of crimson velvet decorated with ermine, and a robe of purple velvet

decorated with ermine over that, and a rich coronet with a cap of pearls and stones on her head; and the old duchess of Norfolk carrying her train in a robe of scarlet with a coronet of gold on her cap, and Lord Burgh, the queen's Chamberlain, supporting the train in the middle.

After her followed ten ladies in robes of scarlet trimmed with ermine and round coronets of gold on their heads; and next after them all the queen's maids in gowns of scarlet edged with white Baltic fur. And so she was brought to St Peter's church at Westminster, and there set in her high royal seat, which was made on a high platform before the altar. And there she was anointed and crowned queen of England by the archbishop of Canterbury and the archbishop of York, and so sat, crowned, in her royal seat all through the mass, and she offered at the said mass. And when the mass was done they left, every man in his order, to Westminster Hall, she still going under the canopy, crowned, with two sceptres in her hands, my Lord Wiltshire her father, and Lord Talbot leading her, and so dined there; and there was made the most honourable feast that has been seen.

The great hall at Westminster was richly hung with rich cloth of Arras, and a table was set at the upper end of the hall, going up twelve steps, where the queen dined; and a rich cloth of estate hung over her head. There were also four other tables along the hall; and it was railed on every side, from the high dais in Westminster Hall to the platform in the church in the abbey.

And when she went to church to her coronation there was a striped blue cloth spread from the high dais of the king's bench to the high altar of Westminster on which she went.

And when the queen's Grace had washed her hands, then came the duke of Suffolk, high constable for that day and steward of the feast, riding on horseback, richly dressed and decorated, and with him, also riding on horseback, Lord William Howard as deputy for the duke of Norfolk in his office of marshall of England, and there came the queen's service followed by the archbishop's with a certain space between, which was all borne by knights; the archbishop sitting at the queen's board, at the end on her left hand. The earl of Sussex was sewer, earl of Essex carver, earl of Derby cup bearer, earl of Arundel butler, Viscount Lisle panter, and Lord Grey, almoner.

The King's "Great Matter"

Henry VIII's wished to make his marriage to Catherine of Aragon null and void rather than look for a divorce. He justified this on the grounds that the original dispensation he received for the marriage to his late brother Arthur's wife, Catherine, was not allowable in canon law. The international implications of his action affected both English relations with Rome, and diplomatic relations between England and its continental neighbours.

The canon law issue hinged on the interpretation of apparently conflicting edicts in the Old Testament. Two passages in Leviticus forbade a man to marry his brother's wife, but did not make it clear whether this rule applied when the brother had died. A text in Deuteronomy stipulated that if a man died without children, his brother had a duty to marry his widow to preserve the line.

The majority of canonists and theologians in England and Europe who debated the conflict of texts favoured Deuteronomy, contrary to Henry's wishes. This may have been why Henry also tried to argue, unsuccessfully, that the original dispensation was invalid for technical reasons.

Although he recognized that papal authority in matrimonial matters was universally accepted in western Christendom, the king may well have hoped that Clement VII, like other popes before him, would prove amenable to the wishes of a monarch who was generally well-disposed towards the papacy; Henry, after all, had given him vigorous support against the Lutheran sweep of protestantism throughout mainland Europe.

However, the political situation in Europe did not work to the king's advantage. In 1525, Charles V, Holy Roman Emperor had won a decisive victory over the French, but although he and the English king had been allies since 1500, he refused England any part of the spoils. To curb imperial power, England and France concluded an alliance against Charles. However, after the sack of Rome in 1527, Charles had Clement at his mercy, and the pope was hardly a free agent when Henry's case was presented in Rome. This political hostility probably counted for more than the fact that the Emperor was Catherine's nephew.

Clement played for time. He first appointed a commission in 1527 to examine Henry's case without empowering it to pass a definitive judgement. Later, in 1529, he sent Cardinal Campeggio to England as legate, to hear, with Wolsey, the king's suit for divorce. Before the hearing, Campeggio urged the queen to retire to a convent, which according to some theologians, was the

Above   Pope Clement VII, who a few years earlier would have granted Henry's divorce without any difficulty.

equivalent of dying to the world, and which would have left Henry free to remarry. Catherine refused to comply, and when the court eventually opened, she continued to assert the lawfulness of her marriage. After considerable delay and vain efforts on Wolsey's part to secure a decision in England, Campeggio adjourned his court on 31 July, and Clement recalled the case to Rome before it could reconvene.

Henry's international position had been weakened by a political settlement in Europe. In 1529 Charles had come to terms with both the French and the pope, and the English king had no option but to bring direct pressure on Clement by attacking papal power in England. Although he maintained diplomatic contacts with the papacy, these moves were unsuccessful. Ultimately, in 1533, the nullity declaration was made in England by Thomas Cranmer, the newly-appointed archbishop of Canterbury.

At one of the four tables sat all the noble ladies, all on one side of the hall, at the second table the noblemen, at the third table the mayor of London with the aldermen, at the fourth table the Barons of the Ports with the Masters of Chancery. The splendid dishes with the delicate meats, the benches which were all gilt, with the noble service performed that day by great men of the realm, the goodly sweet harmony of the minstrels and other things would take too long to tell, but it was a goodly sight to see and behold.

And when she had dined and washed her hands she stood for a while under the canopy of state, and looked through the hall, and then spices were brought with other delicacies, which were all borne in great high plates of gold, from which she took a little refreshment, and gave the rest amongst the lords and ladies; and that done she went up to the White Hall, and there changed her dress, and so left secretly by water for York Place, which is called White Hall, and stayed there all night.

To much rejoicing Princess Elizabeth was born in the latter part of this year.

On Sunday 7 December between three and four o'clock the queen delivered a fair lady and the duke of Norfolk came home to the christening. For the queen's good deliverance a Te Deum was sung and great preparation was made for the ceremony. The mayor and his brethren and eleven of the chief citizens were commanded to be at the christening the following Wednesday.

On this day the mayor, Stephen Peacock, wearing a gown of crimson velvet, and al his aldermen in scarlet, and the city council all took the barge to Greenwich. There were there many lords, knights and gentlemen assembled.

All the walls of the church were hanged with cloth from Arras and the font was made of silber and stood in the middle of the church, three steps high, and was covered in fine cloth and various gentlemen in qowns and with towels around their necks were attending to it, making sure that no filth should enter it. Over it hung a square canopy fringed with gold, and around it a rail covered with red satin. Between the choir and the body of the church was a closed area with a pan over fire, to make the child ready.

When all these things were in place the child was brought to the hall and each man came forward. First ordinary citizens two by two, then gentlemen, esquires and chaplains, then the aldermen and then the mayor alone. Next, in groups, came barons, bishops, earls, and the the earl of Essex.

Soon, trumpets blew and the child was brought to the altar, and the gospel was said. After this the archbishop of Canterbury immediately confirmed the child, the marchioness of Exeter being the godmother.

This year also a town clerk of the city of London hanged himself because he could not abide to hear the gospel in English, and I myself heard him say to me once that if the king set forth the scripture in English and let it be read by the people on his authority, he would cut his own throat, but he broke his promise as you have heard because he hanged himself, but of what mind and intent he did this let God be the judge.

1534

The Act in Restraint of Appeals of the previous year was the first formal repudiation of papal jurisdiction, but it was not until the following year that the positive corollary, the Royal Supremacy, was recognized and established by another statute.

In this year on 3 November the king's highness held his high court of parliament, in which were concluded and made many and various good, wholesome and godly statutes. Amongst them all was one special statute, which authorized the king's highness to be Supreme Head of the Church of England, by which the pope with all his college of cardinals with all their pardons and indulgences was utterly abolished out of this realm, for which God be ever praised. In this parliament also the king's highness was given the first fruits and tenths of all dignities and spiritual promotions. And at the end of that parliament the king's majesty most graciously granted, and willed it by the same Parliament to be established, his most gracious and general free pardon.

1535

By this time, with the Royal Supremacy firmly in place, Henry was steering a delicate and distinctive ecclesiastical course. On 4 June he had burned 22 heretics, most of them anabaptists, but those who adhered to the old faith were in equal danger.

This year on 11 June were arraigned in the king's bench at Westminster three monks of the Charterhouse of London, and there condemned of high treason against the king, and sentenced to be drawn, hanged, disembowelled, beheaded and quartered. One of them was called Francis Nitigate, another Master Exmew, storekeeper of the same place, and the third was called Master Middlemore, vicar of the same place. This year also on 17 June was arraigned at Westminster in the king's bench John Fisher, bishop of Rochester, for treason against the king, and he was condemned there by a jury of knights and esquires (the lord chancellor sitting as high judge), who passed this sentence on him; that the said John Fisher should go from thence to the place where he came from, which was the Tower of London, and from thence to be drawn through the City of London to Tyburn, there to be hanged, cut down alive, his bowels taken out of his body and burnt before him, his head cut off, and his body be divided into four parts and his head and body be set in such places as the king should assign. The effect of the treason was denying the king to be Supreme Head of the Church of England, according to a statute, The Act of Supremacy, made in the last session of Parliament.

On 19 June, a Saturday, the three monks of the Charterhouse, aforementioned, were drawn from the Tower to Tyburn, and there executed according to their sentence, and their heads and bodies hung at different gates around the city.

Also on 22 June, Tuesday, John Fisher, bishop of Rochester, was beheaded at Tower Hill, and the rest of his execution pardoned. His body was buried in Barking churchyard, next to the Tower of London, and his head was set on London Bridge.

This year also on 1 July, being Thursday, Sir Thomas More, sometime chancellor of England, was arraigned at Westminster for high treason and there condemned, and the Tuesday after, being 6 July, he was beheaded at Tower Hill and his body was buried within the chapel in the Tower of London, and his head was set on London Bridge. The effect of his death was for the same cause that the bishop of Rochester died for.

1536

The birth of Elizabeth, instead of a male heir, in September 1533 was a great blow to both Henry and Anne, and although the latter retained her power and position, her relationship with Henry began to cool, and she did not become pregnant again until late in 1535. In January 1536 Catherine died, and Anne was no longer protected by the threat of her return to favour. Soon after Anne miscarried of a son, and Henry began to suspect that this marriage, too, was displeasing to God. At the end of April, for reasons which are not at all clear, the king became convinced that she had been guilty of adultery, and she was condemned on very slender evidence. Her arch-enemy, Eustace Chapuys, reported her downfall to his master the emperor, after her execution on 19 May.

The joy shown by the people every day, not only at the ruin of the concubine but at the hope of princess Mary's restoration is inconceivable, but as yet the king shows no great disposition towards the latter; indeed he has twice shown himself obstinate when spoken to on the subject by his council. I hear that, even before the arrest of the concubine, the king, speaking with Mistress Jane Seymour of their future marriage, the latter suggested that the princess should be replaced in her former position; and the king told her she was a fool, and ought to solicit the advancement of the children they would have between them, and not any others. She replied that in asking for the restoration of the princess she conceived she was seeking the rest and tranquility of the king, herself, her future children, and the whole realm; for, without that neither your majesty nor this people would ever be content.

I will endeavour by all means to make her continue in this vein; I hope also to go and speak with the king within three days, and with members of the council in general. I think the concubine's little bastard Elizabeth will be excluded from the succession, and that the king will get himself requested by parliament to marry. To cover the affection he has for the said Seymour he has lodged her seven miles away in the house of a grand esquire, and says publicly that he has no desire in the world to marry again, unless he is constrained by his subjects to do so. Several have already told me and sent to say that, if it cost them their lives, when parliament meets they will urge the cause of the princess to the utmost.

The very evening the concubine was brought to the Tower of London, when the duke of Richmond went to say goodnight to his father, and ask his blessing after the English custom, the king began to weep, saying that he and his sister, meaning the princess, were greatly bound to God for having escaped the hands of that accursed whore, who had determined to poison them; from which it is clear that the king knew something about it.

Master Norris, the king's chief butler, Master Weston who used to lie with the king, Master Brereton gentleman of the chamber, and the groom of whom I wrote to your majesty by my man, were all condemned as traitors. Only the groom confessed that he had been three times with the said whore and concubine. The others were condemned upon presumption and certain indications, without valid proof or confession.

The concubine and her brother were condemned for treason by all the principal lords of England, and the duke of Norfolk pronounced sentence. I am told the earl of Wiltshire was quite as ready to assist at the judgement as he had done at the condemnation of the other four. Neither the whore nor her brother was brought to Westminster like the other criminals. They were condemned within the Tower of London, but the thing was not done secretly, for there were more than 2,000 persons present. What she was principally charged with was having cohabited with her brother and other accomplices; that there was a promise between her and Norris to marry after the king's death, which it thus appeared they hoped for; and that she had received and given to Norris certain medals, which might be interpreted to mean that she had poisoned the late queen, and intrigued to do the same to the princess. These things she totally denied and gave to each a plausible answer. Yet she confessed she had given money to Weston, as she had often done to other young gentlemen. She was also charged, and her brother likewise, with having laughed at the king and his dress, and that she showed in various ways she did not love the king, but was tired of him. Her brother was charged with having cohabited with her by presumption, because he had once been found a long time with her, and with certain other little follies. To all he replied so well that several of those present wagered 10 to 1 that he would be acquitted, especially as no witnesses were produced against either him or her, as it is usual to do, particularly when the accused denies the charge.

I must not omit that among other things charged against him as a crime was, that his sister had told his

Sexual politics

The reason for Henry's decision to do away with his second wife has always been baffling. We know that after the decision was taken the king talked of having been deceived by witchcraft, and referred to Anne as a 'cursed whore' who had endeavoured to poison his children. However, there is no sign of such an extreme alienation, even a few days before her arrest, and as late as the middle of April it seemed likely that the Boleyns would win the factional struggle which was undoubtedly going on in the court. It is reasonable to suppose that he was already attracted to Jane Seymour, and a knowledge of that developing relationship may well have affected Anne's demeanour during the last few months of her life. She was not so foolish as to play the injured wife in public, but may well have made her feelings plain in private, as she had done before. However, a mere personal estrangement of that nature cannot explain either the suddenness or the vehemence of Henry's reaction.

One theory is that the queen was simply the victim of a court conspiracy. Her ascendency, and that of her family had been deeply offensive, not only to former supporters of Catherine such as the Marquis of Exeter, but also to more neutral interest groups. According to this view, she was simply framed, with the active connivance of her former ally Thomas Cromwell, to whom her presence, and her active commitment to a new diplomacy with the French had become an increasing embarrassment. Realizing that the king was amenable to being turned against Anne, and extremely sensitive to any reflection upon his own sexual activities, they simply invented the most damning sequence of sexual crimes that they could think of, and created a superficially persuasive case. The only substance behind this farago was provided by the fact that her brother, Lord Rochford, was a notorious womaniser, and that she spent a lot of time in his company. The weakness of this theory is that it makes the king appear even more gullible and volatile than he is known to have been. When Catherine Howard was guilty of genuine, if less imaginative, misdemeanours of a similar nature a few years later, he was angry and deeply distressed, but showed no signs of instant paranoia.

An alternative view is that the male foetus of which she is known to have miscarried in January was in some way deformed, and that Henry took this to be proof that he could not have been responsible for its conception. Such a view is plausible in terms of contemporary opinion, especially as Henry had become extremely superstitious on the subject of divine judgement.

Above   Arguments against the existence of purgatory by Hugh Latimer, with Henry's comments in the margin.

Above right   Thomas Cranmer, archbishop of Canterbury, who championed Henry's divorce from Catherine of Aragon.

Moreover, a child conceived in an incestuous union would have been far more likely to bear the marks of such a judgement than one which had merely been conceived in adultery. So, if the foetus had been deformed, it is quite possible that the king would have reacted in such a way. However, the only evidence for such deformity – if it can be called evidence – occurs in a work of catholic polemic written in the reign of Elizabeth. There was no suggestion of any such problems during the weeks between Anne's miscarriage and her arrest. Chapuys, who was Anne's enemy, and who had been given a detailed physical description of the foetus only a few days after the event, made no allusion to any abnormality. So the mystery remains.

At the same time, Anne's hold over the king had always been primarily sexual. Like others, he had been fascinated by her wit and courtly accomplishments, but the fascination which had sustained a frustrating courtship over something like five years had been physical. Maintaining such a hold over a man like Henry once he had been gratified would probably have been impossible for any woman, and although there is no evidence that Anne resorted to magical aids to preserve her allure, the king could easily have been persuaded to the contrary. Whoever suggested to Henry that Anne had bewitched him knew exactly what note to strike in order to provoke a violent and irrational response, and the true solution may lie no deeper than that.

Anne was also a friend and patron to the religious reformers, particularly Cranmer, supported the proposal for a translation of the Bible, and endeavoured to persuade the king of the virtues of both William Tyndale and Simon Fish. This activity may explain some of the animosity against her, and Cromwell, who was also a patron of the reformers, may have felt that her lack of discretion was becoming a liability. She later understandably became a heroine of the reformation to such protestants writers as John Foxe.

wife that the king was impotent. This he was not openly charged with, but it was shown him in writing, with a warning not to repeat it. But he immediately declared the matter, in great contempt of Cromwell and some others, saying he would not in this point arouse any suspicion which might prejudice the king's issue. He was also charged with having spread reports which called in question whether his sister's daughter was the king's child. To which he made no reply. They were judged separately and did not see each other. The concubine was condemned first, and having heard the sentence, which was to be burnt or beheaded at the king's pleasure, she preserved her composure, saying that she held herself ready to greet death and that what she regretted most was that the above persons, who were innocent and loyal to the king, were to die for her. She only asked a short time for confession. Her brother, after his condemnation, said that since he must die, he would no longer maintain his innocence, but confessed that he had deserved death. He only begged the king that his debts, which he recounted, might be paid out of his goods.

Although everybody rejoices at the execution of the whore there are some who murmur at the mode of procedure against her and the others, and people speak variously of the king; and it will not pacify the world when it is known what has passed and is passing between him and Jane Seymour. Already it sounds ill in the ears of the people, that the king, having received such ignomiy, has shown himself more glad than ever since the arrest of the whore; for he has been going about banqueting with ladies, sometimes remaining after midnight, and returning by the river. Most of the time he was accompanied by various musical instruments, and, on the other hand, by the singers of his chamber, which many interpret as showing his delight at getting rid of a thin, old and wicked fool with hope of change, which is a thing especially agreeable to this king. He supped lately with several ladies in the house of the bishop of Carlisle, and showed an extravagant joy, as the said bishop came to tell me next morning, who reported moreover that the king had said to him, among other things, that he had long expected the issue of these affairs, and that thereupon he had before composed a tragedy, which he carried with him; and so saying the king drew from his bosom a little book written in his own hand, but the bishop did not read the contents. It may have been certain

ballads that the king has composed, at which the whore and her brother laughed as foolish things, which was objected to them as a great crime.

Three days after the concubine's imprisonment the princess was removed, and was honourably accompanied both by the servants of the little bastard and by several gentlemen who came of their own accord. Many of her old servants and maids at this news went to her, and although her governess allowed them to remain, she was warned by me not to accept or retain anyone but those given her by the king her father. What I most fear as regards her is, that when the king is asked by parliament to restore her to her rights, he will refuse his consent unless the princess first swears to the statutes invalidating the first marriage and the pope's authority. To this, I think, she will not easily yield, although I should advise her to acquiesce in everything as far as she can without prejudice to her conscience.

Chapuys' fears were entirely justified. To her horror and astonishment, Mary found that her disfavour was not entirely the result of Anne Boleyn's influence. Henry insisted on her complete submission, both in respect of her legitimacy and the papal supremacy. After holding out for a dangerous month, Mary capitulated on 22 June in this letter:

"Most humbly prostrate before the feet of your most excellent majesty, your most humble, so faithful and obedient subject, who has so extremely offended your most gracious highness that my heavy and fearful heart dare not presume to call you father, deserving of nothing from your majesty, save that the kindness of your most blessed nature does surmount all evils, offences and trespasses, and is ever merciful and ready to accept the penitent calling for grace, at any fitting time. Having received this Thursday, at night, certain letters from Mr Secretary to whom I had lately written advising me to make my humble submission immediately to your self, which I dared not, without your gracious licence, presume to do before, and signifying that your most merciful heart and fatherly pity had granted me your blessing, with the condition that I should persevere in what I had commenced and begun; and that I should not again offend your majesty by the denial or refusal of any such articles and commandments as it may please your highness to address to me, for the perfect trial of my heart and inward affection, for the perfect declaration of the depths of my heart.

Sir Thomas Wyatt and courtly love

The elder Thomas Wyatt was born in 1503, the son of Sir Henry Wyatt, a distinguished courtier and royal servant. Sir Henry's loyal service to Henry VIII began before the king came to the throne but his first high office was only secured in 1523 when he became Treasurer of the Chamber.

Thomas Wyatt was introduced to the court in 1516, and after spending time at St John's College, Cambridge, where he did not take his degree but acquired a good humanist education, he returned to the court in 1520 as an Esquire of the Body. In 1524 his father secured his appointment as Clerk of the King's Jewels, and in 1526 Thomas gained his first diplomatic experience in France. He became High Marshall of Calais in 1529, and was appointed to the king's council in 1533. He was knighted in 1537, just six months before his father's death, after which diplomacy entirely dominated his career.

A man of the "new learning", he was a protégé of Thomas Cromwell, and after Cromwell's fall in 1540 Wyatt was arrested on charges of treasonable misconduct. These were probably without foundation, and after two months imprisonment Sir Thomas was released in March 1541 and resumed his career. He died of pneumonia in 1542 on his way to meet the Holy Roman Emperor Charles V's ambassador.

Although Sir Thomas' career was distinguished, his significance is in what he wrote about and experienced at Henry VIII's court. The writing of poetry, like composing and performing music, was supposed to be a courtly accomplishment, but few courtiers possessed the gift. Sir Thomas, like his friend and contemporary Henry Howard, earl of Surrey, was an exception. He wrote sharply satirical poems about the intrigues, moral compromises and over-heated atmosphere of court life, and was a master of the language of courtly love. This chivalric dalliance was a part of the Burgundian tradition, one of the rules of which was that the gallant should address passionate and flattering verses to the lady of his choice. He might also wear her favour when jousting, and would be expected to send her a gift on St Valentine's day. Such gestures seldom bore any relationship to a genuine romantic attachment: although sexual intrigue was common enough, people normally had more sense than to advertise their intentions.

However, Sir Thomas' poetic skill was such that the verses he addressed to Anne Boleyn in this conventional mode have been taken as evidence of a true infatuation. He may indeed have been one of her

Top   Thomas Wyatt, poet and master of the language of courtly love.

Above   A love letter of Henry to Anne Boleyn, ". . . no more to you now mine own darling for lack of time, but that I would you were in mine arms or I in yours . . ."

aspiring lovers in the 1520s, before she caught the king's eye, and he remained an adherant of the Boleyn party at court until its eclipse in 1536. He was not, however, guilty of any misconduct during the 1530s when the works were written. The poem containing the famous lines: ". . .Noli me tangere, for Caesar's I am, and wild for to hold, although I seem tame," would certainly have caused trouble had it been taken seriously. Most courtiers paid a professional, such as John Skelton, to express their devotion; Sir Thomas did not need to, and the misunderstandings this caused have followed him down the centuries.

First, I acknowledge myself to have most unkindly and unnaturally offended your most excellent highness, in that I have not submitted myself to your most just and virtuous laws; and for my offence therein, which I must confess was in me a thousandfold more grievous than it could be in any other living creature, I put myself wholly and entirely at your gracious mercy; at whose hands I cannot receive that punishment for the same which I have deserved.

Secondly, to open my heart to your grace, in these things which I have before refused to condescend to, and have now written with my own hand, sending them to your highness herewith, I shall never beseech your grace to have pity and compassion on me if ever you shall perceive that I shall, secretly or openly, vary or alter from one piece of that which I have written and subscribed, or refuse to confirm, ratify or declare the same, wherever your majesty shall appoint me.

Thirdly, as I have and will, knowing your excellent learning, virtue, wisdom and knowledge, put my soul under your direction, and by the same have and will in all things henceforth direct my conscience, so I wholly commit my body to your mercy and fatherly pity; desiring no state, no condition, nor no manner or degree of living but such as your grace shall appoint unto me; knowing and confessing that my state cannot be so vile as either the extremity of justice would appoint to me, or as my offences have required and deserved. And whatsoever your grace shall command me to do, touching any of these points, either for things past, present or to come, I shall gladly do the same as your majesty can command me.

Most humbly, therefore, beseeching your mercy, most gracious sovereign lord and benign father, to have pity and compassion on your miserable and sorrowful child; and with the abundance of your inestimable goodness, so to overcome my iniquity towards God, your grace, and your whole realm that I may feel some sensible token of reconciliation; which is all I desire, as God is my judge, to whom I shall daily pray for the preservation of your highness with the queen's grace, and that it may please him to send you issue. From Hunsdon, this Thursday, at 11 o'clock at night.

Your Grace's most humble and obedient daughter and handmaid, Mary."

The following document accompanied Mary's letter to Henry:

"The confession of me, Lady Mary, made upon certain points and articles written below; in which I do now plainly and with all my heart confess and declare my inward sentence, belief and judgement, with due conformity of obedience to the laws of the realm; so, minding for ever to persist and continue in this determination without change, alteration or variance, I do most humbly beseech the king's highness, my father, whom I have obstinately and disobediently offended in the denial of the same up to now, to forgive my offences therein, and to take me to his most gracious mercy.

First I confess and acknowledge the king's majesty to be my sovereign lord and king, in the imperial crown of this realm of England; and do submit myself to his highness and to each and every law and statute of this realm, as it becomes a true and faithful subject to do; which I shall also obey, keep, observe, advance and maintain according to my bounden duty with all the power, force and qualities with which God had endued me, during my life.

I do recognize, accept, take, repute and acknowledge the king's highness to be supreme head on earth, under Christ, of the church of England; and do utterly refuse the bishop of Rome's pretended authority, power and jurisdiction within this realm, formerly usurped, according to the laws and statutes made on that behalf, and by all the king's true subjects humbly received, admitted, obeyed, kept and observed.

And I do also utterly renounce and forsake all manner of remedy, interest and advantage which I may by any means claim by the bishop of Rome's laws, processes, jurisdiction or sentence, at this time or in any way hereafter, by any manner of title, colour, means or cause that is, shall or can be devised for that purpose.

I do freely, frankly and for the discharge of my duty towards God, the king's highness and his laws, without other respect, recognize and acknowledge that the marriage formerly had between his majesty and my mother, the late princess dowager, was by God's law and man's law incestuous and unlawful."

The parliament which assembled on 8 June 1536 reorganized the succession, bastardizing Elizabeth in addition to Mary, and settling the succession on the king's

Jane Seymour

The fall of Anne Boleyn in the spring of 1536 left Henry VIII still without a male heir. Although it is not known whether Thomas Cromwell's claim that he had deliberately used Jane Seymour to entice Henry away from the queen was true, it is certain that the king's affection for her grew rapidly. He had first shown an interest in her in 1534 and she remained ideally suited to attract his attention – Henry preferred short women, with small, childlike faces. Within days of Anne's execution Jane Seymour became the king's third wife; and with both previous wives now dead – Catherine had died at the beginning of the year – any male child Jane bore would be generally recognized as the kingdom's rightful heir.

This was the only marriage to provide Henry with a legitimate son: the future Edward VI, born on 12 October 1537. The king hurried to Hampton Court when he heard the news. God had pronounced in his favour at last! Tragically, Jane died just 12 days after the birth of her son. In testimony to her success as the mother of his heir, Henry decided that he would arrange to be buried next to her.

Below   Henry VIII with Jane Seymour and Edward, Prince of Wales with, in the detail above, Princess Mary waiting ominously in the wings. The picture was not painted from life as Jane Seymour died in childbirth.

offspring by Jane Seymour. At the same time the convocation approved a set of reforming religious articles, known as "The Bishop's Book", which omitted many traditional formulas and definitions, without being explicitly protestant. Monasteries worth less than £200 per annum were dissolved by statute, and their property placed at the king's disposal. Not everyone accepted these changes peacefully. In October, first Lincolnshire and then Yorkshire broke out in rebellion.

These articles ordained and delivered to the people. The inhabitants of the North parts being at that time very ignorant and rude, knowing not what true religion meant, but altogether nursed in superstition and popery, and also by means of certain abbots and ignorant priests not a little stirred and provoked by the suppression of certain monasteries, and by the abolishing of the bishop of Rome, now took the excuse of this book, saying see friends now four of the seven sacraments are taken from us, and soon you will lose the other three also, and thus the faith of holy church will utterly be suppressed and abolished. And therefore suddenly they spread abroad and raised great and shameful slanders only to move the people to sedition and rebellion, and to kindle in the people hateful and malicious minds against the king's majesty and the magistrates of the realm, saying let us fully apply ourselves to the maintenance of religion, and rather than suffer it thus to decay to die in the field.

And amongst them also were so many, even of the nobility, who did not a little provoke and stir up the ignorant and rude people the more stiffly to rebel and stand therein, faithfully promising them both aid and succour against the king and their own native country (like foolish and wicked men), thinking by so doing to have given God high pleasure and service. There were also certain other malicious and busy persons who added oil, as the adage says, to the furnace. These made open clamours in every place where there was an opportunity, that the Christian religion would be utterly violated, despised and set aside, and that rather than have it so it behoved and was the part of every true Christian man to defend it even to the death, and not to allow and suffer by any means the faith (in which their forefathers so long and so many thousand years had lived and continued) now to be subverted and destroyed. Amongst these were many priests who deceived the people also with many false stories and venomous lies and fabrications (which could never enter nor

Dissolution of the monasteries

In 1530 there were over 800 religious houses in England staffed by about 10,000 monks, nuns and friars. The largest and wealthiest houses dated from the Saxon period, but the majority had their roots in the 12th century. Some of these had also become rich – notably the great Cistercian houses of Yorkshire – but the majority were small institutions surviving on a moderate income.

The idea of closing down small monasteries and redeploying their income to such purposes as education was not new and had been tried by many bishops after 1485, notably Cardinal Wolsey. In the 1530s Thomas Cromwell was determined to continue this policy by a sustained attack on the smaller religious houses, and in doing so solve some of the financial problems of the Crown. He prepared his ground in 1535 by initiating two great surveys, one of the monastic resources – the *Valor Ecclesiasticus* – and the other of the state of morale within the houses – the *Compendium Compertorum*. Armed with evidence from these surveys Cromwell persuaded parliament to pass the Suppression Act of 1536. In many ways a limited and conservative piece of legislation, only the smallest monasteries with an income of less than £200 per annum were to be closed, with many exemptions, while redundant monks were to receive pensions or were to be given the option of transferring to one of the larger houses.

In the spring and summer of 1536, groups of commissioners travelled around the country to carry out the closures. Jewels and ornaments were seized for the Crown, and a new lay farmer was put in possession of the house to manage it until it was sold off.

If Cromwell calculated that by the conditions of his Act he would not alienate people, the swiftness and brutality of its execution provoked an angry reaction. Serious disturbances broke out in Lincolnshire and Yorkshire – collectively known as the Pilgrimage of Grace – and in some areas abbots and monks of the larger houses were seen to be involved.

The successful suppression of the Pilgrimage gave Cromwell the ideal pretext to act against the larger monasteries, but now he proceeded with greater stealth.

By 1540 all of the English religious houses had been closed, though they had by no means vanished. Some of the largest survived as new cathedral foundations, for example, Winchester and Peterborough, while others lived on as parish churches, such as Bath and Tewkesbury. Many were converted into country houses such as Newstead, Nottinghamshire, and Woburn, Bedfordshire.

The king was indeed enriched by the exercise, but he did not enjoy the overall benefits which Cromwell had hoped for: many of the monastic estates were sold off to fund the wars with France and Scotland in the 1540s. The real beneficiaries of the Dissolution were the county families who were the tenants of the monks already and who bought their lands from the Court of Augmentations.

And what of the monks? Some, particularly heads of houses, had sensed that dissolution was on the way and had set themselves up very comfortably on the strength of leases of monastic property. Those monks who were priests were often redeployed into parochial work, while the younger men frequently married, learned trades and were absorbed into the secular world. Only the oldest monks struggled along on their small pensions lamenting the ''good old days''.

Far left   Title page of the Valor Ecclesiasticus, giving the valuations of church property in England and Wales.

Below left   The remains of Fountains Abbey in Yorkshire, dissolved in 1536.

Below   Rievaulx Abbey in Yorkshire.

Overleaf   Hatfield House in Hertfordshire, seized from the bishop of Ely.

take place in the heart of any good man or faithful subject), saying that all manner of prayer and fasting and all God's service would be utterly destroyed and taken away, that no man should marry a wife, or be a partaker of the sacraments, or even should eat a piece of roast meat but that he should for the same first pay to the king a certain sum of money, and that they should be brought into more bondage and a more wicked way of life than the Saracens are under the Great Turk. The people thus instructed (or as I may more truly say) deceived and mocked with these and other such errors and slanderous tales, being too credulous, hastily they stiffly and stoutly conspired and agreed to the help and maintenance of the once established religion. And in a part of Lincolnshire they first assembled and shortly after joined into an army, being (as it was supposed) of men apt and fit for war about twenty thousand in number.

Against these traitorous rebels the king, with all possible haste and speed, in person and furnished with a goodly and warlike army lacking nothing that such a company needed, marched towards them. But these rebels hearing that his majesty was present with his power and royal army, feared what would be the outcome, and those noblemen and gentlemen who before had favoured them began to withdraw, so they were destitute of leaders. And at last they made certain petitions to the king in writing, professing that they never intended hurt towards his royal person. The king received their petitions, and answered them as follows:

"First we begin and answer the fourth and sixth articles, because on them depends much of the rest. Concerning the choosing of councillors, I have never read, heard nor known that princes' councillors and prelates should be appointed by rude and ignorant common people, nor that they were fit persons or of the ability to discern and choose worthy and sufficient councillors for a prince. How presumptuous then are you, the rude commons of one shire, and that one of the most brute and beastly of the whole realm, and of the least experience, to find fault with your prince for his choice of councillors and prelates, and to take it upon you, contrary to God's law and man's law, to rule your prince whom you are bound by all laws to obey and serve with your lives, lands and goods, and to withstand for no worldly cause? You have attempted the contrary, like traitors and rebels and not like the true subjects you call yourselves.

As to the suppression of the religious houses and monasteries, we wish that you and all our subjects should well know that this is granted us by all the nobles, spiritual and temporal, of this realm, and by all the commons in the same by act of parliament, and not set forth by any councillor or councillors upon their mere will and whim, as you quite falsely would persuade our realm to believe.

And where you allege that the service of God is much diminished, the truth is the opposite, for there are no houses suppressed where God is well served, but where there was most vice, mischief and abomination of living, and that appears clearly by their own confessions, signed with their own hands at the time of their visitations, and yet we allowed a great many of them to remain, wherein if they do not amend their living we have more to answer for than for the suppression of all the rest. And as for the hospitality for the relief of the poor, we wonder you are not ashamed to affirm that they have been a great relief to poor people, when a great many or the majority had not more than four or five religious persons in them, and some only one, who spent the substance of the goods of their houses in nourishing vice and abominable living. Now what unkindness and unnaturalness may we impute to you and all our subjects of a like mind, who had rather such unthrifty, vicious persons should enjoy such possessions, profits and emoluments as accrue from the said houses for the maintenance of their unthrifty life, than we, your natural prince, sovereign lord and king, who does and has spent of our own more in your defence than six times their worth?"

Jousting was not the King's only form of entertainment, as Edward Hall's description of the May Day celebrations in this year testifies. Nor did Henry's devotion to pastimes diminish his political effectiveness, and Wolsey received the Cardinal's hat on his nomination.

The King and the Queen, accompanied by many lords and ladies, rode to the high ground of Shooter's Hill to take the open air, and as they passed on the way they espied a company of tall yeomen clothed all in green with green hoods and bows and arrows, to the number of 200. Then one of them, who called himself Robin Hood, came to the king desiring him to see his men shoot, and the king was content. Then he whistled and all the 200 archers shot and loosed their arrows at once, and then he whistled again and they likewise shot then he whistled again and they likewise shot again;

their arrows whistled so craftily that the noise was strange and great, and much pleased the king and queen and all the company. All these archers were of the king's guard and had thus appareled themselves to give pleasure to the king.

Then Robin Hood desired the king and queen to come into the greenwood and to see how the outlaws live. The king demanded of the queen and her ladies whether they dared adventure to go into the wood with so many outlaws. Then the queen said that if it pleases him she was content; then the horns blew until they came to the wood beneath Shooter's Hill, and there was an arbour made of boughs with a hall, and a great chamber and an inner chamber, very well made and covered with flowers and sweet herbs, which the King much praised. The Robin Hood said, Sir, outlaws' breakfast is venison, and therefore you must be content with such fare as we have. Then the king and queen sat down, and were served with venison and wine by Robin Hood and his men, to their great content.

Then the king and his company departed, and Robin Hood and his men conducted them, and as they were returning there met them two ladies in a rich chariot drawn by five horses, and every horse had his name on his head, and on every horse sat a lady with her name written. On the first courser called Cawde sat Humidity or Humid; on the second courser called Memeon rode Lady Vert; on the third called Phaeton sat Lady Vegetive; on the fourth called Rimphon sat Lady Pleasance; on the fifth called Lampace sat sweet Odour, and in the chariot sat the Lady May accompanied by the Lady Flora, richly appareled, and they saluted the king with several goodly songs, and so brought him to Greenwich. At this Maying there was a great number of people to behold their pleasure and enjoyment.

The same afternoon the king, the duke of Suffolk, the marquis of Dorset and the earl of Essex, their trimmed armour and skirts of green velvet and cloth of gold, came into the field on great chargers, waited upon by several gentlemen in silk of the same colour. On the other side entered 16 lords and gentlemen, all richly appareled according to their devices, and so they valiantly ran their appointed courses; and afterwards they ran 'volant' so fast that one might overtake another, which was a goodly sight to see. And when all was done they departed and went to a goodly banquet.

This summer the king took his progress west wards and visited his towns and castles there, and heard the complaints of his poor commons, and always as he rode he hunted and liberally gave away the venison.

And in the middle of September he came to his manor of Oking and there the Archbishop of York came to him, whom he heartily welcomed and showed him great kindnesses. And while he was staying there a letter was brought to the Archbishop from Rome, certifying that he was elected to be a Cardinal. He immediately showed it to the king, saying he was unworthy, although he did not mean it, and the king encouraged him and wished him to take the order upon him, and so called him My Lord Cardinal, but neither his hat, nor his bull nor any other ceremonial was yet come.

In september of this year the king of Scots sent his commissioners to the town of Newcastle, Thomas Clifford and Ralph Elderkare. At first the Scots without any long communication demanded great amends, saying that the Englishmen had robbed and spoiled them to their loss, and that the king of England must satisfy them if he were to be called honourable.

It was answered by the commissioners that that the Scottish nation would never keep peace, and while they were making treaties, others were still robbing. The Scots demanded recompense for burning their towns and destroying many of their strong castles. The commissioners replied that if they wrote a letter to the king of their doings and of their desire for peace, and of their being weary of war, then peace could be concluded.

He then went on to the Act of Uses, which regulated the practice of enforcement to use, a technical device designed to reduce royal control over certain military tenures. This was objected to by the gentry rather than the commons.

We marvel what madness is in your brain, or upon what ground you would take authority on you to cause us to break those laws and statutes which have been granted and assented to by all the nobles, knights and gentlemen of this realm (whom the same chiefly concerns), since it in no way concerns you, the base commons of our realm. Also the grounds of all those uses were false and never admitted by any law, but usurped against the prince, contrary to all equity and justice, as it has been openly argued and declared by all the well-learned men of the realm of England in Westminster Hall; whereby you may well perceive how mad and unreasonable your demands are, both in that and the rest, and how unfitting it is for us, and dishonourable, to grant or assent to, and less worthy and decent for you in such a rebellious way to demand the same of your prince.

Concerning the fifteenth from which you demand we release you, think you that we are so fainthearted that by force you of one shire, were you a great many more, could compel us with your insurrections and such rebellious demeanor to remit the same? Or think you that any man will or can take you to be true subjects, who first make and show a loving grant and then by force would compel your sovereign lord and king to release you from the same? The time of payment whereof is not yet come, yes, and seeing the grant will not amount to the tenth penny of the charges which we daily do sustain for your care and safeguarding; be sure, by your pretexts for these your ingratitudes, unnaturalness and unkindness to us now administered, you give us cause, who has always been as much dedicated to your wealth as any king ever was, not so much to plan or study for the promoting of the same, seeing how unkindly and untruly you now deal with us, without any cause or excuse. And do not doubt, although you have no grace nor naturalness on you to consider your duty of allegiance to your king and sovereign lord, the rest of our realm undoubtedly has, and we and they shall so look upon this cause, that we trust it shall be to your confusion, if according to your former letters you do not submit yourselves.

Concerning the first fruits, the first year's revenue of an ecclesiastical benefice; traditionally a church tax, now granted to the king.

We let you know it is a thing granted to us by act of parliament also, to defray part of the great and excessive charges which we support and bear for the maintenance of your wealths and our other subjects. And we have known also that you our commons have much complained in times past that the most part of the goods, lands and possessions of the realm were in the spiritual men's hands; and yet, loving subjects as you may be, you cannot find it in your hearts that your prince and sovereign lord should have any part thereof (and yet it is in no way prejudicial to you, our commons), but rebel and unlaw-

fully rise against your prince, contrary to the duty of allegiance and God's commandment. Sirs, remember your follies and traitorous demeanours, and shame not your native country of England, and offend no more so grievously your undoubted king and natural prince, who has always shown himself most loving to you, and remember your duty of allegiance, and that you are bound to obey us, your king, both by God's commandment and the law of nature.

Therefore we charge you again upon the foresaid bonds and pains, that you withdraw yourselves to your own houses, every man, and no more assemble contrary to our laws and your allegiances, and you cause those who provoked you to this mischief to be delivered to our lieutenants' hands or ours, and yourselves submit to such fitting punishment as we and our nobles shall think worthy. For do not think that we or our nobles can or will suffer this injury at your hands unrevenged, if you do not give place to our sovereignty, and show yourselves as bounden and obedient subjects, and no more meddle henceforth with the weighty affairs of the realm, the direction of which appertains only to us, your king, and such noblemen and counsellors as we like to elect and chose to order the same.

And thus we pray to almighty God to give you grace to do your duties, to use yourselves towards us like true and faithful subjects however we may have cause to order you thereafter, and rather obediently to consent amongst you to deliver into the hands of our lieutenant a hundred persons, to be dealt with according to their deserts at our will and pleasure, than by your obstinacy and willfulness to put yourselves, your wives, children, lands, goods and chattels, besides incurring the indignation of God, to the risk of total destruction and utter ruin by force and violence of the sword."

After the Lincolnshire men had received this, the king's answer to their petitions, each mistrusting the other as to who should be noted to be the greatest meddler, they very slowly began to shrink, and out of hand they were all divided, and every man at home in his own house in peace. But the captains of these rebels did not all make a clean escape, but were after apprehended, and treated as they deserved. He who took upon himself to be captain of this rout named himself Captain Cobbler, but it was a monk called Doctor Makerel with several others who afterwards were taken and executed.

Local government

Early Tudor England was more centralized than most European kingdoms, but although the authority of Westminster was followed in the Midlands and the South, elsewhere in the kingdom a number of private franchises retained special privileges in administering justice. In the North, several great lordships built up in the early Middle Ages as a defence against the Scots were still in the hands of private lords; the bishop of Durham's palatinate was in formal terms the most independent jurisdiction in England. Even those controlled by the monarch kept their separate status. One consequence of these jurisdictions was that large areas of the North, Lancashire, Cheshire and Durham, were not represented in parliament.

Wales also presented a host of administrative problems. Although Edward I had formally united it with England in 1284, it remained excluded from parliament and internally disunited: old Welsh princely jurisdictions long annexed to the crown lay side-by-side with Anglo-Norman lordships, many of which were still in private hands. Despite the fact that the murderous results of the Wars of the Roses had placed some of them in the grasp of the monarchy, it was still easy for a criminal to slip from area to area to avoid justice, aided by the fact that, unlike the independent franchises in England, Welsh jurisdictions had different laws from area to area.

Cromwell, Henry VIII's spiritual deputy, in promoting revolutionary religious change, preferred to do so with the consent of parliament. It was therefore useful to widen the regional representation of MPs. In 1536, Parliament converted the franchises into normal counties, with sheriffs and justices of the peace, where the king's writ ran as in the rest of the realm. There was no serious resistance, even from the great palatinate of Durham, whose bishop, Cuthbert Tunstall would have been horrified at any suggestion that he should resist Henry VIII's wishes. The complex process of turning Wales into a governable part of the realm was completed by further major legislation in 1543. The Welsh lost the remains of their customary law, but also lost their inferior, colonial status. Wales was still different from England – the Council in the Marches of Wales gained rather than lost powers in the principality, and the English border counties and the crown kept its theoretical right, inherited from the Welsh princes, to change or modify laws in Wales. Finally, a different structure of supervising justice was created. Instead of the assize circuits of England, "great sessions" were introduced; these courts controlled groups of Welsh counties, and were not answerable to

Above   Henry attending parliament in 1523. This was the assembly in which Sir Thomas More, as Speaker, made his well-known claim to freedom of speech. Wolsey bungled a demand for extra taxation.

the central courts at Westminster.

Although the North boasted a formidable collection of noblemen with minds of their own, in particular the Percys and the Dacres, Cromwell's ingenuity broke their power, and the defeat of the Pilgrimage of Grace in 1537 provided the opportunity to strengthen the crown's hand in the North. Direct government from Westminster was impractical, so part of the solution was to give the wardenships of the Scottish border to reliable royal servants, and part was to increase the criminal jurisdiction of the Council of the North, a body which the Tudors had taken over from Richard III, who had established it while ruling the North before his accession to the throne. At the same time it was relieved of its responsibilities for administering royal estates. Parliamentary representation was also extended as it had been in Wales, with southern patterns of government brought to the North. Similar experiments in local administration were tried in the south-west in 1539 in the aftermath of the execution of Henry Courteney. Courteney was executed, and his son imprisoned, on dubious charges of treason arising from the fact that he was a grandson of Edward IV, via his mother Catherine. The council established to bring direct royal government to the region lapsed in little more than a year.

All these things thus ended, the country appeased, and all things quiet, the king's majesty retired and broke up his army.

The next disturbance to Henry's plans was the Pilgrimage of Grace.

But, even within six days after, the king was truly informed that there was a new insurrection made by the northern men, who had assembled themselves into a huge and great army of warlike men, well appointed with captains, horse, armour and artillery, to the number of 40,000 men, who had encamped themselves in Yorkshire. And these men had bound themselves to each other by their oath to be faithful and obedient to their captain.

They also declared, by their proclamation solemnly made, that their insurrection should extend no further than to the maintenance and defence of the faith of Christ and the deliverance of holy church, sore decayed and oppressed, and to the furtherance also of private and public matters in the realm concerning the wealth of all the king's poor subjects. They called this, their seditious and traitorous voyage, a holy and blessed pilgrimage; they also had certain banners in the field whereon was painted Christ hanging on the cross on one side, and a chalice with a painted cake in it on the other side, with various other banners of similar hypocrisy and feigned sanctity. The soldiers also had a certain cognizance or badge embroidered or set upon the sleeves of their coats which was a representation of the five wounds of Christ, and in the midst thereof was written the name of Our Lord, and thus the rebellious garrison of Satan set forth and decked themselves with his false and counterfeited signs of holiness, only to delude and deceive the simple and ignorant people.

After the king's highness was informed of this newly arisen insurrection he, making no delay in so weighty a matter, caused with all speed the dukes of Norfolk and Suffolk, the marquis of Exeter, the earl of Shrewsbury and others, accompanied by his mighty and royal army which was of great power and strength, immediately to set upon the rebels. But when these noble captains and counsellors approached the rebels and saw their number and how they were determined on battle, they worked with great prudence to pacify all without shedding blood.

But the northern men were so stiff-necked that they would in no way stoop, but stoutly stood and maintained their wicked enterprise. Therefore the abovesaid nobles, perceiving and seeing no other way to pacify these wretched rebels, agreed upon a battle; the battle was appointed and a day was assigned. But the night before the day appointed for the battle a little rain fell, nothing to speak of, but yet as if by a great miracle of God the water, which was a very small ford which the day before men might have gone over dry shod, suddenly rose to such a height depth and breadth that no man who lived there had ever seen before, so that on the day, even when the hour of battle should have come, it was impossible for one army to get at the other.

After this appointment made between both the armies, disappointed, as it is to be thought, only by God who extended his great mercy and had compassion on the great number of innocent persons who in that deadly slaughter would have been likely to have been murdered, could not take place. Then by the great wisdom and policy of the said captains a consultation was held and a pardon obtained from the king's majesty for all the captains and chief movers of this insurrection, and they promised that such things as they found themselves aggrieved by, all would be gently heard and their reasonable petitions granted, and that their articles should be presented to the king, so that by his highness' authority and the wisdom of his council all things should be brought to good order and conclusion. And with this order every man quietly departed, and those who before were bent as hot as fire on fighting, being prevented by God, went now peaceably to their houses, and were as cold as water.

In this time of insurrection, and in the rage of hurly burly, even when the king's army and the rebels were ready to join battle, the king's banner being displayed and the king's majesty then lying at Windsor, there was a butcher living within 5 miles of Windsor who caused a priest to preach that all those who took part with the Yorkshiremen, whom he named God's people, did fight and defend God's quarrel. And further the said butcher in selling his meat, when someone offered him a lower price for a sheep than he asked for it, he answered, "Nay, by God's soul, I had rather the good fellows of the North had it amongst them, and a score more of the best I have." This priest and butcher were accused by the king's council of the abovesaid treason on

The Pilgrimage of Grace

The Pilgrimage of Grace was the worst political crisis of Henry VIII's reign. The grievances that inspired it stretched back to 1485 and the policy that Henry and his father had followed towards the traditional nobility of the North, especially the Lumley, Percy and Neville families, whose status and authority had been dented by court oriented forces such as the embryonic 'council' at York, leaving them emasculated before their followings and angry at the new-found power of upstart nobles and gentry.

The pace of change quickened with the advent of Thomas Cromwell's administration in the 1530s. Here was a man whose sympathies were plainly with the protestants. The Statute of Uses prevented the gentry from bestowing their property by will, and people began to ask what other rights and privileges were likely to fall before Cromwell's assault. There were rumours of heavier taxation; conscription; and even that poor men were to be forbidden to eat white bread.

Harvests had been bad in the mid-1530s and the rise in prices caused landlords to seek a better profit from their lands by raising rents and entry fines and by converting arable land to pasture by enclosing fields. The fabric of society seemed to be under threat, and from lord to peasant there were those who saw Cromwell as the architect of their problems.

Lord Hussey wrote to Chapuys, the Holy Roman Emperor's ambassador to Henry's court, suggesting that if Charles V sent troops to England it would lead to the restoration of Catherine of Aragon, and catholicism and traditional values.

However, he was soon overtaken by events. In October 1536 the commons of north Lincolnshire rebelled when they heard rumours that feast days were no longer to be kept as holidays, and at Louth, where the local community was particularly proud of its magnificent parish church, St Grace, it appeared as if covetous eyes were being cast on its treasures and ornaments. On hearing these remarks, one of the assembled company "fashioned to draw his dagger, saying that Louth. . .should make the King and his master Cromwell such a breakfast as he never had." The disturbances spread to the nearby towns of Caistor and Horncastle. The commons nominated their own leaders and marched on Lincoln where the bishop's palace was sacked and a council of war held in the cathedral chapter house. The fragile unity of the movement then began to break up.

However, it soon transpired that worse trouble was to come. At the height of the movement, in November 1536, over 40,000 men advanced to Doncaster, and the king had nothing like sufficient forces available to contain them. However the movement was uncertain of its methods, as well as somewhat diverse in its aims. The leaders insisted that they were not rebels, but loyal servants of the king was were trying to point out to him the error of his ways. It was Henry who insisted that they were rebels, and forced many noblemen to choose between their sympathies and their allegiance.

Below   St Grace's church in Louth, where the most serious rebellion in Henry VIII's reign began.

Monday in the morning, and the same day they were both sent for, and confessed their treason, and so according to the martial law they were sentenced to die. And so on the said Monday they were both examined, condemned and hanged; the butcher was hanged on a new pair of gallows set at the end of the bridge before the castle gate; and the priest was hanged on a tree at the foot of Windsor bridge.

In December this year the Thames of London was all frozen over, therefore the king, with his beautiful spouse queen Jane, rode through the City of London to Greenwich. And this Christmas the king, by his messengers and heralds, sent down into the North his general pardons to all capital offenders. And shortly afterwards came Aske to London, and so to the court, to the king. This Aske was the chief captain of the last rebellion in the North, and was now both pardoned by the king, and his grace received him into his favour and gave to him apparel and great rewards, but as you will later see Aske did not enjoy his new friend the king's kindness for a year and a day, and it was a pity that he had any favour at all, for there lived not a truer wretch as well in person as in disposition and deeds, especially against his anointed governor and sovereign lord.

1537

On 3 February Thomas FitzGerald, late earl of Kildare, and five of his uncles, were drawn, hung and quartered at Tyburn for high treason.

Also in the same month Nicholas Musgrave, Thomas Tilby and others began a new rebellion at Kirkby Stephen in Westmoreland, with 8,000 persons, and besieged the city of Carlisle, from whence they were beaten by the power of the city alone, and on their return the duke of Norfolk, who then was made lieutenant of the North, met them and took the captains, and according to martial law arraigned 74 of them, and hanged them on Carlisle's walls, but Musgrave escaped. And in the same month of February yet another insurrection began by the incitement of Sir Frances Bigod, a man no doubt who loved God and feared his prince with a right obedient and loving fear; but being deceived and provoked to it by false rebellious persons it was his fortune to taste the end which belongs to rebels. Such are men when God leaves them to themselves, and when they will try to do the thing which God's holy word forbids. This Bigod was apprehended and brought to the Tower of London.

Fisher and More's opposition to divorce

In 1527, when he became involved in Henry VIII's search for an annulment of his first marriage, John Fisher of Rochester was one of England's most senior and respected bishops. He had preached Henry VII's funeral sermon, and had been one of the cautious clerical councillors whom the young king had inherited from his father. Originally a protégé of Margaret Beaufort, Henry's mother, he was celebrated for his learning and for his austere way of life.

When the king began to convince himself that he had offended against Divine law, Fisher was appealed to by both sides. He did not hesitate to endorse the queen's position, and soon became her most vociferous and effective champion; he later claimed to have written seven books on her behalf. He preached constantly against the king, and vigorously opposed the anti-clerical legislation passed in 1529 by the first session of the reformation parliament.

Henry showed a great deal of restraint in dealing with Fisher and even allowed him to become one of

Above The title page of Thomas More's book, *Utopia, a sophisticated political and social satire.*

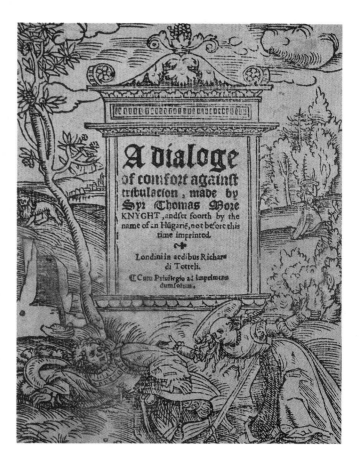

Catherine's official counsel for the trial at Blackfriars in 1529. In 1530 he was one of the 15 senior clerics charged with praemunire for having connived at the exercise of Wolsey's ecclesiastical jurisdiction!

Fisher was threatened twice with treason charges, and was briefly imprisoned. However, he refused to be silenced and became increasingly provocative as the king finally took the law into his own hands. In 1533 he was the only bishop still resisting and secretly appealed to the Holy Roman Emperor, Charles V, to use force to stop Henry's proceedings. Charles had no intention of intervening, and the bishop's action was not known at the time. Eventually, in April 1534, Fisher was arrested for refusing to swear to the Succession Act, which he believed to involve an implicit acceptance of the king's authority over the church. He remained obdurate and was executed in 1535, a few weeks after he had been promoted to the College of Cardinals.

Sir Thomas More's opposition was totally different. He was a layman, a highly respected lawyer and royal servant who had been Speaker of the House of Commons in the parliament of 1523. Like Fisher, he refused to be convinced of the validity of the king's matrimonial cause; unlike the bishop, he was willing to remain silent on the subject and even accepted the lord chancellorship after Cardinal Wolsey's fall. For three years, however, he worked hard behind the scenes to frustrate Henry's purpose, justifying his conduct on the grounds that it was in the best interest of the realm, and of the king himself.

More finally resigned as lord chancellor in 1532 when the clergy surrendered their autonomy to the king: he was no longer able to serve a master who had so offended against the laws of the Church. Having failed to prevent the annulment, or Henry's marriage to Anne Boleyn, More was willing to continue his silence in retirement, but the king was not satisfied.

Like Fisher, More was arrested in 1534 for refusing the oath of succession, and was executed in the following year for persisting in his refusal. However, unlike Fisher, he had not been guilty of an overt act of treason. Of the two men, More is most commonly remembered today as a victim of Henry VIII's ruthlessness. At the time it was the execution of Fisher, a prince of the Church, that horrified Europe.

Also at the latter end of this year the Lord Darcy, Aske, Sir Robert Constable, Sir John Bulmer and his wife, Sir Thomas Percy, brother to the earl of Northumberland, Sir Stephen Hamilton, Nicholas Tempest esquire, William Lumley, son to the Lord Lumley, began again to conspire, although they before had, every one of them, their pardons; and now they were all taken and brought to the Tower of London.

Eustace Chapuys had been in contact with many malcontents in England, including the leaders of the Pilgrimage of Grace. He was as sympathetic to their cause as the chronicler Edward Hall was hostile, and in this letter to the Empress Isabella he describes the progress of events for the benefit of his master's consort. He hints broadly at the need for Imperial intervention.

"I hear from a gentleman, one of the chief officers in the royal army, that the duke of Norfolk, Talbot, the marquis of Dorset, the earl of Rutland and other captains have held a conference with the rebels in the North who, as stated in a former dispatch have risen in arms against this king. They could not have acted more prudently, for otherwise both the king and his kingdom might have been placed in jeopardy.

No one knows yet what resolution the king will take in the present emergency. It is however to be feared that his own arrogance, and the persuasions of those by whom he is surrounded, will prevent him from acceding as he ought to the demands of the northern people; also because it is said that king Francis has promised to come personally to his aid with 40,000 or 50,000 men if he should want them. The rebels on the other hand are sufficiently numerous to defend themselves, and there is every appearance that, instead of diminishing, their number will increase, especially if they only get some assistance in money from abroad. This is particularly his holiness' concern, and if he would only send here Cardinal Pole, who is now in Rome much good might be done.

Reginald Pole was often an outspoken critic of the king's policies.

Henry was not alone in his earnest desire for a son to settle the succession. Many of his subjects were just as concerned, and saw the news of Jane Seymour's pregnancy as an evident sign of God's approval, both of the marriage and of the king's "proceedings" against Rome. This time their prayers were to be answered.

On 27 May 1537, Trinity Sunday, there was a *Te Deum* sung in St Paul's cathedral for joy at the queen's quickening of her child, my lord chancellor, lord privy seal and various other lords and bishops being then present; the mayor and aldermen with the best guilds of the city being there in their liveries, all giving laud and praise to God for joy about it. The bishop of Worcester, Dr Latimer, made an oration before all the lords and commons after the *Te Deum* was sung, explaining the reason for their assembly, which oration was marvellously fruitful to the hearers. And also the same night various great fires were made in London, with a hogshead of wine at every fire for the poor people to drink as long as it lasted. I pray Jesus, if it be his will, to send us a prince.

The summer of 1537 saw the executions of many of the leaders of the Pilgrimage of Grace, which made a grim catalogue when compressed in the manner of the following entry.

"M. Warren, Mayor

Then was my Lord FitzGerald, the earl of Kildare's son in Ireland, and five of his uncles drawn from the Tower to Tyburn, and there hanged, beheaded and quartered, on Saturday the day after Candlemass. On Friday 25 May, Sir John Bulmer was drawn from the Tower of London to Tyburn and there hanged and beheaded, and his wife at the same hour burned at Smithfield, both for treason; and Sir Stephen Hamerton, Sir Nicholas Tempest, the abbot of Fountains, the prior of Guisborough, and Pickering, a doctor, were drawn from the Tower to Tyburn and there hanged, beheaded and quartered. On Saturday 2 June Sir Thomas Percy, Lord Lumley's son, Sir Francis Bigod, the abbot of Jervaulx, in Yorkshire, and another monk were drawn from the Tower to Tyburn and there hanged, beheaded and quartered. On St Peter's eve my Lord Hussey and Sir Robert Constable and Master Aske, who was the chief captain of all, were sent home to the north country, and there they suffered death; and master Aske was hanged in York castle upon the walls in chains. On Saturday 30 June my Lord Darcy was beheaded on Tower Hill. On St Edward's eve, Friday, in the morning Prince Edward was born, the true son of King Henry VIII and Queen Jane, his mother at Hampton Court. His godfathers were the duke of Norfolk, the duke of Suffolk and the bishop of Canterbury; and his godmother was his own sister, who was the daughter of Queen Catherine aforesaid. On

Wednesday, St Crispin's eve, Queen Jane died in child bed, and is buried in Windsor Castle."

1538

The religious reforms introduced under the Royal Supremacy, and implemented by Thomas Cranmer, archbishop of Canterbury and Thomas Cromwell, vice-regent in spirituals, included a vigorous campaign against idolatry and superstition, which revealed numerous weaknesses in the traditional piety of England. The English bible was first authorized in the same year.

This year also in February an image of the crucifix of Christ which had been long used for a great pilgrimage at the abbey of Boxley near Maidstone in Kent, called the Rood of Grace, was taken from there and brought to the king at Westminster, because of certain idolatry and craft which had been perceived in the said rood, for it was made to move the eyes and lips by strings of hair when they wished to show a miracle, and never discovered until now. The archbishop of Canterbury had searched this image at his visitation, and so, at the king's commandment, it was taken from there so that the people might leave the idolatry which had been used there. Also the said rood was first set in the market place at Maidstone, and there the people were openly shown the workings for moving the eyes and lips, so that all the people might see the illusion which had been used in that image by the monks of that place for many years, time out of mind, by which they had got great riches from deceiving the people into thinking that the image had moved by the power of God, which now plainly appeared to be the contrary.

Also it was proclaimed in the star chamber at Westminster, at the end of the Hilary term, in the presence of the lord chancellor and the lords of the king's Council, with several justices of the peace of various shires in England, that the said justices should cause the Bible and Testament in English to be had in their shires, and see that the curates and priests should preach the word of God sincerely and truly to the people, and let the people have the Bible and Testament in English, and to see that they accused no person of heresy, but that he should be examined and tried before the justices in their sessions, and there make their answers and trials according to the statues of this realm about the same, upon pain of the king's displeasure.

On 24 February the image of the rood from the abbey of Boxley in Kent, called the Rood of Grace, was brought to Paul's Cross, and there, at the sermon preached by the bishop of Rochester, the abuses of the ornaments and engines used in olden times in the image were declared, which image was made of paper and cloth from the legs up, each leg and arm was of timber, and so the people had been deluded and caused to do great idolatry by the said image, for a long time, to the derogation of God's honour and great blasphemy of the name of God, as he substantially declared in his sermon by scripture. And also he showed how other images in the church, used for great pilgrimages, had caused great idolatry in this realm, and how he thought that the idolatry will never be left until the said images are taken away; and that the boxes which they have to gather the offerings of the people should be taken away first, so that they should have nothing used to put the charity of the people in; but if there were any persons who wished to offer to such images, the offering could be given straight to poor people, and the people should be shown that they should offer no more to the said images, and then he did not doubt that in a short time they would agree that the said images might be taken away. Also he said that he confessed a woman 20 years ago in Oxford, which woman was the wife of the miller near the abbey of Hailes, and that she showed him that the abbot there had given her many jewels which had been offered there at the holy blood, and how he would have given her one jewel which she knew very well hung about the said holy blood, and said to the abbot that she would not have that "blood" because she was afraid since it hung by the holy blood, and the abbot said "Tush, thou art a fool, it is but duck's blood". And this, said the bishop, showed that it was true, and he besought god that he might be damned if it were not as he said. He also said that he had told the king and council of the same, and that it would be known more openly afterwards. Also, after the sermon was done, the bishop took the image of the rood into the pulpit and broke its workings; then he gave it back to the people, and then the rude people and boys broke the image into pieces, so that not one piece was left whole.

Like every reforming campaign, that of Cranmer and Cromwell at times got out of hand, and the decline of traditional ecclesiastical discipline led to a variety of eccentric performances.

This year, in June and July, a bricklayer called Henry

Daunce (in Whitechapel parish without Aldgate in London) used to preach the word of God in his own house in his garden, where he set a tub to a tree, and preached therein several Sundays and other days, early in the morning and at 6 o'clock at night, and he had a great audience of both spiritual and temporal people. He had no book-learning, in English or any other tongue, and yet he declared scripture as well as if he had studied at the universities. But at last he caused the bishops such indignation because the people followed him, that they sent for him to go to my lord of Canterbury, where he was asked many questions; they could lay nothing to his charge, but prohibited him from preaching because of the great number of people drawn to his sermons.

Also this year, on Bartholomew's Eve, the rood at the north door of St Paul's was taken down by the dean of St Paul's, who was the bishop of Chichester, by the king's commandment, so that the people should do no more idolatry to the said image, and the image of St Uncumber also, in the same church.

St Uncumber, or Wilgifors, was a popular saint of dubious origin, supposed to assist women in getting rid of unwanted husbands.

Also all manner images which were used for common pilgrimages in England and Wales were taken down throughout the realm in every shire by the king's command, so that the people should use no more idolatry to them.

Antipapal propaganda took many forms in the later years of Henry's reign; from serious polemical treatises like Stephen Gardiner's De Vera Obedientia Oratio, to stage plays and carnival antics.

On 17 June there was a triumph on the Thames in front of the king's palace at Westminster, where two barges were prepared with ordnance of war, such as guns and darts of reed, one for the bishop of Rome and his cardinals, and the other for the king's grace, and so they were rowed up and down the Thames from Westminster Bridge to King's Bridge; and the pope and his cardinals made their defiance against England and shot their ordnance one at the other, and so had three courses up and down the water; and at the fourth course they joined together and fought hard. But at last the pope and his cardinals were overcome, and all his men cast overboard into the Thames. However none were drowned for they were persons chosen who could swim, and the king's barge lay hovering nearby to take them up as they were cast overboard, which was a goodly pastime. The king's grace with his lords and certain ladies stood on the leads over his private stairs, which was covered with canvas and set with green bows and roses properly made, so that rosewater sprinkled down from them into the Thames upon the ladies and gentlemen who were underneath in barges and boats to see the pastime. And also two other barges rowed up and down with banners and pennants of the arms of England and St George, in which were sackbuts and waits, who played on the water, and so it finished.

1539

When Jane Seymour died, Henry at once began to search for a new wife, and that search became urgent when Charles V and Francis I signed a ten-year truce in the summer of 1538. England was temporarily isolated, and exposed to a papally orchestrated attack. Negotiations with the Lutheran princes of Germany bore no fruit, but in October 1539 a marriage treaty was signed with the duke of Cleves, a reforming catholic. Despite this favourable account the king was not pleased with his bride.

This year on St John's day, 27 December, Lady Anne, daughter of the duke of Cleves in Germany, landed at Dover at 5 o'clock at night, and there was honourably received by the duke of Suffolk and other great lords, and so lodged in the castle. And on the following Monday she rode to Canterbury where she was honourably received by the archbishop of Canterbury and other great men, and lodged at the king's palace at St Austin's, and there highly feasted. On Tuesday she came to Sittingbourne.

1540

On New Year's Eve the duke of Norfolk with other knights and the barons of the exchequer received her grace on the heath, two miles beyond Rochester, and so brought her to the abbey of Rochester where she stayed that night and all New Years Day. And on New Years Day in the afternoon the king's grace with five of his privy chamber, being disguised with mottled cloaks with hoods so that they should not be recognized, came secretly to Rochester, and so went up into the chamber where the said Lady Anne was looking out of a window to see the bull-baiting which was going on in the courtyard, and suddenly he embraced and kissed her, and showed her a token which the king had sent her for a New Year's gift, and she being abashed and not knowing who it

Marriage to Anne of Cleves

When Henry VIII rejected papal authority and annulled his marriage to Catherine of Aragon in 1533, he knew he was incurring the wrath of the Holy Roman Emperor, Charles V, who was Catherine's nephew. Nevertheless he thought he could exploit the long-standing enmity between the Empire and France, and so protect himself from attack. In 1539, however, Francis I and the Emperor signed the Treaty of Toledo. By this, and earlier accords, the two monarchs bound themselves to sever relations with England and co-operate against the enemies of Christendom – by which they meant protestant heretics as well as Turks. At the same time, Pope Paul III was organizing a Catholic crusade against him.

Henry responded to this unforeseen threat by disposing of potential usurpers, rebuilding the defences of his realm, reasserting his Catholic orthodoxy and seeking allies abroad. Negotiations with the protestant princes of Germany and Thomas Cromwell's promptings, drew him, in January 1540, into marriage with Anne, the sister of duke William of Cleves.

The marriage proved a major embarrassment. Henry found his unfortunate bride, whom he referred to as ''the Flanders mare'' physically repulsive. Furthermore, diplomatic efforts to detach France from the Empire soon showed signs of bearing fruit, rendering the English king's new ally redundant. Henry gave in to the pressures exerted by Cromwell's enemies and their charming protégée Catherine Howard, a future queen for Henry, in July 1540, freed himself from the German entanglement by annulling the marriage. The king endowed Anne with a substantial income and she lived out the remainder of her life in some style in England.

Above   Anne of Cleves found Henry a reluctant husband more interested in reducing his political isolation.

Below   Deal Castle in Kent, built to Continental specifications. One of the coastal fortifications built in 1538 and 1539, during the invasion scare of those years. The Cleves marriage was an alternative security precaution.

was thanked him, and so he spoke with her. But she regarded him little, but always looked out of the window at the bull baiting, and when the king saw that she took so little notice of his coming he went into another chamber and took off his cloak and came in again in a coat of purple velvet. And when the lords and knights saw his grace they did him reverence, and then her grace, seeing the lords doing their duties, humbled herself lowly to the king's majesty, and his grace saluted her again, and they talked together lovingly, and afterwards he took her by the hand and led her to another chamber where their graces amused themselves that night and on Friday until the afternoon. And then his grace took his leave, and left for Gravesend, and there went on his barge and so went to Greenwich that night, and she rode to Dartford that night and lodged there until the morning.

And on Saturday she also went towards Greenwich where, at the foot of Shooters Hill, there was a pavilion set up for her grace, where she was met by the earl of Rutland, who was her grace's chamberlain, with the Lady Douglas, the duchesses of Richmond and of Suffolk, and various other ladies and gentlewomen who were appointed to attend her grace daily at court, with also her grace's servants and yeomen. And there she alighted and changed her dress, and put on a rich gown of cloth of gold, and so mounted her horse again and rode slowly towards Greenwich. And about a mile and more from Greenwich, on Blackheath, the king's majesty met her grace, richly dressed in a coat of cloth of gold, with all his lords and knights, and after they had greeted each other the king's grace and she rode slowly to Greenwich, all the way from there the road being lined by gentlemen in coats of velvet with great chains around their necks, and the mayor of London riding in a coat of crimson velvet with a rich collar of gold round his neck, in front of the king's majesty.

And all the aldermen, with the council of the city and six score of the citizens, all in coats of black velvet with chains of gold around their necks, stood along by the park side where she would pass by, and 24 merchants of the steelyard in coats of velvet with chains, more than 500 people and more than 2,000 of their servants on horseback in new liveries; and also all the guilds of London lay in barges on the Thames at Greenwich, their barges being well trimmed with banners and shields, and various musical instruments, with also two bachelors' barges of the guild of mercers, richly hung with cloth of gold, which was a goodly sight.

So she came to Greenwich that night, and was received as queen. And the next day, being Sunday, the king's grace kept a great court at Greenwich, where his grace with the queen offered at mass, richly dressed. And on Twelfth Night, which was Tuesday, the king's majesty was married to the said queen Anne solemnly, in her closet at Greenwich, and his grace and she went publicly in procession that day, she having a rich coronet of stones and pearls set with rosemary on her hair, and a gown of rich cloth of silver, richly hung with stones and pearls, with all her ladies and gentlewomen following her, which was a goodly sight to behold.

1541

Henry's marriage to Anne of Cleves was annulled by convocation and parliament in July 1540, not long after the fall of its principal architect, Thomas Cromwell. By that time Charles V and Francis I were again at odds, and the international implications of the king's decision were minor. Before the end of July Henry had embarked upon his fifth marriage, with a nineteen year old niece of the duke of Norfolk, named Catherine Howard. Catherine was attractive and experienced, but totally lacking in responsibility and discretion. By the end of October 1541 a damning sequence of infidelities had been proved against her, to Henry's intense anger and distress.

This year on 13 November Sir Thomas Wriothesley, secretary to the king, came to Hampton Court to the queen, and called all the ladies and gentlewomen and her servants into the great chamber, and there openly before them declared certain offences she had committed in misusing her body with certain persons before the king's time, because of which he there discharged all her household; and the morning after she was taken to Sion, with my Lady Bainton and two other gentlewomen and certain of her servants to wait on her there until the king's further pleasure. And various people were taken to the Tower of London, such as my Lady Rochford, Master Culpepper, one of the king's privy chamber, and others.

On 1 December Thomas Culpepper, one of the gentlemen of the king's privy chamber, and Francis Dorand, gentleman, were arraigned at the Guildhall in London, for high treason against the king's majesty, in misdemeanour with the queen, as appeared

Cromwell's fall

In 1538 Thomas Cromwell used his authority as Henry VIII's Ecclesiastical Deputy to issue Injunctions to the clergy which were intended to advance the process of the reformation significantly. These ordered the removal of idolatrous images from churches, prohibited rituals such as creeping to the cross, which were not justified by Scripture, and required an English translation of the Bible to be made available in every parish church.

The Injunctions, and Cromwell's continuing support for the cause of reform, added fuel to the furious conflicts already raging in the pulpits of London, between reformers such as Robert Barnes, Thomas Garret and William Jerome and conservative preachers appointed by John Stokesley, bishop of London. This presented the king's government with serious problems: some of the reformers were as concerned with remedying social grievances – for example, inequalities in the distribution of wealth – as they were with religious reforms. Their preaching could be interpreted as subversive, and the increasing public disorder which accompanied their sermons could be seen as a sign of a fatal slide towards anarchy.

Henry was not merely faced with the problem of restoring order and maintaining established authority, he also had to avert the possibility of a Catholic crusade against him, a result of the recently established amity between Francis I of France and the Holy Roman Emperor Charles V. This threat gave Cromwell's enemies in the Privy Council – prominent among them Stephen Gardiner, bishop of Winchester, and Thomas Howard, 3rd duke of Norfolk – the opportunity to undermine his position and strike a heavy blow for the ancient faith. They were able to argue convincingly that the enforcement of Catholic orthodoxy, albeit within an independent national church, would re-establish domestic harmony and reduce the likelihood of foreign invasion.

Accordingly, Henry took considerable pains to see that the parliament of 1539 passed the Act of Six Articles – the "whip with six strings". This reaffirmed the essentials of the Catholic faith, restored the powers of the episcopal courts to deal with heresy, and provided a range of ferocious penalties for dissent, including death by burning for denial of the real presence in the elements of the eucharist.

The Act, however, did not end the war of the pulpits in London or resolve the factional conflicts at court. Cromwell not only survived the crisis of 1539, he also fought back and seemingly strengthened his position, being created earl of Essex and winning appointment as

Above   A contemporary painting of Francis I of France and the Holy Roman Emperor Charles V renewing their friendship.

Lord Great Chamberlain in April 1540. This enabled him, though at some risk, to continue his support for the increasingly outspoken reformers, who defied the new legislation and challenged the authority of government to decide questions of religion.

He was not, however, able to deal with his enemies on the council, who used the king's personal distaste for the marriage which Cromwell had arranged with Anne of Cleves against him, while also exploiting the continuing unrest arising from religious controversies. In June 1540, they convinced Henry that Cromwell was a radical heretic, though there is no convincing evidence that he was any more than a reformer with a zealous belief in the primacy of the Bible and the importance of preaching. He was arrested suddenly at a council meeting, declared a traitor by Act of Attainder, and beheaded by a clumsy and incompetent headsman on 28 July 1540.

by their indictment which they confessed to, and they were sentenced to be drawn, hanged and quartered, the lord mayor sitting there as chief, the lord chancellor on his right hand, and the duke of Norfolk on his left hand, the duke of Suffolk, the lord privy seal, the earls of Sussex, of Hertford, and various others of the king's council sitting with all the judges also in commission that day. And on 10 December the said Culpepper and Dorand were drawn from the Tower of London to Tyburn, and there Culpepper, after exhorting the people to pray for him, stood on the ground by the gallows, knelt down and had his head struck off; and then Dorand was hanged, dismembered, disembowelled, beheaded and quartered. Culpepper's body was buried at St Sepulchre's church near Newgate, and their heads were set on London Bridge.

1542

By the end of this year Henry was again moving towards war with France, and he deliberately provoked hostilities with Scotland in order to prevent a repetition of the invasion of 1513. In responding to this provocation, James V suffered a major defeat at Solway Moss on 23 November.

The King of Scots, hearing that the army was returned, raised an army of 15,000 men chosen from all parts of his realm under the guidance of lord Maxwell, lord warden of his West Marches, boasting that they would stay as long in England as the duke of Norfolk did in Scotland. And so on Friday they crossed the Water of Esk and burnt some of the houses of the Grahams, right on the Border. Thomas, Dacre's bastard, and Jack of Musgrave sent word to Sir Thomas Wharton, the king's warden on the West Marches, to come to their help. But the two valiant captains, although the Scots attacked fiercely, manfully and courageously set upon them with 100 light horse, and left a detachment on the side of a hill, which dismayed the Scots amazingly: either they thought that the duke of Norfolk had come to the West Marches with his great army, or they thought that some greater army was coming, when they saw Sir Thomas Wharton coming with only 300 men. But at that time God so ordained it that at the first brunt they fled and the Englishmen followed, and there were taken prisoner the earls of Cassilis and Glencairn, lord Maxwell, admiral and warden, lord Fleming, lord Somerville, lord Oliphant, lord Gray, Sir Oliver Sinclair, the king's

The return to war

In October 1540, the good relations between the Holy Roman Emperor Charles V and Francis I of France broke down, when Charles gave his son Philip the duchy of Milan. This freed Henry VIII from the fear of a joint Franco-Imperial invasion and gave him the opportunity to settle scores with his French and Scottish neighbours.

He turned first to James V of Scotland, whom he wished to detach from his French alliance and allegiance to Rome. Employing a combination of threatening embassies and raids across the border, he did his best to browbeat the Scottish king into entering an alliance that would have turned Scotland almost into a vassal kingdom.

When these measures failed, he embarked on a full-scale war and in November 1542, at Solway Moss, inflicted a humiliating defeat on the Scots. James V died three weeks later, supposedly of a broken heart, leaving his throne to Mary, his six-year-old daughter.

With Scottish military power broken and a minor on the throne of Scotland, Henry held all the cards he needed to achieve a resounding diplomatic coup. He overplayed his hand badly, however. He embarked on a war with France in 1543 as an ally of Charles V, before he had settled matters in Scotland. At the same time he tried to press entirely unrealistic demands on the Scots, among them a marriage between his son Edward and the baby queen, together with Mary's surrender into English hands after the union.

These demands were repugnant to Scots of every political complexion, and consequently Henry secured far less, in the Treaty of Greenwich of July 1543, than he had hoped for. Namely, no more than peace, and an agreement that Mary and Edward would one day marry. Even this apparent success proved an illusion –

Francis I sent troops to Scotland to bolster the pro-French party and protect his interests there. This enabled Cardinal Beaton, archbishop of St Andrews, to take control of government and in December to repudiate the treaties.

Henry's policy in Scotland was wrecked and he was obliged to renew his war there and significantly extend hostilities against France. In May 1544 he sent Edward Seymour, 1st earl of Hertford, to ravage the Lowlands, and in July he invaded France in person at the head of an army of 40,000 men.

The campaign went relatively well at first, although there was little co-operation between Henry and his imperial ally. The king displayed unexpected energy and enthusiasm, and secured a significant success when Boulogne surrendered to him in September. But on the very day of this triumph Charles V withdrew from the war, leaving Henry to face the French alone – while the war with Scotland dragged on.

The situation was precarious for much of 1545. Francis I assembled an army of 50,000 men, sent

Above   The fortification at Dover, built to guard against possible attacks from France.

Far left   James V of Scotland with Mary of Guise.

reinforcements to Scotland, laid siege to Boulogne, and prepared a fleet of over 200 ships for an attack on the English coast. The French raided the Solent in July which led to the loss, with over 500 hands, of one of Henry's finest ships, the *Mary Rose*, when she capsized.

The English fleet, whose size, strength and efficiency had improved greatly during Henry's reign, took the offensive and after a series of inconclusive engagements regained control of the Channel. Francis was unable to prevent Henry from supplying Boulogne by sea; he could not protect his own coastline from attack, and was fearful that Charles V would intervene against him. He therefore had little option but to make peace on the best terms available. These, negotiated at Ardres in June 1546, obliged him to abandon the Scots, allowed the English to occupy Boulogne for eight years, and required him to pay an indemnity.

minion, John Ross, lord of Oragy, Robert Erskine, the lord Maxwell's two brothers, John Lesley, bastard of the earl of Rothes, and two hundred more gentlemen, and over eight hundred common people, so many that some men, yes and women too, had three or four prisoners. They took also twenty-four guns, four carts with spears and ten pavilions. This was done by the hand of God, for the cardinal of Scotland promised them heaven for the destruction of England.

1543

After the fall of Thomas Cromwell three years earlier, the pace of religious reform was checked, and the orthodox doctrine of the mass again began to be enforced with some rigour. John Marbeck had a narrow escape.

In this month there were indicted, arraigned and condemned at New Windsor four men, namely, Anthony Pearson, a priest, Robert Testwood, a singing man, Henry Filmer, a tailor, and John Marbeck, a singing man. All these men were at the same time, as I have said, arraigned and condemned of heresy, by force of the Six Articles. These are the heresies they were condemned for, as is alleged in their indictments. Firstly that Anthony Pearson preached for two years before he was arraigned in a place called Winkfield, and there said: "That as Christ was hung between two thieves, even so when the priest is at mass, and has consecrated and lifts him up over his head, then he hangs between two thieves, unless the priest preaches the word of God truly, as he has taken it upon him to do."

Also he said to the people from the pulpit: "You shall not eat the body of Christ as he hung upon the cross, gnawing it with your teeth so that the blood runs about your lips, but you shall eat it today as you will eat it tomorrow, the next day and every day, for it refreshes not the body but the spirit."

Also, after he had preached and commended the scripture, calling it the word of God, he said as follows: "This is the word, this is the bread, this is the body of Christ."

Also, he said that Christ, sitting with his disciples, took bread and blessed it, and broke it, and gave it to his disciples saying, "This is my flesh, take it and eat it," and likewise took the wine and blessed it, and gave it to his disciples saying: "Take and drink it, this is my blood". "What is this to us, but to take the scripture of God, and to break it to the people."

Henry Filmer, the tailor, was arraigned of this article, that he said that the sacrament of the altar is nothing but a symbol and a ceremony. And also, if God is in the sacrament of the altar, I have eaten twenty Gods in my life.

Robert Testwood was arraigned of this article, that he said, at the time when the priest was lifting up the sacrament, "What, will you lift him up so high, what yet higher, take heed, let him not fall."

John Marbeck was arraigned, that he had with his own hand gathered from various men's writings certain things which were expressly against both the mass and the sacrament of the altar.

These four persons were arraigned, condemned, and burned for the abovesaid, except John Marbeck, whose honesty and innocence purchased for him the king's pardon; the other three were burned at Windsor.

1544

Shortly after the defeat of his forces at Solway Mass, James V died.

In this year also the king's majesty prepared two great armies for France. One was conducted and led by the duke of Norfolk and the gentle Lord Russell, lord privy seal; it encamped at Muttrell and besieged the town where they stayed a long time, and left the town as they found it. The other army was led by the valiant duke of Suffolk, who was the king's lieutenant for that army and was accompanied by the lord chamberlain, the earl of Arundel, marshall of the field, and Sir John Gage, comptroller of the king's house, and Sir Anthony Brown, master of the king's horse, with many other different captains. On 19 July they encamped before Boulogne on the east side on a hill, where after many sharp skirmishes they gained first the citadel and shortly after lower Boulogne.

On 14 July the king's majesty in his royal person crossed the sea from Dover to Calais and on 26th day encamped himself before Boulogne on the north side within less than half a mile from the town, where his grace remained until the town was surrendered to his majesty. This town was so sore assaulted and so besieged with such an abundance of great ordinance that there was never a more valiant assault made, for besides undermining the castle, tower and walls the town was so beaten with ordinance that

The Church after 1540

In the final years of his reign, Henry VIII presided over what was, in effect, a two-party Church. Religious conservatives and radicals both supported royal supremacy, but disagreed vehemently about the future nature of the national Church.

The conservatives, headed by Stephen Gardiner, bishop of Winchester, held the ascendancy until the summer of 1543, and, with the support of the king, introduced a programme of reform consonant with the Act of Six Articles of 1539, which had reaffirmed the Catholic doctrine of the sacraments. The most striking products of this were the "King's Book", *A Necessary Doctrine and Erudition for Any Christian Man*, and an Act for the Advancement of True Religion. The former upheld the doctrine of transubstantiation, sanctioned prayers and masses for the dead, and denied the doctrine of justification by faith alone. The latter mitigated the severity of the heresy laws and limited access to Thomas Cromwell's *Great Bible*.

The radicals, headed by Thomas Cranmer, archbishop of Canterbury, exploited the king's personal affection for the archbishop, and benefited from the decline in conservative influence following the execution of Catherine Howard and Henry's marriage to Catherine Parr in July 1543. This enabled them to contribute to the continuing process of reform – for example, to publish a new English Litany and a Primer for schoolmasters, and to prepare a Book of Homilies and a new Order of Communion, which were issued in Edward VI's reign.

The king himself was fully aware of this dangerous division within his Church, and took pains to avoid becoming the instrument of either party. His own religious beliefs at this time are hard to pin down. He was a convinced believer in royal supremacy, and firmly committed to the traditional doctrine of the mass, but there are signs that he may have been moving towards protestantism at the end of his life.

In 1545 he told the parliament that his subjects should bring their doctrinal disputes to himself or his council for resolution, because it was his responsibility to ensure that true doctrine was taught.

Above A portrait of Thomas Cranmer, archbishop of Canterbury, by Gerald Flicke. His personal influence over the king not only enabled him to survive several conspiracies designed to convict him of heresy, but also maintained the momentum of reform through the 1540s.

there was not one house left whole within it. And the Frenchmen were pressed so sorely that after the king had assaulted them for about a month they sent from the town to the king two of their chief captains called Monsieur Semblemound and Monsieur de Haies, who declared that the chief captain of the town with his retinue was content to deliver the town to his grace if they might leave with bag and baggage, which request the king's majesty mercifully granted. And so on the next day the duke of Suffolk rode into Boulogne and to him in the king's name they delivered the keys of the town. And in the afternoon all the Frenchmen left Boulogne.

The noble men of war, who were strong and gallant, who came out of the town were of horsemen 67, of footmen 1,563, of gunners 800, of injured men 87, of women and children 1,927. So there were in all who came out of the town 4,444, besides a great number of aged, sick and injured persons who were not able to leave. The last person who came out was Monsieur de Veruine, grand captain of the town, who when he came near the place where the king stood, got down from his horse and came to the king. And after he had talked to him a while the king took him by the hand and he, reverently kneeling on his knees, kissed his hand, and afterwards mounted his horse and left.

Two days later the king's highness, with a naked sword borne before him by the lord marquis of Dorset, rode into Boulogne like a noble and valiant conqueror, and the trumpeters standing on the walls of the town sounded their trumpets at his entry, to the great comfort of all the king's true subjects who beheld it. And on his entry he was met by the duke of Suffolk who delivered to him the keys of the town, and so he rode towards his lodging which was prepared for him on the south side of the town. Within two days after the king rode about all the town within the walls, and then commanded that Our Lady's church in Boulogne should be defaced and taken down, and there he appointed a mount to be made, for the greater defence and strength of the town.

When the king had set all things there in such order as to his wisdom seemed best, he returned to England to the great rejoicing of all his subjects.

1545

Francis had no intention of accepting the loss of Boulogne, and as Anglo-Imperial relations became strained in the summer of 1545, he prepared a major counter attack.

The court in Henry's final years

When, on 28 July 1540, Henry VIII married Catherine Howard, the niece and protégé of Thomas Howard, 3rd duke of Norfolk, he had many reasons to celebrate his good fortune. He had disposed of Thomas Cromwell, the minister whose support for religious radicals had become a grave danger. He had freed himself from Anne of Cleves and the diplomatic entanglements associated with marriage to her. And he had, it seemed, won the passionate love of a vivacious young woman, in spite of the 30 years difference in their ages. The situation, however, was less rosy than it may have appeared, and the king's fifth marriage did not inaugurate an Indian summer for his reign.

Cromwell's fall, and the Act of Precedence of 1539, giving priority to the great officers of state, had enabled the minister's enemies, led by Norfolk and Stephen Gardiner, bishop of Winchester, both religious conservatives, to turn the Privy Council into a formally organized board of government whose membership was dominated by aristocratic – and conservative – office holders. However, Cromwell had exploited the opportunities created by his factional victories in 1536–9 to take control of the court and to pack the Privy Chamber with his own adherents, educated radicals like himself. The victory of the conservatives could not be complete until these men were removed from their proximity to the volatile and suggestible king.

In view of the influence which could be exerted through the queen, the Council and the new Lord Great Chamberlain, Robert Radcliffe, 1st earl of Essex, it seemed that the conservatives would root out their enemies in time. Catherine's behaviour, however, made this unlikely. Tiring of a husband who was grossly overweight, bald, partially incapacitated by ulcers on his legs, and increasingly preoccupied with theology, she embarked on recklessly dangerous affairs with Francis Dereham, a former lover, and Thomas Culpeper, a Gentleman of the Privy Chamber. When Henry learned of her misbehaviour, he sent her to the block, in February 1542, and severely punished the Howard family for her treason.

In July 1543, the king married again, for the sixth and last time. His new wife was Catherine Parr the 31-year-old widow of John Neville, Lord Latimer. Far from being a creature of the conservative faction like her predecessor, she was a devout and committed reformer who arranged for regular sermons and scripture classes in her chambers. She encouraged radical preachers such as Hugh Latimer and Miles Coverdale, and ensured that

the royal nursery was staffed with reforming humanists, among them John Cheke and Anthony Cooke. Furthermore, her brother William, 1st earl of Essex, and a Privy Councillor, and her brother-in-law Sir William Herbert, a Chief Gentleman of the Privy Chamber, supported two men of reformist persuasion whose successes in the wars with France and Scotland brought them into political prominence. These were John Dudley, Viscount Lisle, who commanded the fleet against the French in the naval war of 1545, and Edward Seymour, 1st earl of Hertford, the king's brother-in-law, who led successful invasions of Scotland in 1544 and 1545, and who also took command in France in 1546. In 1545, Dudley and Seymour entered into an alliance with the radicals of the Privy Chamber that successfully challenged the conservative supremacy in the Privy Council.

The continuing antagonism between radical Privy Chamber and conservative Council virtually institutionalized faction, and ensured that Henry was kept under constant pressure from his feuding servants and councillors. It is hardly surprising that he became increasingly morose and unpredictable in his pain-racked final years.

Above   Catherine Parr, Henry's last queen. Both her learning and her influence have been much over stated, but her sympathy with the reformers helped them to regain the king's ear.

Above left   The king in later life, playing the harp and accompanied by his long serving jester, Will Somers.

On 18 July at 9 o'clock at night began thunder and lightning with some rain which continued all night until 8 o'clock the next morning, and that afternoon all the French king's navy came out of Newhaven and Dieppe and arrived off the coast of England in Sussex, before Brighton, in all over 300 ships besides 24 galleys which they had. And there they set certain of their soldiers on shore to burn, but the beacons were fired and the men of the country came down so thick that the French men fled and did little harm.

On 20 July the Mary Rose, one of the king's great ships, by great misfortune due to leaving the port holds open, sank as she turned and all the men in her except for 40 drowned, above 500 persons. Sir George Carew, who was captain, was drowned. This was done off Portsmouth harbour.

On 21 July the French galleys and navy came off Portsmouth harbour, and landed some of their army in the Isle of Wight, and about 2,000 men burned and camped there, and at every tide they came with their galleys and shot their ordinance at the king's ships in the harbour. But the wind was so calm that the king's ships could carry no sail, which was a great discomfort for them.

On 24 July the City of London sent 1,500 men towards Portsmouth, who mustered in St George's Field, the under-chamberlain and the sword-bearer having charge of them all. To assist them an honest citizen was appointed from every ward until they got to Portsmouth. But when they got to Farnham they were sent home again by the king's command, for the Frenchmen were gone from the Isle of Wight, and many of them slain and drowned.

For the provision of those soldiers there was levied upon the citizens in every ward certain sums of money like the rate of a fifteenth, which the aldermen of every ward paid out of hand and afterwards gathered back from their wards, and every soldier had paid to him at his setting forth 3s. and at Farnham on returning to London again 2s. more to bring them home.

Thanks to the major changes which had been brought about by the reformation parliament of 1529–36, the power of statute had been considerably augmented. Henry welcomed this development, because he saw the parliament as an apt instrument for his own hand, rather than any sort of limitation or potential rival.

Above all he saw it as an ally in the enforcement of his own distinctive brand of reformed religion – a religion of which he was the sovereign arbiter.

On 24 December the king's majesty came into the parliament house, to give his royal assent to such acts as had been passed there, where the speaker made to him an eloquent oration, to which it has always been the custom for the lord chancellor to answer, but at this time it was the king's pleasure that it should be otherwise, for the king himself answered, as follows word for word, as near as I was able to report it.

"Although my Chancellor for the time being has been used, before this time, very eloquently and substantially to answer such orations as have been set forth in this high court of parliament, yet he is not so able to open and set forth my mind and meaning and the secrets of my heart in so plain and ample manner as I myself can. Wherefore, taking it upon myself to answer your eloquent oration, master speaker, I say that where you, in the name of our well beloved commons, have both praised and extolled me for the notable qualities which you have conceived to be in me, I most heartily thank you all that you have reminded me of my duty, which is to endeavour myself to obtain and get such excellent qualities and necessary virtues as a prince or governor should or ought to have, of which gifts I recognize myself both bare and barren. But for such small qualities as God has endowed me with I render to his goodness my most humble thanks, intending with all my wit and diligence to get and acquire for myself such notable virtues and princely qualities as you have alleged to be incorporated in my person. Having first remembered these thanks for your loving admonition and good counsel, I next thank you again because, considering our great charges (not for our pleasure but for your defence, not for our gain but to our great cost) which we have lately sustained, as well in defence against our and your enemies as for the conquest of that fortress which was to this realm most displeasant and noisome, and shall be by God's grace hereafter most profitable and pleasant to our nation, you have freely of your own decision granted to us a certain subsidy, specified here in an act, which truly we take in good part, regarding more your kindness than the profit thereof, as he that sets more by your loving hearts than by your substance. Besides this hearty kindness I cannot a little rejoice when I consider the perfect trust and

The Struggle for control

The last two years of Henry VIII's reign were turbulent, characterized by vicious factional conflicts whose outcome remained uncertain almost until the end.

The principal reason for this was that the king's deteriorating health made it probable that he would die before his heir, Prince Edward, attained his majority. In the context of the Succession Act of 1544, this meant that when Edward succeeded his father, England would be governed by a regency council nominated by the old king. Since this council would have the power to advance or reverse the cause of religious reform, and to dispose of royal patronage, its composition was of crucial importance.

The conservatives and reformers intensified their struggle to destroy each other and capture Henry's support. Plot and counter-plot followed in bewildering succession until, in the summer of 1546, the conservatives, headed by Thomas Howard, 3rd duke of Norfolk and Stepehen Gardiner, bishop of Winchester, played their last card: they attempted to prove to the king that his own wife, Queen Catherine Parr, was a heretic.

Henry declined publicly to be convinced, and this gave the reformers, headed by Edward Seymour, 1st earl of Hertford, and counselled by Sir William Paget, one of the wiliest politicians of the time, the opportunity to counterattack. In December, they

Above Henry VIII in old age.

Below Apothecary's bills listing drugs and medical supplies, such as maidenhair, scolopender, and syrup of vinegar. Henry had always been a hypochondriac and genuine illness made him an apothecary's dream.

accused Henry Howard, earl of Surrey, Norfolk's son, of planning to stage a treasonable coup. Since the earl had been recklessly outspoken about his own royal blood, and his determination to see his father head the regency council, the accusation probably rang true to the dying king. As a result he had both father and son arrested, and the latter sent to the block.

sure confidence which you have put in me, as men having undoubted hope and unfeigned belief in my good deeds and just proceedings for you, since without my desire or request you have committed to my order and disposition all chantries, colleges, hospitals and other places specified in a certain act, firmly trusting that I will order them to the glory of God and the profit of the commonwealth. Surely if, contrary to your expectation, I should suffer the ministries of the church to decay, or learning (which is so great a jewel) to be diminished, a poor and miserable people to be unrelieved, you might say that I, being put in so special a trust as I am in this case, were no trusty friend to you, nor a charitable man to my fellow christians, nor a lover of the public wealth, nor yet one who feared God, to whom account must be rendered of all our doings. Doubt not, I pray you, that your expectations will be fulfilled more Godly or goodly than you will wish or desire, as you will plainly see afterwards.

Now, since I find such kindness on your part towards me, I cannot chose but to love and favour you, affirming that no prince in the world more favours his subjects than I do you, and no subjects or commons more love and obey their sovereign lord than I see you do me, for whose defence my treasure shall not be hidden, nor if necessity requires it will my person be not risked. But although I with you and you with me are in this perfect love and concord, this friendly amity cannot continue unless both you, my lords temporal, and you, my lords spiritual, and you, my loving subjects, study and take pains to amend one thing which is surely amiss and far out of order, which I most heartily require you to do, which is that charity and concord is not amongst you, but discord and dissension bears rule in every place. St Paul wrote to the Corinthians, in the 12th chapter; 'Charity is gentle, Charity is not envious, Charity is not proud,' and so on in that chapter. Behold then what love and charity is amongst you when one calls another heretic and anabaptist and he calls him back papist, hypocrite and pharisee. Are these tokens of charity amongst you? No, no, I assure you that this lack of charity amongst yourselves will be the hindrance and assuaging of the fervent love between us, as I said before, unless this is healed and clearly made whole. I must judge the fault and occasion of this discord to be partly the negligence of you, the fathers and preachers of the spirituality. For if I know a man who lives in adultery I must judge him to be a lecherous and carnal person; if I see a man boast and brag about himself I cannot but deem him a proud man. I see and hear daily that you of the clergy preach against each other without charity or discretion. Some are too stiff in their old 'Mumpsimus', others are too busy and curious in their new 'Sumpsimus'. Thus almost all men are in variety and discord, and few or none truly and sincerely preach the word of God as they ought to do. Shall I now judge you to be charitable persons who do this? No, no, I cannot do so. Alas, how can the poor souls live in concord when you preachers sow amongst them in your sermons debate and discord? They look to you for light and you bring them darkness. Amend these crimes, I exhort you, and set forth God's word truly, both by true preaching and giving a good example, or else, I, whom God has appointed his vicar and high minister here, will see these divisions extinct, and these enormities corrected, according to my true duty, or else I am an unprofitable servant and an untrue officer.

Although, as I say, the spiritual men are at some fault that charity is not kept amongst you, yet the temporality are not clean and unspotted with malice and envy, for you rail against bishops, speak slanderously of priests, and rebuke and taunt preachers, both against good order and Christian brotherhood. If you know for certain that a bishop or preacher errs or teaches perverse doctrine, come and declare it to some of our council or to us, to whom is committed by God the high authority to reform and order such causes and behaviour. But be not judges yourselves, according to your own fantastical opinions and vain expositions, for in such high causes you may easily err. And although you are allowed to read holy scripture and to have the word of God in your mother tongue, you must understand that you are licensed to do so only to inform your own conscience and instruct your children and family, not to dispute and make scripture a railing and taunting stock against priests and preachers (as many light people do). I am very sorry to know and hear how irreverently that precious jewel, the word of God, is disputed, rhymed, sung and jangled in every alehouse and tavern, contrary to the true meaning and doctrine of the same. And yet I am equally sorry that the readers of scripture follow it in their deeds so faintly and coldly. For I am sure of this, that charity was never so faint amongst you, and virtuous and godly

Henry's Will

When Henry VIII died on 28 January 1547, he left behind a will of extraordinary political significance.

It specified the line of succession to the throne of England. Put simply it provided for the Crown to pass first to Prince Edward, and then if necessary to Princess Mary, Princess Elizabeth, and finally to the descendants of Henry's younger sister Mary, duchess of Suffolk.

The will also named the 16 members of the regency council which would govern England while the new king was still a minor. It excluded prominent conservatives such as Thomas Howard, 3rd duke of Norfolk, who was under sentence of death in the Tower, and Stephen Gardiner, the bishop of Winchester. The will vested the 16 councillors with co-equal authority, and provided for corporate rule.

Finally, the will provided generous legacies for the king's executors and other councillors and servants. Significantly, one clause required the executors to honour any promises of rewards the king might have made, even if these had not been set down in proper legal form. This, and Sir William Paget's convenient memory of his conversations with the dead monarch, facilitated the promotion of four peers – Hertford, Essex, Lisle and Wriothesley – the creation of four new barons, and the distribution of lands worth the huge sum of £3,200 per annum.

The effect of Henry's will was to bring Prince Edward to the throne and confirm the position of the illegitimate princesses Mary and Elizabeth in the line of succession.

However, it is virtually certain that Henry never signed the will. The document was drafted by Sir William Paget, corrected after several discussions with the dying king, and authenticated with the dry stamp, which produced a replica of the royal signature, under the supervision of Sir Anthony Denny, one of the Chief Gentlemen of the Privy Chamber. And although Henry may have approved the use of the stamp – he was on his death-bed, and perhaps incapable of providing a signature – it may have been applied to a document of whose contents he was not fully aware, and what is more, applied after his death.

He would have approved of the arrangements for the succession, since the essentials had already been spelt out in the 1544 Succession Act; and the membership of the regency council would have been exactly as he wished, since a recently discovered draft of the will makes it clear that the list of names was drawn up at a time of the arrest of the Howards, in early December 1546, when the king was still sound in mind. The list

Top Henry's will which he finally approved with his stamp on 30 December 1546.

Above Henry's seal.

was not changed. It is likely that Paget tampered with the will without the king's knowledge, inserting the crucial clauses about the powers of a Regency Council majority and the honouring of promised rewards in order to help Hertford buy the support he needed to win and retain the protectorate.

living was never less found, nor God himself was never, amongst Christians, less reverenced, honoured and served. Therefore, as I said before, be in charity with one another, like brother and brother; love fear and serve God (to which I, as your supreme head and sovereign lord, exhort and require you) and then I doubt not but that love and league which I spoke of in the beginning shall never be dissolved or broken between us. As to the making of laws, which are now made and concluded, I exhort you the makers to be as diligent in putting them into execution as you were in making and furthering them, or else your labour will be in vain and your commonwealth in no way relieved. Now to your petition concerning our royal assent to be given to such acts as have passed both houses: they shall be read openly so that you may hear them." Then they were openly read, and to many his grace assented, and some he assented not to. This, the king's oration, was to his subjects there present such a comfort that the like joy could not be given to them in this world. And thus the acts read, as the custom is, and his assent given, his grace rose and departed.

1546

The circumstances of Henry VIII's decline and death were of great importance to his successor. He was intermittently unconscious during his last weeks, and there was a good deal of controversy over his exact intentions for the minority government that was to follow him. The 17th-century historian Gilbert Burnet presents a vivid account, based partly on oral tradition.

The king was now overgrown with corpulency and fatness, so that he became more and more unwieldy. He could not go up or down stairs, unless he was raised up or let down by an engine. And an old sore in his leg became very uneasy to him, so that all the humours in his body sinking down into his leg, he was much pained, and became exceedingly perverse and intractable, to which his inexcusable severity to the duke of Norfolk and his son may be in great measure imputed. His servants scarcely dared speak to him, to put him in mind of his approaching end. And an Act of Parliament which was made for the security of the king's life had some words in it against the foretelling of his death, which made everyone afraid to speak to him of it, lest he in his angry and imperious humours should have ordered them to be indicted on that statute. But he felt nature declining apace, and so made the will, that he had left behind him at his last going into France, be written over again, with this difference only, that Gardiner, bishop of Winchester, whom he had appointed one of the executors of his will and one of the counsellors to his son until he came of age, was now left out. Of which, when Anthony Brown put the king in mind of it, thinking it was only an omission, he answered that he knew Gardiner's temper well enough, and though he could govern him, yet none of them would be able to do it, and that he would give them much trouble. And when Brown at another time repeated the motion to the king, he told him if he spoke more of it he would strike him out of his will too.

Henry's will named a group of executors to act as his son's regency council, but the councillors themselves immediately applied for reappointment in the name of the new king, and made arrangements for the minority which apparently contravened Henry's intentions. The king's own chronicle records these events, of which he can have been only dimly aware, with characteristic detachment. The last months of Henry's life also saw the eclipse of conservative influence completed by the fall of the Howards. His will then named as his executors a group of men who were predominantly of the reforming party. These executors were supposed to form the regency council for his son.

About Michaelmas in this present year Thomas, duke of Norfolk and Henry, earl of Surrey, his son and heir, upon certain suspicions of treason were committed to the Tower of London. And immediately after the following Christmas, the King then being at the extremity of death, the said Earl was arraigned in the Guildhall before the Lord Mayor of London, the Lord Chancellor of England and various other lords and judges in commission there. The special charge against him was bearing certain arms supposed to belong to the King and to the Prince. Bearing them he denied not, but justified the same as belonging by right to him and all his ancestors, Dukes of Norfolk, and being born by them time out of mind without challenge or impeachment. But to his indictment he pleaded not guilty. And since he was not a Lord of Parliament he was forced to be tried by a common inquest of his country, which found him guilty, and thereupon he was sentenced to death and shortly after was executed at Tower Hill; his death was greatly lamented by many for he was a gentleman endowed with great learning and many excellent virtues.

The Duke his father never came to any trial, but was supposed to be attainted by Parliament, which supposed attainder was upon good and just consideration reversed in the first year of Queen Mary, when there not only appeared the innocence of the said Duke, but to his great honour and commendation he was declared to be a right valiant and true servant of the crown of England.

The King, as said before, now languishing and lying on the verge of death, made his last will and testament, in which he not only yielded himself to almighty God, but also ordered that during the minority of his son Prince Edward, his executors who numbered 16, whose names will be shown hereafter, that they, I say, should also be the counsellors and helpers of the said Prince in all his affairs, both private and public. Their names were these:

Thomas Cranmer, archbishop of Canterbury.

Thomas Wriothesley, Lord Chancellor.

Sir William Paulet, knight of the order, Lord St John, and Lord Great Master.

Sir Edward Seymour, knight of the order, Earl of Hertford, High Chamberlain of England.

Sir John Russel, knight of the order, Lord Privy Seal.

Sir John Dudley, knight of the order, and Viscount Lisle and High Admiral of England.

Cuthbert Tunstall, bishop of Durham.

Sir Anthony Brown, knight of the order, Master of the Horse.

Sir Edmund Montague knight, Chief Justice of the Common Pleas.

Thomas Bromley knight, one of the justices of the King's Bench.

Sir Edward North knight, Chancellor of the Augmentations.

Sir William Paget, knight of the order, Chief Secretary.

Sir Anthony Denny Knight.

Sir William Herbert knight.

Sir Edward Wootton knight.

Nicholas Wootton, dean of Canterbury and York.

As soon as the aforesaid noble King had finished his last will and testament as above said he then yielded his spirit to almighty God, and departed this world on 28 January in the 39th year of his reign and in the year of our lord 1546. His body, according to his will, was conveyed with all funeral pomp to the College of Windsor, there to be interred.

Part III

Edward VI
1547-1553

The reign of Edward was directed by the men with whom he had been surrounded after his accession by his first Protector and Governor, Edward Seymour, duke of Somerset. Minority governments were always afflicted by problems, and those of Edward VI had to cope with serious economic breakdown and social unrest, as well as with the religious strife which they had provoked. By 1551 mounting financial difficulties had also enforced a humiliating retreat from international commitments. However, it was only at the beginning of 1553 that the king's impending majority ceased to dominate the horizon and determine the actions of those in power. The preoccupation then became his imminent death, and what could be done to salvage the Reformation and the Dudley ascendancy.

(Opposite   Edward VI)

1547

After the death of King Henry VIII, his son Edward, Prince of Wales, was come to at Hertford by the earl of Hertford and Sir Anthony Brown, Master of the Horse, for whom beforehand was made great preparation that he might be created Prince of Wales, and afterwards he was brought to Enfield, where he was first told of his father's death, and the same day the death of his father was reported in London, where there was great lamentation and weeping, and suddenly he was proclaimed king. The next day, being the last of January, he was brought to the Tower of London where he stayed for three weeks. And in the meantime the council sat every day for the perform-

ance of the will. During this time the late king was buried at Windsor with much solemnity, and the officers broke their staffs, hurling them into the grave. But they were restored to them again when they came to the Tower.

Only a few days elapsed between Henry's funeral and his son's coronation. The ceremonies of the latter were cut short out of consideration for his youth. Charles Wriothesley gives a brief description.

On 19 February the king's majesty rode from the Tower to Westminster through the City of London, which was richly hung with rich cloths and several pageants, the conduits running wine, the guilds standing in their dress and the aldermen, the lord mayor riding in a crimson velvet gown with a rich collar of gold, with a mace in his hand, in front of the king. And when his majesty came where the aldermen stood, the recorder made a speech to his majesty, and afterwards the chamberlain gave his majesty a purse of cloth of gold as a present from the City, which he thankfully took.

On 20 February, being Quinquagesima Sunday, the king's majesty Edward VI, aged nine years and three months was crowned king of this realm of England, France and Ireland within the church of Westminster with great honour and solemnity. And a great feast was kept that day at Westminster Hall, which was richly hung, his majesty sitting all through dinner with his crown on his head. And after the second course was served, Sir Edward Dymmock came riding into the hall in a full white armour, richly gilded, and his horse richly decked, and threw his gauntlet to wage battle against all men who would not take him as the rightful king of this realm, and then the king drank to him and gave him a cup of gold. And after dinner the king made many knights, and then he changed his clothes and so rode from there to Westminster Place.

Popular ballads reflected the relief that, after so many uncertainties, the Tudor succession had been secured without dispute. This lyrical example was recorded by the 18th-century historian, John Strype, from a manuscript, now lost.

A Ballad sung to King Edward in Cheapside as he passed through London to his coronation.

Sing, up heart, sing, up heart, and sing no more down,
But joy in King Edward that weareth the crown.

Sir, song in time past hath been down a down,
And long it hath lasted in tower and town,
To have it much meeter, down hath been added;
But up is more sweeter to make our hearts gladded.
Sing up heart etc.

King Edward up springeth from puerility,
And toward us bringeth joy and tranquility;
Our hearts may be light and merry cheer,
He shall be of such might, that all the world may him
   fear.
Sing up heart etc.

His father late our sovereign both day and also hour
That in joy he might reign like a prince of high power,
By sea and land hath provided for him eke,

That never king of England had ever the like.
Sing up heart etc.

He hath gotten already Boulogne, that goodly town,
And biddeth sing speedily up, up, and not down.
When he waxeth wight and to manhood doth spring,
He shall be straight then of four realms the king.
Sing up heart etc.

Ye children of England, for the honour of the same,
Take bow and shaft in hand, learn shootage to frame.
That you another day may so do your parts,
To serve your King as well with hands as with hearts.
Sing up heart etc.

Ye children that be towards sing up and not down,
And never play the cowards to him that weareth the
   crown:
But always do your care his pleasure to fulfill,
Then shall you keep right sure the honour of
   England still.
Sing up heart etc.

Venetian diplomats were professional observers and the best trained in Europe. Their reports also had the advantage of being dispassionate and impartial. This description by the retiring ambassador Daniel Barbaro is a particularly good example.

The country is at present subject to the king of England by right, as the eldest hereditary male heir to the Crown. In default of the male line it passes to the female line; but as the sovereignty is undivided, the eldest daughter becomes sole heir; or to the next of kin should there be no daughters.

Besides the succession and heirship, the consent of the lords and commons is requisite so that, before the king's coronation, the people are solemnly asked thrice whether they approve of the king-elect; and the election being confirmed unanimously, the confirmed king takes oath to observe the laws; and is thus crowned, consecrated, anointed, and hailed king. It is indeed true that after the confirmation the king may have to quell insurrection on the part of the nobility, should they consider themselves in any way wronged, as they are many in number, and consider themselves no less noble than their sovereign. But ordinarily the people love their king and put up with anything to retain him, especially when he keeps the promises made them.

If the king comes to the crown at mature age, the government is conducted by his majesty in person and by the lords and commons who sit in Parlia-

Protector of the realm

As Henry VIII lay dying, the earl of Hertford and Sir William Paget secretly agreed that, regardless of the old king's wish for a regency council, Hertford should take over as protector with Paget as first minister. Hertford rode through the early hours of 28 January to reach his nephew, the new king, who was brought to the security of the Tower of London on 31 January. There the council met and agreed to Paget's nomination of the protector. Only then was the demise of the crown made public and Edward VI proclaimed. There followed a prolific distribution of titles and sinecures – Hertford being advanced to the dukedom of Somerset. He played a leading part in the coronation on 20 February.

But his authority was not yet fully secured. He had headed off an irritating challenge from his brother Thomas – though by bringing him into the council he opened the way for others more senior, but likewise excluded by Henry to claim a place there. More serious was the discontent of the conservative, lord chancellor, Wriothesley, created earl of Southampton in the accession honours. Somerset's position so far rested only on the executors' verbal agreement, not on letters patent, which only the Great Seal, held by the chancellor, could authenticate.

Early in March Somerset was able to exploit irregularities in the chancellor's neglect of the legal side of his responsibilities to force his resignation from the council. The Great Seal went to Lord Rich, and was almost at once affixed to the patent giving Somerset the formal authority he sought: in particular he was empowered to appoint whoever he wanted to the Privy Council. He duly brought in some of the older and more experienced men who had not been Henry VIII's executors. But having taken control of the council, Somerset proceeded very largely to ignore it, using its meetings merely to endorse his decisions. When they did meet, the protector was domineering, tactless and rude – one colleague was reduced to tears by his savage tongue. Paget repeatedly warned him that his arrogant behaviour was self-destructive, but Somerset no more listened to him than he did to anyone else. For a time the principal secretaries of state were supplanted by the protector's personal secretaries, Thomas Smith and William Cecil.

Somerset's autocracy is most evident in the vast use he made of proclamations, ruling by edict to a greater extent than any other head of government in the Tudor age. Yet he had for a long time, a widespread reputation for benevolence, as the friend of the poor, ''the good duke''. This derived predominantly from one Act of the

Above   Edward Seymour, Lord Protector for his nephew Edward.

first parliament of the reign which repealed the new treason laws of Henry VIII along with medieval and more recent laws against heresy. That there was a measure of relaxation is undoubted; but it was nothing more than was commonplace at the beginning of a new reign, and Somerset can claim no personal involvement in its drafting. Conversely there is no strong reason to associate him directly with the notorious 1547 Vagrancy Act, which proposed to deal with the problem of long-term unemployment by capital punishment.

It cannot, in fact, be supposed that Somerset had any special consideration for the humbler classes of society. He exploited them, as he did the Crown and the Church, amassing vast estates in the west country and building a great house in London. There seems no truth in the story that he contemplated knocking down Westminster Abbey to provide materials for Somerset House. This apart, little can be said in the protectors favour. He was simply unequal to the eminence to which Henry VIII's brief romance with his sister had chanced to bring him.

ment. If a minor, as at present, they give him governors or protectors, though at present this title of protector has become generally odious, the uncle of the present king having been deprived of it, for the reasons written in the reporter's letter to the senate, dated 6 October 1549. In addition to which it was the intention of the present king's father to leave the care of his son not to one individual, but to several persons with equal authority, although this was not practised, owing to the neglect of many or to the extreme diligence and curiosity of one alone, who in Barbaro's time ruled everything, whence arose endless confusion.

The late king had considered the great danger which threatened the kingdom in case the nobility maintained the power it then possessed; and also that it was not safe to give his son, who at the time of his death was ten years old, in ward to a kinsman. So first of all by strange methods he chose to depress the nobility, leaving them their titles and depriving them of all jurisdiction, so that there is neither duke nor lord in the whole realm who can by law put any one to death, nor who derives his entire revenue from the places of which he is lord.

To secure his son and the crown the late king also gave equal authority to 16 regents, not making any of them chief, that they might rule the ward and the realm. Which was in truth well judged, had not all his orders, by some misfortune unknown to the reporter, been altered after his death, so that his last will and testament was published in another form than the true one, and everything is going daily from bad to worse, nor does anything remain, save the reputation of the present king, who is of a good disposition, and the whole realm hopes the best for him, as he is handsome, affable, of becoming stature, seems to be liberal, commences interesting himself about public business, and in bodily exercises, literary studies, and knowledge of languages appears to surpass his comrades and competitors as also his own years, in number 14.

The Venetian diplomat continues his report . . .

I will now tell of the navy of England, whose position being insular save where it touches Scotland, the English therefore by reason of their numerous harbours and islands have a very great quantity both of ships and sailors, and are very powerful at sea. In case of need they can fit out 500 vessels, of which upwards of 100 are decked; and many men-of-war

Edward's education

Edward's first years were spent under female tutors and under regulations of the strictest order, one being, for example, that nobody less than a knight might visit him. He had learned to read and write English by 1544 when, at the age of six, he was entrusted to two principal tutors. The first, Richard Cox, was a career academic and churchman, a committed but moderate reformer. The king thus identified his son's, and therefore the nation's future with the protestant cause. The other tutor, John Cheke, was regius professor of Greek at Cambridge and the most distinguished humanist scholar in the land. Other specialist teachers were also employed, such as John Belmain for French and Philip van Wilder for the lute. Edward was also trained in appropriately aristocratic pursuits such as archery, rackets and hunting. After six months of tuition he was competent in Latin grammar, and ready to begin on the simpler authors such as Cato and Aesop. He was a keen pupil, though attempts by his teachers to enliven classical and biblical stories with topical events did not always hold Edward's attention. Once at least he received caning.

By the time of his accession, he was well founded in Latin and was beginning Greek. His courteousness to his masters did not change when he became king. He began to share his studies with a dozen or so contemporaries, among them Henry Brandon, duke of Suffolk, and Warwick' son Robert Dudley, who was

Below.   A coin struck commemorating the succession of Edward VI.

later to become earl of Leicester. It was, however, with the most lowly of these youths that Edward struck up the only personal and lasting friendship of his life. Barnaby Fitzpatrick was the son of an Irish peer, as a pledge of whose loyalty he had been dispatched to England. He became a Gentlemen of the Privy Chamber and, on a visit to the French court, the recipient of many letters from Edward which contain almost the only evidence that he possessed something of the natural exuberance of a teenager.

Cox's tutorship came to an end in 1550, and Cheke's two years later. Edward's formal instruction was now over, but his intellectual development continued. Court preachers such as Latimer and Hooper were important influences. There are many testimonies to the king's accomplishments; apart from the classics, he knew modern languages, history, geography and astronomy. He wrote with a fine italic hand. His most notable literary memorial is the *Chronicle*, begun perhaps at the time of his accession as a schoolroom exercise, but latterly becoming something of a personal diary. It suggests a lively interest in foreign, military and diplomatic events, as well as home affairs, court appointments and martial sports.

From one who is often depicted as a fanatical protestant, there is very little recorded of religious matters, save what touched his own supremacy in the Church. He personally revised the statutes of the Order of the Garter to conform with protestant ideas, and revelled in the pageantry of his admission to the French Order of St Michael. But these enthusiasms were exceptional. For the most part Edward seems to have been an austere,

Above   Part of Edward VI's autobiographical journal.

Below   The coronation procession passing through the streets of London. The procession is leaving the Tower of London on the left of the picture and moving along East Cheap, past Bow Church, and then down the Strand to Charing Cross and Westminster.

reserved person; fully aware of the consequences of his rank, self-confident, but also cautious. He was highly intelligent, and coped well with the formidable education which was devised for him. How wise a king it would have made him we will never know.

are stationed permanently in several places. There are also some 20 ships which they call galleons, not very high but long and wide, with which, in the late wars, they fought all their battles.

They do not use galleys, because of the very great strength of the tides in the ocean, so that, as the reporter was told by the prior of Capua, when he went with six galleys to fetch the queen of Scotland, the navigation of those seas differs from that of all others, as unless the tide be favourable the wind is of very little use. On the shores the sea rises to the height of a tall house, so quickly that it is marvellous; for it chokes the mouths of the rivers and swells them to a distance of 70 or 80 miles up stream, so that two galleys are always kept in readiness for whatever may occur.

The naval affairs are directed by the lord high admiral, one of the chief officers of state, on whom many magistracies and offices connected with the fleet depend. And they issue awards from a tribunal of their own called the admiralty court, whose jurisdiction embraces maritime affairs exclusively, and what occurs on the high seas, they taking cognisance of whatever relates to piracy and shipwrecks; and their sentences are based on civil law, and the president of the court is a lawyer.

The punishment inflicted upon corsairs is to hang them in such a way that their toes well nigh touch the water, so they are generally hanged on the banks of rivers and on the sea shore.

The claims on wrecked property are in like manner decided according to the laws of England, which decree that such as is stranded belongs either to the king or to the proprietor of the soil near the shore if the king concede it, but with regard to other things the laws are more humane, even in the case of enemies, as all aliens and especially merchants are fully authorized to go all over the kingdom; and if of a hostile nation enquiry is made first of all how Englishmen are treated in their country, and as they do by others, so is it done by them. In conclusion, all men registered for military or naval service are exempt by law from all taxes on real and personal property and live under the king's protection.

Protector Somerset inherited a war against Scotland, which he was determined to prosecute with vigour. Mustering a large army, on 4 September 1547 he crossed into Scotland at Eyemouth, north of Berwick and on 10 September was confronted by the Scottish army at Pin-

kie Cleugh, just east of Edinburgh. William Patten, who travelled with the army, wrote a pamphlet describing the action in the easily recognizable style of wartime propaganda.

It waxed very hot on both sides, with pitiful cries, horrible roars, and terrible thundering of guns besides. The day darkened overhead with the smoke of shot: there was the sight and appearance of the enemy at hand in front, the danger of death on every other side. The bullets, pellets and arrows were flying everywhere so thick and landing so uncertainly that nowhere was there any certainty of safety. Every man was stricken with a dreadful fear, not so much perhaps of death as of hurt; which things, although they were only certain to some, yet were they doubted by all. There was assured cruelty at the enemy's hands, without hope of mercy. It was death to fly and danger to fight.

The whole of the field, at this point of joining battle was to both the eye and the ear so heavy, so deadly, lamentable, outrageous, terribly confused, and so quite against the quiet nature of man. If, for our nobility the regard of their honour and fame, for the knights and captains the estimation of their worth and honesty, and for us all generally the natural motion of bounden duty, our own safety, hope of victory and the favour of God which we trusted we had for the rightness of our quarrel, had not been a more vehement cause of courage than the danger of death was cause of fear, the very horror of the thing would have been able to make any man forget both prowess and policy.

But lord marshal and the others, with presence of mind and courage, warily and quickly continued their course towards them: and my lord's grace, duke of Somerset, was then at his post, aloft by the ordinance.

The enemy were in a fallow field, whose furrows lay sideways towards our men.

Besides those furrows, next to us and a stone's throw from them, there was a cross ditch or drain which our men needed to cross to come to them. In that many who could not leap over stuck fast, to no small danger of themselves and some disorder of their fellows.

The enemy, seeing our men's fast approach, disposed themselves to bear the brunt, and in this order stood still to receive them.

The earl of Angus, next to us in their forward was captain of the same, with 8,000 men, and four or five pieces of ordnance on his right side, and 4,000 horsemen on his left.

Behind him, somewhat westward, was the governor with the main body, with 10,000 inland men as they call them, counted the choicest men of their country.

And the earl of Huntly was in the rear, near the main body on the left side, with 8,000 men also. There were 4,000 Irish archers as a wing to them both, last indeed in order and first, as they said, who ran away.

Their main body and rear were also guarded by their ordnance.

Edward Shelley, lieutenant under my lord Grey of his men from Boulogne, was the first on our side to get over the ditch, my lord Grey was next, and after them two or three ranks of the leading bands. But as yet they could only make their race badly because the furrows lay crosswise to their course. They went on notwithstanding, although they were not likely to be able to form a front to hurt them, both because the Scottish men's pikes were as long or longer than their staves, and because their horses were all naked, without breastplates; although there were many among us not one was put on, since at our coming forth in the morning we looked for nothing less than for battle that day. But my lord and Shelley and the rest so valiantly and strongly made the charge upon them that, whether or not it was by their prowess or power, the left side of the enemy which his lordship set upon, although their order remained unbroken, was compelled to sway a good way back and give much ground; and all the rest of them stood much amazed.

Before this, as our men were very nearly at them, they stood very brave and boasting, shaking their pike-points and crying "Come here, rascals! Come here, dogs! Come here, heretics!", for they are hardly fair-mouthed men. Although they meant little kindness, yet they showed by this much civility, both of fair play, to warn before they struck, and of formal order, to chide before they fought.

Our captains who were behind (perceiving at a glance that because of the unevenness of the ground, the sturdy order of the enemy, and because their own men were so nearly straight in front of them,

they were not able to maintain this onset to any advantage) according to the plan made for that situation therefore turned and made a slow retreat up towards the hill again.

However, it may sound to anyone, I will never admit, for any affection towards country or kin, to be so partial as to wittingly bolster falsehood or bury the truth; for in my opinion honour gained that way would be unworthily won and a very vile gain. However by this I cannot count any lost, where only a few lewd soldiers ran out of order with no standard or captain, because of no need but a mere indiscretion and madness. A madness indeed! For first the Scots were not able to pursue them, because they were foot soldiers; and, if they could, what could they hope for by flight, so far from home in their enemy's land, where there was no place of refuge!

This plan shows the coming into ranks again of our horsemen upon the hill; the placing of the hackbutters against the enemy; the shooting of our archers: and then the coming down of our horsemen afterwards for the chase and slaughter of the enemy.

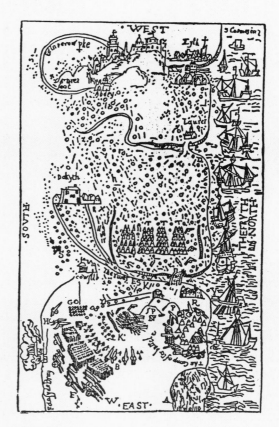

But my lord Grey and my lord Edward by some mercy returned, but neither all in safety, nor without evident marks that they had been there: for the one, with a pike through his mouth, was torn along from the tip of the tongue, and thrust that way very dangerously, more than two inches into the neck; and my Lord Edward had his horse sore wounded under him with swords, and I think fatally.

Likewise, a little before this onset, Sir Thomas Darcy as he approached the enemy was struck a glancing blow on the right side by a bullet from one of their field pieces; and by this his body was bruised with the bowing in of his armour, his sword hilt broken, and the forefinger of his right hand beaten flat. Also, upon the parting of this fray, Sir Arthur Darcy was slashed at with swords, and so hurt on the wedding finger of his right hand that it was thought best by the doctors to have it cut away.

About the same time some of the Scots ran out hastily to the king's majesty's standard of the horsemen, borne by Sir Andrew Flammack, and laying fast hold of its staff they cried "A King! A King!", and if both his strength, his heart and his horse had not been good, and if he had not been helped in these straits by Sir Ralph Coppinger of the king's personal guard, he would have been slain and the standard lost. Nevertheless the Scots held so fast to it that they broke and carried away the lower end of the staff up to the ring, and they tried so hard to gain the standard that Sir Andrew, as luck would have it, escaped home safe and without other hurt.

There were also here Cavarley, the standard bearer of the men at arms, and Clement Paston, a pensioner, each of whom was wounded in the leg with a pike, and Don Philip, a Spaniard, in the knee; several other were maimed and hurt, and many horses were badly wounded also.

By this time our foreward had gained the full advantage of the hillside, and stood sideways on to the enemy. They were nevertheless not able in all parts to stand full square in rank because at their west end, upon their right hand and towards the enemy, there was a square plot enclosed with turf, which is their manner of fencing in those parts. One corner of this hindered the square of their ranks. Our main body in good order stood next to them, in continuing ranks. The forward part of them stood upon the hillside, the rest upon the plain, and he rear were wholly on the plain.

Establishing religion

Henry VIII's break with Rome had left the doctrine and worship of the English Church largely unaltered. Edward VI's coronation was celebrated with traditional ceremony, shortened only to avoid tiring the young sovereign. It was widely expected, however, that Somerset, guided by archbishop Cranmer, would swiftly establish an altogether Protestant order. There was much speculation and radical talk from the pulpits, and to restrain this Cranmer published his book of *Homilies*, which were prepared sermons. In the following month injunctions ordered every parish church to acquire the *Paraphrases*, biblical commentaries, of Erasmus. Elaboration in church ritual and music was curtailed and experiments began with English services. In some places this was spontaneous, elsewhere it was officially inspired: in the Chapel Royal compline was heard in English as early as April, and at the Mass at Westminster Abbey for the opening of Parliament in November, the *Gloria* and other choral parts were rendered in English. The parliamentary session thus inaugurated included a second and comprehensive act for dissolution of the chantries, completing the appropriation of all endowments for prayer for the dead, from the simple requiem in a parish church to the maintenance of whole colleges of priests. Only the cathedral and academic communities were spared, along with St George's Chapel, Windsor. So the chantry and college priests followed the monks and friars: henceforth the English would be familiar with only parish clergy.

The other principal religious measure of this parliamentary session was the repeal of the 1539 Act of Six Articles, by which Henry VIII had sought to restrain the spread of radical protestantism. Early in 1548 the government ordered the destruction of images, and abolished the colourful popular devotions of Candlemas, Ash Wednesday and Holy Week, all now regarded as superstitious. That Easter a new Order of the Communion allowed the laity to receive the sacrament under both bread and wine for the first time, in an English section written into the Latin Mass. This piecemeal progress was too slow for some, whose agitation provoked the government first to restrict preaching to those licensed for the purpose, and then in September to ban it altogether. By now Cranmer and other scholars were working on a complete translation of the liturgy. Their task was completed by the end of the year. The first Book of Common Prayer was authorized by the First Act of Uniformity in January 1549, and came into use on the following Whitsunday.

The book was innovative not only for being in the

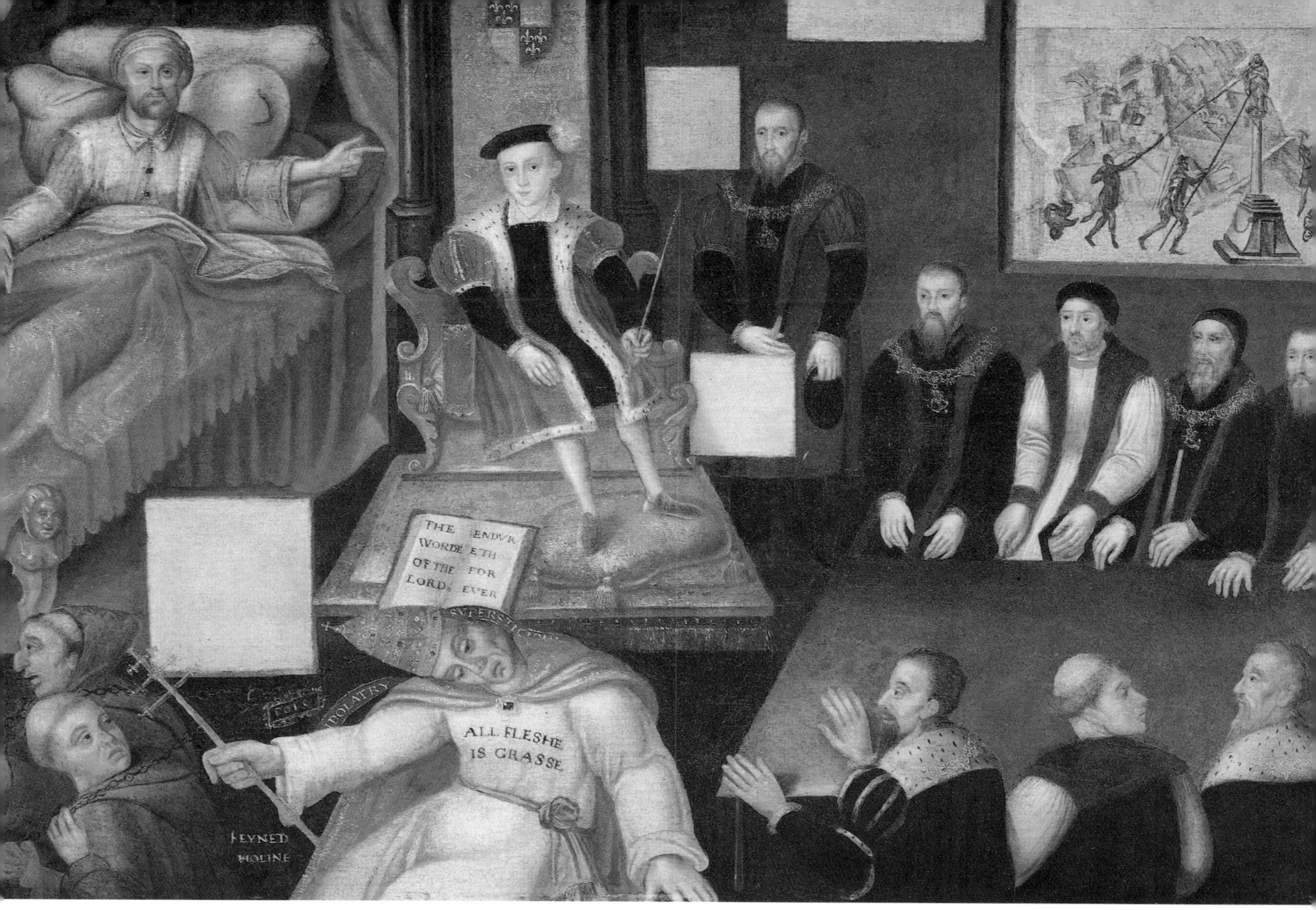
THE ENDVR
WORDE ETH
OF THE FOR
LORD EVER
ALL FLESHE
IS GRASSE
FEYNED
HOLINE

vernacular, but also because it contained almost all the services in one volume and was common to a country which had hitherto known a variety of uses. Its relatively conservative format disappointed many, yet it was too revolutionary for others. Princess Mary would have none of it. Neither would those who rebelled in the west country demanding restoration of the old customs and services: some Cornishmen claimed they could not understand the English; Cranmer wondered if they had understood the Latin any better. Opposition within the hierarchy came principally from bishops Gardiner of Winchester and Bonner of London. Gardiner protested after the 1547 injunctions, whose legality he questioned. Bonner, whose diocese was of key importance, repeatedly refused the orders of Cranmer and the government to implement and preach in favour of the reforms. He was ousted in October 1549. Two other bishops were to be deprived, and another resigned. The majority of bishops, as with the clergy and people at large, however, accepted protestantism as the state religion.

Above *The deathbed of Henry VIII, an anti-papal allegory painted in about 1548. Henry is seen gesturing to his son and successor Edward. To Edward's left are members of the Council of Regency: Edward Seymour, John Dudley, Cranmer and John Russell. The pope is shown being crushed by the new Prayer Book.*

Below *The papists being banished from England in favour of the protestant religion.*

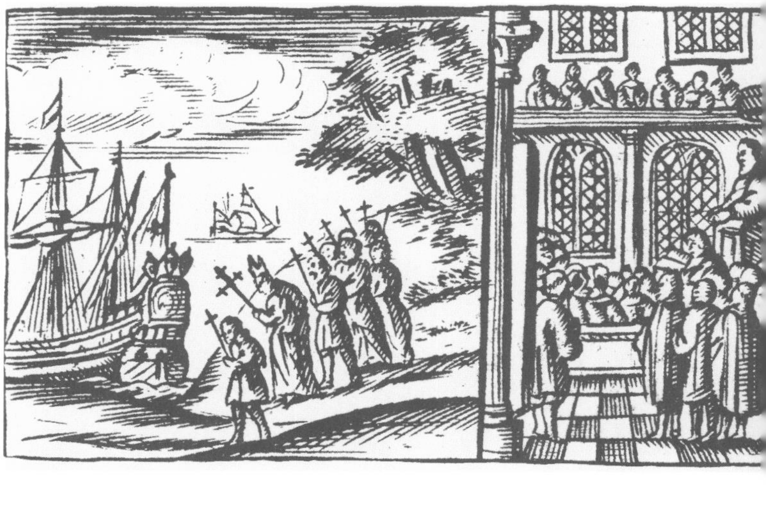

So by the placing and ordering of our army in this way we showed ourselves, in a way, to surround them, so that they should in no way escape us; which by our power and number we were as well able to do as a spinner's web to catch a swarm of bees. However for heart and courage we meant to meet with them, if they had been as many again more.

1548

Protector Somerset and archbishop Cranmer made it clear, within a few weeks of Henry's death, that they intended to take the country further in a Protestant direction. In the summer of 1547 Cranmer had issued a set of Homilies, some of which were distinctly Protestant. Henry's conservative Act of Six Articles was also repealed, along with the heresy laws. Another statute of the same parliament, which convened on 4 November, dissolved the Chantries and conveyed their property to the Crown. By March 1548 the process of enforcement had begun, and an English order of communion had been issued. Wriothesley describes the next steps in the process.

In the beginning of March the king sent his commissioners into every shire in England to survey all colleges, free chapels and chantries. Also in May the king's majesty sent his proclamation with a book for the order of receiving of the holy communion of the body and blood of Christ in both kinds, of bread and wine, which shall be ministered by the priest to all persons at Easter, and at all times after when the people will require the same.

In May St Paul's choir, with various other parishes in London, sang all the service in English, both matins, mass and evensong, and kept no mass unless some received communion with the priest.

On 12 May 1548 King Henry VII's aniversary was kept at Westminster, the mass sung all in English, with the consecration of the sacrament also spoken in English, the priest leaving out all the canon after the creed except for the "Pater noster", and then administering the communion according to the King's Book; at which mass was made a sermon by Mr Tong, the king's chaplain.

Throughout this year a commission headed by the archbishop of Canterbury had been preparing a full English liturgy. This was based on the Sarum rite, but with a number of modifications drawn from other liturgies, both ancient and modern. Its emphasis was mildly, but distinctly Protestant. When the second parliamentary session of the reign met on 24 November, a Bill of Uni-

formity was introduced to enforce its general use. Burnet's account is virtually a reproduction statute.

The next act that passed in this parliament was about the public service, which was put to the House of Commons on the 9 December, and the next day was also put to the House of Lords. It lay a long time before them, and was not agreed until the 15 January. The earl of Derby, the bishops of London, Durham, Norwich, Carlisle, Hereford, Worcester, Westminster and Chichester, and the lords Dacre and Windsor protesting. The preamble of the acts sets forth "That there had been several forms of service, and that of late there had been great difference in the administration of the sacraments, and other parts of divine worship; and that the most effectual endeavours could not stop the inclinations of many to depart from the former customs; which the king had not punished, believing they flowed from a good zeal. But so that there might be a uniform way over all the kingdom the king, by the advice of the lord protector and his council, had appointed the archbishop of Canterbury with other learned and discreet bishops and divines to draw up an order of divine worship, having respect to the pure religion of Christ taught in the scripture, and to the practice of the primitive church, which they by the aid of the Holy Ghost had with one uniform agreement, concluded upon. Wherefore the parliament, having considered the book, and the things which were altered or retained in it, gave their most humble thanks to the king for his care about it, and prayed that all who had formerly offended in these matters, except those who were in the Tower of London or the prison of the Fleet, should be pardoned.

This alludes principally to Stephen Gardiner, bishop of Winchester, imprisoned in the tower in July 1548 for his opposition to official religious policy.

And it was enacted that from the feast of Whitsunday next all divine offices should be performed according to it, and that such of the clergy as should refuse to do it, or continue to officiate in any other manner, should on the first conviction be imprisoned for six months and forfeit a year's profit from their benefice; for the second offence forfeit all their church preferments and suffer a year's imprisonment; and for the third offence should be imprisoned for life. And all who should write or put out things in print against it, or threaten any clergymen for using it, were to be fined £10 for the first offence,

£20 for the second, and forfeit all their goods and be imprisoned for life for a third offence. Only at the universities might they use it in Latin and Greek, except for the office of communion. It was also lawful to use other psalms or prayers taken out of the Bible, so these in the book were not omitted. This act was variously censured by those who disliked it. Some thought it too much that it was said that the book was drawn up "by the aid of the Holy Ghost"; but others said this was not to be so understood, as if they had been inspired by extraordinary assistance, for then there would be no room for any correction of what was done now; and therefore it was only to be understood in the sense that all good moves and consultations are directed or assisted by the secret influence of God's Holy Spirit, which do often help good men even in their imperfect actions, where the good that is done is justly ascribed to the grace of God. Others censured it because it was said to be done by uniform agreement, although four of the bishops employed in drawing it up protested against it. These were the bishops of Norwich, Hereford, Chichester, and Westminster. But these had agreed to the main parts of the work, although they were not satisfied in a few particulars, which made them dissent from the whole.

1549

Thomas Seymour, the protector's brother, was a man of high ambition, and deeply dissatisfied with the barony and office of lord admiral, which were granted to him in 1547. He wanted to be governor of the king's person, and intrigued in the privy chamber to that end. He sought Edward's personal favour with gifts of money. He married the queen dowager, Catherine Parr, in 1547 and after her death in childbirth in 1548, attempted to establish a relationship with princess Elizabeth. By the beginning of 1549 his pretensions could no longer be ignored. The following account of his fate is taken from the proceedings of the Privy Council of 17 January 1549.

After various conferences, held at sundry times, by the lord protector with the lords and others of the privy council concerning such information as had been given to him of the great attempts and disloyal practices of the lord Seymour of Sudeley, admiral of England, tending to the danger of the king's majesty and the lord protector and council, and the subversion of the whole state of the realm, some points of which are touched on in this decree and the rest appear with several others and their circumstances

in the examinations and depositions of the said admiral and his adherents. This day the whole council assembled to consult and decide upon a certain order for the prevention and repression of the admiral's attempts. First they remembered how last year, that is in the first year of the reign of our sovereign lord, his majesty then being only 10 years of age, newly entered in to his kingdom, at open war with the Scots, at some grudge with France, not in the most sure relations with the emperor, the people at home in some argument about religion, in the parliament time the said admiral, as appeared by information given to the lord protector, forgetting all duty, love and kindness which he owed to his sovereign, his country and his brother, out of his great pride and ambitious intentions would have laid hands upon the person of the king's majesty and taken him under his order and disposition (if he had not been prevented by God's grace and wisdom), to the great peril and danger of his majesty and the subversion of the state of the whole realm. And failing in his purpose that way, to serve his mischievous plans another way he induced the king's majesty, without the advice or knowledge of the lord protector or council, to write letters of his devising to the parliament, intending by them to have sown sedition in the realm. And by this, as he said himself to several noblemen, he intended to have made the blackest parliament that there ever was in England. All these great offences and disloyal attempts the Protector and the council thought best to pass over in silence for the better service of his majesty and safety of his person, and quietness of the realm, and to avoid such slanders and perils which might have followed from foreign parts on knowledge of tumult here at home. Because of that the admiral, persevering in his former mischievous intention and determination, did straightaway renew his efforts: that is to say to subvert the state of the realm, to depose the protector and council, to dispose of the king's majesty's person at his will and pleasure, and especially to appoint the council about his majesty and the marriage of his majesty. And with this intention, or worse, as by great circumstantial evidence appears, not only corrupted with money and rewards several persons of the Privy Chamber and nearest to his majesty's person, but also persuaded by various means sundry noblemen and others to conspire and take part with him. And finally, despite the good advice given to the contrary by the lord protector and other of his friends of the council, he schemed to marry the Lady Elizabeth, one of his majesty's sisters, and the second in line after his majesty to the crown. The protector and council, carefully weighing the great danger imminent and even at hand by these means to the person of the king's majesty, and the great trouble, mischief and inconvenience which would thereby have ensued to the whole realm, have thought it their most bounden duties to stop and prevent the same in time; and for that purpose, after good and mature deliberation, have decreed and ordered with one whole mind, consent and agreement, to commit the admiral to prison within the Tower of London, there to remain until further order be taken with him, as the case afterwards on more ample consultation shall require for the greatest safety of the king's majesty and the realm."

In 1548 there were a number of scattered risings in the Midlands and South, ostensibly caused by resentment against the enclosure of arable and common land for pasture. These enclosures had been taking place since the middle of the previous century, and it is now generally believed that the "dearth" or high prices, which were then blamed upon enclosure, were caused by other factors. The issue was the subject of great debate, as the following passages from a husbandman, capper, merchant and knight express their views in turn.

Truly these enclosures do unto us all, for they make us pay dearer for our land which we occupy, and cause us to be able to have no land for our money to put to tillage; all is taken up for pasture, either for sheep or the grazing of cattle. I have known lately of a dozen ploughs within less than six miles around me laid down in these 7 years; and where 40 people had their living, now one man and his shepherd has all. This thing is not the least cause of these uproars, for because of these enclosures men lack livelihoods and are idle. And therefore for very necessity they desire change, hoping to come to something thereby, and certain that whatever happens to them, it can be no harder for them than it was before. Moreover all things are so dear that by their daily labour they are not able to live.

And the capper intervenes . . .

I have good experience of that, for I am willing to give journeymen 2d. a·day more than I used to do, and yet they say they cannot sufficiently live on it. And I know for a fact that the best manager of them all can save only a little at the year's end. And because of the dearth you speak of we who are

Printing and the Reformation

The early months of Edward VI's reign saw a great increase in radical, often scurrilous pamphlets and ballads attacking the Church, the bishops and Catholic ritual in particular. Some were the products, often crudely made, of a flourishing underground press. But there were serious polemicists too, such as John Bale, Thomas Becon and William Turner. There also emerged between 1547 and 1549 metrical versions of the psalms by Thomas Sternhold and John Hopkins; the foundation of the English Protestant collection of hymns. Most printers were in London; of other centres the most prolific was Ipswich, where in 1548 one printer brought out ten books by Calvin and other continental reformers.

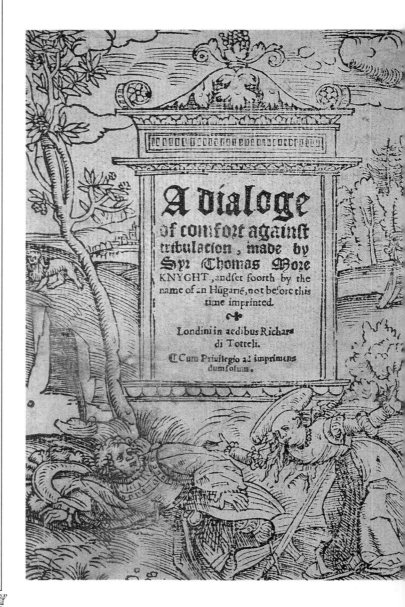

It seems that the government was at first content to allow a lapse of the stringent regulations Henry VIII had made against the import of books and for censorship of the domestic press. In May 1547 Stephen Gardiner, bishop of Winchester, complained of the unfettered flow of Protestant literature from abroad. In the same month, however, the government condemned rumours of religious change, asserting that they had nothing of the sort in mind.

The parliament which met in November 1547 removed the threat of execution for heresy and certain treasons, but re-established the treason of writing and speaking against the king's control of the Church, known as the royal supremacy. A subsequent outburst of anti-clericalism prompted a proclamation, while Parliament was still sitting, deploring the physical assaults and indignities the clergy had suffered. Fear of extremism in religion led to further measures intended to restrain debate about the eucharist and experimental forms of worship. In August there was a return to firm censorship of the press and the stage, and in September all preaching, which had earlier been restricted, was halted.

Many who had come to England from the continent when Edward's accession had seemed to signal the likely implementation of full protestantism, were temporarily silenced. Some were returning exiles – notably John Hooper, who became chaplain to Somerset and, in 1550, a reluctant bishop of Gloucester. Thousands of foreigners, many of them seeking refuge after the defeat of the German Protestant princes by Charles V in April 1547, also came to England. Some forty divines came at the invitation of Thomas Cranmer, archbishop of Canterbury, to help shape the new Protestant national church. The most prominent of these were Martin Bucer from Strasbourg, who was appointed regius professor of divinity at Cambridge, and the Italian, Peter Martyr, who occupied the equivalent chair at Oxford. Another Italian, Bernadino Ochino, was made a canon of Canterbury, where a number of the refugees settled. Cranmer tried but failed to entice the even more eminent Philip Melanchthon, Martin Luther's lieutenant. The archbishop was looking for a compromise between the teaching of Luther and that of the more extreme Zwingli and Calvin, to which most of the new arrivals adhered. Their criticisms of the 1549 prayer book contributed to the more advanced protestantism developed after 1550.

Foreigners were permitted their own forms of worship and church discipline. In July 1550 the former Augustinian friary in London was granted to those who had settled in the city; it became known as the "temple of Jesus" and the king appointed the Polish divine, John à Lasco, as the first superintendant. A community of Flemish weavers under the leadership of Valérand

Above   A great number of new presses were established during Edward's reign which were helpful in putting across the protestant message.

Left   The views of Thomas More found a ready audience.

Poulain was established under Somerset's protection at Glastonbury abbey. They, too, were allowed their own liturgy. However, these new arrivals had hardly time to organize themselves before Edward's reign ended and, for them and many others, a new exile began.

craftsmen can keep few or no apprentices as we were used to do. Therefore the city, which was before well inhabited and wealthy, as you know every one of you, is fallen for lack of occupiers into great desolation and poverty.

The thoughts of the merchant highlight what was happening around the country . . .

So have most of the towns in England, except London. And not only are the good towns sorely decayed in their houses, streets and other buildings, but also the country in their highways and bridges. For such poverty reigns everywhere that few men have enough to spare to give anything to the repair of such ways, bridges and other common conveniences. And although there are many things put down now which before were occasions of much expense, such as stage plays, interludes, May games, wakes, revels, wagers at shooting, wrestling, running and throwing the stone or bar, and as well pardons, pilgrimages, offerings and many other such things, yet I see we are not wealthier but rather poorer. Why this is I cannot well tell, for there is such a general dearth of all things such as I have never known, not only of things growing in this realm but also of other merchandise which we buy overseas, such as silks, wines, oils, woad, madder, iron, steel, wax, flax, linen cloth, fustians, worsteds, coverlets, carpets and all arrases and tapestry, spices of all sorts and all haberdashers' goods such as paper, both white and brown, glasses for drinking and looking and glazing windows, pins, needles, knives, daggers, hats, caps, brooches, buttons and laces. I well know that all these cost me more now by a third than they did only seven years ago. Then all kinds of food are as dear or dearer again, and it is none of God's doing as far as I can see; for I never saw more plenty of corn, grass and cattle of all sorts than we have at present and have had these three years past continually, thanked be our lord. If these enclosures were the cause of it, or any other thing, it would be a pity if it were not removed.

However, the knight disagrees that enclosures are the cause of hardship . . .

Since you have plenty of all things from corn and cattle, as you say, then it would not seem that the dearth should be caused by these enclosures; for it is not because of scarceness of corn that we have this dearth, for thanks to God corn is very cheap, and has been so these last three years continually. It cannot be caused by dearth of cattle, for enclosures nourish them more than anything else. But I confess there is a wonderful dearth of all things; and I and all men of my sort suffer most from it, as we have no wares to sell or occupation to live by, but only our lands. For all you three, I mean you my neighbour the husbandman, and you master merchant and you goodman capper, and all sorts of craftsmen may save themselves right well; for as much as all things are dearer than they were, so much do you raise the price of your wares and occupations which you sell. But we have nothing to sell which we might advance the price of to balance those things which we must buy.

1549

In the summer of this year widespread civil disorders again arose in the south of England. In some areas these were aggravated by discontent over the new English liturgy, which was due to be introduced at Whitsun. There was also a widespread undercurrent of social hostility directed against the gentry. By this time the king was sufficiently interested for his observations to lapse into the first person.

The people began to rise in Wiltshire, where Sir William Herbert did put them down, overrun and slay them. Then they rose in Sussex, Hampshire, Kent, Gloucestershire, Suffolk, Warwickshire, Essex, Hertfordshire, part of Leicestershire, Worcestershire and Rutlandshire, where by fair persuasions, partly of honest men among themselves and partly by gentlemen, they were often appeased, and again, because certain commissions were sent down to pull down enclosures, they rose again.

The French king, seeing this, caused war to be proclaimed and, hearing that our ships lay at Jersey, sent a great number of his galleys and certain ships to surprise our ships; but they, lying at anchor, beat the French so that they were fain to retire with a loss of a thousand of their men. At the same time the French king passed by Boulogne to Newhaven with his army and took Blackness by treason and the German camp, which done, Newhaven surrendered. There were also, in a skirmish between 300 English footmen and 700 French horsemen, six noblemen slain. Then the French king came with his army to Boulogne, which, they seeing, raised Bolemberg. But because of the plague he was compelled to retire, and Gaspard de Coligny, Seigneur de Chatillon was left behind as governor of the army.

In the meantime, because there was a rumour that I was dead, I passed through London.

After that they rose in Oxfordshire, Devonshire, Norfolk and Yorkshire.

Lord Grey of Wilton was sent to Oxfordshire with 1,500 horsemen and footmen, whose coming, and the assembling of the gentlemen of the county, so abashed the rebels that more than half of them ran away, and of those who stayed some were slain, some taken and some hanged.

The lord privy seal, John Russell, was sent to Devonshire, and with his band, which was only small, lay at Honiton while the rebels besieged Exeter, which raised several pretty feats of war. For after several skirmishes, when the gates were burned they in the city continued the fire until they had made a rampart within. Also afterwards when they were undermined and powder was laid in the mine, those within drowned the powder and the mine with water which they cast in. The lord privy seal hearing this thought to have gone to reinforce them by a by-way, but the rebels having a spy about this cut all the trees between Ottery St Mary and Exeter. For which cause the lord privy seal burned the town and thought to return home. The rebels kept a bridge behind his back and so compelled him, with his small band, to set upon them which he did, and overcame them, killing 600 of them and returning home without any loss of men. Then the Lord Grey and Paolo Spinola, the Italian mercenary captain with their bands came to him, and afterwards Grey with 200 from Reading, and being reinforced with those bands he came to raise the siege at Exeter since they were short of food. And as he passed from Honiton he came to a little town of his own, from which came only two roads, which they had reinforced with two bulwarks made of earth and had put about 2,000 men to defend them, and the rest they had laid, some at a bridge called Honiton Bridge, partly at a certain hedge in a highway, and most at the siege of Exeter. The rearguard of the horsemen, of which Travers was captain, set upon one bulwark; the vanguard and the main body on the other. Spinola's band kept them occupied at their wall. At length Travers drove them into Clyst St Mary, which the lord privy seal burned. Then they ran to a bridge nearby, being driven from which there were in a plain about 900 of them slain. The next day about another 2,000 of them were met at the entry of a

highway; they first desired to talk, and in the meantime fortified themselves, and when this was seen they ran away, and that same night the city of Exeter was delivered from the siege.

After that they gathered at Launceston, where the lord privy seal and Sir William Herbert went and overthrew them, taking their chief heads and executing them. Nevertheless some sailed to Bridgewater and went about sedition, but were quickly repressed. So much for Devonshire.

At this time the "Black Galley" was taken.

This was an English ship lost to the French in August 1549.

Now to Norfolk. The people suddenly gathered together in Norfolk and increased to a great number, against whom the lord marquis of Northampton was sent with 1,060 horsemen who, winning the town of Norwich kept it one day and one night, and the next day in the morning, with loss of 100 men, departed out of the town; among whom the lord Sheffield was slain. There were taken various gentlemen and serving men, to the number of thirty, with which victory the rebels were very glad. But afterwards, hearing that the earl of Warwick came against them, they began to stand upon a strong plot of ground on a hill near to the town of Norwich, having the town confederate with them. The earl of Warwick came with 6,000 men and 1,500 horsemen and entered the town of Norwich, which having won, it was so weak that he could scarcely defend it, and often the rebels came into the streets killing several of his men and were repulsed again, yes and the townsmen were given to mischief themselves. So having endured their assaults for three days, and having stopped their supplies, the rebels were forced by lack of food to remove, and the earl of Warwick followed them with 1,000 Germans and all his horsemen, leaving the English footmen in the town, and he overcame them in plain battle, killing 2,000 of them and taking Robert Kett of Wymondham, their captain, who in January following was hanged in Norwich and his head displayed. Kett's brother William was also taken and punished alike.

News of the 1549 insurrections travelled widely, and Somerset was very anxious to correct the impression received by many unsympathetic governments, such as that of the emperor, that England was upon the brink of anarchy. Sir Philip Hoby was the ambassador resident with Charles V. This letter to the ambassador from the duke of Somerset concerns the suppression of the insurrection in the west, and in Norfolk.

After our right hearty commendations; we have before advised you of the troublesome business, uproars and tumults practiced in sundry places of the realm by a number of lewd, seditious and ill-disposed persons, to the great disquiet both of the king's majesty and all his highness' quiet and loving subjects. These tumults and commotions, although at the beginning they were spread in many parts of the realm, in the end they were well pacified and quieted, except Devon, Cornwall and Norfolk, where they continued their rebellion so stubbornly that the king's majesty was forced to send the king's highness' lieutenant with a power both ways, the sooner to suppress them and bring them to their duty: lord privy seal for Devon and Cornwall, and the earl of Warwick into Norfolk. We have before told you of the proceedings of lord privy seal in his journey, who by his policy and wise handling of the matter, after the slaughter of more than a thousand of the rebels and execution of some of the ringleaders, has, thanks be to God, so honourably achieved and finished that not only does the country remain in present good order, but the multitude repent of their former detestable and naughty doings so that they abhor to hear themselves spoken of.

In the same way you shall understand that in Norfolk the living God has so wrought by the wisdom and manliness of Lord Warwick, that they also are brought to subjection by such means as follow. The said rebels, having tried for a month to allure to them such numbers of light persons as they could, and partly by that means and partly by force and violence had at last assembled together a great number, afterwards encamped themselves near the city of Norwich. That city they had at their commandment, and had placed in it their food and other provisions, of which they had got a large store. Lord Warwick coming to those parts, after he had thoroughly understood the state of the rebels, knowing most of them to be simple persons who were either constrained by force or otherwise seduced by those of the worse sort, thought it best to use such means of subduing them which would cause the least loss of blood and would punish only the heads and captains; and for this reason, trying first to cut off their food supplies, approached the city of Norwich, which within a short time he took, and in the taking

Social and political discontent

Commodity prices were beginning to rise by 1547, and although people were accustomed to shortages when the harvest failed, they were puzzled and alarmed by these increases. Harvests were good, and corn plentiful, yet food was becoming more expensive. One reason for this inflationary trend was the growth in population which resulted in an increased demand for land and higher rents when leases became due for renewal. Another was that Henry VIII had tampered with the currency to pay for his wars with Scotland and France; coinage debasement, particularly of the silver currency, meant that the intrinsic value of some coins was no more than 30% of their face value. Confidence was heavily undermined and traders put up their prices. Despite protests, Somerset insisted on continuing the Scottish war; pressure on the royal revenues did not ease and debasement continued.

Blame for increasing rents was placed upon enclosers and engrossers. The former were those who took their land out of the common field system and fenced it off. At best this deprived their neighbours of common grazing and foraging rights; at worst it meant the land was converted from tillage to pasture for sheep, a move that resulted in a drastic reduction in the labour force. This depopulation enclosure had been a concern of the government and of social reformers since at least the 1520s. Engrossers were those particularly wealthy gentlemen who brought up a number of adjacent farms and turned them into a single holding, irrespective of whether or not the land was enclosed.

Somerset issued proclamations denouncing enclosures, and draft legislation criticizing noble and gentle landlords and proposing a heavy tax on large flocks of sheep was introduced into parliament. He was determined upon reforms which the aristocracy, both in parliament and outside, were equally determined to prevent.

The aristocracy, and particularly his fellow councillors saw Somerset as a hypocrite with demagogic tendencies, and feared he could become a tyrant. Since the summer of 1547 he had largely ignored the council which had elevated him, governing by proclamation and filling the court with his creatures. He had pursued the war with Scotland obsessively, and, in spite of his reforming principles, had amassed a large landed estate that was by no means free from the abuses he so violently fiercely denounced in others. At the same time, his controversial programme of religious change provoked opposition of a different kind. With the full

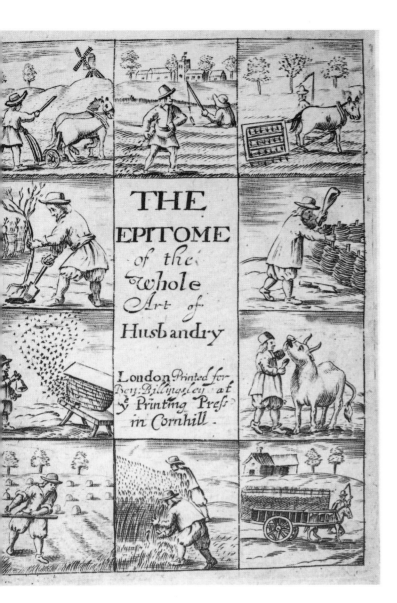

Above Families were forced to move from town to town in search of work when they were unable to use common land to grow food.

Left Everyday rural scenes in the mid-fifteenth century. Many landowners moved from arable farming to the more profitable sheep farming.

support of Thomas Cranmer, archbishop of Canterbury, he had set about converting the schismatic, but still largely catholic Church which Henry VIII had left, into a fully protestant one. Priests were allowed to marry, an English Prayer Book was authorized by parliament for introduction at Whitsun 1549.

There had been widespread anti-enclosure riots in the Midlands in the summer of 1548, and in June 1549 a major insurrection in East Anglia, which threatened to engulf the whole of south-east England, coincided with a rebellion in Devon and Cornwall which rose against the Prayer Book. The East Anglians were, if anything, sympathetic to the new religion, and claimed that they were not rebels, but were attempting to enforce a policy to which the protector was committed. At first Somerset hesitated, not because he accepted their arguments but because he did not have the resources to do anything else; but again his hesitancy was misconstrued. The aristocracy, however, defended their interests vigorously. Lord Rich suppressed

disorders in Essex; Sir Thomas Wyatt and other gentry hanged the leaders of a rising in Kent on 13 May; in July, Lord Grey executed the principal rebels in Oxfordshire and Berkshire; the earl of Arundel prevented threatened disorders in Surrey.

In Devon and Norfolk the local gentry did not have the resources or organization to cope with the riots. Exeter, whose townsmen were more protestant than their rural neighbours and did not share their social grievances, held out against the rebels until the end of July when it was relieved by Lord John Russell with an army consisting largely of German and Italian mercenaries. In Norfolk the rioters led by Robert Kett, took the city of Norwich, and beat off the first force sent against them led by William Parr, marquess of Northampton, and it was late August before a second army of sufficient strength, led by a tough and experienced soldier, John Dudley, earl of Warwick, could be raised. Warwick defeated Kett's forces in a pitched battle and executed many of the survivors.

of it overthrew a great number of the rebels. By this means he so bridled them and cut off their food that they had to live for three days with water for drink, and eat their meat without bread. On Thursday last, issuing out of their camps onto a plain nearby, they determined to fight, and like mad, desperate men ran upon the sword; a thousand of them being slain the rest were content to crave pardon.

One Kett, a tanner, from the beginning a chief doer among them, fled; and the rest of the rebels, casting away their weapons and armour and asking pardon on their knees with weeping eyes, were by lord of Warwick sent home without injury and pardoned, the chief heads, ringleaders and officers excepted. Kett, with three of his brothers and three other chief captains, all vile persons, were also taken and are still held to receive that which they have deserved.

Thus are these vile wretches, who have for a long time troubled the realm and have done their utmost to destroy and utterly undo the same, come to confusion. So that we trust, truly, that these traitors, mutineers and rebellions are now at an end, praised be God etc. And thus we bid you heartily well to fare. 1 September, 1549.

The lord privy seal, Lord John Russell, to the council, concerning the defeat of the rebels in the west.

On Friday we marched from Exeter to Crediton; seven miles of the way was very cumbersome, and on that day we went no further.

On Saturday we marched towards the camp at Sampford Courtney, and on the way our scouts and the rebel scouts met suddenly on the Sunday, and in a skirmish between them one, Maunder, was taken, who was one of the chief captains. Order was given to Lord Grey and Sir William Herbert, to win time, to take good part of our army and with it to make with all possible speed towards that camp, to view it and see what service could be done for its invasion. They found the enemy strongly encamped, both because of the lie of the ground and their entrenchment. They kept them busy with large ordnance until a more convenient way was made by the pioneers; this done they were assaulted with good courage, on one side by our footmen, and on the other side by the Italian hackbutters in such a way that it was not long before they turned their backs and fled back to the town which they had before fortified for all events. While this was happening I was still

behind with the rest of the army, conducting the carriage, Humphrey Arundel with his whole force came on the back of our vanguard who were busy with the assault of the camp. His sudden appearance caused such fear in the hearts of our men that we wished our strength was a great deal more, not without good cause. To remedy this lord Grey had to leave Herbert at the enterprise against the camp, and to retire to our last horsemen and footmen, who he caused to turn their faces to the enemy in a show of battle against Arundel. There was nothing for an hour except shooting of ordnance to and fro. Sir William Herbert in the meantime followed the first attempt, and pressing still upon them never breathed until he had driven them to a plain fight. To the chase came forth horsemen and footmen, in which five or six hundred of the rebels were slain, and among them one, Underhill, was slain, who had the charge of that camp.

As our men were retiring I arrived, and as it was growing late I thought it good to lose no time, but appointed Sir William Herbert and Sir Anthony Kingston, with their footmen and horsemen, to set to on one side, my lord Grey to set to opposite them, and I with my company to come on the other side: at this sight the rebels' stomachs so fell from them that they fled without any blow. The horsemen followed the chase, and slew up to 700 and took a far greater number. Great executions would have followed if the night had not come on so fast.

All this night we sat on horseback, and in the morning we had word that Arundel had fled to Launceston, and he immediately began to plot with the townsmen and the guard of Greenfield and other gentlemen to have them murdered that night. The guards so much abhorred this cruelty that they immediately set the gentlemen free and gave them their help, with the help of the town, for the apprehension of Arundel, whom they have imprisoned with four or five ringleaders. I have immediately sent Sir George and Sir Peter Carew with a good band to keep the town in check. And this morning I hurry there with the others.

We have taken fifteen pieces of ordnance, some brass and some iron. Of our side there were many hurt, but not more than ten or twelve killed. Lord Grey and Sir William Herbert have served notably. Every gentleman and captain did their part so well that I do not well know who first to commend. I

Somerset's fall

Somerset's handling of the south western and Norfolk rebellions in the summer of 1549 destroyed the credibility of his rule. The Privy Council, to which he persistently refused to listen, wanted him removed. John Dudley, earl of Warwick colluded with Henry Fitzalan, 16th earl of Arundel and Thomas Wriothesley, 1st earl of Southampton, in an effort to dislodge the protector and the religious reformation he had introduced.

They gathered in London where they gained the support of the civic leadership, and took control of the Tower of London. Meanwhile Somerset was at Hampton Court with Edward VI, accompanied by Thomas Cranmer, archbishop of Canterbury, Sir William Paget and other stalwarts. Realizing his isolation, on 5 October the protector appealed in the king's name for all subjects to come to his aid. On several occasions he wrote personally to John Russell, 1st earl of Bedford, and Sir William Herbert, who were returning with their army from the west country, denying rumours that he had sold Boulogne and withheld soldiers' pay.

The London councillors countered the next day with a warning that the king was endangered by Somerset's treason. That night between 9 and 10 o'clock, having emptied the Hampton Court armoury, Somerset, the king and their followers left for Windsor Castle. There, on 7 October, Somerset made a further call for men to join him. However, no forces came to Windsor except some of the king's guard whom the councillors in London sent for Edward's own protection. An exchange of letters and emissaries followed.

A few days later, the coup was accomplished. Sir Anthony Wingfield, vice-chamberlain of the household, arrived at Windsor Castle, removed Somerset from his quarters next to the king's, and placed him under strong guard in the lieutenant's tower. Edward, suffering from a cold brought on by the night ride from Hampton Court and aggravated by the dank atmosphere of the castle, greeted Wingfield and his men as liberators, and expressed his confidence in the London lords.

On 13 October, the protectorate was abolished and Somerset, with many of his dependants, was a prisoner in the Tower. It was not the end of his career; he reappeared as a member of the Privy Council in April 1550. However, he was unappreciative of this reprieve, and his attempts to recover his old authority led to a second arrest in October 1551 and his execution in the following January.

Overleaf   London in 1550, showing the Court of Star Chamber on the left, London Bridge and the Tower of London on the right.

Below   Protector Somerset on the scaffold at Tower Hill where he was executed for treason following Northumberland's charge against him.

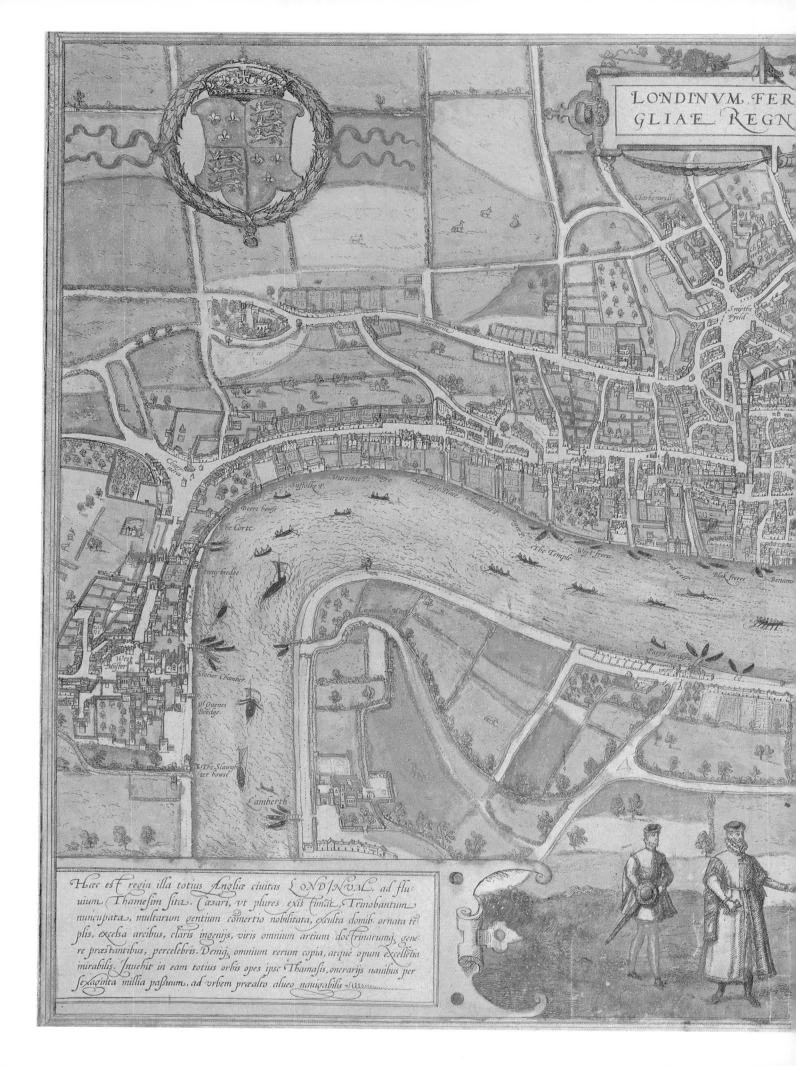

LONDINVM, FER
GLIAE REGN

Clarkenwell

Smythe
Fyeld.

Fenchurne

Suffolke P. Duresme P. Somerset Hale
Beere howse
The Corte
The Temple Whyl frere.
Grimbull
Trenyhrealye Blak freres
Benam

Lambeth Marfh
Payes garden

West
Munster
Steban Chamber
Ye Quenes
Bredge.
The Slaugh
ter howse

Lamberth

Hæc est Regia illa totius Angliæ ciuitas LONDINVM, ad flu-
uium Thamesin sita. Cæsari, vt plures exis timut, Trinobantum
nuncupata, multarum gentium comertio nobilitata, exculta domib. ornata te
plis, excelsa arcibus, claris ingenijs, viris omnium artium doctrinarunq, gene
re præstantibus, percelebris. Deniq, omnium rerun copia, atqúe opum excellétia
mirabilis. Inuehit in eam totius orbis opes ipse Thamasis, onerarijs nauibus per
sexaginta millia passuum, ad vrbem præalto alueo nauigabilis.

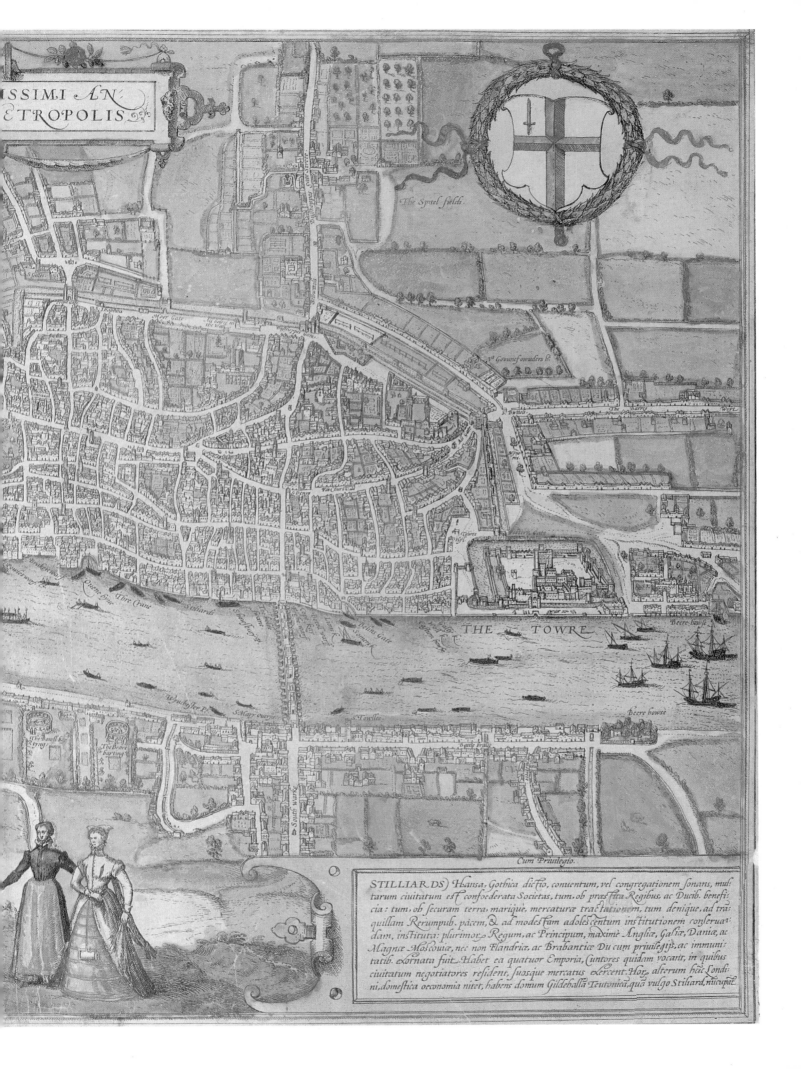

ISSIMI AN·
ETROPOLIS

The Spvel fields.

The Spttel

Thapbus
Moor Gate
Aldegate in
Highgate Crosse
Bishoppgate strete

N? Geovrie powders s?

The Barry
West

Bottia

Hartes
Gate

Aldgate
High

Watre Gate

THE TOWRE
Beere house

The Crane
Stillarde
Queen Hive
Ebbing Lane
Bellins Gate

Beere house

Winchester P.
S.Mary over

S. Tovlles

Beere house

The Bovll &
baytyng

The Beare
bayting

South warke

Cum Priuilegio.

STILLIARDS) Hansa, Gothica dicto, conuentum, vel congregationem sonans, multarum ciuitatum est confoederata Societas, tum ob praestita Regibus, ac Ducib. benefi-cia: tum, ob securam terra, marique, mercaturae tractationem, tum denique, ad trãquillam Rerumpub. pacem, & ad modestam adolescentum institutionem conseruãdam, instituta: plurimor Regum, ac Principum, maximè Angliae, Galliae, Daniae, ac Magnae Moscouiae, nec non Flandriae, ac Brabantiae Du cum priuilegijs, ac immunitatib. exornata fuit. Habet ea quatuor Emporia, (untores quidam vocant, in quibus ciuitatum negotiatores resident, suasque mercatus exercent. Hor. alterum hcic Londini, domestica oeconomia nitet, habens domum Gildehallã Teutonica, quã vulgo Stiliard, nũcupat.

have given order to all the ports so that none of the rebels' ships shall pass that way.

Officially, the captured rebels were tried by commission of Oyer and Terminer, but the niceties of criminal justice were not always observed, and the use of martial law during the uprising in the South West offered scope to Sir Anthony Kingston's black sense of humour. Richard Grafton provides some examples.

And amongst other offenders in this rebellion I thought it well to note two, for the manner of their execution seemed strange. The first was one, Bowyer, who was mayor of a town in Cornwall called Bodmin. This mayor had been busy among the rebels, but some who loved him said he was forced to it, and that if he had not agreed with them they would have destroyed him and his house. But however it was, this was his end. On a certain day Sir Anthony Kingston, being provost-marshal in the field, wrote to the said mayor declaring that he and certain others would come and dine with him on such and such a day. The mayor seemed to be very joyous at this, and made very good preparation for him. And at the appointed time Sir Anthony Kingston and his company came and were right heartily welcomed by the mayor. And before they sat down to dinner Sir Anthony called the mayor aside and showed him that there must be an execution in the town, and therefore wished him with all speed to cause a pair of gallows to be made, so that they might be ready by the end of dinner. The mayor went diligently about it, and caused it to be done. When dinner was ended Sir Anthony called the mayor to him and asked him if that was ready of which he had spoken to him, and he answered it was ready. Then he took the mayor by the hand and prayed him to bring him to the place where it was, and he did so. And when Sir Anthony saw them he said to the mayor: "think you they are strong enough?" "Yes Sir," he said, "that they are." Well then," said Sir Anthony, "get you up to them, for they are provided for you." The mayor cried: "I trust you mean no such thing to me." "Sir," sayeth he, "you have been a busy rebel, and therefore this is appointed for your reward." So that without longer respite or tarrying there was the mayor hanged.

At the same time, and near to that place, there was a miller who had been a very busy varlet in that rebellion, whom Sir Anthony Kingston also sought for. But the miller had warning, and he, having a good tall fellow as his servant, called him to him and

said, I must go forth; if any come to ask for me say that you are the owner of the mill, and that you have kept it these last four years, and in no way name me. The servant promised his master to do so. Afterwards came Sir Anthony Kingston to the miller's house and called for the miller. The servant answered that he was the miller. "Then," said Kingston, "how long have you kept this mill?" and he answered "three years." "Well then," said he, "come on, you must go with me," and he caused his servants to lay hands upon him, and brought him to the next tree saying, "you have been a rebellious knave and therefore here shall you hang. Then he cried and said he was not the miller, but the miller's servant. "Well then," said Kingston, "you are a false knave to tell two tales, therefore hang him up," said he; and so he was hanged. After he was hanged someone who stood by said to Sir Anthony, surely this was only the miller's man? What then, said he, could he ever have done his master better service than to hang for him?

Unsuccessful war in Scotland, civil disturbances in England, and his necessary severity against his brother, lord Seymour, had seriously weakened the protector's position by the autumn of 1549. At the same time his autocratic methods, and neglect of the council caused a number of nobles, led by Thomas Wriothesley, earl of Southampton, and John Dudley, earl of Warwick, to plot his overthrow. The king recorded the outcome in his journal with extraordinary detachment.

In the meantime in England rose great stirs, likely to increase much if it had not been well foreseen. The council, about nineteen of them, were gathered in London, thinking to meet with the lord protector and to make him amend some of his disorders. He, fearing his position, caused the secretary in my name to be sent to the lords to know for what cause they gathered their powers together and, if they meant to talk with him, to say that they should come in a peaceable manner. The next morning, being 6 October and Saturday, he commanded the armour to be brought out of the armoury of Hampton Court, about 500 harnesses, to arm both his and my men with it, the gates of the house to be fortified, and people to be raised. People came abundantly to the house. That night with all the people at nine or ten o'clock at night I went to Windsor, and there watch and ward was kept every night. The lords sat in the open places of London, calling gentlemen before them and declaring the causes of accusing the lord protector, and caused the same to be proclaimed.

The rise of Dudley

After Somerset's deposition, the conservatives, led by Thomas Wriothesley, 1st earl of Southampton, and Henry Fitzalan, 12th earl of Arundel, were in the majority; it seemed likely that the Reformation would be halted, if not reversed. The imprisoned bishops, Stephen Gardiner of Winchester and Edmund Bonner of London, expected release, while prominent radicals like John Hooper went in fear of their lives. Yet within a short time John Dudley, earl of Warwick had turned the coup inside out and emerged as the head of a regime more Protestant than its predecessor. At first he had appeared to side with the conservatives, but was alarmed by their hope of having Princess Mary appointed regent, and so secure an alliance with the Holy Roman Emperor Charles V. His ambition for power could therefore only be sustained by the Protestant faction, to which he attached himself.

Each side sought to gain supporters. Warwick was particularly concerned to prevent Sir Thomas Arundell, who was known to be Mary's special agent, from becoming a councillor. By placing his brother Sir Andrew Dudley and other close friends in attendance on the king, and through Thomas Cranmer, archbishop of Canterbury, he blocked Sir Thomas's appointment and secured instead that of Thomas Goodrich, bishop of Ely. The conservative cause was damaged when Charles V refused help to defend Boulogne against the French resulting in the subsequent withdrawal of Sir William Paget. By the end of November 1549 the council was meeting at Warwick's house.

Southampton's final move was to promote Somerset's execution. Warwick, realizing that he was the real target, as he would be implicated in any treason found against his former colleague, saved the deposed protector by arranging for Parliament to accept a submission from him instead of pressing charges. He was then able to dismiss the conservatives, and in February 1550 assume the presidency of the council. Warwick was in effect the new ruler of England.

Above   John Dudley, earl of Warwick, who became President of the Council when he outmanoeuvred Somerset.

After which time few came to Windsor, but only the men of my own guard who the lords willed, fearing the rage of the people so lately quieted. Then the protector began to treat by letters, sending Sir Philip Hoby, lately come from his embassy in Flanders to see his family, who brought on his return a very gentle letter to the protector which he delivered to him, another to me, another to my household, to declare his faults, ambition, vainglory, entering into rash wars in my youth, negligence about Newhaven, enriching himself from my treasure, following his own opinions, and doing all by his own authority etc., which letters were openly read, and immediately the lords came to Windsor, took him and brought him through Holborn to the Tower. Afterwards I came to Hampton Court where they appointed by my consent six lords of the council to be attendant on me, at least two, and four knights. Lords – the marquis of Northampton, the earls of Warwick and Arundel, lords Russell, St John and Wentworth. Knights – Sir Andrew Dudley, Sir Edward Rogers, Sir Thomas Darcy, Sir Thomas Wroth. Afterwards I came through London to Westminster. Lord Warwick was made admiral of England. Sir Thomas Cheney was sent to the emperor for relief, which he could not obtain. Mr Nicholas Wootton was made secretary. The lord protector, by his own agreement and submission, lost his protectorship, treasurership, marshalship, all his movables and nearly £2,000 of lands, by act of Parliament.

1550

The earl of Warwick's victory, first over Somerset, and then over the earl of Southampton, made life very difficult for the king's conservative elder sister, Mary. By 1550 she had extensive estates of her own in East Anglia, but was increasingly distressed by the progress of religious policy. She had for many years been dependent upon the support of her cousin the Emperor Charles V, and asked his ambassador, Van der Delft, to arrange her escape by sea from one of her minor residences at Woodham Walter, near Maldon in Essex. Van der Delft instructed his secretary, Jean Dubois, to carry out the operation, and he arrived at Maldon disguised as a corn factor. Afterwards, he reported to the Emperor's sister, Mary of Hungary.

Soon after six in the evening my brother returned with the said Henry, who brought me a horse to carry me to my lady, saying that he would lead me by a secret way. This he did, without anyone seeing me who could possibly recognize me. I was met by the controller, Sir Robert Rochester and had a long talk with him while my lady was making ready to receive me. He told me he had reported our former conversation to my lady, and then went on in the same strain as before, saying that the emperor was wise in considering that my lady might wait until she had been further pressed, in order to go with greater justification, for it must not be forgotten that she would lose all chance of the succession. He told me as a mighty secret, adjuring me to give no hint of it to anyone, that he was quite persuaded the king could not outlast the year; for he and others knew his horoscope to say so. I remarked that his mistress and he must know what facts they had to take into consideration, though on the same facts my lady had twice declared that she wished to go. I myself had been present on the latter occasion, and had asked her grace by my master's orders, before taking leave of her, whether she was quite decided to go. She had replied in the affirmative, as I had told him before dinner. I would be so bold as to make no secret of my thankfulness to the Creator now that all these difficulties were coming up, that my lady's letter had reached me at Antwerp, that I had presented it to Queen Mary of Hungary, regent of the Netherlands after my master's death, and that it had been sent to the emperor; for it might otherwise have been imagined that we had given a false account in our reports. God knew that my master's illness had partly been brought about by his disappointment when he learned he was decieved in his hopes that the undertaking might be carried out when he left the country, after the many letters he had written to his majesty on the subject. However, there was no reason why they should consider themselves obliged to act in one way rather than another, and if my lady wished to stay she should be welcome, and no harm done, except that the whole business was so near being discovered that it was most improbable that it could be kept secret.

"For the love of God," said he, "do not say that to my lady! She is a good woman and really wants to go; but neither she nor you see what I see and know. Great danger threatens us!" I told him I would take care to say nothing that might unnecessarily alarm my lady, but I could not conceal from her anything that she might afterwards regret she had not know. I knew we were on the point of making peace with the Scots, and would have done so already on

The Peace of Boulogne

On 8 August 1549, Henry II of France declared his intention to recover Boulogne, taken by Henry VIII in 1544, and immediately moved against his objective, which was in need of both reinforcements and supplies. The campaign was unsuccessful because the French were unable to command the sea, and in spite of the turmoil which followed Somerset's fall in October, provisions and reinforcements were organized and shipped from England.

Bombardment and direct assault failed, and the longer the campaign continued the greater the probability became that the Holy Roman Emperor Charles V would intervene on the English side. Charles V had already warned Henry II that he was bound by a treaty obligation to defend the English interest in Calais, and, although he had refused to extend that guarantee to Boulogne, when the English appealed to him again in late October 1549, he allowed troops to be recruited from his lands in East Friesland, though he again declined to become directly involved in Boulogne's defence.

By November John Dudley, the 1st earl of Warwick, had taken over the reins of government in England. He realized that the country could not afford a prolonged campaign in France, and that with no immediate Imperial help, the best course was to negotiate. The French king was willing, and by late January 1550 formal commissioners had been appointed by both sides. The English negotiators, led by Sir William Paget, concluded that the French were talking from a position of strength and that it would be better to cede Boulogne. At the end of March it was agreed that Boulogne would be returned to France for a payment of 400,000 crowns in two instalments. The formalities of surrender were completed in April, and the final treaty signed at the end of May.

Below   Boulogne, bought back by the French in 1549. The strength of the English navy had prevented the French king, Henry II, from taking back the town forcibly.

advantageous terms had it not been for this matter. Once peace was made the emperor would have no pretext for keeping at sea the armed ships which he had ordered to serve an additional month for this purpose. For my part, I added, I could see no peril greater than that incurred by delaying and neglecting to seize this opportunity, such as it was. Some of our ships' company had been heard to say that they suspected they were going for the princess of England, as they had done ten years before, as my lady might know better than I. Also one of my men told me that he had been in a house at Maldon where the council's dissatisfaction with my lady, because of her religion, was discussed, and someone had said they would be glad to see her out of the country, and with the emperor.

While talking we were summoned to my lady's presence. According to her custom, she enquired after the emperor's and queen's health, expressed her gratitude and regretted the trouble M. d'Eecke and I were taking on her behalf. I replied that our trouble was small if it could do her any service; but that time pressed as I had written in bad Latin to her controller. "I have your letter here" said she, "and also the one you wrote before; but I am as yet ill-prepared, and it seems you wish it to be for tonight." I replied, "Any time your majesty pleases; but I have spoken and written to your controller the reasons for which prolonged delay appears to me dangerous."

She then mentioned the preparations she had made, packing up some of her property in great long hop-sacks, which would not look as if they contained anything heavy. I made so bold as to say that once she had crossed the water she should lack nothing, and that her effects did not matter so much, for the great thing was to conduct her person to safety, which was the point upon which she must now make up her mind. "I do not know," said she, "how the emperor would take it if it turned out to be impossible to go now, after I have so often importuned his majesty on the subject." I replied that if she was satisfied the emperor would also be content, and she might safely write such a message and send it by me. "And were I to do so," said she, "would you take my rings now?" I answered that I would do anything her majesty commanded me, but she already knew how that question had been considered, as it would be dangerous to send things first that might betray the principal secret. I humbly begged her first to take care of her person, for as she

was minded to risk her rings she might as well go with as after them. She then spoke with her controller, and also called in her principal woman of the bed-chamber, who was keeping the door. They all three then appeared to come to a decision, and my lady turned to me saying that she could not be ready before the day after next, Friday; but that she could then leave her house at four in the morning under the pretext of going to amuse herself and purge her stomach by the sea, as her ladies did daily. Four o'clock was just the time when the watch retired; and my lady asked me whether the tide would also serve. I replied that it would do very well, and that the queen had also approved of carrying out the enterprise at day-break or evening, rather than at night; but it was to be feared that in the meantime the council might be informed that our warships were so near. "Well then," said she, "the queen and I are of one mind. And know you that the very day your master left London two of the king's galleys, called the Sun and the Moon, also left and came up to Stansgate, where they stayed three or four days? Such craft have never been known to come so far up the river. And their captain was the vice-admiral, the greatest heretic on earth. It is more than time I was hence, for things are going worse than ever. A short time ago they took down the altars in the very house my brother lives in."

While we were consulting as to how the affair had best been managed for Friday, and how we might let M' d'Eecke know, so that he might retire for a day or two, there came a knock at the door of the room where we were, and the controller went out. In the meantime I asked my lady why she did not avail herself of her house at St Osyth, of which her controller had spoken to me. She answered that it was too much under observation, for a lord was residing there who had just been admitted to the council. The controller came in at this point, with: "Our affair is going very ill. There is nothing to be done this time, for here is my friend Mr Schurts, who has ridden hard from Maldeon to warn me that the bailiff and other folk of the village wish to arrest your boat (this to me), and suspect you of having some understanding with the warship at Stansgate. Some men from the village have been to see the ship, but were not allowed to go on board. Therefore they intend to send expressly on behalf of the village by next tide, and ask the ship its business, holding you and your men in the meantime to examine you here." In fact

Reforming the church

Introduction of the Prayer Book of 1549 failed to satisfy demands for reform of the Church. Even Thomas Cranmer, archbishop of Canterbury, had seen it as no more than a provisional first step, and any hope he might have had that it would find widespread acceptance were soon undermined when Stephen Gardiner, bishop of Winchester, declared that its formulas were consistent with Catholic belief. Some of the harshest criticisms came from the foreign divines who had come to England at Cranmer's invitation, to speed up the process of reformation.

In 1550 their viewpoint gathered allies. They could count on the support of powerful friends at court, and, in addition take encouragement from the growing indications that the young king also favoured a decisive move towards protestantism. Carefully trained by godly tutors, Edward had absorbed his lessons well: writing to a childhood friend at the French court in 1551, he solemnly advised him to avoid any contamination by Catholic worship; rather he should: "Read the scripture, or else some good book, and give no reverence to the mass at all".

The tensions between the radical and moderate wings of the Church first came to a head with the publication of the Ordinal of January 1550, a form of consecration for bishops and priests based on the Lutheran rite. This order, in the drafting of which Cranmer had taken a prominent role, was immediately subjected to a scathing attack by John Hooper, the leading radical figure among English reformers. Hooper used a series of Lenten sermons preached before the king, to denounce the order for its popish remnants. When in July the Privy Council decided to appoint Hooper bishop of Gloucester, the matter took on more than symbolic significance: Hooper refused to take the oath or to be consecrated in the required vestments Cranmer and the Council urged him to comply and when he refused he was eventually committed to Fleet prison.

The confrontation with Hooper was a decisive moment for English Protestantism. By enforcing their authority on the reluctant bishop, who after three weeks in the Fleet gave way and was consecrated according to the required form, Cranmer and the church leadership asserted the crucial principle that in matters of organization and church practice, the English church had the right to develop independently of continental models, whether Lutheran or Calvinist. Hooper's defeat was therefore a great defeat for advocates of radical Protestantism, and an important step towards the establishment of a distinctly independent English church. With his authority

Top   A bloated pope and his minions are tormented in hell.

Above   The contrast of authority, the word of God, on the left, against the word of the Pope, right.

assured, Cranmer was able to proceed with his long-planned reform of the Prayer Book. Finally enacted in 1552, it swept away many of the remaining ceremonies offensive to Protestants, and adapted an unambigiously Protestant teaching on many doctrines.

he represented the matter as so serious that we might expect to see the beacon-fires, that are wont to be lit on the approach of enemies, blazing along the coast by the following evening. He added that he was thankful I had not stayed to dinner, for it would have proved the destruction of his friend Schurts. We were greatly troubled by these tidings, and knew not what to do or say. I put some questions to the controller, wishing to know exactly what was happening; but he went out again, saying he would obtain fuller details. Meanwhile, my lady said, "What shall we do? What is to become of me?" And she also asked me what the emperor had said when my master returned, and when I took the despatch to him at Aix-la-Chapelle. I replied that I knew nothing, for I had addressed myself to M' d'Arras, who sent me back again as soon as he had spoken to the emperor; for his majesty had decided to leave the conduct of the undertaking to the queen.

The controller then came in and said, "I see great danger. My friend here says there is something mysterious in the air and that you had better depart at once, for these men of the town, Maldon, are not well-disposed." I told him that I could not go before the tide, and if I was going to be arrested it would mean too grave danger for my lady in case I were recognized; so it would be better to hide me than to risk discovery by my arrest. But as the matter was so desperate, it might be best of all to take my lady down to the boat and get her off in secret, as I also should have to go; for if I failed to escape, my lady's danger would be as great as if she had made the attempt. "No," said the controller, "that is impossible, for they are going to double the watch tonight, and what is more post men on the church-tower, whence they can see all the country round – a thing that has never been done before. So all we can do is to see to getting you out of this." We went on discussing for some time in great perplexity, my lady repeating "but what is to become of me?" all the while, until at last I said we must come to some decision, for it was beginning to get dark, and once the watch was set I should be unable to go. The controller then went out once more, and on his return said that he had asked his friend to wait, and given him to understand that I had come for the money for my corn; he would take me with him and get me past the watch. I was to say I had received my money and he, the controller's friend Mr Schurts, would enable me to return in safety and go at the next tide. I asked

whether I might be certain that all would go as he said, for though it was very important for me, I cared much more for what concerned my lady. "I assure you truly it will," he replied, "and I have told Schurts to request the bailiff on my behalf not to give you any trouble, saying I have friends in your country whom I would not like to know that you had been bothered with my knowledge, especially after I had bought from you."

In addition to being a king, Edward was also a boy; and underneath the veneer of formal language and protocol, his natural curiosity and exuberance occasionally appear. He was particularly interested in military displays, and in feats of physical skill, which he occasionally expressed, as in this entry from June 1550.

I went to Deptford, being bidden to supper by Lord Clinton, where before supper I saw certain men stand upon the end of a boat without holding anything, and run one at another until one was cast into the water. At supper Mons, Vidame and Hunaudaye supped with me. After supper a fort was made upon a great lighter on the Thames, which had three walls, and a watch-tower in the midst, of which Mr Winter was captain, with forty or fifty other soldiers in yellow and black. To the fort also belonged a galley of yellow colour with men and munition in it for defence of the castle. There came four pinnaces, with their men handsomely dressed in white, and intending to assault the castle, they first drove away the yellow pinnace, and after with clods, squibs, canes of fire, darts made for the occasion and bombards they assaulted the castle; and at length they came with their pieces and burst the outer walls of the castle, beating those of the castle into the second ward; they afterwards issued out and drove away the pinnaces, sinking one of them, out of which all the men in it, more than twenty, leaped out and swam in the Thames. Then came the admiral of the navy with three other pinnaces and won the castle by assault and burst the top of it down and took the captain and under-captain.

The relaxation of traditional ecclesiastical discipline after the repeal of the heresy laws, and the lack of strict censorship of the press, produced an upsurge of strange and extreme beliefs, but there were limits to what could be tolerated. The earl of Warwick, who threw in his lot with the radical reformers after the fall of Somerset, made these limits clear as lord president of the council.

On 8 September there was one Gryg, a poulterer

Mary's wait

Princess Mary was heiress to the throne under the terms of Henry VIII's will and, because of her unyielding adherance to the mass, the great hope of all who opposed further reform of the Church. Although she argued strongly with the king and his ministers in private, she did not make her feelings public, asking only that matters be left as in her father's time until Edward came of age.

In 1549, having refused to accept the new liturgy, she was permitted, as a temporary measure, to hear Mass with as many as 20 of her household. This was not so much a gesture of toleration as a diplomatic move to assuage the emperor Charles V, Mary's cousin and supporter, whose military co-operation England required. The 1549 coup against Somerset was orchestrated by the conservative lords, Arundel and Southampton, who hoped to have Mary appointed regent – less for religious reasons than to prevent one councillor again assuming supreme power.

Warwick, sensing a threat to his own ambitions, engineered the triumph of the radical party. The conservative cause suffered when the emperor failed to prevent the loss of Boulogne by the English. Improved relations with France from 1550 lessened the case for tolerating the princess's Mass, and in 1551 a further attempt was made to stop it, though this was stoutly resisted. Northumberland's government, like its predecessor, did not realistically suppose that Mary could be forced into hearing the new Prayer Book service, nor that the emperor would invade if she were. Nevertheless written permission for the household

Mass was always refused. Mary's fears for her own safety were without foundation; the emperor warned her against the extravagant views of her small band of supporters. In the summer of 1550 she had sought exile, and various plans were made to ferry her away; but increased security measures impeded any such attempt. Mary was destined to remain in England, but almost always away from court, until Edward VI's death.

Above Edward's coronation in 1547 led Mary to begin fearing for her safety.

Below left Princess Mary; her determined resistance to the introduction of the Prayer Book made her the natural leader of the religious conservatives.

Below right Mary after her accession, with her husband, Philip of Spain.

in Surrey, who was taken amongst the people of London for a prophet for curing various people only by saying prayers over them, saying he took no money, so that people would follow him as if he had been a god. But after he had been examined by the earl of Warwick and others of the council, he was commanded to be set first at Croydon in Surrey on a scaffold with a paper on his breast on Saturday last, which was the 6 September, and this day he was set on a scaffold in Southwark, on a scaffold before the pillory in the afternoon when the lord mayor and his brethren were to ride through the fair, and he there desired the lord mayor and all the people whom he had deceived to forgive him, which penance was enjoined upon him by the council, for he was a very dissembling person, and took money from many, and coats and other things, and he had been a very great deceiver of the people, in selling his wares such as coneys and others in the market in Cheap.

1551

As the expenses of war mounted in the latter part of his reign, Henry VIII had begun to debase the currency. The gold coin was little affected, but the silver went through a series of debasements after 1545, with the result that the exchange rate of sterling was reduced by a half, and domestic prices shot up. By 1551 the earl of Warwick realized that the problem of inflation would have to be tackled, but instead of calling in the debased coinage, he endeavoured to reduce its value by proclamation. This effect was less than satisfactory, as Wriothesley records.

On 8 May a proclamation was made and set forth by the king's majesty and his Privy Council for the diminishing of the coin of shillings and groats, from the last day of August next, the shilling to go for 9d. and no more, and the groat for 3d. and no more.

After this proclamation was made the people within the City of London murmured greatly, and put up their wares and victuals at higher prices, whereupon the council sent for the lord mayor to the court at Greenwich on Sunday 10 May, and gave him sore words for the disobedience of the people, whereupon the mayor called a common council, and the wardens of every guild within the City of London to the Guildhall on 12 May. There, by the mouth of Mr Recorder, it was declared to the Commons that the king's council was so discontented with the citizens for the disobedience of the people in murmuring at the proclamation and enhancing their wares and victuals, giving them straight charge

and commandment on behalf of the king our sovereign lord to call all their company before them immediately, and to admonish them to keep and sell their victuals and wares at no higher prices than they did before the proclamation was made. And declaring further to them that they should admonish all their companies, that if they heard any person rail against any of the king's council, that they should inform on them to the mayor or some of the council. For the earl of Warwick declared to the lord mayor, at the court, that as he rode by Eastcheap to the court he asked the price of a carcass of mutton, and the butcher held it at 13s. and he said that was too much; and another said 16s. and then he answered that it would be better to be hanged; whereupon there arose tales that the earl had said the day would come when a mutton would be worth 20s. Which slanderous words, and the report that he had said where we had one foreigner we would have a hundred, and other slanderous words cause the king's majesty's council to be highly displeased with the citizens of London, who by their good obedience should give an example to all England. And they were now not so stubborn as they were, therefore Mr Recorder exhorted them to take heed from henceforth that such enormities and reports should be put right, as they caused the king's majesty high displeasure and indignation.

And if they heard any such ill reports they should bring forth the parties, or else it would lead to the utter destruction of the City and people for ever, and cause all the whole realm to be forever against them.

Having failed to take her opportunity to escape in July 1550, by the following March Mary was under renewed pressure to give up the illegal mass in her household. On this occasion the king, whose personal convictions were strongly protestant, also became involved. Mary, as always, appealed to the Emperor. Edward's journal recorded the crisis laconically.

The lady Mary, my sister, came to me to Westminster, where after greetings she was called with my council into a chamber where it was declared how long I had suffered her mass, in hope of her reconciliation, and how now, there being no hope as I saw by her letters, unless I saw some speedy amendment I could not bear it. She answered that her soul was God's and her faith she would not change, nor hide her opinion with dissembled doings. It was said

I did not constrain her faith but willed her only as a subject to obey. And that her example might lead to too much inconvenience.

On 19 March the emperor's ambassador came with a short message from his master of threatened war, if I would not allow his cousin the princess to use her mass. No answer was given to this at the time.

The following day the bishops of Canterbury, London and Rochester, Thomas Cranmer, Nicholas Ridley and John Scory, concluded that to give licence to sin was sin; to allow and wink at it for a time might be born as long as all possible haste was used.

Notwithstanding the emperor's forceful intervention, the council continued its pressure on Mary over the celebration of the mass. Several of her chaplains were arrested, and Robert Rochester, her controller, was summoned and given strict instructions to see the law obeyed. Rochester was both unable and unwilling to comply. He was imprisoned, and a special delegation of councillors was sent down into Essex, to persuade or cajole her into compliance. Their report was recorded in full in the council register.

A note of the report of the message taken to the Lady Mary's grace by us, the lord Rich, lord chancellor of England; Sir Anthony Wingfield, knight of the order and controller of the king's majesty's most honourable household; and Sir William Petre, one of his majesty's two principal secretaries; and of her grace's answers to the same, reported by all we three to the king's majesty and the lords of his majesty's privy council at Windsor, 29 August 1551.

First, having received commands and instructions from the king's majesty we went to the said Lady Mary's house at Copthall in Essex last Friday 28 August in the morning. There shortly after our coming I, the lord chancellor, delivered his majesty's letters to her, which she received on her knees, saying that for the honour of the king's majesty's hand with which the letters were signed she would kiss the letter, and not for the matter contained in them, for the matter (she said) I take to proceed not from his majesty but from you of the council.

While reading the letter, which she read privately to herself, she said these words in our hearing, "Ah! good Master Cecil took much pain here."

When she had read the letters we explained the matter of our instructions to her, and as I, the lord chancellor, began, she prayed me to be brief for, said she, "I am not well at ease, and I will make you a short answer, although I have already declared and written my own mind to his majesty plainly with my own hand."

After this we told her at good length how the king's majesty, having used all the gentle means and exhortations he might to reduce her to the rites of religion and order of divine service set forth by the laws of the realm, and finding her in no way conformable but still remaining in her former error, had resolved, by the agreement of the whole of his majesty's privy council and with the consent of several others of the nobility, that she should no longer use the private mass, nor any other divine service than is set forth by the laws of the realm. And here we offered to show her the names of all those who were present at this consultation and resolution, but she said she cared not for any rehearsal of their names, for, said she, "I know you are all of one sort about that."

We told her further that the king's majesty's pleasure was that we should also give strict charge to her chaplains that none of them should presume to say any mass or other divine service than what is set forth by the laws of the realm, and like charge to all her servants that none of them should presume to hear any mass or other divine service than aforesaid. Her answer was this: First she protested that to the king's majesty she was, is and ever will be his majesty's most humble and most obedient subject and poor sister, and would most willingly obey all his commandments in any thing saving her conscience. Yes, and would willingly and gladly suffer death to do his Majesty good, but rather than agree to use any service than that which was used at the death of the late king, her father, she would lay her head on a block and suffer death. But said she, "I amd unworthy to suffer death in so good a quarrel. When the king's majesty shall come to such years that he shall be able to judge these things himself, his majesty shall find me ready to obey his orders in religion, but now in these years, although he, good sweet king, has more knowledge than any other of his years, yet it is not possible that he can be a judge in these things. For if ships were to be sent to sea, or any other thing done touching the policy and government of the realm I am sure you would not think his highness yet able to consider what should be done, and much less (said she) can he in these years discern what is fittest in matters of divinity. And if my chaplains say no mass, I can hear none, no more can my poor servants. But as for my servants, I know it will be against their wills as it will be against mine, for if they could come where it was said, they would hear it with good will. And as for my priests, they know what they have to do. The pain of your laws is only imprisonment for a short time, and if they refuse to say mass for fear of that imprisonment, let them do as they will. But none of your new service shall be used in my house, and if any is said in it I will not stay in the house."

And after this we declared to her grace, according to our instructions, for what reasons the lords of the king's majesty's council had appointed Rochester, Inglefield and Walgrave, being her servants, to introduce the subject of her, and how ill and untruly they behaved in the charge committed to them, and besides that how they had manifestly disobeyed the king's majesty's council. To this she said it was not the wisest counsel to appoint her servants to control her in her own house, and that her servants knew her mind about that well enough, for of all men she might worst endure any of them persuading her in such matters, and for their punishment my lords use them as they think good. And if they refused to take the message to her and her chaplains and servants, as aforesaid, they are, said she, "more honest men, for they would have spoken against their own consciences."

After this, when we had at good length declared to her the effect of our instructions about the promise which she claims to have been made to the emperor, and besides had explained to her at length all such things that we knew and had heard about it, her answer was that she was well assured the promise was made to the emperor, and that the same was once granted before the king's majesty in her presence, seven of the council being there, despite the denial thereof at my last being with his majesty. "And I have," said she, "the emperor's signature testifying that this promise was made, which I believe better than all of you of the council. And though you esteem little the emperor, yet you should show more favour to me for my father's sake, who made most of you almost of nothing. But as for the emperor, if he were dead I would say as I do, and if he would give me now other advice I would not follow it; nevertheless," said she, "to be plain with you, his ambassador

The North-East passage

Although Henry VIII bequeathed a fleet of almost 100 ships and a sophisticated naval administration to his son Edward VI, he had not been interested in exploration or long distance trade. At a time when Spain and Portugal were developing great colonial empires in the Far East and the Americas, and when the French were trying to establish themselves in Canada and Brazil, English voyages were few and unproductive. The merchants of Bristol had developed the fishing grounds off Newfoundland, but did not trade regularly beyond the Canaries and the Azores.

Within a few months of Henry's death, however, Sebastian Cabot was tempted back into English service. The energetic 70 year old had been Pilot Major to the Holy Roman Emperor Charles V for many years, and his navigational techniques and training was unrivalled. At the same time a protracted quarrel with the Hanseatic League, which controlled trade routes into the Baltic, and a crisis in the export of English cloth to Antwerp convinced the Privy Council and many London merchants that fresh commercial initiatives were needed. The first English trading voyage to Morocco was probably made in 1551, and in the following year three ships traded with, and explored, the Barbary Coast in North Africa. By 1553 an organized expedition, accompanied by two warships, had reached the Guinea coast to the South, but Spain made it clear that further attempts in that direction would be resisted.

The real necessity was an alternative route to Cathay and the riches of the east, and in 1553 the talented geographer and cartographer John Dee argued that it would be possible to reach China by sailing around the north of Russia. The ice free waters of the North Cape, well known to Norwegian seamen, appeared to confirm this theory, and convinced Sir William Cecil, Edward's secretaries, of its practicality. A new company was

formed to trade with the east by way of a new route, yet to be discovered.

In May 1553 Sir Hugh Willoughby assumed command of three small ships, the *Bona Esperanza* of 120 tons, the *Edward Bonaventure* of 160 tons, and the *Bona Confidentia* of 90 tons, with Richard Chancellor as Pilot Major. The expedition was meticulously planned, even down to a commendatory letter "towards the great empire of Cathay", requesting full protection and permission to trade. However, in early August the ships were separated in a storm off the North Cape, and in late September Willoughby, with the *Bona Esperanza* and the *Bona Confidentia* made landfall on an uninhabited part of Lappland, near Kegov. An apparent abundance of fish and game, and the onset of the first snows of winter, persuaded them to stay, but they could not survive the harsh conditions. Their bodies were found the following summer by Russian fishermen.

Richard Chancellor in the *Edward Bonaventure*, more by good luck than skill, found his way to Archangel in north-east Russia and travelled overland from there to Moscow. He was warmly welcomed by the Czar, Ivan IV, and started negotiations which resulted two years later in a formal treaty and the establishment of the Muscovy Company: the first of a long series of trading companies which eventually carried English goods and the English flag, all over the known world.

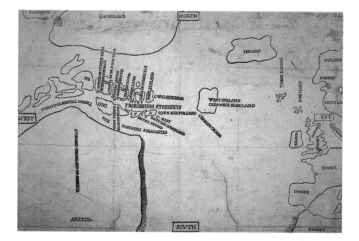

Above The north west passage began to attract English seamen in Edward's reign, although exploration beyond Hudson's Bay did not come until later.

Far left Navigation was becoming a sophisticated science, as these direction cards indicate.

Below The French were the first to colonise Canada, although it is extremely unlikely that they found unicorns!

shall know how I am used at your hands." After this we told her of his majesty's pleasure for someone to attend upon her grace to fill Rochester's place during his absence, as in the instructions. To this her answer was that she would appoint her own officers, and that she was old enough for that purpose; and if we left any such man there she would go out of her gates, for they would not both dwell in one house. And said she, "I am sickly, yet I will not die willingly, but will do the best I can to preserve my life. But if I shall chance to die I will protest openly that you of the council are the causes of my death. You give me fair words, but your deeds are always ill towards me."

And having said thus she departed from us into her bedchamber and delivered to me, the lord chancellor, a ring most humbly upon her knees, with very humble recommendations, saying she would die his true subject and sister, and obey his commandments in all things except this matter of religion concerning the mass and the new service, but yet, said she, this will never be told to the king's majesty.

After her departure we called the chaplains and the rest of her household before us, giving them strict commandment, on pain of their allegiance, that neither the priests should from henceforth say mass or any other divine service than what is set forth by the laws of the realm, nor that they, the rest of the servants, should presume to hear any. The chaplains, after some talk, all promised to obey the king's majesty's commandment signified by us.

We gave similar commandment to them, and every one of them, upon their allegiance, to give notice to some one of the council at least if any mass or divine service other than that which is set forth by the laws of this realm should be hereafter said in that house.

Finally, when we had said and done as is foresaid and were gone out of the house, waiting there for one of her chaplains who was not with the rest when we gave the foresaid charge to them, the lady Mary's grace sent for us to speak with her one word at the window. When we were come into the court, although we offered to come up to her chamber, she insisted on speaking out of the window, and prayed us to speak to the lords of the council that her Controller might shortly return, for, said she, "since his departure I take account myself of my expenses and

learn how many loaves of bread are made from a bushel of wheat, and you know my father and mother never brought me up to baking and brewing, and to be plain with you I am weary with my task and therefore, if my lords will send my officer home, they will give me pleasure. Otherwise, if they will send him to prison, I curse him if he does not go to it merrily and with a good will. And I pray God to send you to do well in your souls and bodies too, for some of you have but weak bodies."

A few months after his fall in October 1549, the duke of Somerset was released from the Tower, and restored to the council in May 1550. But his reconciliation with Warwick, duke of Northumberland from November 1551 was skin deep, and the marriage between Warwick's eldest son, Lord Lisle, and Anne Seymour in June 1550 did not end the feud. Fearing Somerset's renewed political influence, in November 1551, Warwick accused him of plotting the deaths of several councillors, himself included. He was tried, and convicted of felony, being executed on 22 January 1552. At his own execution the following year, Northumberland confessed that the charges were fabricated. This chronicler, who was writing in about 1563, traces the history of their relationship, interspersed with notes for his own guidance.

The marriage between the two dukes at Shene.

How Northumberland suspected he was to be betrayed there, and therefore did not go there.

How Sir R. Morrison was sent as ambassador to the emperor and Sir William Pickering to the Flemish king.

Look for either of their letters.

The second taking of the duke of Somerset and of Arundel Palmer.

That the duke should aspire to – of which he was acquitted, but condemned of felony, for he was suspected to have planned to have killed Northumberland, for which he was condemned.

The rejoicing of the people when they heard he was acquitted, thinking he was acquitted of all.

The good will of the people to Somerset at his execution.

Fane said it was Penshurst which had offended, which the duke had often before asked for, but he would not part with it because it was given him in respect of taking the earl of Huntley.

The court of the young king

The court of a minor was very different from that of an adult sovereign and his consort. Henry VIII's two barbers were of no use to the nine-year-old Edward VI, and were demoted to grooms. Many others were even less fortunate: almost £1,000 was spent in pensioning staff made redundant at the start of the reign. At the centre of the court which remained was the Privy Chamber, to which access was strictly controlled; its officials were the king's most intimate companions and servants as well as being part of the government. To begin with, 18 Gentlemen of the Privy Chamber attended the king, taking turns to sleep, armed, next to his bedchamber. Five grooms were always on duty, one of whom kept watch at night. Somerset made Sir Michael Stanhope, his brother-in-law, the chief Gentleman, with charge of the keys, the finances, and the dry stamp for embossing Edward's signature.

From October 1549, the governorship of the king's person was transferred from the fallen Somerset to a group of six lords and four knights who were added to the Privy Chamber. When John Dudley, earl of Warwick, became president of the council in February 1550 he brought many new men into the Privy Chamber – among them, in August 1551, Edward's friend Barnaby Fitzpatrick. There was also a quadrupling of the guard, with men made available after the peace with France, when in May 1550 Warwick cautiously allowed Somerset back into the council.

The Privy Chamber itself was used as a store room for valuables and money. However, despite the proximity of riches, Edward was kept short of funds by Somerset, and it was Thomas Seymour, in his attempts to displace his brother as protector who sent the money that enabled the king to give presents such as £20 to the preacher Latimer, £5 to his virginals teacher, and £1 to young Barnaby.

Edward's court was much duller than his father's. In the first four years of his reign, less was spent on entertainments, principally at Shrovetide and Christmas, than Henry VIII had been known to lavish on a single display. Edward took part in some martial sports, but was never strong enough to emulate his father. He acted in an anti-papal play in his coronation pageant, and took occasional parts in court drama. The spectacle which seems to have interested him most was a mock sea fight put on by Edward Clinton, the lord high admiral, at Deptford in June 1550. Christmas 1551 was marked by much more extensive celebration at court, probably to divert the king's mind from the impending execution of his uncle, Somerset.

Above 'Mother Jak' was Mrs Jackson, Edward's nurse. The person actually represented in this drawing is now thought to be Magaret Griggs, Sir Thomas More's foster daughter. The origin of the mis-identificaiton is not known.

Until the last year of his life, Edward had seen only London and its immediate surroundings. In July 1552 he began what was intended to be the first in a series of stately progresses. He set off with 15 councillors and a retinue estimated at 4,000 – so huge that it had to be reduced after only two days. They inspected the defences of Portsmouth, then went on to Southampton and Salisbury, returning to Windsor in September. Edward recorded in detail the stages of his journey, and the hospitality he received in the houses of his nobility. It was the only venture he made around his kingdom.

How, after it was concluded by the council that the duke of Somerset should be protector and governor of the king, the earl of Warwick said to the admiral, Sir Thomas Seymour, that he would do well to move in council that, his brother being protector, he might be the king's governor, as though that office had not been granted, when he certainly knew it was determined before, and promised the admiral all his help and support, and that if he wanted it he would declare that he meant what he said. The admiral accordingly did move it in the council which, as soon as the duke heard, he suddenly got up and spoke not one word, and so the council was dissolved. Afterwards Warwick came to the duke and said thus: your grace may see this man's ambition. In such ways he procured and maintained hatred between the brothers, so that he might despatch one and then at length the other, and in the end rule himself alone.

The cause of the falling out of the protector and the admiral was the ambition of the admiral and the envy that he had that his brother should be further advanced than he.

How immediately after Henry's death he began to make bands and to keep a great household and how he so conferred with various members of the government of the realm, and condemned his brother because of his simplicity.

How, being admiral, he would not go in person on the journey against Scotland.

How, when his brother was in Scotland, he practiced to have the government of the king, and how at the return Wroth, Cheke and various others of the privy chamber were put out because they were suspected of furthering his ambition.

Of the hatred between the queen and the duchess of Somerset, and how the duchess hated the admiral and on the other side how the admiral sought the disinheritance of her children and would have had the duke's children by his first wife to be his heirs. How the brothers were once pacified, but the love continued not.

How the admiral made the act of confirmation of letters patent a great matter against his brother, surmising that he would thereby give away Calais, and what stir was caused in parliament by that means.

How the act of repeal of capital laws was made partly to allure the Scots and partly to win favour of the nobility. And how many honest men of the council were against it in general, because it was thought a great security for the king in his minority, and how the papists accused the protestants of being papists because they spoke against it.

The admiral's wife, Queen Catherine died, and afterwards as it was supposed he made efforts to marry Lady Elizabeth.

The admiral is committed to the Tower, charged with how he went about the marriage with Lady Elizabeth by which he sought the crown, how he maintained pirates and had part of the spoil, and how he was associated with Sherrington in coining shillings, his commission being revoked, and because he spoke for Sherrington to the council. And how he had fortified and victualled the castle of Holt. The examination of his treason by law was committed to Montague the king's serjeant and attorney, and to Goderick and Gosnall. Goderick and Gosnall said that his fault was not treason but misprision at the most, if it could be proved that Sherrington had done what was laid to his charge, and that the admiral consented to it, as it was not proved that the commission was revoked. Well, said Montague, if you were incited as we are you would not stick at this matter. Goderick answered, if you take this matter to be treason let him be indicted and tried by the order of the common law. No, not so, said Montague, it will be better done by the parliament. For if he is condemned by order of the common law, later when the king comes of age we might be blamed. If it is done by parliament we are discharged. Sir William Sherrington confesses this fault and has his pardon, of life, lands and goods. The admiral is attainted and executed at Tower Hill. How it was said he had written with a cipher of an oration in paper, and sewed it in his shoe, and being on the scaffold willed his man to remember what he said, who disclosed it. Some say it was only invented by the duchess of Somerset and counterfeited by J. Godsalve. Look what Mr Latimer preached after him, and how by that sermon he had great hatred from many. Inquire for the end at the admiral's death.

The rebellion was throughout the realm, which began at Bury.

The rebellion in the west.

The rebellion of Kett in Norfolk, and how it was

The succession crisis

In the opening months of 1553 it became clear that the young king was seriously ill; perhaps even dying. Until then Edward's health had not been generally bad. Through 1551 and 1552 he had joined enthusiastically in court entertainments, and his journal records his steady interest and growing maturity in state affairs. But in February 1553 he fell sick, and it gradually became clear that this was much more serious than the chill and fever initially diagnosed. By the spring those close to the centre of power were aware that he was dying. He was suffering from acute pulmonary tuberculosis, a disease incurable in the sixteenth century.

The king's illness presented Northumberland with an acute dilemma. He could be in no doubt that Mary's accession would lead to the reversal of his guiding policies and his eclipse from power; and he could not rule out the possibility that like his father Edmund, Henry VIII's adviser who had been executed on charges of treason, he would be used as a convenient scapegoat for an unpopular regime. However, Henry VIII's will had left unambiguous instructions that in the case of Edward's death without male heirs, the crown was to pass to the king's sisters, first Mary and then Elizabeth.

As Edward's health ebbed away, Northumberland embarked on a desperate venture to shore up his position. On 21 May his fourth son Guildford was married to Lady Jane Grey, who, through descent from Henry VIII's sister Mary, possessed a tenuous place in the line of succession. It was also about this time that Edward and Northumberland drew up a document, the *Device*, that excluded Mary and Elizabeth from the line of succession. The ambiguities of this document caused by hasty and careless drafting, have fuelled debate over who was ultimately responsible for the plan to make Lady Jane queen. Initially the provisions of the *Device* left the crown to no living person, but to the future male hiers of the four women of the Grey line; an alteration willed the crown to Jane and her male heirs alone, making her the immediate beneficiary.

For a time his gamble seemed likely to succeed. On 21 June the scheme to divert the succession was presented to the leading councillors and justices, who gave their assent, though many were reluctant. When the king died on 6 July little seemed to stand in Northumberland's way: the fleet and fortifications were in the hands of apparently loyal supporters, and he commanded the only substantial military force. The failure to capture princess Mary before Edward's death was all that seemed to stand in the way of a successful coup when Jane was proclaimed queen on 9 July.

Above   Lady Jane Grey, the eldest daughter of Henry Grey, duke of Suffolk, and his wife Frances, née Brandon. Frances Brandon was the elder daughter of Henry VIII's sister, Mary, through her marriage to Charles Brandon, duke of Suffolk. Jane became puppet-queen at the age of sixteen for nine days.

supposed that the Lady Mary and her counsel were privy to it.

How Sir R. Southwell was accused by Sir Edmund Knight of being one of the authors of this rebellion.

How when the duke of Somerset was first taken Cecil the secretary was committed to ward.

And how then Southwell searched his chamber at the Savoy and took away the disposition of E. Knyvet against him. And how, afterwards, none of the council resorted to Kett in the Tower but only Southwell.

How the duke of Somerset was first taken, and how, Warwick being at Stondon, Balthazar's son brought letters thither from his wife and Sir R. Southwell.

How Sir M. Stanog and Wolfe laid in wait with bands of men to kill Warwick by the way, and how at supper Warwick would eat nothing, but suddenly in the middle got up and went into the gallery and there walked. But it seemed all this was without cause, and purposely devised to bring Somerset into more hatred.

How the duke was taken and carried to the tower.

How Wriothesley was sent for and made one of the councillors.

Enquire for the articles on which the duke was examined and for this confession which was drawn by Paget.

The examination of Sir R. Fane, only that he should rob Henry when he went for the Germans to be brought to Boulogne.

How Sturmins and Brune were ambassadors in France at that time for the peace, and how by Brune's means the army went not forward.

How the duke was delivered.

How Sir R. Fane had been several times before in prison for Warwick's sake, and how he was once his man.

How Warwick was lodged with Somerset in his house for fear of his brother the admiral.

How the first cause of the breach between Somerset and Warwick was that Warwick wished to have money coined and the duke, with tears, denied it.

How after Somerset was deprived all the lords had base money coined in the Tower, which was a great damage.

How Warwick was made duke of Northumberland and Herbert earl of Pembroke.

How bands of horsemen were devised, and how they were distributed, and what was their wages.

How they continued not long because of the great cost.

What exchanges of lands Northumberland made with the king, and what gifts he and others had from the king.

1552

Somerset was generally mourned by the common people, and Northumberland hated for his role in bringing about the execution. Henry Machyn, a London undertaker, who probably recorded his impressions very soon after the event, reflects that feeling.

On 22 January, soon after 8 o'clock in the morning, the duke of Somerset was beheaded on Tower Hill. There was as great a company as has been seen, ... the king's guard being there with their halberds and a thousand more with halberds of the privilege of the Tower, Ratcliffe, Limehouse, Whitechapel, St Katherine's and Stratford Bow, as well as Hoxton and Shoreditch; and the two sheriffs being present there, seeing the execution of my lord, and his head being cut off, and shortly after his body was put into a coffin and carried into the Tower, and there buried in the church, on the northside of the choir of St Peter's, and I beseech God to have mercy on his soul, amen! And there was a sudden rumbling a little before he died, as if it had been guns shooting and great horses coming, so that a thousand fell to the ground for fear, for they who were at one side thought no other but that one was killing another, so that they fell down to the ground, one upon another with their halberds, some fell into the ditch of the Tower and other places, and a hundred into the Tower ditch, and some ran away for fear.

1553

The fourth session of Edward's first parliament, in 1552, had passed a second Act of Uniformity, imposing a revised prayer book of a more specifically protestant nature. By the end of the year the king was ailing, and in January 1553 he drew up his "Device" for the succes-

sion, excluding both Mary and Elizabeth in favour of the Suffolk line. By the time that his second parliament met he was seriously ill, although that was not fully apparent at the time. The "Device", which needed parliamentary ratification, was not presented. Wriothesley records the proceedings briefly.

The first day of March began the first session of the second Parliament of our sovereign lord King Edward VI, all the lords spiritual and temporal assembling that day in the king's majesty's court of Whitehall at Westminster in their robes. First a sermon was made by Doctor Ridley, bishop of London, in the king's chapel, and after the communion was kept; the king's majesty with several other lords received the communion that day.

The following day all the bishops and deans of the spirituality assembled at St Paul's for their convocation in their robes, the bishop of Rochester, Mr Scory, making the sermon before them in Latin, in the Lady Chapel behind the choir.

On the last day of March, being Good Friday, parliament broke up and was clearly dissolved at the king's palace at Whitehall at 7 o'clock at night, the king's majesty sitting on his robes in the great chamber on the king's side, where the first session began, with all the lords spiritual and temporal in their robes likewise.

The rapid development of Edward's illness overtook the plans which he, or Northumberland, had made for the succession. In June Lady Jane Grey, the eldest daughter of the duke of Suffolk, and recently married to Northumberland's fifth son, Guildford, was declared the heir, in spite of the fact that her mother, through whom she derived her claim, was still alive. Edward forced his council and judges to ratify his choice, but it was unpopular, even in protestant London, and Jane survived just nine days as queen. Henry Machyn was loyal, but unenthusiastic.

On 6 July died the noble King Edward VI, in the seventh year of his reign, son and heir to the noble King Henry VIII. And he was poisoned, as everybody says, for which now, thanks be to God, there are many of the false traitors brought to their end, and I trust God that more will follow as they may be spied out.

On 7 July a proclamation was made that all penthouses should be no lower than 10 foot, and all private lights be condemned.

The same day an old man was set on the pillory for counterfeit, false writings.

The same day there came to the Tower the lord treasurer, the earl of Shrewsbury, and the lord admiral with others; and there they discharged Sir James Croft of the constableship of the Tower, and there they put in the said lord admiral, and he took his oath and charge of the Tower, and the next day after he conveyed into all places in the Tower and ... great guns, such as the White Tower on high.

On 9 July all the head officers and the guard were sworn to Queen Jane as queen of England . . . . . daughter of the duke of Suffolk, and served as queen of . . . . . .

The following day queen Jane was received into the Tower with a great company of lords and nobles of . . . after the queen, and the duchess of Suffolk her mother, bearing her train, with many ladies, and there was a firing of guns and chambers such as has not often been seen, between 4 and 5 o'clock; by 6 o'clock began the proclamation on the same afternoon of Queen Jane, with two heralds and a trumpet blowing, declaring that Lady Mary was unlawfully begotten, and so went through Cheapside to Fleet Street, proclaiming Queen Jane. And there was a young man taken at that time for speaking certain words about Queen Mary, that she had the true title.

On 11 July, at 8 o'clock in the morning the young man was set on the pillory for speaking this, and both his ears were cut off. There was a herald and a trumpeter blowing, and he was quickly taken down. And the same day the young man's master, dwelling at St John's Head, whose name was Sandur Onyone, and another Master Owen, a gun-maker at London Bridge, living at Ludgate, were drowned.

On 12 July by night were carried to the Tower 3 carts full of all manner of ordnance, such as great guns and small, bows, bills, spears, morrish pikes, armour, arrows, gunpowder and stakes, money, tents and all manner of ordnance, a great number of cannon balls, and a great number of men at arms; and it was for a great army near Cambridge; and two days after the duke and various lords and knights went with him, and many gentlemen and gunners, and many men of the guard and men of arms towards Lady Mary's grace, to destroy her grace, and so to Bury, and all was against him, for his men forsook him.

Epilogue

*W*hen Edward VI died on 6 July 1553 the female succession which England had so long dreaded became inevitable. Apart from Edward, Henry VIII had left two daughters, Mary and Elizabeth. Both had been declared illegitimate by parliament, but both had been included in the succession to the throne. Moreover, by a quirk of fate, all the living descendants of Henry's two sisters, Margaret and Mary, were also women, with the exception of the young Henry Darnley, the grandson of Margaret's second marriage to Archibald, earl of Angus. Darnley was too remote to be a realistic claimant, and Mary Stuart, Queen of Scots, the grand-daughter of Margaret Tudor's first marriage, had been excluded by the Act of Succession.

In one sense the prophets of doom were quickly justified. Within a year Mary was married to Philip of Spain, the only legitimate son of the Emperor Charles V. Nevertheless, the government of England was carried on very much as before, and the administrative machinery which had successfully weathered a troubled minority soon proved to be capable of surviving a diligent but not particularly effective Queen. There were important changes, particularly in the court, which was the centre of government and patronage.

But with the advent of a female ruler, the importance of the Privy Chamber collapsed overnight. A queen needed women about her, and the Gentlemen of the Privy Chamber were reduced to a handful of officers and ushers. The ladies who replaced them might represent the political interests of their fathers, husbands or brothers, but they held no offices in their own right. The close links which had been established over the years between Privy Council and Privy Chamber were dissolved, and the Council was left without any serious competitor in the crucial business of influencing the sovereign's mind. At least, that was what should have happened, but Mary was soon to demonstrate that alternative sources of advice could be discovered; first the Emperor's ambassador, Simon Renard, then her husband, King Philip, and finally Cardinal Reginald Pole. For the first time, after 1553 a Tudor monarch was looking to outsiders for essential support, and her subjects were not particularly pleased.

Below   The Great Court of Trinity College, Cambridge, one of Henry VIII's two major academic foundations. The other was Christ Church, Oxford.

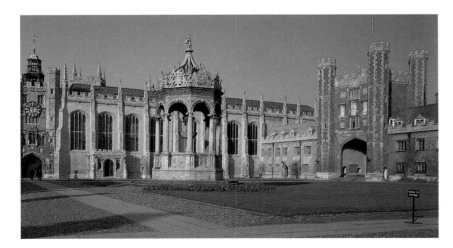

Europe after Edward VI

When Edward died in 1553, Europe was firmly, if not very clearly, divided into confessional camps, which by then had taken territorial and political shape. The division of the Holy Roman Empire along these lines was to be confirmed by the Peace of Augsberg in 1555. By that time Scandinavia, England and most of northern Germany adhered to protestantism in one or other of its forms. France, Spain, Portugual, Italy and most of southern Germany were catholic; while Poland and the Netherlands were increasingly divided. With Charles V's abdication in 1555 his great Empire was divided between his brother Ferdinand and his son Philip. Habsburg-Valois rivalry was about to give way to religious war.

SCOTLAND

Edinburgh

NORTH SEA

IRELAND

Dublin

York

ENGLISH

MONARCHY

WALES   ENGLAND

R. Thames

London

Plymouth

Calais

Amsterdam

NETHERLANDS

Antwerp

Munster

Cologne

HOL

ROMA

DANISH

DENMARK

HOLSTEI
Hambu

Bremen

Rouen

Amiens

Rheims

Paris

Verdun

Worms

Frankfurt

PALATINATE

Metz

Speier

ATLANTIC OCEAN

Nantes

Blois

Tours

R. Seine

Toul

EMPI

R. Loire

FRANCH
COMTE

Augsbu

Basel

Bern

SWITZERLAND

Bordeaux

Lyon

Geneva

R. Garonne

NAVARRE

Turin

MILAN

Oporto

Valladolid

ANDORRA

Toulouse

Avignon

Montpellier

Genoa

Marseille

Floren

TUSCAN

PORTUGAL

CASTILE

Madrid

ARAGON

Saragossa

Barcelona

CORSICA

Lisbon

R. Tagus

Toledo

Valencia

Balearic Islands

SARDINIA

SPANISH

Seville

GRANADA

Granada

MON

Cadiz

Gibraltar

Ceuta

MEDITERRANEAN   SEA

Bona

Tunis

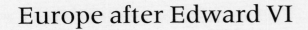

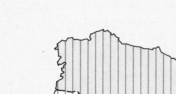

A Guide to Peers

HENRY VII

Bath Philibert de Chandee, earl; created 1486.

Bedford Jasper Tudor, duke; (Henry's uncle), created 1485; died without issue 1495.

Clarence George Plantagenet, duke; (Edward IV's brother); killed 1478.

Derby Thomas Stanley, 1st earl; created 1485; died 1504.

Devon Edward Courtenay, earl; created 1485; died 1509. William Courtenay, earl; (son of Edward); attainted 1504; created 1511; died 1511.

Dorset Thomas Grey, 1st marquess; created 1475; forfeited 1483; restored 1485; died 1501.

Essex Henry Bourchier, 2nd earl; died 1540.

Kent George Grey, 2nd earl; died 1503.

Kildare Gerald FitzMaurice FitzGerald, 8th earl; forfeited 1494; restored 1495; died 1513.

Lincoln John de la Pole, earl; killed at Stoke, 1487.

Northumberland Henry Percy, 4th earl; present at Bosworth; killed April 1489. Henry Algernon Percy, 5th earl; a minor until 1499.

Oxford John de Vere, 13th earl; forfeited 1475; restored 1485; died 1513.

Shrewsbury George Talbot, 4th earl; 1468–1538.

Suffolk Edmund de la Pole, 2nd duke; surrendered dukedom 1493, thereafter earl; forfeited 1504.

Surrey Thomas Howard, earl; forfeited 1485; restored 1489.

Warwick Edward Plantagenet, earl; (son of the duke of Clarence), executed 1499.

York Richard Plantagenet, duke; (father of Edward IV) killed 1460. Richard Plantagenet, duke; (son of Edward IV) killed 1483.

HENRY VIII

Arundel Thomas Fitzalan, 5th earl; inherited 1487, died 1524. William Fitzalan, 6th earl; inherited 1524, died 1544. Henry Fitzalan, 7th earl; inherited 1544, died 1580.

Bath John Bourchier, 1st earl; created 1536, died 1539. John Bourchier, 2nd earl; inherited 1539, died 1561.

Buckingham Edward Stafford, duke; inherited 1485 (as a minor), executed 1521.

Cumberland Henry Clifford, 1st earl; created 1525, died 1542. Henry Clifford, 2nd earl; inherited 1542, died 1570.

Derby Thomas Stanley, 2nd earl; inherited 1504, died 1521. Edward Stanley, 3rd earl; inherited 1521, died 1572.

Devon William Courtenay, 1st earl; created May 1511, died June 1511. Henry Courteny, 2nd earl; inherited 1511, marquess of Exeter 1525.

Dorset Thomas Grey, 2nd marquess; recognized 1511, died 1530. Henry Grey, 3rd marquess; inherited 1530, duke of Suffolk 1551.

Essex Thomas Cromwell, earl; created April 1540, executed July 1540. William Parr, earl; created 1543, marquess of Northampton 1547.

Exeter William Courtenay, earl of Devon, marquess; created 1525, executed 1538.

Hertford Edward Seymour, viscount Beauchamp, earl; created 1537, duke of Somerset 1547.

Huntingdon George Hastings, 1st earl; created 1529, died 1544. Francis Hastings, 2nd earl; inherited 1544, died 1560.

Lincoln Henry Brandon (son of the Duke of Suffolk), earl; created 1525, died still a minor 1534.

Lisle Arthur Plantagenet, viscount; created 1523, died 1542. John Dudley, viscount; created 1542, Earl of Warwick 1547.

Norfolk Thomas Howard, earl of Surrey, 2nd duke; restored 1514, died 1524. Thomas Howard, earl of Surrey, 3rd duke; inherited 1524, forfeited 1547, restored 1553, died 1554.

Northampton William Parr, earl of Essex, marquess; created 1547, forfeited 1553, restored 1559, died 1571.

Northumberland Henry Algernon Percy, 5th earl; (see Henry VII); died 1527. Henry Percy, 6th earl; inherited 1527, died 1537, leaving the king as his heir.

Nottingham Henry Fitzroy (see Richmond); earl; created 1525, died 1536.

Oxford John de Vere, 13th earl; restored 1485, died 1513. John de Vere, 14th earl; inherited 1513, died 1526. John de Vere, 15th earl; inherited 1526, died 1540. John de Vere, 16th earl; inherited 1540, died 1562.

Pembroke Anne Boleyn, marquess; created 1532, executed 1536.

Richmond Henry Fitzroy (Henry VIII's illegitimate son), duke; created 1525, died 1536.

Rutland Thomas Manners, Lord Ros, 1st earl; created 1525, died 1543. Henry Manners, 2nd earl; inherited 1543, died 1563.

Salisbury Lady Margaret Pole, Countess; restored 1513, forfeited 1539, executed 1541.

Shrewsbury George Talbot, 4th earl; inherited, as a minor, 1473, died 1538. Francis Talbot, 5th earl; inherited 1538, died 1560.

Southampton William Fitzwilliam, earl; created 1537, died 1542.

Suffolk Charles Brandon, viscount Lisle, duke; created 1514, died 1545. Henry Brandon, 2nd duke; inherited 1545, died, still a minor, 1551.

Surrey Thomas Howard, earl (see Henry VII); duke of Norfolk, 1514–1524. Thomas Howard, earl; inherited 1514; duke of Norfolk, 1524–1547, 1553–4. Henry Howard, earl (the poet); executed 1546.

Sussex Robert Radcliffe, viscount Fitzwalter, 1st earl; created 1529, died 1542. Henry Radcliffe, 2nd earl; inherited 1542, died 1557.

Westmorland Ralph Neville, 4th earl; inherited 1499, died 1549.

Wiltshire Henry Stafford, earl; created 1510, died 1523. Thomas Boleyn, Viscount Rochford (Anne Boleyn's father), earl; created 1929, died 1539.

Worcester Charles Somerset, Lord Herbert, 1st earl; created 1514, died 1526. Henry Somerset, 2nd earl; inherited 1526, died 1549.

EDWARD VI

Bedford John Russell, 1st earl; created 1550, died 1555.

Northumberland John Dudley, earl of Warwick, duke; created 1551, executed 1553.

Pembroke William Herbert, 1st earl; created 1551, died 1570.

Somerset Edward Seymour, earl of Hertford, duke, created 1547, executed 1552. Lord Protector.

Southampton Thomas Wriothesley, 1st earl; created 1547, died 1550.

Suffolk Henry Grey, 3rd marquess of Dorset, duke; created 1551, executed 1554. Father of Lady Jane Grey.

Warwick John Dudley, viscount Lisle, earl; created 1547, duke of Northumberland 1551. John Dudley, earl; inherited 1551, died 1554.

Westmorland Henry Neville, 5th earl; inherited 1549, died 1564.

Wiltshire William Paulet, Lord St. John, earl; created 1550, marquess of Winchester 1551.

Winchester William Paulet, earl of Wiltshire, 1st marquess; created 1551, died 1572. The Lord Treasurer.

Worcester William Somerset, 3rd earl; inherited 1549, died 1589.

Glossary

Attainder The legal corruption of blood, following conviction for high treason. Frequently confirmed by Act of Parliament.

Bachelor A journeyman, or craftsman who has not yet achieved master status; the junior members of guilds or fraternities without their own businesses.

Banneret A knighthood conferred for valiant deeds upon the battlefield, or in the king's presence.

Barons of the Cinq Ports The civic officers of the jurisdictional liberty known as the Cinq (five) Ports — Sandwich, Dover, Hythe, Winchelsea and Hastings, who provided ships for the king's service in return for their privileges.

Beadsman A petitioner, or a person who seeks a favour of some kind. Normally used of a social inferior, in relation to a superior.

Bearing sheet The winding sheet, normally of woollen cloth, in which a corpse was wrapped in preparation for burial.

Caparisoned The wearing of ornamental or heraldic drapery by a horse.

Challengers In a tournament, those who issued the challenge to combat; the initiators or protagonists of the joust.

Charterhouse A house of strictly reformed monks, known as Carthusians. The Carthusians lived in individual cells, and shared only their worship.

Coin A groat, worth 4d. The ducat at this period was worth about 6s 8d sterling, or 24 groats, and there was no coin worth 6d.

Our Lady of Coleyn The confraternity, or fellowship, of the Rosary of our Lady of Cologne. A society of lay people associated with this particular cult.

Double horses Matched in pairs.

The house of the English nation The headquarters of the Merchant Adventurers in Antwerp, which enjoyed certain jurisdictional immunities and privileges.

Fellowships The Livery companies of the City of London. Can be used by a guild, or any similarly organized society.

Fifteenth A traditional parliamentary tax upon the value of moveable property; invariably coupled with a tenth of real property. By the early 16th century the assessments for these taxes has fossilized at £29,000.

Jubilee A year of remission, in which plenary indulgences for sin might be obtained by making a pilgrimage to Rome.

Largesse Bounty; the granting of alms for charitable purposes, especially upon ceremonial occasions.

Legate A papal emissary or representative of the highest rank or status. The status was also attached, ex officio, to certain senior ecclesiastical posts, such as the archbishopric of Canterbury.

Patent A formal document conferring a grant, which could be land, a title, an office, or an annuity.

Pomegranate The badge of Catherine of Aragon; very frequently employed in courtly heraldry between 1509 and 1525.

Praemunire An offence at common law, originating in a statute of 1393. The exercising of ecclesiastical jurisdiction without the king's consent.

Prise out Seek out, or discover by diligent search.

Progress A provincial tour, or visitation, usually by the monarch. A progress was distinguished from less formal travel by the existence of 'geistes' or itineraries.

Sacrament of the altar The consecration of the host during the mass, also known as the eucharist. To catholics of this period one of the central mysteries of the faith, in which the substance of bread and wine were converted into the body and blood of Christ.

Upon six or seven To gamble, or hazard ones fortunes rashly; also to be careless in making preparations.

Sophistical Excessively refined or over elaborate distinction or definition; a pretentious quibble.

Stradiates Light cavalry

Steelyard The London headquarters of the Hanseatic League — an association of German trading towns enjoying certain privileges which were much resented by the Londoners.

Bibliography

Social and Economic

Andrews K.R., *Trade, plunder and settlement; maritime enterprise and the genesis of the British Empire, 1480–1630*, Cambridge, 1984

Bridbury A.R., *Economic growth; England in the later middle ages*, 2nd ed., London, 1979

Clark P., *English provincial society from the Reformation to the Revolution; politics and society in Kent 1500–1640*, Brighton, 1977

Clark, P., and Slack, P., eds., *Crisis and Order in the English towns 1500–1700*, London, 1972

Clark, P., and Slack, P., eds., *English Towns in transition, 1500–1700*, Oxford, 1976

Clay C.G.A., *Economic expansion and social change: England 1500–1700*, Cambridge, 1984

Coleman D.C., *The Economy of England 1450–1750*, Oxford, 1977

Cornwall J., *The Revolt of the Peasantry, 1549*, London, 1977

Ellis S.G., *Tudor Ireland; Crown, community and the conflict of cultures, 1470–1603*, London, 1985

Hatcher J., *Plague, population and the English Economy, 1348–1530*, London, 1977

Hoskins W.G., *The Age of Plunder; the England of Henry VIII, 1500–1547*, London, 1976

Kerridge E., *Agrarian problems in the sixteenth century and after*, London, 1969

Lander J.R., *Government and community: England 1450–1509*, London, 1980

O'Day R., *Education and society, 1500–1800*, London, 1982

Prior M., ed., *Women in English Society, 1500–1800*, London, 1985

Pugh T.B., ed., *The Marcher Lordships of South Wales, 1415–1536*, Cardiff, 1963

Pythian Adams C., *The desolation of a City; Coventry and the Urban Crisis of the Later Middle Ages*, Cambridge, 1979

Simon J., *Education and society in Tudor England*, Oxford, 1984

Stone L., *Family, sex and marriage in England, 1500–1800*, London, 1977

Thomson J.A.F., *The Transformation of Medieval England, 1370–1529*, London, 1985

Wolffe B.P., *The Crown Lands, 1461–1536*, London, 1970

Politics, Law and Finance

Allen J.W., *A history of political thought in the sixteenth century*, London, 1928; reprinted 1964

Anglo S., *Spectacle, Pageantry and Early Tudor Policy*, Oxford, 1969

Bernard G.W., *The power of the early Tudor nobility; a study of the fourth and fifth earls of Shrewsbury*, Brighton, 1985

Bindoff S.T., *The House of Commons, 1509–1558*, London, 1982

Bradshaw B., *The Irish constitutional revolution of the sixteenth century*, Cambridge, 1979

Bush M.L., *The Government policy of Protector Somerset*, London, 1975

Challis C.E., *The Tudor Coinage*, Manchester, 1978

Chambers R.W., *Thomas More*, London, 1935

Chrimes S.B., *English constitutional ideas in the fifteenth century*, Cambridge, 1936

Chrimes S.B., *Henry VII*, London, 1972

Dietz F.C., *English Public Finance, 1485–1558*, 2nd ed., London, 1964

Elton G.R., *England under the Tudors*, 2nd ed., London, 1974

Elton G.R., *The Tudor Revolution in Government*, Cambridge, 1953

Elton G.R., *Politics and Police*, Cambridge, 1972

Fox A.G., and Guy J.A., eds., *Reassessing the Henrician Age; Humanism, Politics and Reform 1500–1550*, Oxford, 1986

Graves M.A.R., *The House of Lords in the Parliaments of Edward VI and Mary; an institutional study*, Cambridge, 1981

Graves M.A.R., *The Tudor parliaments; Crown, Lords and Commons 1485–1603*, London, 1985

Griffiths R.A., and Thomas R.S., *The making of the Tudor dynasty*, Gloucester, 1985

Gunn S.J., *Charles Brandon, Duke of Suffolk*, Oxford, 1988

Guy J.A., *The Cardinal's Court: the impact of Thomas Wolsey in Star Chamber*, Brighton, 1977

Guy J.A., *The Public Career of Thomas More*, Brighton, 1984

Guy J.A., *Tudor England*, Oxford, 1989

Harris B.J., *Edward Stafford, Third Duke of Buckingham, 1478–1521*, Stanford Ca, 1986

Heinze R.W., *The proclamations of the Tudor Kings*, Cambridge, 1976

Hoak D.E., *The King's Council in the reign of Edward VI*, Cambridge, 1976

Ives, E.W., *Anne Boleyn*, Oxford 1986

Jordan W.K., *Edward VI: the threshold of power*, London, 1970

Jordan W.K., *Edward VI: the young king*, London, 1968

Kelly H.A., *The matrimonial trials of Henry VIII*, Stanford Ca, 1978

Lander J.R., *Crown and nobility, 1450–1609*, London, 1976

Lehmberg S.E., *The later parliaments of Henry VIII, 1536–1547*, Cambridge, 1977

Loades D.M., *Politics and the nation, 1450–1660*, 3rd ed., London, 1986

Loades D.M., *The Tudor Court*, London, 1986

Loach J., and Tittler R., eds., *The Mid-Tudor polity 1540–1560*, London, 1980

MacCulloch D., *Suffolk and the Tudors*, Oxford, 1986

MacFarlane K.B., *England in the fifteenth century; collected essays*, London, 1981

McConica J.K., *English Humanists and Reformation Politics*, Oxford, 1965

Marius R., *Thomas More*, New York, 1984

Miller H., *Henry VIII and the English nobility*, Oxford, 1986

Pollard A.F., *Wolsey*, London, 1929

Richardson W.C., *The history of the Court of Augmentations 1536–1554*, Baton Rouge, La, 1961

Richardson W.C., *Tudor Chamber Administration 1485–1547*, Baton Rouge, La, 1952

Ridley J., *Thomas Cranmer*, Oxford, 1962

Ross C.D., *Richard III*, London, 1981

Scarisbrick J.J., *Henry VIII*, London, 1968

Slavin A.J., *Politics and Profit; a study of Sir Ralph Sadler, 1507–1547*, Cambridge, 1966

Smith A.G.R., *The Emergence of a nation state; 1529–1660*, London, 1984

Smith L.B., *Henry VIII; the mask of royalty*, London, 1971

Starkey D., ed., *The English Court from the wars of the Roses to the Civil War*, London, 1987

Starkey D., *The reign of Henry VIII: politics and personalities*, London, 1985

Starkey D., and Coleman C., eds., *Revolution Reassessed; revisions in the history of Tudor government and administration*, Oxford, 1986

Warnicke R.M., *The rise and fall of Anne Boleyn*, Cambridge, 1989

Willen D., *John Russell, first Earl of Bedford: one of the King's men*, London, 1981

Williams P., *The Tudor Regime*, Oxford, 1979

Wilkie W.E., *The Cardinal Protectors of England; Rome and the Tudors before the Reformation*, Cambridge, 1974

Youings J.A., *Sixteenth Century England*, Harmondworth, 1984

Warfare

Bernard G.W., *War, taxation and rebellion in early Tudor England; Henry VIII, Wolsey and the Amicable Grant of 1525*, Brighton, 1986

Gillingham J., *The Wars of the Roses*, London, 1981

Goodman A., *The Wars of the Roses; military activity and English society, 1452–1497*, London, 1981

Young, A. *Tudor and Jacobean Tournaments*, London 1987

Art and Literature

Bennett H.S., *English books and readers, 1475–1557* Cambridge, 1952

Fox A.G., *Thomas More: History and Providence*, Oxford, 1982

Strong, R. *The English Renaissance Miniature*, London, 1983

Walker G., *John Skelton and the politics of the 1520s*, Cambridge, 1988

Ecclesiastical

Aston M., *England's Iconoclasts*, Oxford, 1988

Bowker M., *The Henrician Reformation; the diocese of Lincoln under John Longland 1521–1547*, Cambridge, 1981

Bowker M., *The secular clergy of the diocese of Lincoln*, Cambridge, 1968

Brigden S.E., *London and the Reformation*, Oxford, 1989

Cooper J.P., *Land, men and beliefs; studies in Early Modern History*, London, 1983

Cross C., *Church and Pope 1450–1669*, London, 1976

Davis J.F., *Heresy and Reformation in South East England 1520–1559*, London, 1983

Davies C.S.L., *Peace, Print and Protestantism 1450–1558*, London, 1976

Dickens A.G., *Lollards and Protestants in the Diocese of York 1509–1558*, Oxford, 1959

Dickens A.G., *The English Reformation*, 2nd ed., London, 1990

Dickens A.G., *Thomas Cromwell and the English Reformation*, London, 1959

Elton G.R., *Reform and Reformation 1509–1558*, London, 1977

Elton G.R., *Policy and Police; the enforcement of the Reformation in the age of Thomas Cromwell*, Cambridge, 1972

Harrison S.M., *The Pilgrimage of Grace in the Lake Counties 1536–7*, London, 1981

Heath P., *The English parish clergy on the eve of the Reformation*, London, 1969

Hughes P., *The Reformation in England*, Vol. 1, London, 1950

Knowles D., *The Religious Orders in England*, Vol. 3; Cambridge, 1959

Kreider A., *English Chantries; the road to dissolution*, Cambridge, Mas, 1979

Oxley J.E., *The reformation in Essex to the death of Mary*, Manchester, 1965

Scarisbrick J., *The Reformation and the English people*, Oxford, 1984

Youings J.A., *The dissolution of the Monasteries*, London, 1971

Index

255